THE BOSPHORUS
Pages 136–149

EXCURSIONS FROM ISTANBUL
Pages 150–171

BEYOĞLU
Pages 100–107

BEYOĞLU   B O S P H O R U S

SERAGLIO POINT
P

ERAGLIO POINT

D0967420

...AHMET
Pages 68–83

0 metres   500

0 yards   500

EYEWITNESS TRAVEL

ISTANBUL

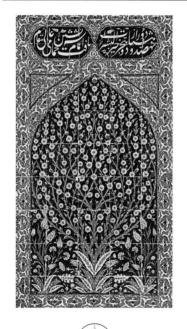

EYEWITNESS TRAVEL
ISTANBUL

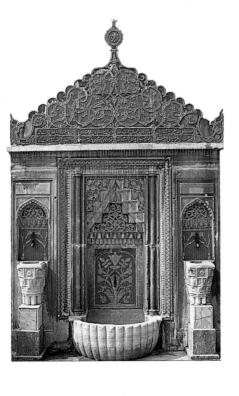

LONDON, NEW YORK,
MELBOURNE, MUNICH AND DELHI
www.dk.com

PROJECT EDITOR Nick Inman
ART EDITOR Kate Poole
EDITORS Claire Folkard, Jane Oliver, Christine Stroyan
DESIGNERS Jo Doran, Paul Jackson
VISUALIZER Joy FitzSimmons

MAIN CONTRIBUTORS
Rosie Ayliffe, Rose Baring, Barnaby Rogerson, Canan Sılay

MAPS
Paul Bates, Anne Rayski, Glyn Rozier (ESR Cartography Ltd)
Neil Cook, Maria Donnelly, Ewan Watson
(Colourmap Scanning Ltd)

PHOTOGRAPHERS
Anthony Souter, Linda Whitwam, Francesca Yorke

ILLUSTRATORS
Richard Bonson, Stephen Conlin, Gary Cross, Richard Draper,
Paul Guest, Maltings Partnership, Chris Orr & Associates,
Paul Weston, John Woodcock

Reproduced in Singapore by Colourscan
Printed and bound in China by Leo Paper Products Ltd

First American Edition, 1998
11 12 13 14 10 9 8 7 6 5 4 3 2 1

Published in the United States by DK Publishing,
375 Hudson Street, New York, New York 10014

Reprinted with revisions 1999, 2000, 2001, 2002, 2004, 2007, 2009, 2011

Copyright 1998, 2011 © Dorling Kindersley Limited, London

Published in Great Britain by Dorling Kindersley Limited.

A CATALOG RECORD FOR THIS BOOK IS AVAILABLE
FROM THE LIBRARY OF CONGRESS.

ISSN 1542-1554
ISBN 978-0-75666-969-0

THROUGHOUT THIS BOOK, FLOORS ARE REFERRED TO IN ACCORDANCE WITH EUROPEAN
USAGE; I.E., THE "FIRST FLOOR" IS THE FLOOR ABOVE GROUND LEVEL.

Front cover main image: Blue Mosque

MIX
Paper from
responsible sources
FSC™ C018179
www.fsc.org

CONTENTS

HOW TO USE
THIS GUIDE **6**

Madonna mosaic in the Church of
St Saviour in Chora

INTRODUCING
ISTANBUL

FOUR GREAT DAYS IN
ISTANBUL **10**

PUTTING ISTANBUL
ON THE MAP **12**

THE HISTORY OF
ISTANBUL **18**

ISTANBUL
AT A GLANCE **34**

Tile panel in the Paired Pavilions
of Topkapı Palace's Harem

◁ The Blue Mosque and the church of Haghia Sophia, dominating Sultanahmet Square

The great 6th-century
Byzantine church of
Haghia Sophia

Men smoking bubble pipes in
Çorlulu Ali Paşa Courtyard

TRAVELERS'
NEEDS

Ferry passing the Karaköy waterfront

Simit seller

BEYOND
ISTANBUL

SURVIVAL GUIDE

Dolmabahçe Mosque with the skyline of Sultanahmet in the distance

HOW TO USE THIS GUIDE

This guide helps you to get the most from your stay in Istanbul. It provides both expert recommendations and detailed practical advice. Introducing Istanbul locates the city geographically, sets Istanbul in its historical and cultural context and gives an overview of the main attractions. Istanbul Area by Area is the main sightseeing section, giving detailed information on all the major sights plus three recommended walks, with photographs, maps and illustrations throughout. Greater Istanbul looks at sights outside the city centre. The Bosphorus guides you through a trip up the straits, and Excursions from Istanbul explores other places within easy reach of the city. Tips for restaurants, hotels, entertainment and shopping are found in Travellers' Needs, while the Survival Guide contains useful advice on everything from personal security to public transport.

FINDING YOUR WAY AROUND ISTANBUL

The centre of Istanbul has been divided into four sightseeing areas, each with its own chapter, colour-coded for easy reference. All sights are numbered and plotted on an area map for each chapter. The major sights are covered in more detail.

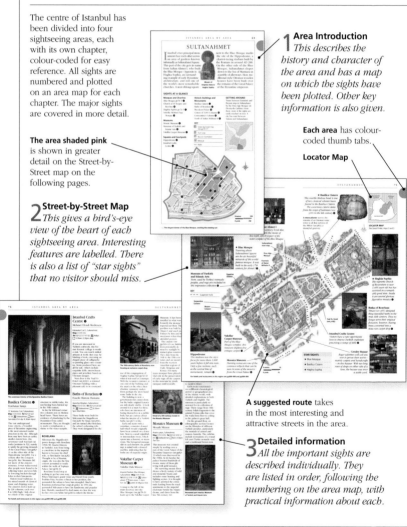

1 Area Introduction
This describes the history and character of the area and has a map on which the sights have been plotted. Other key information is also given.

Each area has colour-coded thumb tabs.

Locator Map

The area shaded pink is shown in greater detail on the Street-by-Street map on the following pages.

2 Street-by-Street Map
This gives a bird's-eye view of the heart of each sightseeing area. Interesting features are labelled. There is also a list of "star sights" that no visitor should miss.

A suggested route takes in the most interesting and attractive streets in the area.

3 Detailed information
All the important sights are described individually. They are listed in order, following the numbering on the area map, with practical information about each.

ISTANBUL AREA MAP

The coloured areas shown on this map *(see inside front cover)* are the four main sightseeing areas used in this guide. Each is covered in a full chapter in *Istanbul Area by Area (pp48–107)*. They are highlighted on other maps throughout the book. In *Istanbul at a Glance (see pp34–43)*, they help you to locate the top sights. The introduction to the Street Finder *(see pp246–263)* shows on which detailed street map you will find each area.

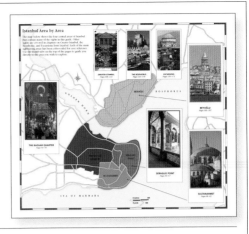

Introductory text gives an overview of the main sights in the Greater Istanbul area.

A map of the city shows Greater Istanbul and the areas covered in the chapter's sub-divisions.

4 Introduction to Greater Istanbul

Greater Istanbul has its own introduction, outlining what the city suburbs have to offer the sightseer. It is divided into five districts, shown on a map.

Practical information is provided in an information block. The key to the symbols used is on the back flap.

5 Introduction to Greater Istanbul areas

An introduction places the area in its historical context and provides a map showing the numbered sights.

The Visitors' Checklist provides detailed practical information.

6 The major sights

These are given two or more full pages. Historic buildings are dissected to reveal their interiors. Where necessary, sights are colour-coded to help you locate the most interesting areas.

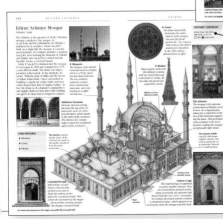

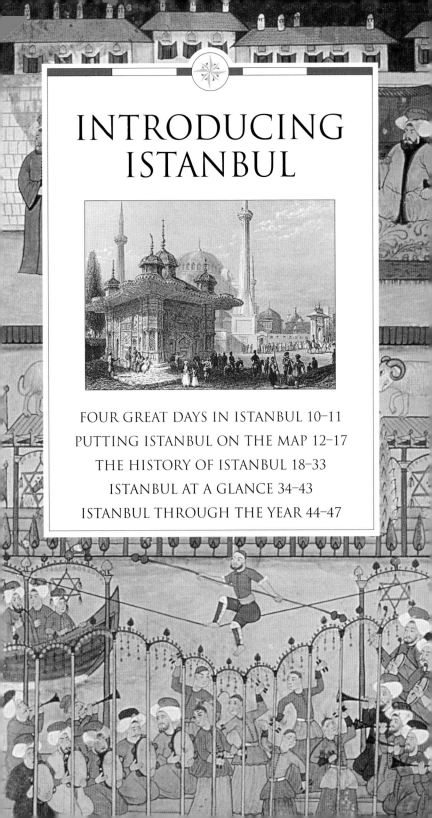

INTRODUCING ISTANBUL

FOUR GREAT DAYS IN ISTANBUL

Istanbul is a frenetic city with a wealth of culture, history and nightlife. Split in two by the Bosphorous Strait, it is the only city in the world to straddle two continents, Europe and Asia, and thus has two contrasting atmospheres. These itineraries

Ceramic plate from the Grand Bazaar

are designed to give you a flavour of the city as a whole. All the sights are cross-referenced to the rest of the guide, so you can look up more information and tailor the day to suit your needs. Price guides include meals, transport and admission fees.

A range of exotic spices for sale in the Spice Bazaar

SHOPPING AND SEAFOOD

- **Refresh your senses in the Spice Bazaar**
- **Shop for antiques in Çukurcuma**
- **Haggle in the Grand Bazaar**
- **Enjoy the buzz on Nevizade Sokak**

TWO ADULTS allow US$105

Morning
The **Spice Bazaar** *(see p88)* is a riot of colour, stalls and smells, where you can buy any number of exotic foodstuffs, including hand-made Turkish delight and creamy goats' cheese. From here, head up to the bustling **Grand Bazaar** *(see pp98–9)*, a labyrinthine Ottoman shopping complex housing thousands of leather, rug, ceramics and jewellery shops. Prices are inflated and price tags often absent altogether so remember to bargain. All this shopping is bound to whet your appetite, so head for the waterfront

district of Kumpkapı, where you will find more than 50 fish restaurants vying for your attention. Again, many outlets do not display prices, so ask before you order.

Afternoon
Revived and restored, take a taxi to the Galata Bridge and stroll over to trendy Tünel and Beyoğlu *(see pp101–7)*, soaking up the view as you go. Take time to browse around the cosy cafés and bars in Tünel, before making your way up İstiklâl Caddesi *(see pp102–3)* to shop for clothes, shoes, books and music. Further up, the district of **Çukurcuma** *(see p107)* is a hunting ground for antique furniture and ornaments. Nevizade Sokak, just off İstiklâl Caddesi, is a narrow street lined with dozens of *meyhanes (see p193)*. The area really comes alive at night, when hundreds of locals flock here and passers-by are serenaded by traditional musicians.

A FAMILY DAY OUT

- **See Istanbul in miniature**
- **A boat trip to Büyükada**
- **A horse-drawn carriage ride around Büyükada**

FAMILY OF FOUR allow US$120

Morning
Catch a bus from Taksim Square to Miniatürk *(see pp222–3)* located in Sütlüce on the northern shore of the **Golden Horn** *(see p89)*. The park displays miniatures of the city's most famous sights, such as Haghia Sophia *(see pp72–5)*, as well as other treasures from around the country that reflect Turkey's rich heritage. There is also a children's park and a museum showcasing photo-graphs of Atatürk, the great Turkish leader of the early 20th century, and the wars in Gallipoli. When you get hungry, head to Miniatürk's attractive café-restaurant that overlooks the Golden Horn.

Bustling dock activity at Eminönü

Afternoon

Head back to Istanbul after lunch and hop on a boat bound for Büyükada, one of the nine islands that make up the **Princes' Islands** *(see p159)*. It is a one-and-a-half hour trip from Kabatas pier (one hour and ten minutes from Kadiköy pier), so there is time to admire the view as Istanbul recedes on the horizon. On arrival, stroll around the main square of Saat Meydani or take a horse-drawn carriage ride around the island. Climb the hill to St George's Monastery for panoramic views and a meal at the hilltop restaurant.

The Fortress of Europe overlooking the Bosphorus

MOSQUES, MUSEUMS AND HAMAMS

- **Byzantine iconography at Haghia Sophia**
- **Glimpse the past at the Museum of Turkish and Islamic Arts**
- **An awe-inspiring visit to Topkapı Palace**

TWO ADULTS allow US$140

Morning

Start at the **Blue Mosque** *(see pp78–9)*, perhaps Istanbul's most elegant Islamic sight, famous for its slender minarets and blue Iznik tiles. Stroll through the well-tended garden at the front before making your way to imposing **Haghia Sophia** *(see pp72–5)*, another of Istanbul's most renowned mosques. Inside is a marvellous array of Byzantine mosaics, friezes and Iznik blue tile decorations, as well as a huge domed ceiling. Then head to the nearby **Museum of Turkish and Islamic Arts** *(see p77)*, which has a wonderful collection of glass and metalwork, carpets and manuscripts from down the centuries, as well as modern art from Turkey and overseas. For lunch, head to Divanyolu Caddesi, which is lined with fantastic traditional restaurants with prices to suit all budgets.

Afternoon

You will need at least three hours to appreciate **Topkapı Palace** *(see pp52–9)*, a sprawling complex of court-yards, gardens, fountains, a harem and a collection of priceless antiques. Then, at the end of a long day, indulge in that most Turkish of pleasures, a visit to a Turkish bath *(see p67)*. Çemberlitas Baths *(see p81)* in Sultanahmet is one of the finest.

Decorative blue tiles in the Haghia Sophia mosque

UP THE BOSPHORUS

- **A boat up the Bosphorus**
- **Enjoy views at Fortress of Europe**
- **Stroll through the pretty village of Bebek**

TWO ADULTS allow US$95

Morning

Catch a bus from Taksim Square or Eminönü bus terminus heading for Sarıyer or Emirgan and get off at Arnavutköy on the Bosphorus *(see p145 for details of boat cruises)*. There are some lovingly restored Ottoman houses and mansions to admire here, most of them painted in pastel shades and trimmed with intricate wooden fretwork. Cafés line the back streets, so sit and linger over a coffee and a pastry. From Arnavutköy, continue walking north-wards, past the fishing boats and pleasure cruisers bobbing on the water, until you reach **Bebek** *(see p138 & p146)*, one of Istanbul's most affluent villages. There are more than enough chic clothes and antiques shops here to tempt visitors to part with their cash and work up an appetite for lunch. Dine in style at the **Poseidon** *(see p206)*. Here you can sip an aperitif and enjoy the splendid view before savouring the menu of fresh fish.

Afternoon

Delve into history at the imposing **Fortress of Europe** *(see pp140–41)*, built in the 15th century as part of the Muslim conquest of Constantinople. There is also a fantastic view of the Bosphorus from here. Afterwards, walk around the delightful 19th-century pavilions of nearby **Emirgan Park** *(see p141)* with its many pine, fir and cypress trees and an ornamental lake.

Putting Istanbul on the Map

Istanbul stands astride the straits of the Bosphorus,
straddling the European and Asian parts of Turkey
and bordered to the south by the Sea of Marmara.
The city is divided not only by the Bosphorus but
also by the Golden Horn, an inlet forming a natural
harbour. Although no longer the capital of Turkey
(*see p31*), Istanbul is still the country's largest and
most monumental city.

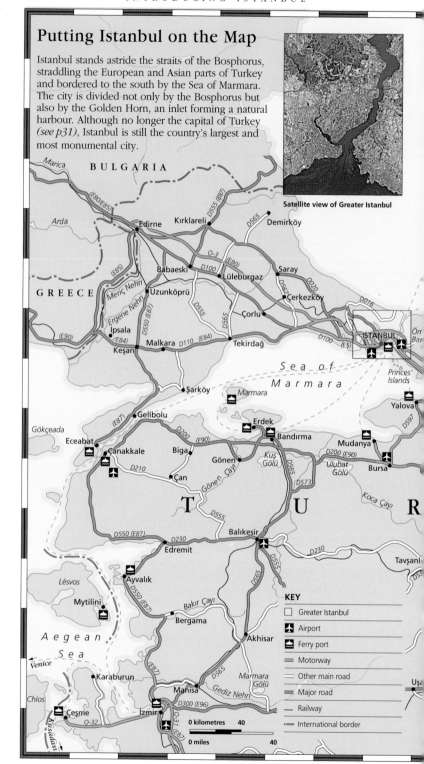

Satellite view of Greater Istanbul

KEY

☐	Greater Istanbul
✈	Airport
⛴	Ferry port
▬	Motorway
─	Other main road
▬	Major road
─	Railway
·–·–	International border

0 kilometres   40

0 miles   40

◁ **Miniature depicting the lavish festivities staged for the circumcision of Ahmet III's sons in 1720**

Istanbul and its Environs

The sights in central Istanbul are covered in detail on pages 48–107 and a Street Finder is provided on pages 246–63. Sights outside the centre are covered on pages 108–49. Places of interest on the Bosphorus and further afield, still within the city boundaries, are explored on pages 134–71.

GREATER ISTANBUL AND ENVIRONS

Gaziosmanpaşa   D020   D016

Kemerburgaz

Beykoz

O-3 (E80)

Halkalı

O-4 (E80)

D020

D100

D100 (E5)

0 kilometres   7

0 miles   4

See next page

Black Sea

Zonguldak

Ereğli

Devrek   D030

Karabük   Yenice Irmağı

Şile

Kandıra   D020

Karasu   D010   Akçakoca   D750

Kocaeli (İzmit)   D100   Sakarya (Adapazarı)   D100   Düzce   Gerede Çayı

D130   D100

Sapanca Gölü

İznik   Bolu   O-4 (E89)

D140   D160   D160   D170   D140

Bilecik

Sakarya Nehri

Nallıhan   Beypazarı   Kirmir Çayı

K   **E**   *Sarıyar Barajı*   **Y**

Eskişehir   D200 (E90)   Milhallıçcık   ANKARA

D200 (E90)   D260

D650

Tuz Gölü

EUROPE AND THE MEDITERRANEAN REGION

DENMARK	ESTONIA
SWEDEN	LATVIA
	LITHUANIA
UNITED	RUSSIAN
REP OF KINGDOM	FEDERATION
IRELAND	BELORUSSIA
NETHERLANDS	POLAND
BELGIUM GERMANY	
LUXEMBOURG CZECH REP.	UKRAINE
FRANCE	SLOVAKIA
SWITZERLAND AUSTRIA HUNGARY	MOLDAVIA
SLOVENIA CROATIA	ROMANIA
ITALY BOSNIA SERBIA	
MONTENEGRO	BULGARIA
	GEORGIA
PORTUGAL SPAIN	Istanbul
	GREECE TURKEY
	LEBANON SYRIA
TUNISIA	ISRAEL IRAQ
MOROCCO ALGERIA	JORDAN SAUDI
LIBYA	EGYPT ARABIA

Odessa

Samsun Trabzon

D010   D755

Greater Istanbul

The expanding metropolis of Istanbul spreads along the Bosphorus to the north, beyond the airport to the west and inland from the Asian shore in the east. Its official population is put at just under 13 million but the actual population is probably much higher. Transport improvements are being made to make getting around this vast urban area easier. Most visitors, however, stay in the historical central parts where the major sights are located.

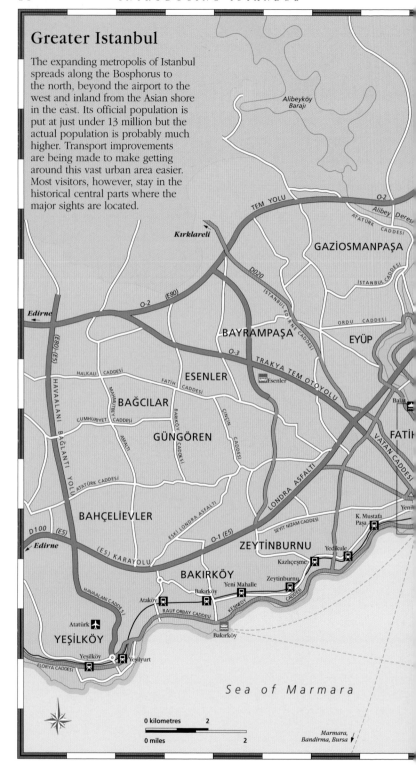

Alibeyköy
Barajı

O-2

Alibey Deresi

ATATÜRK CADDESİ

TEM YOLU

GAZİOSMANPAŞA

Kırklareli

İSTANBUL CADDESİ

D020

ORDU CADDESİ

O-2 (E80)

BAYRAMPAŞA

EYÜP

Edirne

(E80) (E5)

O-3

TRAKYA TEM OTOYOLU

HALKALI CADDESİ

İSTANBUL EDİRNE CADDESİ

Esenler

ESENLER

FATİH CADDESİ

HAVAALANI BAĞLANTI YOLU

MAMMURBEY CADDESİ

BAĞCILAR

Balat

CUMHURİYET CADDESİ

BARKÖY CADDESİ

ÇINÇIN CADDESİ

ASFALT

GÜNGÖREN

FATİH

VATAN CADDESİ

ATATÜRK CADDESİ

Yeni

LONDRA ASFALTI

BAHÇELİEVLER

K. Mustafa
Paşa

SEYİT NİZAM CADDESİ

D100 (E5)

ESKİ LONDRA ASFALTI

O-1 (E5)

ZEYTİNBURNU

Yedikule

Edirne

(E5) KARAYOLU

Kazlıçeşme

BAKIRKÖY

Yeni Mahalle

Zeytinburnu

CADDESİ

HAVAALANI CADDESİ

Ataköy

Bakırköy

KENNEDY

RAUF ORBAY CADDESİ

Atatürk

Bakırköy

YEŞİLKÖY

Yeşilköy

Yeşilyurt

ELORYA CADDESİ

Sea of Marmara

0 kilometres   2

0 miles   2

Marmara,
Bandırma, Bursa

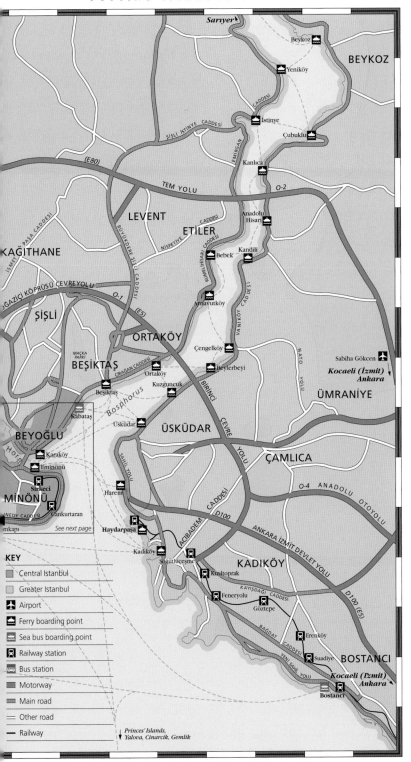

Sarıyer

BEYKOZ

Beykoz

Yeniköy

İstinye

Çubuklu

Kanlıca

(E80)

TEM YOLU

O-2

LEVENT

ETİLER

Anadolu
Hisarı

KAĞITHANE

Bebek

Kandilli

ŞİŞLİ

Arnavutköy

ORTAKÖY

Çengelköy

Sabiha Gökcen

Kocaeli (İzmit)
Ankara

BEŞİKTAŞ

MAÇKA
PARKI

Ortaköy

Beylerbeyi

ÜMRANİYE

Kuzguncuk

Beşiktaş

Bosphorus

BİRİNCİ

Kabataş

BEYOĞLU

Üsküdar

ÜSKÜDAR

ÇAMLICA

O-4 ANADOLU OTOYOLU

Karaköy

Eminönü

Sirkeci

Harem

MİNÖNÜ

Cankurtaran

D100

ANKARA İZMİT DEVLET YOLU

See next page

Haydarpaşa

Kadıköy

Söğütlüçeşme

KADIKÖY

D 100 (E5)

KEY

	Central Istanbul
	Greater Istanbul
✈	Airport
	Ferry boarding point
	Sea bus boarding point
	Railway station
	Bus station
	Motorway
	Main road
	Other road
	Railway

Kızıltoprak

Feneryolu

Göztepe

Erenköy

Suadiye

BOSTANCI

Kocaeli (İzmit)
Ankara

Bostancı

Princes' Islands,
Yalova, Cinarcik, Gemlik

Central Istanbul

Shoe shine man outside the New Mosque

This guide divides central Istanbul into four distinct areas, each with its own chapter. Three areas lie on the southern side of the Golden Horn. Seraglio Point is a raised promontory on which stands the sumptuous Topkapı Palace. Two architectural masterpieces, Haghia Sophia and the Blue Mosque, dominate the area of Sultanahmet. The pace of life is quite different in the Bazaar Quarter, a maze of narrow streets filled with frenetic commerce. North of the Golden Horn is Beyoğlu, which for centuries was the preferred place of residence of Istanbul's foreign communities, and is still markedly cosmopolitan in atmosphere.

İstiklâl Caddesi, Beyoğlu
Old-fashioned trams shuttle up and down the pedestrianized street that forms the backbone of this area (see pp100–107).

The Grand Bazaar, in the Bazaar Quarter
This quaint former coffee house stands at a junction in the labyrinthine old shopping complex at the heart of the city's Bazaar Quarter (see pp84–99).

KEY

▩	Major sight
⚓	Ferry boarding point
🚉	Railway station
Ⓜ	Metro
🚊	Tram stop
🚊	Nostalgic Tram stop
🚡	Underground funicular stop
ℹ	Tourist information
◐	Turkish bath
C	Mosque
✝	Church
⊠	Post office
🚓	Police station

Map labels:

İSKENDER CADDESİ
ŞİŞHANE SOK
YOLCUZADE
FÜTUHAT SOK
TERSANE CAD
Atatürk Köprüsü
Atatürk Bridge
Golden Horn
G o l d e n H o
Haliç H
ATATÜRK BULVARI
RAGIP GÜMÜŞPALA CAD
ÇARDAK CAD
Emin
CAM ME
KAZANCILAR CAD
YENİ HAYAT SOK
HACI KADIN CADDESİ
KİBLE ÇEŞME CADDESİ
MURAT EFENDİ
ÇİÇEK PAZARI SOK
Süleymaniye Mosque
FETVA YOKUŞU SOK
NAMAHREM SOK
SİYAVUŞ PAŞA SOK
UZUNÇARŞI CAD
VASIF ÇINAR CAD
AŞİ
KATİP ÇELEBİ CADDESİ
DAĞLIOĞLU SOK
SARI BEYAZIT CAD
CEMAL YENER TOSYALI CAD
REVANİ ÇELEBİ SOK
DÖKMECİLER SOK
KIRAZLI MESCİT SOK
BOZDOĞAN KEMERİ CADDESİ
SÜLEYMANİYE
FULATPAŞA CAD
ORUÇ
ŞEHZADE BAŞI CAD
BÜYÜK DERE
PAŞA
BEŞİM ÖMER PAŞA CADDESİ
ÇARÇIKAR SOK
MAHMUTPAŞA
THE BAZAAR QUARTER
SELİM PAŞA SOKAĞI
GENÇTÜRK CADDESİ
FETHİ BEY CAD
MAHFİL
ZEYNEP KAMİL SOK
VEZNECİLER CAD
ÜNİVERSİTE CAD
ÇADIRCILAR CAD
BEZCİ
SEREF
Grand Bazaar
⊠
Aksaray
KURULTAY SOK
ORDU CADDESİ
YENİÇERİLER
Beyazıt
Laleli-Univ
CAD
ŞAİR HAŞMET SOK
AĞA ÇEŞME S/SOK
BEYAZIT KARAKOL CAD
TİYATRO CAD
Çembe
MESİH PAŞA CADDESİ
DÖNEM
YAĞLIKÇILAR SOK
GEDİKPAŞA CAD
SİNAN ALİ
KÂTİP SİNAN CAD
TÜLCÜ SOK
OZBEKL SOK

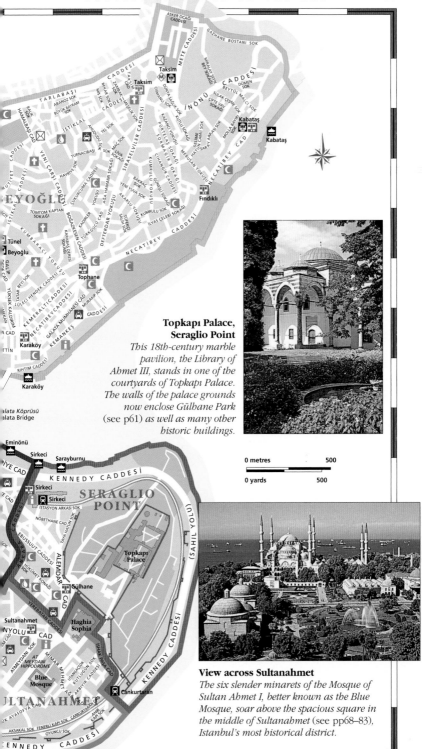

**Topkapı Palace,
Seraglio Point**
*This 18th-century marble
pavilion, the Library of
Ahmet III, stands in one of the
courtyards of Topkapı Palace.
The walls of the palace grounds
now enclose Gülhane Park
(see p61) as well as many other
historic buildings.*

0 metres   500

0 yards   500

View across Sultanahmet
*The six slender minarets of the Mosque of
Sultan Ahmet I, better known as the Blue
Mosque, soar above the spacious square in
the middle of Sultanahmet (see pp68–83),
Istanbul's most historical district.*

THE HISTORY OF ISTANBUL

I stanbul was founded in the 7th century BC on a naturally defensive site from which trade along the Bosphorus could be controlled. For 16 centuries it was a great imperial capital, first of the Byzantine Empire and then of the Ottoman sultans. Some knowledge of the histories of these two civilizations helps the visitor to appreciate the magnificent monuments found throughout the city.

The topography of Istanbul was formed at the end of the last Ice Age, when meltwaters created the Bosphorus. The Stone Age cultures in the area were replaced by Copper Age villages and walled Bronze Age towns (notably Troy, *see p171*). The Bosphorus was an important trade route in the ancient world along which ships carried wine and olive oil north from the Mediterranean,

Septimius Severus, who devastated the city in the 2nd century AD

and grain, skins, wool, timber, wax, honey, salted meat and salted fish south from regions around the Black Sea.

The area around the Bosphorus was subjugated by a series of peoples, starting with the Mycenaeans (1400–1200 BC). Between 800 and 680 BC the region was controlled by the kingdom of Phrygia. Later, in 676 BC, Greek expeditionaries founded the city of Chalcedon (on the site where modern Kadıköy now stands).

THE FOUNDATION OF BYZANTION

The foundation of Istanbul is usually dated to 667 BC when, according to legend, a Greek colonist, Byzas, led an expedition from the overcrowded cities

of Athens and Megara to establish a colony on the European side of the Bosphorus. This colony, known as Byzantion, grew to be a successful independent city-state, or *polis*, one of the 40 most important such states throughout the Ancient Greek world. During the next few centuries, Byzantion worked in partnership with Chalcedon, using the same coinage and sharing the tolls exacted from passing sea trade.

But Byzantion had to struggle to maintain its independence in the mercurial politics of the ancient world. It endured Lydian (560–546 BC), Persian (546–478 BC), Athenian (478–411 BC) and Macedonian (334–281 BC) rule before briefly regaining its autonomy. In 64 BC it was subsumed into the Roman Empire as Byzantium. The city was almost destroyed in AD 195 by Septimius Severus because of its support for his rival for the imperial throne, Pescennius Niger. It survived the Goths' devastation of Chalcedon in AD 258 but trade in the region dramatically declined in the following years.

TIMELINE

Alexander the Great

c.676 BC Chalcedon, a Greek settlement, founded on Asian shore	**340 BC** Philip II of Macedonia unsuccessfully besieges city		**AD 195** Roman emperor Septimius Severus destroys Byzantium but later rebuilds it and creates the Hippodrome
600 BC	**400 BC**	**200 BC**	**AD 1**	**AD 200**
c.667 BC Byzantion reputedly founded by Greek colonists from Athens and Megara, led by Byzas	**334 BC** Alexander the Great crosses the Hellespont (Dardanelles) and conquers Anatolia	**64 BC** Pompey brings Byzantion into the Roman Empire, renaming it Byzantium	**AD 258** Goths destroy Chalcedon

◁ **The Byzantine emperor Justinian the Great shown with one of his prefects in a mosaic**

CONSTANTINE THE GREAT

In AD 324, after defeating his co-emperor Licinius, Constantine the Great (324–37) became sole ruler of the Roman Empire. One of his greatest achievements was to move the capital of the empire from Rome to Byzantium. Initially, Constantine preferred the site of Troy *(see p171)* for his capital, but was persuaded by advisers that Byzantium held a superior position for both defence and trade. Constantine's city was officially styled the "New Rome" but became widely known as Constantinople. The emperor quickly started on an ambitious programme of construction work, which included the Great Palace *(see pp82–3)* and various public buildings.

Gold aureus of Constantine

Constantine was also instrumental in the spread of Christianity. According to legend, he saw a vision of the cross before a battle in 312. Although not actually baptized until just before his death, he worked hard to create a coherent system of Christian belief out of the variant practices of the day. All the early church councils took place in the city or nearby, the first being held in Nicaea, (modern-day İznik, *see p160*), and the second in Constantinople itself.

A successor of Constantine, Theodosius I (379–95), divided the Empire between his two sons, Honorius and Arcadius. When the

Latin-speaking Western Empire fell to barbarian armies during the 5th century, the Greek-speaking Eastern Empire, thereafter known as the Byzantine Empire, survived.

THE AGE OF JUSTINIAN

The 6th century was dominated by the extraordinary genius of Justinian (527–65), who developed Constantinople into a thriving city and almost succeeded in reconquering the lost provinces of the Western Empire from the barbarians. At the time of his death the empire had expanded to its greatest size, and covered Syria, Palestine, Asia Minor, Greece, the Balkans, Italy,

Empress Theodora, wife of Justinian

southern Spain and many territories in northern Africa, including Egypt.

Justinian's formidable wife, the ex-courtesan Theodora, had a great deal of influence over him. In 532 she persuaded the emperor to use mercenaries to put down an angry mob in the most notorious event of his reign, the Nika Revolt. In the carnage that followed 30,000 were killed inside the Hippodrome *(see p80)*.

Justinian was also responsible for much of the city's great architecture, including Haghia Sophia *(see pp72–5)*, Haghia Eirene *(see p60)* and parts of the Great Palace.

Relief from the Egyptian Obelisk *(see p80)*, showing Theodosius I and his courtiers

TIMELINE

324 Constantine becomes ruler of the Roman Empire	**330** Inauguration of Constantinople	**395** On the death of Theodosius I, the empire is divided into two	**476** The Western Roman Empire falls to barbarians **532** Nika Revolt is put down by mercenaries; 30,000 are killed	**674** Five-year-long siege of Constantinople initiated by the Saracens

300	400	500	600	700

325 First church council meets at Nicaea	**337** Constantine is baptized a Christian on his deathbed	**412** Construction work begins on the Walls of Theodosius II *(see p22)*	**537** Emperor Justinian dedicates the new Haghia Sophia *Walls of Theodosius II*	**726** Leo III issues a decree denouncing idolatry, and many icons are destroyed

THE BYZANTINES AT WAR

The Byzantine Empire never again attained the splendour of the reign of Justinian, but throughout the first millennium it remained rich and powerful. During the early Middle Ages, Constantinople was an oasis of learning, law, art and culture at a time when Europe was plunged into a

"Greek fire", used by the Byzantines against the Arabs

dark age of ignorance and illiteracy. Considering themselves to be the leaders of Christianity, the Byzantine rulers dispatched missionaries to spread their religion and culture among the Slavic nations, especially Russia.

During this period, Constantinople produced some capable emperors, in particular Heraclius (610–41), Basil the Macedonian (867–86), Leo the Wise (886–912) and Basil the Bulgar-Slayer (976–1025). Between them these rulers contributed a number of buildings to the city and recaptured lost provinces.

Never without enemies greedy for a share of the prodigious riches that had been amassed in the city, Constantinople was besieged by Slavs, Arabs, Avars, Bulgars, Persians and Russians, all without success because of the protection of the land walls. The surrounding seas, meanwhile, were under the control of Constantinople's powerful navy. Its main ship

A 6th-century ivory carving of a Byzantine emperor, possibly Anastasius I (491–518)

was the dromon, an oared vessel which could ram another ship but above all deliver the dreaded "Greek fire", an early form of napalm.

In 1059 Constantine X, the first of the Dukas dynasty of emperors, ascended to the throne. The state over which the dynasty presided was a weakened one, divided between the over-privileged bureaucracy in the capital and the feudal landlords of the provinces. At the same time increasing dependency on foreign mercenaries placed the empire's defence in the hands of its most aggressive neighbours. These included the Normans from southern Italy, the Venetians and Turkic no-mads from the east. The Byzantine imperial army was totally destroyed at the Battle of Manzikert (1071) and again, a century later, at the Battle of Myriocephalon (1176) by the Seljuk Turks from the east. These losses effectively ended Byzantine rule of Anatolia, which had for so long been the backbone of the empire. The remarkable Comnenus dynasty (1081–1185) ruled for a century after the Dukas emperors, between these two defeats. Their main achievement was to succeed in holding the rest of the empire together.

Haghia Sophia mosaic

The City of Constantinople

Mosaic of the Virgin, St Saviour in Chora

For almost a thousand years Constantinople was the richest city in Christendom. It radiated out from three great buildings: the church of Haghia Sophia *(see pp72–5)*, the Hippodrome *(see p80)* and the Great Palace *(see pp82–3)*. The city also had a great many other fine churches and palaces, filled with exquisite works of art. Daily life for the populace centred on the four market squares, or *fora*. Meanwhile, their need for fresh water was met by an advanced network of aqueducts and underground water cisterns.

Walls of Theodosius
Theodosius II's great chain of land walls (see p114) *withstood countless sieges until the Ottoman conquest of the city in 1453 (see p26).*

THE CITY IN 1200

At its height the magnificent city of Constantinople probably had about 400,000 inhabitants. The population density was relatively low, though, and there was space within the city walls for fields and orchards.

Mocius Cistern

The Golden Gate was a ceremonial gate through the city's ramparts.

Church of St John of Studius *(see p116)*

Walls of Constantine (now totally destroyed)

Forum of Arcadius

Harbour of Theodosius

BYZANTINE CHURCH ARCHITECTURE

Early Byzantine churches were either basilical (like St John of Studius) or built to a centralized plan (as in SS Sergius and Bacchus). From the 9th century, churches, like the typical example shown here, were built around four corner piers, or columns. Exteriors were mostly unadorned brickwork, but interiors were lavishly decorated with golden mosaics. Although the Ottomans converted Constantinople's churches into mosques after their conquest of the city, many original features are clearly discernible today.

TYPICAL LATE BYZANTINE CHURCH

A central apse is flanked by two smaller side apses.

Four columns support the dome.

Brickwork may alternate with layers of stone.

The narthex, a covered porch, forms the entrance to the church.

Golden mosaics cover the ceilings and upper walls.

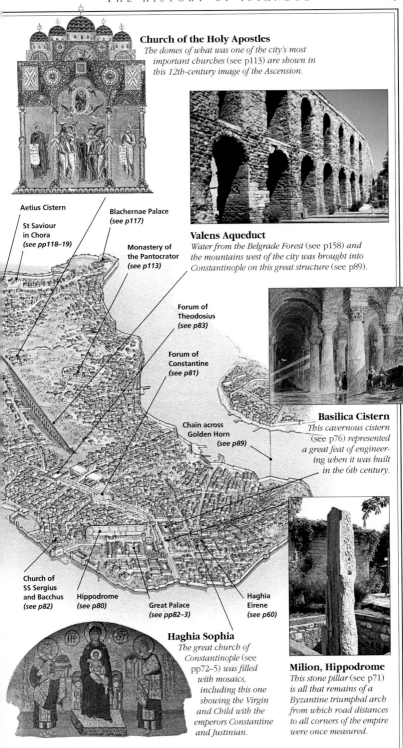

Church of the Holy Apostles
The domes of what was one of the city's most important churches (see p113) are shown in this 12th-century image of the Ascension.

Aetius Cistern

St Saviour in Chora
(see pp118–19)

Blachernae Palace
(see p117)

Monastery of the Pantocrator
(see p113)

Valens Aqueduct
Water from the Belgrade Forest (see p158) and the mountains west of the city was brought into Constantinople on this great structure (see p89).

Forum of Theodosius
(see p83)

Forum of Constantine
(see p81)

Chain across Golden Horn
(see p89)

Basilica Cistern
This cavernous cistern (see p76) represented a great feat of engineering when it was built in the 6th century.

Church of SS Sergius and Bacchus
(see p82)

Hippodrome
(see p80)

Great Palace
(see pp82–3)

Haghia Eirene
(see p60)

Haghia Sophia
The great church of Constantinople (see pp72–5) was filled with mosaics, including this one showing the Virgin and Child with the emperors Constantine and Justinian.

Milion, Hippodrome
This stone pillar (see p71) is all that remains of a Byzantine triumphal arch from which road distances to all corners of the empire were once measured.

The capture of Constantinople during the Fourth Crusade of 1202–4

THE FOURTH CRUSADE

In 1202, an army of 34,000 responded to an appeal from Pope Innocent III for a new crusade to the Holy Land. This unruly force of Christians lacked the funds to get beyond Venice, where it needed to hire ships. It consequently fell under the influence of Enrico Dandolo, the manipulative Doge of Venice. With his backing, the crusaders were soon diverted to Constantinople where they helped the young Alexius IV take the throne.

However, six months later, when they realized they were unlikely to receive their promised financial reward from the emperor, the crusaders lost patience and launched a new attack, ousting Alexius in favour

Icon of St Michael, now in Venice, an example of the fine Byzantine art plundered by the Venetians during the Fourth Crusade

of one their own, Baldwin I, Count of Flanders. Through the dark years that followed, known as the Latin Empire, the once great city was reduced by pillage, misrule and emigration to a scattering of disconnected villages grouped behind the city walls. Outside Constantinople, the exiled Byzantine emperors survived the turmoil, biding their time as the rulers of the Empire of Nicaea, just to the south, which included modern-day İznik *(see p160)*.

CONSTANTINOPLE IN DECLINE

In 1261, Constantinople was recaptured for Byzantium by Michael VIII Palaeologus (1258–82), who met almost no resistance in the process. He did this with the aid

TIMELINE

1202 An army assembles in Venice to launch the Fourth Crusade

1204 Alexius IV is deposed and Baldwin I is crowned emperor of a new Latin Empire

1203 Dandolo, Doge of Venice, diverts the Fourth Crusade to Constantinople. He cuts the chain across the Golden Horn *(see p23)* and storms the city

1261 Michael VIII Palaeologus recaptures Constantinople from the Venetians

1299 Osman I founds the Ottoman Empire

Bronze horses taken by Dandolo from the Hippodrome (see p80) to Venice

1326 Prusa (Bursa) is taken and becomes Ottoman capital

1331 Ottomans capture Nicaea (modern İznik)

1321 Outbreak of disastrous 33-year-long Byzantine civil war

| 1200 | 1225 | 1250 | 1275 | 1300 | 1325 |

of the Italian city of Genoa, which was naturally disposed to fight against her rival Venice. Yet she still exacted a crippling price for her assistance. The Genoese established the colony of Pera across the Golden Horn from Constantinople, and effectively took control of the city's trade.

Constantinople's recapture and reconstruction caused a flowering of scholarship and artistic activity, known as the Palaeologue Renaissance after the family of emperors. An example of the many beautiful buildings dating from this period is the Church of St Saviour in Chora *(see pp118–19)*.

Two-headed Byzantine eagle

During this period the double-headed eagle was adopted as the imperial crest, with the two heads symbolizing the western and eastern halves of the empire. Yet, within a few decades there was further discord in Constantinople, when a quarrel arose between Andronicus II (1282–1328) and his grandson Andronicus III (1328–41) over the succession. This led to the disastrous civil war of 1321–54.

THE RISE OF THE OTTOMANS

The Ottoman state was born in 1299 when Osman I, a leader of warriors who were fighting for the Muslim faith on the eastern frontier of the Byzantine Empire, declared his independence. The new state quickly expanded and in 1326 captured Prusa (modern-day Bursa, *see pp162–8)*, which became its capital. The judicious piety of the Ottomans soon won them the support of the general population of their territories, and even of some Christian brotherhoods. Meanwhile, a professional core of Janissaries *(see p127)* was created to add stability to an army which was otherwise too dependent on Turkic and renegade volunteer cavalry.

By 1362, with the Ottoman capture of Adrianople (Edirne, *see pp154–7)*, Byzantium had been reduced to the city-state of Constantinople and a few minor outposts, isolated within Ottoman domains. Only a Mongol incursion in 1402 delayed the Ottoman invasion of Constantinople itself. In 1422 the Ottoman army made its first attack on the city's colossal land walls. As the threat increased, the Byzantine emperor made a last ditch effort to win the support of the Latin West in 1439. The Hungarians alone answered his call for help, forming a 25,000-strong crusade. However, in 1444 they were defeated en route by the Ottomans at the Battle of Varna on the Black Sea.

Mosaic of the Virgin and Child in St Saviour in Chora

1362 Murat I conquers Adrianople (Edirne), which then becomes the Ottoman capital. Byzantium is reduced to the city of Constantinople

1451 Mehmet II succeeds to the Ottoman throne and orders construction of the Fortress of Europe *(see p140)* to seal the Bosphorus

1350	1375	1400	1425	1450

1348 The Galata Tower is built by the Genoese inhabitants of the city as a watchtower over the Pera quarter

1422 First Ottoman siege of Constantinople by Murat III

1444 A Hungarian army on its way to help Constantinople is destroyed by the Ottomans at Varna on the Black Sea. Constantinople's last hope of survival is lost

Galata Tower

THE CONQUEST OF CONSTANTINOPLE

On 29 May 1453 Sultan Mehmet II (1432–81), known as "the Conqueror", entered Constantinople after a 54-day siege during which his cannon had torn a huge hole in the Walls of Theodosius II *(see p114)*. Mehmet's first task was to rebuild the wrecked city, which would later become known as Istanbul. The Grand Bazaar *(see pp98–9)* and Topkapı Palace *(see pp54–7)* were erected in the years following the Muslim conquest. Religious foundations were endowed to fund the building of mosques such as the Fatih *(see p113)* and their associated schools and baths *(see pp38–9)*. The city had to be

Sultan Mehmet II, "the Conqueror"

repopulated by a mixture of force and encouragement. People from all over the empire moved to Istanbul, and Jews, Christians and Muslims lived together in a cosmopolitan society.

Mehmet and his successors pushed the frontiers of the empire across the Middle East and into Europe. In the early 16th century, Selim I (1512–20) conquered Egypt and assumed the title of caliph *(see p29)*, as well as establishing the Ottomans as a sea power. He is also notorious for killing all his male relatives bar one son, to ensure that there were no rivals for the succession.

SÜLEYMAN THE MAGNIFICENT

Selim's one surviving son was Süleyman I, "the Magnificent" (1520–66), under whose rule the Ottoman Empire reached its maximum extent. At the time of his death the empire stretched from Algiers to the Caspian Sea and from Hungary to the Persian Gulf. Much of western Europe only just escaped conquest when an Ottoman army was driven back from the gates of Vienna in 1529. Süleyman's reign was a time of great artistic and architectural achievements. The architect Sinan *(see p91)* designed many mosques and other great buildings in the city, while the Ottoman arts of ceramics *(see p161)* and calligraphy *(see p95)* also flourished.

OTTOMAN EMPIRE
◻ *Maximum extent (1683)*

Depiction of the unsuccessful siege of Vienna

TIMELINE

1453 Mehmet the Conqueror enters Constantinople on 29 May

1456 The Ottomans occupy Athens

1461 Trebizond on the Black Sea, the last part of the Byzantine Empire, is conquered

1536 Grand Vizier İbrahim Paşa is killed on the orders of Süleyman's wife, Roxelana *(see p76)*

1561 Süleyman executes his son Beyazıt on suspicion of treason

1571 Defeat of the Ottoman navy at the Battle of Lepant

|1450|1475|1500|1525|1550|

1455 Yedikule Castle *(see p115)* is built and work begins on the Grand Bazaar

1478 Topkapı Palace completed

1470 Fatih Mosque is built over the Church of the Holy Apostles

1533 Hayrettin Paşa, better known as Barbarossa, is appointed grand admiral

1556 Inauguration of Sinan's Süleymaniye Mosque *(see pp90–91)*

Süleyman I

THE SULTANATE OF WOMEN

Süleyman's son Selim II (1566–74), "the Sot", was not such a capable ruler, although he added Cyprus to the empire. The defeat of his navy by the Venetians at the Battle of Lepanto was a heavy blow to Ottoman ambitions to be a seafaring power. This era was also

The Battle of Lepanto, a defeat for the Ottoman navy

the start of the so-called "Sultanate of Women", when Selim's mother (the valide sultan, *see p28*) and Nur Banu, his principal wife (the first *kadın*), effectively took over power and exercised it for their own ends. Corruption and intrigue became endemic, and after Selim's death Nur Banu kept her son, Murat III (1574–95), distracted by the women of the harem so that she could maintain her control over imperial affairs.

Osman II (1618–22) was the first sultan to try to reverse the decline of the empire. But when the Janissaries *(see p127)* learnt of his plans to abolish their corps, they started a revolt which eventually led to his assassination. Murat IV (1623–40) enjoyed more success in his attempts at reform and significantly reduced corruption

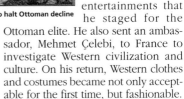

Osman II, who failed to halt Ottoman decline

during his stable period of rule.

The late 17th century saw many years of capable government by a succession of grand viziers from the Albanian Köprülü family. Yet their efforts were not sufficient to stem

the decline in imperial fortunes, symbolized by a failed attempt to capture Vienna in 1683. The Treaty of Karlowitz in 1699 marked the start of the Ottoman withdrawal from Europe.

THE TULIP PERIOD

Ahmet III (1703–30), on his succession to the throne, left power in the hands of his capable grand vizier, İbrahim Paşa. The sultan preferred pleasure to politics. During his reign, beautiful Baroque palaces, such as Aynalı Kavak Palace *(see p127)*, fountains, mosques and yalis *(see p139)* were built. Formal gardens were laid out and filled with tulips, Ahmet's favourite flower, which lent their name to the period of his rule. The sultan even ordered tulips to be scattered over the floor at the lavish festivals and entertainments that he staged for the Ottoman elite. He also sent an ambassador, Mehmet Çelebi, to France to investigate Western civilization and culture. On his return, Western clothes and costumes became not only acceptable for the first time, but fashionable.

1616 The Blue Mosque *(see pp78–9)* is finished after eight years of construction work by the architect Mehmet Ağa

1699 The loss of Hungary under the Treaty of Karlowitz marks the Ottomans' retreat from Europe

| 00 | 1625 | 1650 | 1700 | 1725 |

1622 Revolt of the Janissaries. They murder Osman II in Yedikule Castle, the Prison of the Seven Towers

Domes of the Blue Mosque

1729 The first Ottoman printing press is set up in Istanbul and begins to print texts in Turkish

Ottoman Society

Beneath the sultan, Ottoman society was divided into a privileged ruling class (the *askeri*, which included the religious hierarchy, or *ulema*) and a tax-paying subject population *(reaya)*. Rank and honour, however, were not hereditary but could be gained through education or service in the army or administration. This social structure was modified during the reforms of the 19th century *(see p30)*, but Ottoman titles were only finally abolished in 1923 after the Turkish Republic was created *(see p31)*.

The grand vizier, the prime minister, was the sultan's right-hand man.

The sultan *was at the apex of the social order and everyone owed allegiance to him. He lived a life of ease and luxury, as seen in this portrait of Mahmut I (1730–54). The Ottoman* (Osmanlı in Turkish) *sultans were always succeeded by one of their sons, but not automatically by the eldest.*

BAYRAM RECEPTION *(c.1800)*

In this painting by Konstantin Kapidagi, Selim III (1789–1807, *see p30*) presides over a parade of high-ranking officials during the celebration of a religious festival *(see p47)* at Topkapı Palace.

Aǧa of the Janissaries

Minister of the Interior

Şeyhülislam (Grand Mufti)

Chief executioner

Men of high rank *could be recognized by their different uniforms, above all their large and distinctive headgear, as seen in this portrait of four Ottoman officials. The turban was abolished by Mahmut II (see p30) in 1829 in favour of the more egalitarian fez.*

THE WOMEN OF THE HAREM

Like all other Ottoman institutions the harem was hierarchical. It was presided over by the sultan's mother, the valide sultana. Next in order of importance came the sultan's daughters. Immediately below them were the four *kadıns*, the official wives or favourites. Then came the *gözdes* (girls who had recently caught the sultan's eye), and the *ikbals* (women with whom he had already slept). Apart from the sultan's family members, all these women had entered the harem as slaves. They were kept under a watchful eye by a powerful stewardess, the *kahya kadın*.

One of the sultan's favourites as depicted in a 19th-century engraving

Black eunuchs

Sword bearer to the sultan

The Gate of Felicity (*see p54*), in the second courtyard of Topkapı Palace, was used for such ceremonial occasions.

The sultan is surrounded by his courtiers. He is the only seated figure.

Şeyhülislam (Grand Mufti)

Chief lackey (footman)

Chief of the sultan's bodyguard

Black eunuchs

Dancing women

Valide sultana

Dwarf

The valide sultana, the most powerful woman in the harem, is the centre of attention in this festive scene. The picture was commissioned in 1689 by Madame Giradin, wife of the French ambassador.

OTTOMAN TITLES

Ağa: leader of an organization. The most influential *ağas* were the commander of the Janissary corps, the sultan's elite troops (*see p127*), and the Ağa of the Abode of Felicity, or chief black eunuch, who was in charge of the harem (*see pp58–9*).

Chief black eunuch

Bey: governor of a district or province. The word is now used simply to mean "Mr".

Caliph: spiritual ruler of the Islamic world. The title was assumed by the Ottoman sultans, beginning with Selim the Grim in 1517.

Gazi: honorary title given to a victorious Islamic warrior.

Kadi: judge charged with interpreting Islamic law and Ottoman administrative codes.

Khedive: viceroy of Egypt under Ottoman rule (1867–1914). The autonomous khedives acknowledged the religious leadership of the Ottoman Empire.

Paşa: title bestowed on a senior civil servant or high-ranking army officer. According to his rank, a *paşa* was entitled to display one, two or three horsetails on his standard (*see p56*).

Sultan: political and religious ruler of the empire.

Şeyhülislam (Grand Mufti): head of the *ulema*, a religious institution which was made up of "learned men" responsible for interpreting and enforcing Islamic law (*sharia*).

Valide sultana: mother of the ruling sultan.

Vizier: minister of state. The four most senior ministers were called "viziers of the dome" because they attended cabinet meetings in the domed hall of the divan in Topkapı Palace (*see pp54–9*). From the 16th century, the divan was presided over by the immensely powerful grand vizier (the prime minister).

Grand vizier

A Janissary leaps to his death in a German painting of the Auspicious Event of 1826

THE REFORMING SULTANS

Abdül Hamit I (1774–89) resumed the work of reform and was succeeded by Selim III, who instituted a wide range of changes to the military and Ottoman society. He was deposed by a Janissary mutiny in 1807. Mahmut II (1808–39) realized that the Janissary corps *(see p127)* could not be reformed, so he established a modern army alongside them, but the Janissaries rebelled and were massacred on 15 June 1826 in the "Auspicious Event". Soon after, in 1829, the sultan introduced further modernizing measures including changes in the dress code.

Later in his reign Mahmut re-organized central government so that a regulated bureaucracy

replaced the old system of rule by military and religious powers. By doing this he paved the way for his sons Abdül Mecit (1839–61) and Abdül Aziz (1861–76) to oversee the Tanzimat (Reordering), a series of legislative reforms. Functionaries were given higher salaries to deter them from taking bribes, and the grand vizier's post was replaced by that of prime minister.

A constitution was declared in 1876, creating parliamentary government. However, the Russian-Turkish War of 1877–88 led to Abdül Hamit II suspending it and ruling alone for the next 30 years. In 1908 a bloodless revolution by a collection of educated men – the so-called Young Turks – finally forced the sultan to recall parliament.

ATATÜRK AND WESTERNIZATION

Throughout the 19th- and early 20th-centuries, the Ottoman Empire steadily lost territory through wars with Russia and Austria, and to emerging Balkan nation-states such as Serbia, Greece and Bulgaria. Then, in World War I, despite famously winning the battle for Gallipoli in a valiant defence of the Dardanelles *(see p170)*, the Ottoman Empire found itself on the losing side. Istanbul was occupied by victorious French and British troops, and much of Western Anatolia by Greek forces.

Artillery in action at Gallipoli

TIMELINE

Dolmabahçe clocktower

1807 Much of the city is destroyed during a Janissary revolt against Mahmut II

1845 First (wooden) Galata Bridge is built over the Golden Horn

1870 Schliemann begins excavation of Troy *(see p171)*

1888 Rail link with Paris leads to first run of the Orient Express *(see p66)*

1800	1825	1850	1875	19

1826 Mahmut II finally destroys the Janissaries in their own barracks in the "Auspicious Event"

1856 Abdül Mecit I abandons Topkapı Palace for the new Dolmabahçe Palace *(see pp128–9)*

1875 The Tünel underground railway system, the third built in the world, opens in Galata

Orient Express poster

The peace treaties that followed rewarded the victors with Ottoman territory and as a result stimulated Turkish nationalists to take over power from the sultan.

The history of modern Turkey is dominated by the figure of Mustafa Kemal Paşa (1881–1938), a military hero turned politician, universally known as Atatürk, or "Father of the Turks". It was at his instigation that the Turkish War of Independence was fought to regain land lost to the Allies and, in particular, Greece. At the end of this war, the present territorial limits of Turkey were

A portrait of Atatürk

established. Atatürk then started a programme of political and social change. The sultanate was abolished in 1922, and religion and state were formally separated a year later, when the country was declared a secular republic. His reforms included replacing the Arabic alphabet with a Roman one, allowing women greater social and political rights, encouraging Western dress (the fez was banned) and obliging all Turks to choose a surname.

MODERN ISTANBUL

Another part of this process was to move the institutions of state from the old Ottoman city of Istanbul to the more centrally located Ankara, which became the capital of Turkey in 1923. Since then, Istanbul has gone through a dramatic transformation into a modern city. As migrants

from Anatolia have poured in, the population has increased, and although small communities of Jews, Arabs, Armenians and Christians remain within the city, they are now vastly outnumbered by Turks.

Modern tram *(see p240)*

A booming economy has led to the building of new motorways and bridges, and the public transport network has been revolutionized with modern trams, light railways and fast catamaran sea buses *(see p243)*. Meanwhile Istanbul has geared itself up for tourism: its ancient monuments have been restored and many new hotels and restaurants were opened in the run up to 2010, Istanbul's year as European Capital of Culture.

But, like Turkey as a whole, Istanbul is forever wrestling with a divided half-Asian, half-European identity. The influences of these contrasting cultures remain widely evident today and create the city's unique atmosphere.

The 1970s suspension bridge spanning the Bosphorus

The Ottoman Sultans

The first Ottomans were the leaders of warlike tribes living on the borders of the Byzantine Empire. From the 13th century, however, the dynasty established itself at the head of a large empire. In their heyday, having captured Istanbul in 1453 (see p26), the Ottoman sultans were admired and feared for their military strength and ruthlessness towards opponents and rival pretenders to the throne. Later sultans often led a decadent life-style while power was exercised by their viziers (see p29).

Murat III (1574–95), whose *tuğra (see p95)* is shown above, fathers over 100 children

Selim II, "the Sot" (1566–74), prefers drinking and harem life to the affairs of state

Selim I, "the Grim" (1512–20), seen here at his coronation, assumes the title of caliph after his conquest of Egypt

Osman Gazi (1299–1326), a tribal chieftain, establishes the Ottoman dynasty

Murat I (1359–89)

Mehmet I (1403–21)

Beyazıt II (1481–1512)

1250	1300	1350	1400	1450	1500	1550

1250	1300	1350	1400	1450	1500	1550

Orhan Gazi (1326–59) is the first Ottoman to bear the title of sultan

Süleyman I, "the Magnificent" (1520–66), expands the empire and fosters a golden age of artistic achievement

Beyazıt I (1389–1402) is nicknamed "the Thunderbolt" because of the speed at which he takes strategic decisions and moves his troops from one place to another

Period of Interregnum (1402–13) while Beyazıt's sons fight each other over the succession

Murat II (1421–51), the greatest of the warrior sultans, gains notable victories against the Crusaders

Mehmet II, "the Conqueror" (1451–81), captures Constantinople in 1453. He then rebuilds the city, transforming it into the new capital of the empire

Mehmet III (1595–1603) succeeds the throne after his mother has but one of his 19 brothers strangl

Mustafa I (1617–18 and 1622–3), a weak and incompetent ruler, reigns for two short periods and is deposed twice

Abdül Mecit I (1839–61) presides over the reforms of the Tanzimat *(see p30)*

Mehmet VI (1918–22), the last Ottoman sultan, is forced into exile by the declaration of the Turkish Republic *(see p31)*

Mahmut II, "the Reformer" (1808–39), finally defeats the Janissaries *(see p127)*

İbrahim, "the Mad" (1640–48), much despised, goes insane at the end of his short but disastrous reign

Mehmet V (1909–18)

Mahmut I (1730–54)

Murat V (1876)

Mustafa II (1695–1703)

Süleyman II (1687–91)

Mustafa III (1757–74)

| 1650 | 1700 | 1750 | 1800 | 1850 | 1900 |

| 1650 | 1700 | 1750 | 1800 | 1850 | 1900 |

Ahmet II (1691–5)

Osman III (1754–7)

Abdül Mecit II (1922–3) is caliph only, the sultanate having been abolished in 1922 *(see p31)*

Abdül Aziz (1861–76)

Mehmet IV (1648–87)

Abdül Hamit I (1774–89)

Murat IV (1623–40)

Mustafa IV 1807–08

Ahmet III (1703–30) presides over a cultural flowering known as the Tulip Period *(see p27)*

Osman II (1618–22)

Abdül Hamit II (1876–1909) suspends parliament for 30 years and rules an autocratic police state until toppled from power by the Young Turk movement

Ahmet I (1603–17) has the Blue Mosque *(see pp78–9)* constructed in the centre of Istanbul

Selim III (1789–1807) attempts Western-style reforms but is overthrown by a revolt of the Janissaries

ISTANBUL AT A GLANCE

More than 100 places worth visiting in Istanbul are described in the *Area by Area* section of this book, which covers the sights of central Istanbul as well as those a short way out of the city centre. They range from mosques, churches, palaces and museums to bazaars, Turkish baths and parks. For a breathtaking view across Istanbul, you can climb the Galata Tower *(see p105)*, or take a ride on a ferry *(see pp242–3)* to the city's Asian shore. A selection of the sights you should not miss is given below. If you are short of time, you will probably want to concentrate on the most famous monuments, namely Topkapı Palace, Haghia Sophia and the Blue Mosque, which are all located conveniently close to each other.

ISTANBUL'S TOP TEN SIGHTS

Topkapı Palace
See pp54–7

Archaeological Museum
See pp62–5

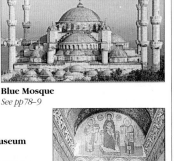

Blue Mosque
See pp78–9

Dolmabahçe Palace
See pp128–9

Haghia Sophia
See pp72–5

Basilica Cistern
See p76

Süleymaniye Mosque
See pp90–91

The Bosphorus Trip
See pp144–9

Grand Bazaar
See pp98–9

Church of St Saviour in Chora
See pp118–19

◁ View of Haghia Sophia in central Sultanahmet, a great Byzantine church later converted into a mosque

Istanbul's Best: Mosques and Churches

Most visitors to Istanbul will immediately be
struck by the quantity of mosques, from the
imposing domed buildings dominating the skyline
to the small neighbourhood mosques which would
pass unnoticed were it not for their minarets. Several mosques were built as churches, but converted
for Islamic worship after the Ottoman conquest
(see p26). Some of the most outstanding of them
have since become national
monuments, but no longer
serve a religious function.

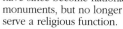

St Saviour in Chora
*The Dormition of the Virgin
is one of many beautiful
mosaics that fill this Byzantine
church (see pp118–19).*

Eyüp Mosque
*The holiest mosque in
Istanbul stands beside
the tomb of Eyüp Ensari,
a companion
of the Prophet
Mohammed
(see p120).*

GOLDEN HO

**Church of the
Pammakaristos**
*An image of Christ
Pantocrator gazes
down from the
main dome of what
was one of the most
important churches
in the city (see p113).*

Fatih Mosque
*Rebuilt after an earth-
quake, this mosque was
founded by Mehmet the
Conqueror after his con-
quest of the city (see p26).
The inner courtyard is
especially fine (see p113).*

Süleymaniye Mosque
*Sinan, the greatest Ottoman
imperial architect, built this
mosque in honour of his patron
Süleyman the Magnificent (see
p26). He placed ablution taps
in the side arches of the mosque
to serve a large number of
worshippers (see pp90–91).*

Atik Valide Mosque
The last major work of Sinan (see p91), this mosque was built in 1583 for the wife of Selim II. Its mihrab (niche indicating the direction of Mecca) is surrounded by İznik tiles (see p131).

Rüstem Paşa Mosque
The fine tiles decorating this mosque date from the mid-16th century, the greatest period of İznik tile (see p161) production (see p88).

Haghia Sophia
One of the world's greatest feats of architecture, Haghia Sophia dates from AD 537. The calligraphic roundels were added in the 19th century (see pp72–5).

BEYOĞLU

B O S P H O R U S

ASIAN SIDE

SERAGLIO
POINT

BAZAAR
ARTER

Blue Mosque
Istanbul's most famous landmark was built by some of the same stonemasons who later helped construct the Taj Mahal in India (see pp78–9).

SULTANAHMET

Church of SS Sergius and Bacchus
An intricate frieze with a Greek inscription honouring the two dedicatees of this former church has survived for 1,400 years (see p82).

| 0 metres | 500 |
| 0 yards | 500 |

Exploring Mosques

Five times a day throughout Istanbul a chant is broadcast over loudspeakers set high in the city's minarets to call the faithful to prayer. Over 99 per cent of the population is Muslim, though the Turkish state is officially secular. Most belong to the Sunni branch of Islam, but there are also a few Shiites. Both follow the teachings of the Koran, the sacred book of Islam, and the Prophet Mohammed (c.570–632), but Shiites accept, in addition, the authority of a line of 12 imams directly descended from Mohammed. Islamic mystics are known as Sufis *(see p104)*.

Overview of the Süleymaniye Mosque complex

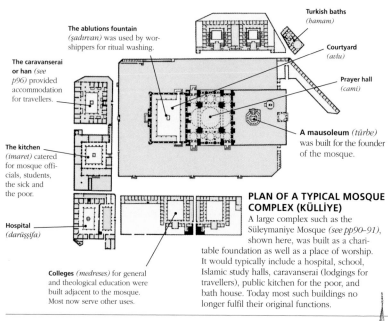

Turkish baths *(hamam)*

The ablutions fountain *(şadırvan)* was used by worshippers for ritual washing.

The caravanserai or han *(see p96)* provided accommodation for travellers.

Courtyard *(avlu)*

Prayer hall *(cami)*

The kitchen *(imaret)* catered for mosque officials, students, the sick and the poor.

A mausoleum *(türbe)* was built for the founder of the mosque.

Hospital *(darüşşifa)*

Colleges *(medreses)* for general and theological education were built adjacent to the mosque. Most now serve other uses.

PLAN OF A TYPICAL MOSQUE COMPLEX (KÜLLİYE)

A large complex such as the Süleymaniye Mosque *(see pp90–91)*, shown here, was built as a charitable foundation as well as a place of worship. It would typically include a hospital, school, Islamic study halls, caravanserai (lodgings for travellers), public kitchen for the poor, and bath house. Today most such buildings no longer fulfil their original functions.

INSIDE A MOSQUE

Visitors will experience a soaring sense of space on entering the prayer hall of one of Istanbul's great mosques. Islam forbids images of living things (human or animal) inside a mosque, so there are never any statues or figurative paintings; but the geometric and abstract architectural details of the interior can be exquisite. Men and women pray separately. Women often use a screened off area or a balcony.

The müezzin mahfili *is a raised platform found in large mosques. The muezzin (mosque official) stands on this when chanting responses to the prayers of the imam (head of the mosque).*

The mihrab, *an ornate niche in the wall, marks the direction of Mecca. The prayer hall is laid out so that most people can see it.*

The minbar *is a lofty pulpit to the right of the mihrab. This is used by the imam when he delivers the Friday sermon (khutba).*

MUSLIM BELIEFS AND PRACTICES

Muslims believe in God (Allah), and the Koran shares many prophets and stories with the Bible. However, whereas for Christians Jesus is the son of God, Muslims hold that he was just one in a line of prophets – the last being Mohammed, who brought the final revelation of God's truth to mankind. Muslims believe that Allah communicated the sacred texts of the Koran to Mohammed, via the archangel Gabriel.

There are five basic duties for Muslims. The first of these is the profession of faith: "There is no God but God, and Mohammed is his Prophet". Muslims are also enjoined to pray five times a day, give alms to the poor, and fast during the month of Ramazan *(see p47)*. Once in their lifetime, if they can afford it, they should make the pilgrimage (hajj) to Mecca (in Saudi Arabia), the site of the Kaaba, a sacred shrine built by Abraham, and also the birthplace of the Prophet.

The call to prayer *used to be given by the muezzin from the balcony of the minaret. Nowadays loudspeakers broadcast the call across the city. Only imperial mosques have more than one minaret.*

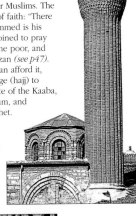

PRAYER TIMES

The five daily prayer times are calculated according to the times of sunrise and sunset, and so change throughout the year. Exact times will be posted up on boards outside large mosques. Those given here are a guide.

Prayer	Summer	Winter
Sabah	5am	7am
öğle	1pm	1pm
İkindi	6pm	4pm
Akşam	8pm	6pm
Yatsı	9:30pm	8pm

When praying, *Muslims always face the Kaaba in the holy city of Mecca, even if they are not in a mosque, where the mihrab indicates the right direction. Kneeling and lowering the head to the ground are gestures of humility and respect for Allah.*

Ritual ablutions *must be undertaken before prayer. Worshippers wash their head, hands and feet either at the fountain in the courtyard or, more usually, at taps set in a discreet wall of the mosque.*

The loge (hünkar mahfili) *provided the sultan with a screened-off balcony where he could pray, safe from would-be assassins.*

The kürsü, *seen in some mosques, is a chair or throne used by the imam while he reads extracts from the Koran.*

VISITING A MOSQUE

Visitors are welcome at any mosque in Istanbul, but non-Muslims should try to avoid prayer times, especially the main weekly congregation and sermon on Fridays at 1pm. Take off your shoes before entering the prayer hall. Shoulders and knees should be covered. Some mosques require women to cover their hair; scarves can usually be borrowed. Do not eat, take photographs with a flash or stand close to worshippers. A contribution to a donation box or mosque official is courteous.

Board outside a mosque giving times of prayer

Istanbul's Best: Palaces and Museums

As the former capital of an empire that spanned from Algeria to Iraq and from Arabia to Hungary, Istanbul is home to a huge and diverse collection of treasures. Some, from musical instruments to priceless jewels, are housed in the beautiful former imperial palaces of the Ottoman sultans, which are worth visiting in any case for their architecture and opulent interiors. Topkapı and Dolmabahçe are the most famous palaces in Istanbul. The Archaeological Museum should also be on any itinerary of the city. This map points out these and other palaces and museums which are worth visiting for their splendid buildings or the exceptional collections they contain.

Aynalı Kavak Palace
This reclusive palace, with its airy feel and intimate proportions, shows subtler aspects of Ottoman taste. It houses a collection of Turkish musical instruments.

Archaeological Museum
Purpose-built in 1896, this superb museum has exhibits ranging from prehistory to the Byzantine era. They include this classical sculpture of the 2nd-century Roman Emperor Hadrian.

Museum of Calligraphy
Some of the texts in Istanbul's collection of Ottoman calligraphy (see p95) are by sultans, such as this panel by Ahmet III (1703–30).

THE BAZAAR
QUARTER

SERAGLIO
POINT

BEYOĞLU

GOLDEN HORN

SULTANAHMET

Museum of Turkish and Islamic Arts
This Seljuk example is one of the many carpets (see pp218–19) included in this museum's display of Turkish heritage. Other collections include glassware and ceramics.

Mosaic Museum
Gladiators fighting a lion are shown in one of the floors from the Great Palace (see pp82–3) displayed in this small museum.

Military Museum
A highlight of this museum is the famous Mehter Band, which gives regular outdoor concerts of Ottoman military music.

Şale Pavilion
One of a group of pavilions built in leafy Yildiz Park by 19th-century sultans, the Şale Pavilion has around 50 splendid rooms, including the Mother-of-Pearl Hall.

BOSPHORUS

THE ASIAN SIDE

Dolmabahçe Palace
This opulent 19th-century palace is home to such marvels as 2-m (7-ft) high vases, a crystal staircase and an alabaster bathroom.

Topkapı Palace
This huge palace was used as the official royal residence for 400 years. The treasury contains a myriad of precious objects including the Kasikci Diamond and this ornate ceremonial canteen.

Beylerbeyi Palace
Adorning one of the principal atriums of this 19th-century imperial summer palace is this elegant marble fountain. The palace was built to entertain visiting foreign dignitaries.

0 metres	750
0 yards	750

Exploring Istanbul's Collections

The *saz*, a type of lute

Each museum in Istanbul contributes a piece to the vast cultural jigsaw of this cosmopolitan city. From Ancient Greek remains and early Chinese ceramics, which arrived in the city along the Silk Route, to 16th-century tiles commissioned for the great mosques and modern industrial machinery, each has its place in the history of Istanbul. Many of the larger museums have a wide range of exhibits and therefore feature under several of the headings below.

The Sarcophagus of the Mourning Women, Archaeological Museum

ARCHAEOLOGY

The archaeological fruits of the expansive Ottoman Empire are displayed in the **Archaeological Museum**, where the exhibits range from monumental 6th-century BC Babylonian friezes to exquisite classical sarcophagi and statues. Classical sculpture fills the ground floor. Upstairs there is a gallery for the archaeology of Syria and Cyprus. Ancient oriental finds are housed in an annexe. The **Museum of Turkish and Islamic Arts** features specifically Muslim artifacts, including early Iraqi and Iranian ceramics as well as beautiful displays of glassware, metalwork and woodwork.

Byzantine mosaic floor in the Mosaic Museum

BYZANTINE ANTIQUITIES

Although Constantinople was the capital of the Byzantine Empire *(see pp20–25)* for over 1,000 years, it can be hard to get a full picture of the city in that period. The best place to start is the **Archaeological Museum**, which has displays illustrating the city's Byzantine history. Its courtyard contains the purple sarcophagi of the Byzantine emperors.

For Byzantine church mosaics, visit the **Church of St Saviour in Chora** near the city walls which has some particularly fine examples vividly depicting the lives of Christ and the Virgin Mary. The impressive **Haghia Sophia** has a few brilliant gold mosaics remaining, some dating back to the reign of Justinian *(see p20)*. The galleries and upper walls of the **Church of the Pammakaristos** are covered with mosaics, although public access is restricted.

The **Mosaic Museum** houses mosaic floors and murals from the now-vanished Byzantine Great Palace *(see pp82–3)*, which were discovered by archaeologists in 1938. The **Sadberk Hanım Museum** also houses several Byzantine antiquities, including icons, ceramics and jewellery.

Mosque lamp from the Archaeological Museum

CALLIGRAPHY

In the days before the printed word, Ottoman calligraphy *(see p95)* developed into a highly skilled artform, widely used both to ornament religious texts and legal documents and decrees. The **Museum of Calligraphy** mounts a continuous series of temporary exhibitions. Early Koranic calligraphy can be viewed in **Topkapı Palace**, the **Museum of Turkish and Islamic Arts** and the **Sakıp Sabancı Museum** *(see p141)*.

CERAMICS

Experts and amateurs come from all over the world to view the collection of Chinese ceramics and porcelain on display in the kitchens of **Topkapı Palace**. The earliest examples provided the inspiration for Turkey's indigenous ceramic production at İznik *(see p161)*. Examples of İznik tiles can be seen on the walls of Topkapı Palace and in the city's mosques. İznik tiles and also pottery are on display in the Çinili Pavilion, an annexe of the **Archaeological Museum**, and at the **Sadberk Hanım Museum**. A wider selection of ceramics from all over the Islamic world can be found in the **Museum of Turkish and Islamic Arts**.

OTTOMAN INTERIORS

The interiors that can be visited in Istanbul run the gamut from the classical Ottoman styling of the older parts of **Topkapı Palace** to extravagant European-inspired 19th-century decor. In the latter category, the huge **Dolmabahçe Palace** set the style. It was decorated with Bohemian glass and Hereke carpets and has an

The opulent Süfera Salon in Dolmabahçe Palace

ornate central stairway fashioned of crystal and brass. The **Pavilion of the Linden Tree** and the Rococo **Küçüksu Palace**, although more intimate in scale, are equally lavish in their interior style.

TEXTILES

The Ottomans were justifiably proud of their textile tradition, which can be admired in the huge imperial costume collection at **Topkapı Palace**, begun in 1850. The palace collection houses older materials, including kaftans dating back to the 15th century. The **Sadberk Hanım Museum** houses magnificent, mostly 19th-century pieces on the top floor and some fine examples of delicate Turkish embroidery.

On a larger scale, there are huge imperial campaign tents in the **Military Museum**, which also has a collection of miniature Janissary *(see p127)* costumes. Uniforms, nomadic tents and a renowned selection of fine carpets are on display in the **Museum of Turkish and Islamic Arts**. The collection includes rug fragments dating back to the 13th century, as well as palatial silks on a larger scale.

Kaftan from
Topkapı Palace

MUSICAL INSTRUMENTS

Examples of typical Turkish instruments, such as the *saz* (lute), can be found in a museum devoted to them at **Aynalı Kavak Palace**. Those played by the Whirling Dervishes are on display at the **Mevlevi Monastery**. Instruments can also be seen, and bought, in two shops situated near the entrance to Gülhane Park *(see p61)*. Traditional Turkish military instruments can be heard being played at the **Military Museum**.

MILITARIA

The beautiful barges in which the Ottoman sultans were rowed around the Golden Horn and the Bosphorus are part of the **Naval Museum** collection. Naval uniforms and paintings of military scenes also feature. Weapons and armour from the 12th–20th centuries can be found in the **Military Museum**, along with a cannon, captured by the Turks during their European campaigns. There is a smaller selection of weaponry in the armoury of **Topkapı Palace**. The **Florence Nightingale Museum**

(located in the Selimiye Barracks on the Asian Side) commemorates the work of the nurse during the Crimean War. It also has some interesting military exhibits.

PAINTING

Close to Dolmabahçe Palace is Istanbul's **Museum of Fine Arts**, which offers a collection of largely late 19th- and early 20th-century Turkish paintings. Those interested in more contemporary works of art may also like to visit the changing exhibitions at the **Taksim Art Gallery**.

SCIENCE AND TECHNOLOGY

Located in a converted warehouse in the heart of Istanbul's docks is the **Rahmi Koç Museum**. It is home to a selection of mechanical and scientific instruments dating from the early years of the Industrial Revolution, as well as an entire reconstructed bridge taken from an early 20th-century ship.

ISTANBUL THROUGH THE YEAR

Istanbul is at its best in late May and early September, when temperatures are mild and sunshine is plentiful. High season, from June to August, is the most expensive, crowded and hottest time to visit, but the summer arts and music festivals are highlights in the city's cultural calendar. Late November until March or April can be damp and dreary. However, Istanbul is still mild in autumn

National Sovereignty Day in Istanbul

and winter and, with fewer tour parties around, you can enjoy the sights in peace. As well as arts and sporting events, several public holidays and religious festivals punctuate the year. It is wise to be aware of these when planning an itinerary as some sights may be closed or else crammed with locals enjoying a day out. Some of these celebrations are also fascinating spectacles in their own right.

Tulips growing in Emirgan Park, scene of the spring Tulip Festival

SPRING

As the winter smog fades and sunshine increases, cafés and restaurants prepare for the first wave of alfresco dining. After a winter's diet of apples and oranges, a welcome crop of spring fruits, including fresh figs, strawberries and tart green plums, arrives in the shops. Toasted sweetcorn is sold from carts *(see p208)*, and a spring catch of sea bream, sea bass and turbot is on the menu. Tulips, hyacinths, daffodils and pansies fill parks and gardens, and the distinctive pink buds of the Judas tree are seen along the Bosphorus. Monuments and museums are generally uncrowded in spring, and discounts are available at many hotels. In May the popular son et lumière shows outside the Blue Mosque *(see pp78–9)* begin and continue until September.

EVENTS

Easter *(March or April)*. Pilgrimage to the Monastery of St George on Büyükada in the Princes' Islands *(see p159)*.
International Istanbul Film Festival *(late March–mid-April)*, selected cinemas. Screening of Turkish and foreign films and related events.
Tulip Festival *(April)*, Emirgan Park *(see p141)*. Displays of springtime blooms.
National Sovereignty Day *(23 April)*. Public holiday marking the inauguration of the Turkish Republic in 1923 *(see pp30–31)*. Children take to the streets in folk costume.
Commemoration of the Anzac Landings *(25 April)*, Gallipoli. Britons, Australians and New Zealanders gather at the location of the Anzac landings at Gallipoli during World War I *(see pp170–71)*.

Spring Day and Workers' Day *(1 May)*. Unofficial public holiday when workers usually attend union-organized rallies.
Kakava Festival *(early May)*, Edirne. A celebration of gypsy music and dance.
Youth and Sports Day *(19 May)*. Public holiday in commemoration of the start of the War of Independence *(see p31)* in 1919, with sporting events and other activities held throughout the city in stadiums and on the streets.
International Istanbul Theatre Festival *(May–June, every two years)*, various venues. European and Turkish productions.
Conquest of Istanbul *(29 May)*, between Tophane and Karaköy and on the shores of the upper Bosphorus. Mehmet the Conqueror's taking of the city in 1453 *(see p26)* is re-enacted in street parades and mock battles.

Colourful evening son et lumière show at the Blue Mosque

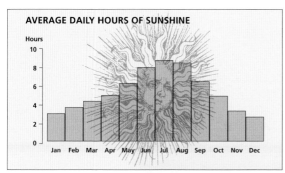

AVERAGE DAILY HOURS OF SUNSHINE

Sunshine Chart
One of Istanbul's attractions is its summer sunshine – there are about 2,500 hours each year. From May to October the city is bathed in light well into the evening, however, bursts of heavy rain are common in high summer. Winter, by contrast, is notoriously deprived of sun.

SUMMER

In contrast to an all-too-brief spring, the warm weather and clear skies of summer can linger on in Istanbul until November. In July and August temperatures soar and although luxury hotels have air conditioning, cheaper ones do not. Popular sights are packed with tourists throughout the high season. Picturesque locations outside Istanbul may, on the other hand, be overrun by locals. At weekends city dwellers trek to the Belgrade Forest and Black Sea beaches *(see p158)* or to health clubs along the Bosphorus. Those who can afford it flee to their coastal summer homes until autumn.

For those who stay behind there is a strong summer culture. This includes a wild nightlife in hundreds of bars and night spots *(see p213)*, and enthusiastic support for many arts festivals, which attract world-famous performers. Look out, too, for events taking place in historical buildings. You may be able to listen to classical music in Haghia Eirene *(see p60)* or enjoy a pop concert in the Fortress of Europe on the Bosphorus *(see pp140–41)*. This is also the best time of year for outdoor sports such as hiking, horse-riding, water sports, golf and parachuting.

In summer, the menu focuses more on meat than fish, but vegetables and fresh fruit – such

Silk Market in Bursa, which operates all year round

as honeydew melons, cherries, mulberries, peaches and apricots – are widely available. In July and August many shops have summer sales *(see p203)*.

EVENTS

Silk Market *(June–July)*, Bursa. Special market for the sale of silk cocoons *(see p164)*.
International Istanbul Music and Dance Festival *(mid-June–July)*. Classical music, opera and dance performed in historic locations. Mozart's *Abduction from the*

Performance of Mozart's *Abduction from the Seraglio* in the Harem of Topkapı Palace

Seraglio is staged annually in Topkapı Palace *(see pp54–9)*.
Bursa Festival *(June–July)*, Bursa Park. Music, folk dancing, plays, opera and shadow puppetry.
Navy Day *(1 July)*. Parades of old and new boats along the Bosphorus.
International Istanbul Jazz Festival *(July)*, various venues. International event with a devoted following.
International Sailing Races *(July)*. Regatta held at the Marmara Islands *(see p169)*.
Grease Wrestling *(July)*, Kırkpınar, Edirne. Wrestlers smeared with olive oil grapple with each other *(see p154)*.
Hunting Festival *(3 days, late July)*, Edirne. Music, art and fishing displays.
Folklore and Music Festival *(late July)*, Bursa. Ethnic dances and crafts displays.
Festival of Troy *(August)*, Çanakkale. Re-enactment of the tale of Troy *(see p171)*.
Victory Day *(30 August)*. Public holiday commemorating victory over Greece in 1922.

AVERAGE MONTHLY RAINFALL

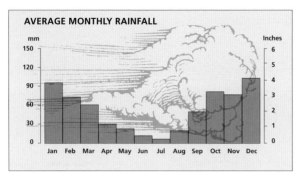

mm / Inches

150 / 6
120 / 5
90 / 4
60 / 3
30 / 2
0

Jan Feb Mar Apr May Jun Jul Aug Sep Oct Nov Dec

Rainfall Chart
Winter is the wettest season in Istanbul. Heavy showers of rain can sometimes continue into April and May, making spring seem shorter. Sudden snowstorms are not uncommon in winter, but these are short-lived and snowfalls will usually melt away as quickly as they come.

AUTUMN

Residents of Istanbul often consider their city to be at its best in autumn. As the summer heat loses its grip, chestnut sellers appear on the streets *(see p208)*, pumpkins are sold in the markets, and fresh figs are eaten in abundance. In the surrounding countryside, cotton, wheat and sunflowers are harvested. Migratory grouper and bonito are among the tastiest types of fish which are caught at this time of year.

A popular beauty spot for its array of autumn colours is Lake Abant, 200 km (125 miles) east of Istanbul. Meanwhile, bird-watchers converge on the hills overlooking the Bosphorus to view great flocks of migratory birds heading for their warm wintering grounds in Africa *(see p141)*.

On the cultural agenda is a world-class arts biennial and an antiques fair which blends Turkish and Western aesthetics. Several public holidays reaffirm Turkey's commitment to secularism, including Republic Day in late October, during which flags are hung from balconies. The bridges over the Bosphorus *(see p138)* are hung with particularly huge flags.

Street-side roasting of seasonal chestnuts

EVENTS

Tüyap Arts Fair *(September)*, opposite the Pera Palas Hotel *(see p104)*. A showcase of Istanbul's artistic talent.
Yapı Kredi Festival *(September)*, various venues. A celebration of music and dance promoting young performers.

Republic Day *(29 October)*. Public holiday commemorating Atatürk's proclamation of the Republic in 1923 *(see p31)*. The Turkish flag adorns buildings in the city.
Akbank Jazz Festival *(October)*, various venues. Jazz music *(see p221)*.
International Istanbul Fine Arts Biennial *(October–November every two years, 2011, 2013)*. International and local avant-garde artists exhibit work in historic locations such as Haghia Eirene and the Imperial Mint *(see p60)*, and the Basilica Cistern *(see p76)*.
Anniversary of Death *(10 November)*. A minute's silence is observed at 9:05am, the precise time of Atatürk's death in Dolmabahçe Palace *(see pp128–9)* in 1938.
Tüyap Book Fair *(October)*, Belikduzu Fair and Congress Centre. Istanbul's premier publishing event showcases prominent writers.
Efes Pilsen Blues Festival *(early November)*, selected venues. Foreign and local blues bands play in popular music venues across the city.
Interior Design Fair *(first week of November)*, Çırağan Palace Hotel Kempinski *(see p123)*. Interior designers and antique dealers display up-market wares in this popular annual show.
Elit's Küsav Antiques Fair *(mid-November)*, Military Museum *(see p126)*. Sale of local and foreign paintings, furniture, carpets, maps, books, porcelain, textiles, silver, clocks and bronze statuary.

Crowds gathering to celebrate Republic Day on 29 October

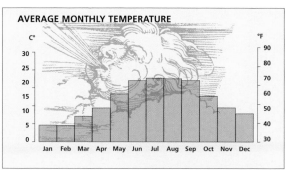

Temperature Chart
The temperature of the city rarely drops below freezing in winter, and even very cold snaps seldom last longer than three days. The heat of the long, humid summer is intensified by the lodos wind, which blows in from the Sea of Marmara. However, the northerly poyraz occasionally provides a cooling breeze.

WINTER

There are distinct bonuses to visiting Istanbul in the winter, when even major sights are uncrowded, although the rain, fog and pollution may be off-putting. Shops in the Akmerkez, Galleria, Capitol and Carousel malls *(see p211)* hold sales, making the city a shopper's paradise for leather, woollens and fashion.

Outside Istanbul, when enough snow has fallen on the mountains, the ski season begins in Uludağ *(see p169)*, one of Turkey's most important winter sports resorts. Meanwhile baklava and cream cakes are consumed in the cosy cafés along the Bosphorus and in the old quarter of Beyoğlu *(see pp100–7)*.

View of Bebek on the Bosphorus *(see pp136–49)* in winter

the founder of the famous Whirling Dervishes.

Christmas *(late December)*. Though Christmas Day is not a public holiday, major hotels organize seasonal festivities.

New Year's Day *(1 January)*. Public holiday incorporating European Christmas traditions including eating turkey, decorating trees and partying. Strings of lights adorn the main roads.

Karadam Ski Festival *(second half of February)*, Uludağ Mountain. Competitions organized by local radio stations and the Uludağ Ski Instructors' Association.

Multitude of lights to welcome in the New Year in Beyoğlu

EVENTS

Mevlâna Festival *(17–24 December)*, Mevlevi Monastery *(see p104)*. Enthusiastic Istanbul devotees perform special dances in honour of

MUSLIM HOLIDAYS

The dates of Muslim holidays vary according to the phases of the moon and therefore change from year to year. In the holy month of **Ramazan**, Muslims refrain from eating and drinking between dawn and dusk. Some restaurants are closed during the day, and tourists should be discreet when eating in public. Straight after this is the three-day **Şeker Bayramı** (Sugar Festival), when sweetmeats are prepared. Two months later the four-day **Kurban Bayramı** (Feast of the Sacrifice) commemorates the Koranic version of Abraham's sacrifice. This is the main annual public holiday in Turkey, and hotels, trains and roads are packed. Strict Muslims also observe the festivals of **Regaip Kandili, Miraç Kandili, Berat Kandili** and **Mevlid-i-Nebi**.

Festivities during Şeker Bayramı

ISTANBUL
AREA BY AREA

SERAGLIO POINT

The hilly, wooded promontory that marks the meeting point of the Golden Horn, the Sea of Marmara and the Bosphorus occupies a natural strategic position. In Byzantine times, monasteries and public buildings stood on this site. Today it is dominated by the grandiose complex of buildings forming Topkapı Palace, the residence of the Ottoman sultans and the women of the harem for 400 years.

Lion relief from the Ishtar Gate

The palace is now open to the public as a rambling museum, with lavish apartments and glittering collections of jewels and other treasures. Originally, the palace covered almost the whole of the area with its gardens and pavilions. Part of the grounds have now been turned into a public park. Adjacent to it is the Archaeological Museum, a renowned collection of finds from Turkey and the Near East.

SIGHTS AT A GLANCE

Museums and Palaces
Archaeological Museum pp62–5 ❷
Topkapı Palace pp54–9 ❶

Churches
Haghia Eirene ❹

Historic Buildings and Monuments
Fountain of Ahmet III ❺
Imperial Mint ❸
Sirkeci Station ⑪
Sublime Porte ❾

Streets and Courtyards
Cafer Ağa Courtyard ❼
Soğukçeşme Sokağı ❻

Parks
Gülhane Park ❽

Turkish Baths
Cağaloğlu Baths ⑩

GETTING AROUND
With little traffic, this area is easily explored on foot. Trams between the Grand Bazaar and the ferry piers at Eminönü stop outside Gülhane Park.

Sirkeci
Sarayburnu
KENNEDY   CADDESI
Sirkeci
İSTASYON ARKASI SOK
MURADİYE CAD
NÖBETHANE CAD
DARÜSSADE SOK
TAYA HATUN JOKAĞI
HÜDAVENDİGÂR CAD
İBNİ KEMAL
EBUSSUUT CADDESİ
 SÜRMELİ SOK
ÇÖPLÜK SOK
EBRİZ SOK
ANKARA CADDESİ
HÜKÜMET KONAĞI SOK
ALAY KÖŞKÜ CAD
ALEMDAR
Gülhane
TEREBATAN CADDESİ
CADDESİ
(SAHİL YOLU)
(YOLU)
İSHAK PAŞA CADDESİ
KENNEDY   CADDESİ
Cankurtaran

| 0 metres | 400 |
| 0 yards | 400 |

KEY

Street-by-Street map
See pp52–3

⛴ Ferry boarding point

🚆 Railway station

🚊 Tram stop

ℹ Tourist information

Ⓒ Mosque

— Walls

◁ **The Circumcision Pavilion in the third courtyard of Topkapı Palace**

Street-by-Street: The First Courtyard of Topkapı

The juxtaposition of Ottoman palace walls, intimately proportioned wooden houses and a soaring Byzantine church lends plenty of drama to the First Courtyard, the outer part of Topkapı Palace. This was once a service area, housing the mint, a hospital, college and a bakery. It was also the mustering point of the Janissaries *(see p127)*. Nowadays, the Cafer Ağa Courtyard and the Fatih Büfe, just outside the courtyard wall, offer unusual settings for refreshments. Gülhane Park, meanwhile, is one of the few shady open spaces in a city of monuments.

Gülhane Park
Once a rose garden in the outer grounds of Topkapı Palace, the wooded Gülhane Park provides welcome shade in which to escape from the heat of the city **8**

Soğukçeşme Sokağı
Traditional, painted wooden houses line this narrow street **6**

Sublime Porte
A Rococo gate stands in place of the old Sublime Porte, once the entrance to (and symbol of) the Ottoman government **9**

Museum of the Ancient Orient

Entrance to Gülhane Park

Gülhane tram stop

Alay Pavilion

0 metres   75
0 yards   75

KEY

– – – Suggested route

Zeynep Sultan Mosque
Resembling a Byzantine church, this mosque was built in 1769 by the daughter of Ahmet III, Princess Zeynep.

Büfes, tiny ornate kiosks, sell drinks and snacks.

Cafer Ağa Courtyard
The cells of this former college, ranged round a tranquil courtyard café, are now occupied by jewellers, calligraphers and other artisans selling their wares **7**

STAR SIGHTS

★ Archaeological Museum

★ Topkapı Palace

★ **Archaeological Museum**
Classical statues, dazzling carved sarcophagi, Turkish ceramics and other treasures from all over the former Ottoman Empire make this one of the world's great collections of antiquities ❷

Çinili Pavilion
(see p65)

The Executioner's Fountain is so named because the executioner washed his hands and sword here after a public beheading.

LOCATOR MAP
See Street Finder maps 3 and 5

Entrance to Topkapı Palace

Topkapı Palace ticket office

★ **Topkapı Palace**
For 400 years the Ottoman sultans ruled their empire from this vast palace. Its fine art collections, opulent rooms and leafy courtyards are among the highlights of a visit to Istanbul ❶

Imperial Mint
This museum houses exhibitions on the historical background to Istanbul ❸

Haghia Eirene
The Byzantine church of Haghia Eirene dates from the 6th century. Unusually, it has never been converted into a mosque ❹

Imperial Gate

Fountain of Ahmet III
Built in the early 18th century, the finest of Istanbul's Rococo fountains is inscribed with poetry likening it to the fountains of paradise ❺

Topkapı Palace ❶

Topkapı Sarayı

Süleyman I's tuğra over the main gate

Between 1459 and 1465, shortly after his conquest of Constantinople *(see p26)*, Mehmet II built Topkapı Palace as his main residence. Rather than a single building, it was conceived as a series of pavilions contained by four enormous courtyards, a stone version of the tented encampments from which the nomadic Ottomans had emerged. Initially, the palace served as the seat of government and housed a school in which civil servants and soldiers were trained. In the 18th century, however, the government was moved to the Sublime Porte *(see p61)*. Sultan Abdül Mecit I abandoned Topkapı in 1853 in favour of Dolmabahçe Palace *(see pp128–9)*. In 1924 Topkapı was opened to the public as a museum. Some areas are currently closed for renovation.

★ **Harem**
The labyrinth of exquisite rooms where the sultan's wives and concubines lived is open to visitors (see pp58–9).

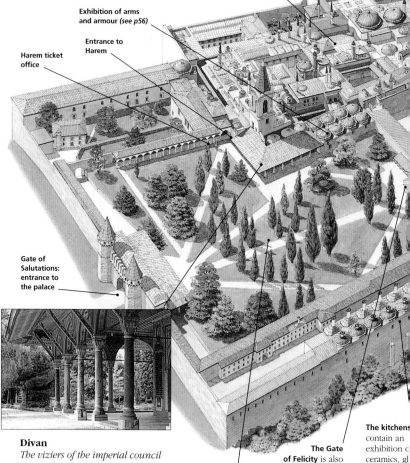

Exhibition of arms and armour *(see p56)*

Entrance to Harem

Harem ticket office

Gate of Salutations: entrance to the palace

Divan
The viziers of the imperial council met in this chamber, sometimes watched covertly by the sultan.

Second courtyard

The Gate of Felicity is also called the Gate of the White Eunuchs.

The kitchens contain an exhibition of ceramics, gl and silverw *(see p56)*.

İftariye Pavilion
Standing between the Baghdad and Circumcision pavilions, this canopied balcony provides views down to the Golden Horn.

VISITORS' CHECKLIST

Babıhümayun Cad. **Map** 3 F3.
Tel (0212) 512 04 80.
Sultanahmet. 9am–4pm
Wed–Mon. **Harem**
9:30am–3:30pm Wed–Mon.
(book early).

Baghdad Pavilion
In 1639 Murat IV built this pavilion to celebrate his capture of Baghdad. It has exquisite blue-and-white tilework.

Circumcision Pavilion

Exhibition of clocks
(see p57)

vilion of the
ly Mantle
e p57)

Exhibition of miniatures and manuscripts
(see p57)

Konyalı Restaurant
(see p198)

The fourth courtyard
is a series of gardens dotted with pavilions.

Third courtyard

Library of Ahmet III
Erected in 1719, the library is an elegant marble building. This ornamental fountain is set into the wall below its main entrance.

Exhibition of imperial costumes
(see p56)

Throne Room

★ Treasury
This 17th-century jewel-encrusted jug is one of the precious objects exhibited in the former treasury (see p57).

STAR FEATURES

★ Harem
★ Treasury

Exploring the Palace's Collections

During their 470-year reign, the Ottoman sultans amassed a glittering collection of treasures. After the foundation of the Turkish Republic in 1923 (see p31), this was nationalized and the bulk of it put on display in Topkapı Palace. As well as diplomatic gifts and articles commissioned from the craftsmen of the palace workshops, a large number of items in the collection were brought back as booty from successful military campaigns. Many such trophies date from the massive expansion of the Otto-man Empire during the reign of Selim the Grim (1512–20), when Syria, Arabia and Egypt were conquered.

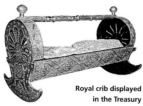

Royal crib displayed in the Treasury

CERAMICS, GLASS AND SILVERWARE

The kitchens contain the palace's collection of glass, ceramics and silverware. Turkish and European pieces are overshadowed by the vast display of Chinese and, to a lesser extent, Japanese porcelain. This was brought to Turkey along the Silk Route, the overland trading link between the Far East and Europe. Topkapı's collection of Chinese porcelain is the world's second best after China itself.

Japanese porcelain plate

The Chinese porcelain on display spans four dynasties: the Sung (10–13th centuries), followed by the Yüan (13–14th centuries), the Ming (14–17th centuries) and the Ching (17–20th centuries). Celadon, the earliest form of Chinese porce-lain collected by the sultans, was made to look like jade, a stone believed by the Chinese to be lucky. The Ottomans prized it because it was said to neutralize poison in food. There are also several exquisite blue-and-white pieces, mostly of the Ming era.

Chinese aesthetics were an important influence on Otto-man craftsmen, particularly in the creation of designs for their fledgling ceramics industry at İznik (see p161). Although there are no İznik pieces in the Topkapı collection, many of the tiles on the palace walls originated there. These clearly show the influence of designs used for Chinese blue-and-white porcelain, such as cloud scrolls and stylized flowers.

Much of the later porce-lain, particularly the Japanese Imari ware, was made specifically for the export market. The most obvious examples of this are some plates decorated with quotations from the Koran. A part of the kitchens, the old confectioners' pantry, has been preserved as it would have been when in use. On display are huge cauldrons and other utensils wielded by the palace's chefs to feed its 12,000 residents and guests. This area is currently closed for renovation.

ARMS AND ARMOUR

Taxes and tributes from all over the empire were once stored in this chamber, which was known as the Inner Treasury. Straight ahead as you enter is a series of horse-tail standards. Carried in processions or displayed outside tents, these proclaimed the rank of their owners. Viziers (see p29), for example, merited three; the grand vizier, five; and the sultan's banner, nine.

The weaponry includes or-nately embellished swords and several bows made by sultans themselves (Beyazıt II was a particularly fine craftsman). The huge iron swords used by European crusaders look crude by comparison. Also on view are pieces of 15th-century Ottoman chainmail and colourful shields. The shields have metal centres surrounded by closely woven straw painted with flowers. This area is currently closed for renovation.

IMPERIAL COSTUMES

A collection of imperial costumes is displayed in the Hall of the Campaign Pages, whose task was to look after the royal wardrobe. It was a palace tradition that on the death of a sultan his clothes were carefully folded and placed in sealed bags. As a result, it is possible to see a perfectly preserved kaftan once worn by Mehmet the Conqueror (see p26). The reforms of Sultan Mahmut II included a revolution in the dress code (see p30). The end of an era came as plain grey serge replaced the earlier luxurious silken textiles.

Sumptuous silk kaftan once worn by Mehmet the Conqueror

TREASURY

Of all the exhibitions in the palace, the Treasury's collection is the easiest to appreciate, glittering as it does with thousands of precious and semi-precious stones. The only surprise is that there are so few women's jewels here. Whereas the treasures of the sultans and viziers were owned by the state and reverted to the palace on their deaths, those belonging to the women of the court did not.

In the first hall stands a full, diamond-encrusted suit of chainmail, designed for Mustafa III (1757–74) for ceremonial use. Diplomatic gifts include a fine pearl statuette of a prince seated beneath a canopy, which was sent to Sultan Abdül Aziz (1861–76) from India.

The Topkapı dagger

The greatest pieces are in the second hall. Foremost among these is the Topkapı dagger (1741). This splendid object was commissioned by the sultan from his own jewellers. It was intended as a present for the Shah of Persia, but he died before it reached him. Among other exhibits here are a selection of the bejewelled aigrettes (plumes) which added splendour to imperial turbans.

In the third hall, the 86-carat Spoonmaker's diamond is said to have been discovered in a rubbish heap in Istanbul in the 17th century, and bought from a scrap merchant for three spoons. The gold-plated Bayram throne was given to Murat III (see p32) by the Governor of Egypt in 1574 and used for state ceremonies until early this century.

It was the throne in the fourth hall, given by the Shah of Persia, which was to have been acknowledged by the equally magnificent gift of the Topkapı dagger. In a cabinet near the throne is an unusual relic: a case containing bones said to be from the hand of St John the Baptist.

MINIATURES AND MANUSCRIPTS

It is possible to display only a tiny fraction of Topkapı's total collection of over 13,000 miniatures and manuscripts at any one time. Highlights of it include a series of depictions of warriors and fearsome creatures known as *Demons and Monsters in the Life of Nomads*, which was painted by Mohammed Siyah Qalem, possibly as early as the 12th century. It is from this Eastern tradition of miniature painting, which was also prevalent in Mogul India and Persia, that the ebullient Ottoman style of miniatures developed.

Also on show are some fine examples of calligraphy (see p95), including texts of the Koran, manuscripts of poetry and several firmans, or imperial decrees. This area is currently closed for renovation.

Cover of a Koran, decorated in gold filigree work

CLOCKS

European clocks given to, or bought by, various sultans form the majority of this collection, despite the fact that there were makers of clocks and watches in Istanbul from the 17th century. The clocks

A 17th-century watch made of gold, enamel and precious stones

range from simple, weight-driven 16th-century examples to an exquisite 18th-century English mechanism encased in mother-of-pearl and featuring a German organ which played tunes on the hour to the delight of the harem.

Interestingly, the only male European eyewitness accounts of life in the harem were written by the mechanics sent to service these instruments.

PAVILION OF THE HOLY MANTLE

Some of the holiest relics of Islam are displayed in these five domed rooms, which are a place of pilgrimage for Muslims. Most of the relics found their way to Istanbul as a result of the conquest by Selim the Grim (see p26) of Egypt and Arabia, and his assumption of the caliphate (the leadership of Islam) in 1517.

The most sacred treasure is the mantle once worn by the Prophet Mohammed. Visitors cannot actually enter the room in which it is stored; instead they look into it from an antechamber through an open doorway. Night and day, holy men continuously chant passages from the Koran over the gold chest in which the mantle is stored. A stand in front of the chest holds two of Mohammed's swords.

A glass cabinet in the anteroom contains hairs from the beard of the Prophet, a letter written by him and an impression of his footprint.

In the other rooms you can see some of the ornate locks and keys for the Kaaba (see p39) which were sent to Mecca by successive sultans.

Topkapı Palace: The Harem

The word Harem derives from the Arabic for "forbidden". A Harem was the residence of the sultan's wives, concubines and children, who were guarded by black slave eunuchs. The sultan and his sons were the only other men allowed access to the Harem, which also included the Cage, a set of rooms where the sultan's brothers were confined to avoid destabilizing succession contests. Topkapı's Harem was laid out by Sultan Murat III in the late 16th century and is a labyrinth of brilliantly tiled corridors and chambers.

Stained-glass window in the Paired Pavilions

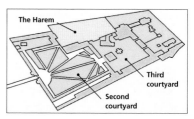

The Harem

Third courtyard

Second courtyard

LOCATOR MAP
See main illustration of the palace on pp54–5

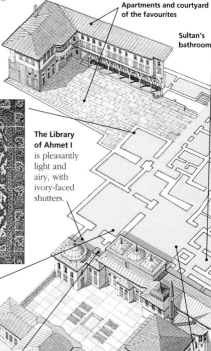

Apartments and courtyard of the favourites

Sultan's bathroom

★ **Paired Pavilions**
These twin apartments, built in the 17th century for the crown prince, boast superb İznik tiles (see p161) and a dome lined with gilded canvas.

The Library of Ahmet I is pleasantly light and airy, with ivory-faced shutters.

The Salon of Murat III, built by Sinan (*see p91*), has fine tiled walls, a handsome fountain and a large hearth.

★ **Dining Room of Ahmet III**
A sumptuous array of fruit and flowers is painted on to the walls of this 18th-century chamber, which is also known as the Fruit Room.

Imperial Hall
The largest room in the Harem, this hall was used for entertainments. Against one wall stands a large throne, from which the sultan would view the proceedings.

LIFE IN THE HAREM

The women of the Harem were slaves, gathered from the furthest corners of the Ottoman Empire and beyond. Their dream was to become a favourite of the sultan (see p28) and bear him a son, which on some occasions led to marriage. Competition was stiff, however, for at its height the Harem contained over 1,000 concubines, many of whom never rose beyond the service of their fellow captives. The last women eventually left in 1909.

A western view of Harem life in a 19th-century engraving

Salon of the Valide Sultana
The sultan's mother, the valide sultana (see p29), was the most powerful woman in the Harem and had some of the best rooms.

The Tower of Justice offers a superb view of Topkapı's rooftops and beyond.

Courtyard of the valide sultan

The Golden Way is so called because new sultans reputedly threw gold coins to their concubines here.

Exit

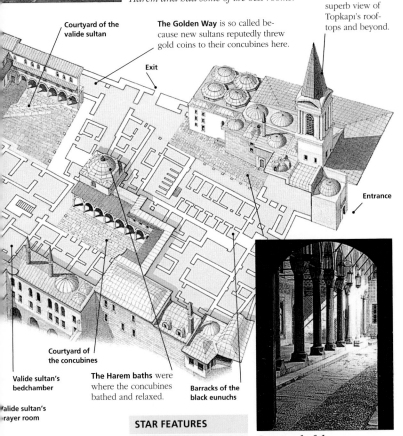

Entrance

Courtyard of the concubines

Valide sultan's bedchamber

The Harem baths were where the concubines bathed and relaxed.

Barracks of the black eunuchs

Valide sultan's prayer room

STAR FEATURES

★ Paired Pavilions

★ Dining Room of Ahmet III

Courtyard of the Black Eunuchs
Marble columns line this courtyard, which still has some old-fashioned, wrought-iron lamps.

KEY

☐ Rooms open to the public

☐ Areas closed to the public

Archaeological Museum ❷

See pp62–5.

Imperial Mint ❸
Darphane-i Amire

First courtyard of Topkapı Palace.
Map 3 E4 (5 F3). 🚇 *Gülhane or Sultanahmet.*

The Ottoman Mint opened here in 1727, but most of what can be seen today dates from the reign of Mahmut II (1808–39), when the complex was extended. In 1967, the mint moved to a new location. The buildings now house laboratories for the state restoration and conservation department, but visitors can look around the exterior of the building during office hours.

Haghia Eirene ❹
Aya İrini Kilisesi

First courtyard of Topkapı Palace.
Map 3 E4 (5 F3). **Tel** *(0212) 522 17 50.* 🚇 *Gülhane or Sultanahmet.* ⬜ *by special permission and for concerts.*

Though the present church dates only from the 6th century, it is at least the third building to be erected on what is thought to be the oldest site of Christian worship in Istanbul. Within a decade of the Muslim conquest of the city

One of the four elaborately decorated sides of the Fountain of Ahmet III

in 1453 *(see p26)* it had been included within the Topkapı Palace complex for use as an arsenal. Today the building, with its good acoustics, hosts concerts during the Istanbul Music Festival *(see p45).*

Inside are three fascinating features that have not survived in any other Byzantine church in the city. The *synthronon*, the five rows of built-in seats hugging the apse, were occupied by clergymen officiating during services. Above this looms a simple black mosaic cross on a gold background, which dates from the iconoclastic period *(see p20),* when figurative images were forbidden. At the back of the church is a cloister-like courtyard where deceased Byzantine emperors once lay in their porphyry sarcophagi. Most have been moved to the Archaeological Museum.

Fountain of Ahmet III ❺
Ahmet III Çeşmesi

Junction of İshak Paşa Cad & Babıhümayun Cad. **Map** 3 E4 (5 F4). 🚇 *Gülhane or Sultanahmet.*

Built in 1729, the most beautiful of Istanbul's countless fountains survived the violent deposition of Sultan Ahmet III two years later. Many of the other monuments constructed by the sultan during his reign, which has become known as the Tulip Period *(see p27),* were destroyed. The fountain is in the delicate Turkish Rococo style, with five small domes, mihrab-shaped niches and dizzying floral reliefs.

Ottoman "fountains" do not spout jets of water, but are more like ornate public taps. They sometimes incorporated a counter, or *sebil,* from which refreshments would be served.

In this case, each of the fountain's four walls is equipped with a tap, or *çeşme,* above a carved marble basin. Over each tap is an elaborate calligraphic inscription by the 18th-century poet Seyit Vehbi Efendi. The inscription, in gold on a blue-green background, is in honour of the fountain and its founder. At each of the four corners there is a *sebil* backed by three windows covered by ornate marble grilles. Instead of the customary iced water, passers-by at this fountain would have been offered sherbets and flavoured waters in silver goblets.

The apse of Haghia Eirene, with its imposing black-on-gold cross

Soğukçeşme Sokağı ❻

Map 3 E4 (5 F3). 🚊 *Gülhane.*

Charming old wooden houses line this narrow, sloping cobbled lane ("the street of the cold fountain"), which squeezes between the outer walls of Topkapı Palace and the towering minarets of Haghia Sophia. Traditional houses like these were built in the city from the late 18th century onwards.

The buildings in the lane were renovated by the Turkish Touring and Automobile Club (TTOK, *see p181*) in the 1980s. Of these, nine buildings form the Ayasofya Pansiyonları *(see p184)*, a series of attractive pastel-painted guesthouses popular with tourists. Another building has been converted by the TTOK into a library of historical writings on Istanbul, and archive of engravings and photographs of the city. A Roman cistern towards the bottom of the lane has been converted into the Sarniç restaurant *(see p198)*.

Traditional calligraphy on sale in Cafer Ağa Courtyard

Cafer Ağa Courtyard ❼

Cafer Ağa Medresesi

Caferiye Sok. **Map** 5 E3. **Tel** *(0212) 513 18 43.* 🚊 *Gülhane.* ◯ *8:30am–8pm daily.*

This peaceful courtyard at the end of an alley was built in 1559 by Sinan *(see p91)* for the chief black eunuch *(see p29)* as a *medrese* (theological college, *see p38*). Sinan's bust presides over the café tables in the courtyard. The former students' lodgings

Restored Ottoman house on Soğukçeşme Sokağı

are now used to display a variety of craft goods typically including jewellery, silk prints, ceramics and calligraphy.

Gülhane Park ❽

Gülhane Parkı

Alemdar Cad. **Map** 3 E3 (5 F2). 🚊 *Gülhane.* ◯ *daily.* **Museum** ◯ *9am–4:30pm Wed–Mon.* 🖼

Gülhane Park occupies what was the lower grounds of Topkapı Palace. Today it has a neglected air but it is still a shady place to stroll and it includes a couple of interesting landmarks.

The History of Islamic Science and Technology Museum, housed in the stables, exhibits the discoveries and inventions of Islamic scientists through the history of Islam.

At the far end of the park is the Goths' Column, a well-preserved 3rd-century victory monument, surrounded by clapboard teahouses. Its name comes from the Latin inscription on it which reads: "Fortune is restored to us because of victory over the Goths".

Across Kennedy Caddesi, the main road running along the northeast side of the park, there is a viewpoint over the busy waters where the Golden Horn meets the Bosphorus.

OTTOMAN HOUSES

The typical, smart town house of 19th-century Istanbul had a stone ground floor above which were one or two wooden storeys. The building invariably sported a *çikma*, a section projecting out over the street. This developed from the traditional Turkish balcony, which was enclosed in the northern part of the country because of the colder climate. Wooden lattice covers, or *kafesler*, over the windows on the upper storeys ensured that the women of the house were able to watch life on the street below without being seen themselves. Few wooden houses have survived. Those that remain usually owe their existence to tourism and many have been restored as hotels. While the law forbids their demolition, it is extremely hard to obtain insurance for them in a city that has experienced many devastating fires.

Sublime Porte ❾

Bab-ı Ali

Alemdar Cad. **Map** 3 E3 (5 E2). 🚊 *Gülhane.*

Foreign ambassadors to Ottoman Turkey were known as Ambassadors to the Sublime Porte, after this monumental gateway which once led into the offices and palace of the grand vizier. The institution of the Sublime Porte filled an important role in Ottoman society because it could often provide an effective counterbalance to the whims of sultans.

The Rococo gateway you see today was built in the 1840s. Its guarded entrance now shields the offices of Istanbul's provincial government.

Rococo decoration on the roof of the Sublime Porte

Archaeological Museum ❷
Arkeoloji Müzesi

Roman statue of Apollo

Although this collection of antiquities was begun only in the mid-19th century, provincial governors were soon sending in objects from the length and breadth of the Ottoman Empire. Today the museum has one of the world's richest collections of classical artifacts, and also includes treasures from the pre-classical world. The main building was erected under the directorship of Osman Hamdi Bey (1881–1910), to house his finds. This archaeologist, painter and polymath discovered the exquisite sarcophagi in the royal necropolis at Sidon in present-day Lebanon. A four-storey wing added later includes the Children's Museum.

★ **Alexander Sarcophagus**
This fabulously carved marble tomb from the late 4th century BC is thought to have been built for King Abdalonymos of Sidon. It is called the Alexander Sarcophagus because Alexander the Great is depicted on it winning a victory over the Persians.

KEY

- ☐ Classical Archaeology
- ☐ Children's Museum
- ☐ Thracian, Bithynian and Byzantine Collections
- ☐ Istanbul Through the Ages
- ☐ Anatolia and Troy
- ☐ Anatolia's Neighbouring Cultures
- ☐ Turkish Tiles and Ceramics
- ☐ Museum of the Ancient Orient
- ☐ Non-exhibition space

The porticoes of the museum take their design from the 4th-century BC Sarcophagus of the Mourning Women.

Sarcophagus of the Mourning Women

Çinili Pavilion

GALLERY GUIDE
The 20 galleries of the main building house the museum's important collection of classical antiquities. The four-storey wing has displays on the archaeology of Istanbul and nearby regions, and includes the Children's Museum. There are two other buildings within the grounds: the çinili Pavilion, which contains Turkish tiles and ceramics, and the Museum of the Ancient Orient.

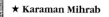

Outdoor café

STAR EXHIBITS

- ★ Alexander Sarcophagus
- ★ Karaman Mihrab
- ★ Treaty of Kadesh

★ **Karaman Mihrab**
This blue, richly tiled mihrab (see p38) comes from the city of Karaman in southeast Turkey, which was the capital of the Karamanid state from 1256–1483. It is the most important artistic relic of that culture.

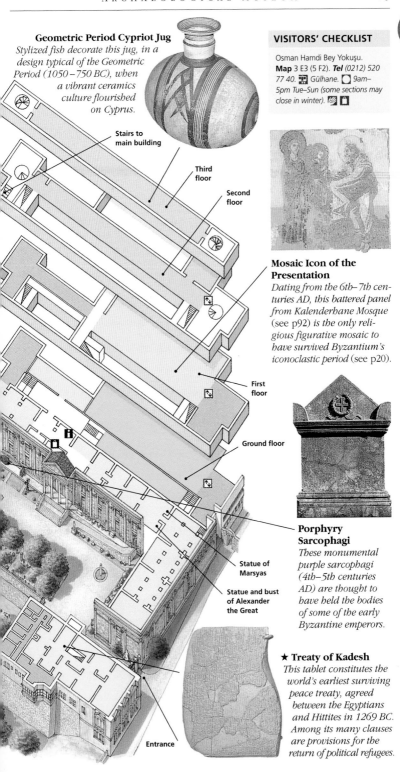

Geometric Period Cypriot Jug
Stylized fish decorate this jug, in a design typical of the Geometric Period (1050–750 BC), when a vibrant ceramics culture flourished on Cyprus.

VISITORS' CHECKLIST

Osman Hamdi Bey Yokuşu.
Map 3 E3 (5 F2). *Tel* (0212) 520
77 40. Gülhane. 9am–
5pm Tue–Sun (some sections may
close in winter).

Stairs to main building

Third floor

Second floor

First floor

Ground floor

Mosaic Icon of the Presentation
Dating from the 6th–7th centuries AD, this battered panel from Kalenderhane Mosque (see p92) is the only religious figurative mosaic to have survived Byzantium's iconoclastic period (see p20).

Porphyry Sarcophagi
These monumental purple sarcophagi (4th–5th centuries AD) are thought to have held the bodies of some of the early Byzantine emperors.

Statue of Marsyas

Statue and bust of Alexander the Great

★ Treaty of Kadesh
This tablet constitutes the world's earliest surviving peace treaty, agreed between the Egyptians and Hittites in 1269 BC. Among its many clauses are provisions for the return of political refugees.

Entrance

Exploring the Archaeological Museum

This enormous collection spans over 5,000 years, from figurines of the Mother Goddess modelled in the 3rd millennium BC to Turkish pottery thrown in the 19th century. To cover everything in one visit is impossible. Visitors with little time should not miss the breathtaking sarcophagi from the royal necropolis at Sidon. To learn more about the history of Istanbul itself you should head for the gallery exploring this theme, on the first floor of the New Building wing. Youngsters may enjoy the displays in the Children's Museum.

CLASSICAL ARCHAEOLOGY

Monumental Bes, the ancient Egyptian god, greets visitors at the door to the main building. Hugely popular in the 1st–3rd centuries, Bes' comically grotesque appearance was an effective deterrent for evil spirits. Rooms 9 and 8 contain the highlights of the museum's entire collection: a group of sarcophagi unearthed in 1887 at Sidon (in present-day Lebanon). These are thought to have been made for a line of Phoenician kings who ruled

Marble bust of Emperor Augustus

in the 6th–4th centuries BC. Their decoration vividly shows the transition from Egyptian to Greek influence in the art of the Near East at that time.

The latest and finest of them is the so-called Alexander Sarcophagus (late 4th century BC). Alexander the Great features in two decorative, high-relief friezes on the longest sides. These show a battle scene and a hunting scene. The friezes survive in almost perfect condition, showing traces of their original colouring, though the metal weapons of the soldiers and hunters have been lost.

The Sarcophagus of the Mourning Women is thought to have been made for King Straton (374–358 BC), who was known for his fondness for women. The grief-stricken females may have been members of his harem.

Rooms 14–20 contain some remarkable statues. Among them is a Roman copy of a 3rd century BC statue of Marsyas, depicting the satyr about to be flayed after daring to challenge Apollo's musical ability. A statue and bust of Alexander the Great (3rd–2nd centuries BC) show the conqueror as the perfect hero, with a meditative expression in his face. Room 18 contains realistic busts of Roman emperors.

CHILDREN'S MUSEUM

Special low cabinets are used in this part of the museum, which is designed for visiting schoolchildren. Paper and coloured crayons are to hand in a bid to stimulate future archaeologists.

THRACIAN, BITHYNIAN AND BYZANTINE COLLECTIONS

This gallery on the ground floor of the New Building wing displays religious and other artifacts from the ancient civilizations of Thrace and Bithynia, and from Byzantium (see pp20–25) – including a statue of Byzantine Emperor Valens. This section of the musuem also covers the architecture of the ancient world.

Bronze head of a snake from the Serpentine Column

ISTANBUL THROUGH THE AGES

With a few well-chosen pieces and explanatory texts in Turkish and English, this gallery brilliantly chronicles Istanbul's archaeological past.

The rare Mosaic Icon of the Presentation (c.AD 600) originally adorned the Kalenderhane Mosque (see p92). One of the three snakes' heads from the Serpentine Column, which has stood headless in the Hippodrome (see p80) since the 18th century, is also displayed here. Look out too for a section of the iron chains that the Byzantines hung across both the Bosphorus and the Golden Horn to stop hostile ships (see p23).

Frieze showing the battle of Issus (333 BC), on the side panel of the Alexander Sarcophagus

Reconstruction of a mausoleum discovered at Palmyra in Syria

ANATOLIA AND TROY

One side of this narrow, long hall chronicles the history of Anatolia (the Asiatic part of modern Turkey) from the Palaeolithic era to the Iron Age. It culminates with a room devoted to the Phrygian culture, which centred on the city of Gordion. The highlight is a recreation of an 8th-century BC royal tomb, which was housed beneath a tumulus in a juniper-wood chamber. As well as cooking utensils, the king was buried with furniture made of oak, box, yew and juniper.

The other side of the gallery traces the excavations of nine different civilizations at Troy (see p171), from 3000 BC to the time of Christ. On display are a few pieces of the gold hoard known as the Schliemann treasure, after the archaeologist who first discovered it in the late 19th century. Most of the pieces were smuggled out of Turkey, however, and are now in museums around the world.

ANATOLIA'S NEIGHBOURING CULTURES

This long gallery is also divided in two, with one side devoted to Cyprus and the other to Syria-Palestine. The Cypriot collection was assembled by the joint American and Russian consul to Cyprus, Luigi Palma di Cesnola, who systematically looted its tombs from 1865–73. Apart from some beautiful pots, the most interesting objects are the figures of plump, naked temple boys (3rd century BC). They are thought to represent boy prostitutes at temples to Aphrodite, the Greek goddess of love.

Among the Syrian exhibits are funerary reliefs, the Gezer Calendar (925 BC) – a limestone tablet bearing the oldest known Hebrew inscription – and a reconstruction of a 1st–3rd-century mausoleum from the trading oasis of Palmyra.

16th-century İznik tiled lunette in the Çinili Pavilion

TURKISH TILES AND CERAMICS

Apart from carpets, the most distinctive Turkish art form is ceramics. This is particularly seen in the sheets of tiles used to decorate the walls of mosques and pavilions such as the Çinili Pavilion, where the entrance archway is plastered with geometric and calligraphic tiles.

In the main room there is an exquisite early 15th-century tiled mihrab from central Anatolia. Rooms 3 and 4 contain tiles and mosque lamps from the famed İznik potteries, the hub of Turkish ceramics production (see p161). With the decline in quality of İznik ceramics in the late 16th century, other centres took over. One of these, Kütahya, also produced pieces of beauty and high quality (rooms 5 and 6).

MUSEUM OF THE ANCIENT ORIENT

Although this collection contains antiquities of great rarity and beauty from the Egyptian and Hittite cultures, pride of place goes to the artifacts from the early civilizations of Mesopotamia (present-day Iraq).

The monumental glazed brick friezes from Babylon's main entrance, the Ishtar Gate, (rooms 3 and 9) date from the reign of Nebuchadnezzar II (605–562 BC), when the capital of Babylon experienced its final flowering. The elegant, 30-kg (65-lb) duck-shaped weight in Room 4 comes from a much earlier Babylonian temple (c.2000 BC).

Room 5 contains some of the earliest known examples of writing, in the form of cuneiform inscriptions on clay tablets, dating from 2700 BC. The famous Treaty of Kadesh (room 7), concluded around 1269 BC between the Egyptian and Hittite empires, was originally written on a sheet of silver. The one in this collection is a Hittite copy. The treaty includes many sophisticated clauses, including one providing for the return of a political refugee, who was "not to be charged with his crime, nor his house and wives and his children be harmed".

Glazed frieze of a bull from Ishtar Gate, Babylon

Cağaloğlu Baths ❿
Cağaloğlu Hamamı

Prof Kazım İsmail Gürkan Cad 34,
Cağaloğlu. **Map** 3 E4 (5 D3).
Tel (0212) 522 24 24.
🚋 Sultanahmet. ⭕ daily 8am–8pm.
www.cagalogluhamami.com.tr

Among the city's more sumptuous Turkish baths, the
ones in Cağaloğlu were built
by Sultan Mahmut I in 1741.
The income from them was
designated for the maintenance
of Mahmut's library in Haghia
Sophia (see pp72–5).
　The city's smaller baths have
different times at which men
and women can use the same
facilities. But in larger baths,

**Corridor leading into the Cağaloğlu
Baths, built by Mahmut I**

such as this one, there are
entirely separate sections. In
the Cağaloğlu Baths the men's
and women's sections are at
right angles to one another and
entered from different streets.
Each consists of three parts: a
camekan, a *soğukluk* and the
main bath chamber or *hararet*,
which centres on a massive
octagonal massage slab.
　The Cağaloğlu Baths are
popular with foreign visitors
because the staff are happy to
explain the procedure. Even
if you do not want to sweat it
out, you can still take a look
inside the entrance corridor and
camekan of the men's section.
Here you will find a small
display of Ottoman bathing
regalia, including precarious
wooden clogs once worn by
women on what would fre-
quently be their only outing
from the confines of the home.
You can also sit and have a
drink by the fountain in the
peaceful *camekan*.

Sirkeci Station ⓫
Sirkeci Garı

Sirkeci İstasyon Cad, Sirkeci. **Map** 3E3
(5 E1). **Tel** (0212) 527 00 50 or 520
65 75. 🚋 Sirkeci. ⭕ daily.

This magnificent railway
station was built to receive
the long-anticipated Orient
Express from Europe. It was
officially opened in 1890, even

**Sirkeci Station, final destination
of the historic Orient Express**

though the luxurious train had
been running into Istanbul for
a year by then. The design, by
the German architect Jasmund,
successfully incorporates features from the many different
architectural traditions of
Istanbul. Byzantine alternating
stone and brick courses are
combined with a Seljuk-style
monumental recessed portal
and Muslim horseshoe arches
around the windows.
　The station café is a good
place in which to escape the
bustle of the city for a while.
Sirkeci serves Greece and
other destinations in Europe
as well as the European part
of Turkey. Istanbul's other
mainline railway station is
Haydarpaşa (see p133), on
the Asian side of the city.

THE WORLD-FAMOUS ORIENT EXPRESS

The Orient Express made its first run from Paris to
Istanbul in 1889, covering the 2,900-km (1,800-mile)
journey in three days. Both Sirkeci Station and the
Pera Palas Hotel (see p104) in Istanbul were built
especially to receive its passengers. The wealthy and
often distinguished passengers of "The Train of
Kings, the King of Trains" did indeed include kings
among the many presidents, politicians, aristocrats
and actresses. King Boris III of Bulgaria even made a
habit of taking over from the driver of the train when
he travelled on it through his own country.
　A byword for exoticism and romance, the train was
associated with the orientalist view of Istanbul as a
treacherous melting pot of diplomats and arms dealers.
It inspired no fewer than 19 books – *Murder on the
Orient Express* by Agatha Christie and *Stamboul Train*
by Graham Greene foremost among them – six films
and one piece of music. During the Cold War
standards of luxury crashed, though a service of
sorts, without even a restaurant car, continued twice
weekly to Istanbul until 1977.

**A 1920s poster for the Orient Express,
showing a romantic view of Istanbul**

Turkish Baths

No trip to Istanbul is complete without an hour or two spent in a Turkish bath *(hamam)*, which will leave your whole body feeling rejuvenated. Turkish baths differ little from the baths of ancient Rome, from which they derive, except there is no pool of cold water to plunge into at the end.

A full service will entail a period of relaxation in the steam-filled hot room, punctuated by bouts of

Ornate wash basin

vigorous soaping and massaging. There is no time limit, but allow at least an hour and a half for a leisurely bath. Towels and soap will be provided, but you can take special toiletries with you. Two historic baths located in the old city, Çemberlitaş *(see p81)* and Cağaloğlu (illustrated below), are used to catering for foreign tourists. Most luxury hotels have their own baths *(see pp180–91)*.

Choosing a Service
Services, detailed in a price list at the entrance, range from a self-service option to a luxury body scrub, shampoo and massage.

The *camekan* (entrance hall) is a peaceful internal courtyard near the entrance of the building. Bathers change clothes in cubicles surrounding it. The *camekan* is also the place to relax with a cup of tea after bathing.

Changing Clothes
Before changing you will be given a cloth (peştemal), to wrap around you, and a pair of slippers for walking on the hot, wet floor.

Corridor from street

Basin and tap for washing

Small, star-like windows piercing the domes

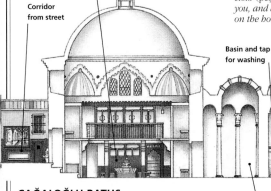

CAĞALOĞLU BATHS
The opulent, 18th-century Turkish baths at Cağaloğlu have separate, identical sections for men and women. The men's section is shown here.

The *soğukluk* (intermediate room) is a temperate passage between the changing room and the *hararet*. You will be given dry towels here on your way back to the *camekan*.

In the *hararet* (hot room), the main room of the Turkish bath, you are permitted to sit and sweat in the steam for as long as you like.

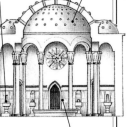

The Exfoliating Body Scrub
In between steaming, you (or the staff at the baths) scrub your body briskly with a coarse, soapy mitt (kese).

The Body Massage
A marble plinth (göbek taşı) occupies the centre of the hot room. This is where you will have your pummelling full-body massage.

SULTANAHMET

I stanbul's two principal monuments face each other across an area of gardens known informally as Sultanahmet Square. This part of the city gets its name from Sultan Ahmet I, who built the Blue Mosque. Opposite is Haghia Sophia, an outstanding example of early Byzantine architecture, and still one of the world's most remarkable churches. A neat oblong square

Mosaic of Empress Irene in Haghia Sophia

next to the Blue Mosque marks the site of the Hippodrome, a chariot-racing stadium built by the Romans in around AD 200. On the other side of the Blue Mosque, Sultanahmet slopes down to the Sea of Marmara in a jumble of alleyways. Here, traditional-style Ottoman wooden houses have been built over the remains of the Great Palace of the Byzantine emperors.

SIGHTS AT A GLANCE

Mosques and Churches
Blue Mosque pp78–9 ⑥
Church of SS Sergius and Bacchus ⑭
Haghia Sophia pp72–5 ①
Sokollu Mehmet Paşa Mosque ⑬

Museums
Marmara University Museum of the Republic ⑨
Mosaic Museum ⑤
Museum of Turkish and Islamic Arts ⑦

Squares and Courtyards
Hippodrome ⑧
Istanbul Crafts Centre ③

Historic Buildings and Monuments
Basilica Cistern ②
Baths of Roxelana ④
Bucoleon Palace ⑮
Cistern of 1,001 Columns ⑩
Constantine's Column ⑫
Tomb of Sultan Mahmut II ⑪

KEY

▨	Street-by-Street map *See pp70–71*
🚊	Tram stop
ℹ	Tourist information
C	Mosque
—	Walls

GETTING AROUND

Trams between Eminönü and Beyazıt stop in Sultanahmet by the Firuz Ağa Mosque on Divanyolu Caddesi. From there, most of the sights are easily reached on foot. A city bus runs between Taksim and Sultanahmet.

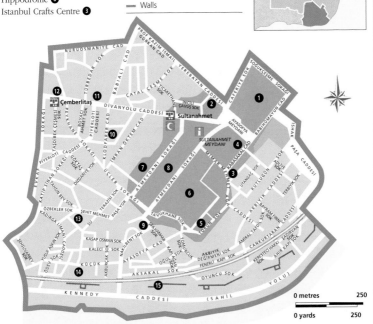

◁ **The elegant domes of the Blue Mosque, catching the evening sun**

Street-by-Street: Sultanahmet Square

Two of Istanbul's most venerable monuments, the Blue Mosque and Haghia Sophia, face each other across a leafy square, informally known as Sultanahmet Square (Sultanahmet Meydanı), next to the Hippodrome of Byzantium. Also in this fascinating historic quarter are a handful of museums, including the Mosaic Museum, built over part of the old Byzantine Great Palace (see pp82–3), and the Museum of Turkish and Islamic Arts. No less diverting than the cultural sights are the cries of the *simit* (bagel) hawkers and carpet sellers, and the chatter of children selling postcards.

Tomb of Sultan Ahmet I
Stunning 17th-century İznik tiles (see p161) adorn the inside of this tomb, which is part of the outer complex of the Blue Mosque.

★ Blue Mosque
Towering above Sultanahmet Square are the six beautiful minarets of this world-famous mosque. It was built in the early 17th century for Ahmet I ➏

Sultanahmet tram stop

Firuz Ağa Mosque

Fountain of Kaiser Wilhelm II

Museum of Turkish and Islamic Arts
Yurts, used by Turkey's nomadic peoples, and rugs are included in this impressive collection ➐

Egyptian Obelisk

KEY

– – – Suggested route

Brazen Column

ATMEYDANI SOK

ATMEYDANI SOK

TAVUKHANE SOK

TORUN S

Hippodrome
This stadium was the city's focus for more than 1,000 years before it fell into ruin. Only a few sections, such as the central line of monuments, remain ➑

Serpentine Column

Mosaic Museum
Hunting scenes are one of the common subjects that can be seen in some of the mosaics from the Great Palace ➎

| 0 metres | 75 |
| 0 yards | 75 |

★ Basilica Cistern

This marble Medusa head is one of two classical column bases found in the Basilica Cistern. The cavernous cistern dates from the reign of Justinian (see p20) in the 6th century ❷

A stone pilaster next to the remains of an Ottoman water tower is all that survives of the Milion (*see p83*), a triumphal gateway.

LOCATOR MAP
See Street Finder maps 3 and 5

★ Haghia Sophia

The supreme church of Byzantium is over 1,400 years old but has survived in a remarkably good state. Inside it are several glorious figurative mosaics ❶

Baths of Roxelana

Sinan (see p91) designed these beautiful baths in the mid-16th century. In recent years the building has housed a carpet shop, but the structure is due to be restored as public baths ❹

Yeşil Ev Hotel
(see p187)

Istanbul Crafts Centre

Visitors have a rare opportunity here to observe Turkish craftsmen practising a range of skills ❸

Cavalry Bazaar

Eager salesmen will call you over to peruse their wares – mainly carpets and handicrafts – in this bazaar. With two long rows of shops on either side of a lane, the bazaar was once a stable yard

STAR SIGHTS

- ★ Blue Mosque
- ★ Basilica Cistern
- ★ Haghia Sophia

Haghia Sophia ❶

Ayasofya

The "church of holy wisdom," Haghia Sophia is among the world's greatest architectural achievements. More than 1,400 years old, it stands as a testament to the sophistication of the 6th-century Byzantine capital. The vast edifice was built over two earlier churches and inaugurated by Emperor Justinian in 537. In the 15th century the Ottomans converted it into a mosque: the minarets, tombs, and fountains date from this period. To help support the structure's great weight, the exterior has been buttressed on numerous occasions, which has partly obscured its original shape. Three mausoleums at the site are also open to the public.

Print of Haghia Sophia from the mid-19th century

Seraphims adorn the pendentives at the base of the dome.

Calligraphic roundel

Kürsü
(see p39)

Byzantine Frieze
Among the ruins of the monumental entrance to the earlier Haghia Sophia (dedicated in AD 415) is this frieze of sheep.

Buttresses

Imperial Gate

Outer Narthex

Inner Narthex

The galleries were originally used by women during services.

Entrance

HISTORICAL PLAN OF HAGHIA SOPHIA

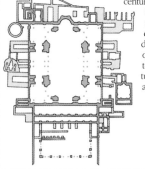

Nothing remains of the first 4th-century church on this spot, but there are traces of the second one from the 5th century, which burnt down in AD 532. Earthquakes have taken their toll on the third structure, strengthened and added to many times.

KEY

⬜	5th-century church
⬛	6th-century church
⬜	Ottoman additions

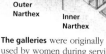

STAR FEATURES

★ Nave

★ The Mosaics

★ Ablutions Fountain

★ Nave
Visitors cannot fail to be staggered by this vast space which is covered by a huge dome reaching to a height of 56 m (184 ft).

Brick minaret

Sultan's loge

Müezzin mahfili (see p38)

★ The Mosaics
The church's splendid Byzantine mosaics include this one at the end of the south gallery. It depicts Christ flanked by Emperor Constantine IX and his wife, the Empress Zoe.

The Coronation Square served for the crowning of emperors.

Mausoleum of Mehmet III

Library of Sultan Mahmut I

Mausoleum of Selim II
The oldest of the three mausoleums was completed in 1577 to the plans of Sinan (see p91). Its interior is entirely decorated with İznik tiles (see p161).

The mausoleum of Murat III was used for his burial in 1599. Murat had by that time sired 102 children.

Exit

The Baptistry, part of the 6th-century church, now serves as the tomb of two sultans.

★ Ablutions Fountain
Built around 1740, this fountain is an exquisite example of Turkish Rococo style. Its projecting roof is painted with floral reliefs.

Exploring Haghia Sophia

Calligraphic roundel

Designed as an earthly mirror of the heavens, the interior of Haghia Sophia succeeds in imparting a truly celestial feel. The artistic highlights are a number of glistening figurative mosaics – remains of the decoration that once covered the upper walls but which has otherwise mostly disappeared. These remarkable works of Byzantine art date from the 9th century or later, after the iconoclastic era *(see p20)*. Some of the patterned mosaic ceilings, however, particularly those adorning the narthex and the neighbouring Vestibule of the Warriors, are part of the cathedral's original 6th-century decoration.

Interior as it looked after restoration in the 19th century

GROUND FLOOR

The first of the surviving Byzantine mosaics can be seen over the Imperial Gate. This is now the public entrance into the church, although previously only the emperor and his entourage were allowed to pass through it. The mosaic shows **Christ on a throne with an emperor kneeling beside him** ① and has been dated to between 886 and 912. The emperor is thought to be Leo VI, the Wise *(see p21)*.

The most conspicuous features at ground level in the nave are those added by the Ottoman sultans after the conquest of Istanbul in 1453, when the church was converted into a mosque.

The **mihrab** ②, the niche indicating the direction of Mecca, was installed in the apse of the church directly opposite the entrance. The **sultan's loge** ③, on the left of the mihrab as you face it, was built by the Fossati brothers. These Italian-Swiss architects undertook a major restoration of Haghia Sophia for Sultan Abdül Mecit in 1847–9.

To the right of the mihrab is the **minbar** ④, or pulpit, which was installed by Murat III (1574–95). He also erected the four **müezzin mahfilis** ⑤, marble platforms for readers of the Koran *(see p39)*. The largest of these is adjacent to the **minbar**. The patterned marble **coronation square** ⑥ next to it marks the supposed site of the Byzantine emperor's throne, or omphalos (centre of the world). Nearby, in the south aisle, is the **library of Mahmut I** ⑦, which was built in 1739 and is entered by a decorative bronze door.

Across the nave, between two columns, is the 17th-century marble **preacher's throne** ⑧, the contribution of Murat IV (1623–40). Behind it is one of several **maqsuras** ⑨. These low, fenced platforms were placed beside walls and pillars to provide places for elders to sit, listen and read the Koran.

In the northwestern and western corners of the church are two **marble urns** ⑩, thought to date from the Hellenistic or early Byzantine period. A rectangular pillar behind one of the urns, the **pillar of St Gregory the Miracle-Worker** ⑪, is believed to have healing powers. As you leave the church you pass through the Vestibule of the Warriors, so called because the emperor's bodyguards would wait here for him when he came to worship. Look behind you as you enter it at the wonderful mosaic of the **Virgin with Constantine and Justinian** ⑫ above the door. It shows Mary seated

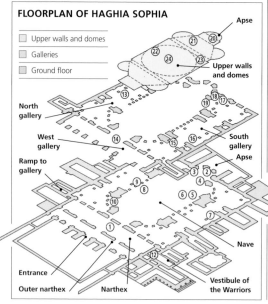

FLOORPLAN OF HAGHIA SOPHIA

- ☐ Upper walls and domes
- ☐ Galleries
- ☐ Ground floor

Apse

Upper walls and domes

North gallery

West gallery

Ramp to gallery

South gallery

Apse

Nave

Entrance

Outer narthex   Narthex

Vestibule of the Warriors

on a throne holding the infant Jesus and flanked by two of the greatest emperors of the city. Constantine, on her right, presents her with the city of Constantinople, while Justinian offers her Haghia Sophia. This was made long after either of these two emperors lived, probably in the 10th century, during the reign of Basil II *(see p21)*. Visitors exit the church by the door that was once reserved for the emperor due to its proximity to the Great Palace *(see pp82–3)*.

Figure of Christ, detail from the Deesis Mosaic in the south gallery

GALLERIES

A ramp leads from the ground floor to the north gallery. Here, on the eastern side of the great northwest pier, you will find the 10th-century mosaic of **Emperor Alexander holding a skull** ⑬. On the west face of the same pier is a medieval drawing of a galleon in full sail. The only point of interest in the western gallery is a green marble disk marking the location of the Byzantine **Empress's throne** ⑭.

There is much more to see in the south gallery. You begin by passing through the so-called **Gates of Heaven and Hell** ⑮, a marble doorway of which little is known except that it predates the Ottoman conquest *(see p26)*.

Around the corner to the right after passing through this dooorway is the **Deesis Mosaic** ⑯ showing the Virgin Mary and John the Baptist with Christ Pantocrator (the All-Powerful). Set into the floor opposite it is the tomb of Enrico Dandalo, the Doge of Venice responsible for the sacking of Constantinople in 1204 *(see p24)*.

In the last bay of the southern gallery there are two more mosaics. The right-hand one of these is the **Virgin holding Christ, flanked by Emperor John II Comnenus and Empress Irene** ⑰. The other shows **Christ with Emperor Constantine IX Monomachus and Empress Zoe** ⑱. The faces of the emperor and empress have been altered.

Eight great **wooden plaques** ⑲ bearing calligraphic inscriptions hang over the nave at the level of the gallery. An addition of the Fossati brothers, they bear the names of Allah, the Prophet Mohammed, the first four caliphs and Hasan and Hussein, two of the Prophet's grandsons who are revered as martyrs.

Mosaic depicting the archangel Gabriel, adorning the lower wall of the apse

UPPER WALLS AND DOMES

The apse is dominated by a large and striking mosaic showing the **Virgin with the infant Jesus on her lap** ⑳. Two other mosaics in the apse show the archangels **Gabriel** ㉑ and, opposite him, Michael, but only fragments of the latter now remain. The unveiling of these mosaics on Easter Sunday 867 was a triumphal event celebrating victory over the iconoclasts *(see p21)*.

Three mosaic portraits of **saints** ㉒ adorn niches in the north tympanum and are visible from the south gallery and the nave. From left to right they depict: St Ignatius the Younger, St John Chrysostom and St Ignatius Theophorus.

In the four triangular, concave areas at the base of the dome) are mosaics of six-winged **seraphim** ㉓. The ones in the eastern pendentives date from 1346–55, but may be copies of much older ones. Those on the western side are 19th-century imitations that were added by the Fossati brothers.

The great **dome** ㉔ itself is decorated with Koranic inscriptions. It was once covered in golden mosaic and the tinkling sound of pieces dropping to the ground was familiar to visitors until the building's 19th-century restoration.

Mosaic of the Virgin with Emperor John II Comnenus and Empress Irene

The cavernous interior of the Byzantine Basilica Cistern

Basilica Cistern ❷
Yerebatan Sarayı

13 Yerebatan Cad, Sultanahmet.
Map 3 E4 (5 E4). **Tel** (0212) 522
12 59. 🚇 Sultanahmet. ⭘ 9am–
5:30pm daily (Oct–Apr 8:30am–4pm).

This vast underground water
cistern, a beautiful piece of
Byzantine engineering, is the
most unusual tourist attraction
in the city. Although there may
have been an earlier, smaller
cistern here, this cavernous
vault was laid out under Justinian in 532, mainly to satisfy
the growing demands of the
Great Palace (see pp82–3) on
the other side of the Hippodrome (see p80). For a century
after the conquest (see p24),
the Ottomans did not know
of the cistern's existence. It
was rediscovered after people
were found to be collecting
water, and even fish, by
lowering buckets through
holes in their basements.

Visitors tread walkways, to
the mixed sounds of classical
music and dripping water. The
cistern's roof is held up by 336
columns, each over 8 m (26ft)
high. The original structure

covered a total area of 9,800
sq m (105,000 sq ft) but today
only about two thirds of it is
visible, the rest having been
bricked up in the 19th century.
Water reached the cistern,
which held about 100 million
litres (22 million gal), from
the Belgrade Forest, 20 km
(12 miles) north of Istanbul, via
the Valens Aqueduct (see p89).

Istanbul Crafts Centre ❸
Mehmet Efendi Medresesi

Kabasakal Cad 5, Sultanahmet.
Map 3 E4 (5 E4).
Tel (0212) 517 67 82. 🚇 Adliye.
⭘ 9:30am–5:30pm daily.

If you are interested in
Turkish craftwork, this former Koranic college is worth
a visit. You can watch skilled
artisans at work: they may be
binding a book, executing an
elegant piece of calligraphy
or painting glaze onto ceramics. Items produced here are
all for sale. Others include
exquisite dolls, meerschaum
pipes and jewellery based
on Ottoman designs.

Next door is the Yeşil Ev
Hotel (see p186), a restored
Ottoman building with a
pleasant café in its courtyard.

Baths of Roxelana ❹
Haseki Hürrem Hamamı

Ayasofya Meydanı, Sultanahmet.
Map 3 E4 (5 E4). 🚇 Sultanahmet.
🔴 for restoration.

These baths were built in
1556 for Süleyman the
Magnificent (see p26) by
Sinan (see p91), and are
named after Roxelana, the
sultan's scheming wife. They
were designated for the use

ROXELANA

Süleyman the Magnificent's
power-hungry wife Roxelana
(1500–58, Haseki Hürrem
in Turkish), rose from being
a concubine in the imperial
harem to become his chief
wife, or first kadın (see p28).
Thought to be of Russian
origin, she was also the first
consort permitted to reside
within the walls of Topkapı
Palace (see pp54–9).

Roxelana would stop at
nothing to get her own way.
When Süleyman's grand vizier and friend from youth,
İbrahim Paşa, became a threat to her position, she
persuaded the sultan to have him strangled. Much later,
Roxelana performed her coup de grâce. In 1553 she
persuaded Süleyman to have his handsome and popular
heir, Mustafa, murdered by deaf mutes to clear the way
for her own son Selim (see p26) to inherit the throne.

Symmetrical red-and-white brick exterior of the 16th-century Baths of Roxelana

Mosaic Museum 5
Mozaik Müzesi

Arasta çarşısı, Sultanahmet.
Map 3 E5 (5 E5).
Tel (0212) 518 12 05.
Sultanahmet.
9am–4:30pm Tue–Sun.

Located near Arasta Bazaar, among a warren of small shops, this museum was created simply by roofing over a part of the Great Palace of the Byzantine Emperors (see pp82–3), which was discovered in the 1930s. In its heyday the palace boasted hundreds of rooms, many of them glittering with gold mosaics.

The surviving mosaic has a surface area of 1,872 sq m (1,969 sq ft), making it one of the largest preserved mosaics in Europe. It is thought to have been created by an imperial workshop that employed the best craftsmen from across the Empire under the guidance of a master artist.

Detail of a 5th-century mosaic in the Mosaic Museum

In terms of imagery, the mosaic is particularly diverse, with many different landscapes depicted, including domestic and pastoral episodes, such as herdsmen with their grazing animals, as well as hunting and fighting scenes. It portrays more than 150 different human and animal figures, including both wild and domestic beasts. There are also scenes taken from mythology, with fantastical creatures featuring on the design. The mosaic is thought to have adorned the colonnade leading from the royal apartments to the imperial enclosure beside the Hippodrome, and dates from the late 5th century AD.

Blue Mosque 6

See pp78–9.

Museum of Turkish and Islamic Arts 7
Türk ve İslam Eserleri Müzesi

Atmeydanı Sok, Sultanahmet.
Map 3 D4 (5 D4). **Tel** (0212) 518 18 05. Sultanahmet.
summer: 9am–7pm Tue–Sun; winter: 9am–5pm Tue–Sun.
www.tiem.org

Over 40,000 items are on display in the former palace of İbrahim Paşa (c.1493–1536), the most gifted of Süleyman's many grand viziers. Paşa married Süleyman's sister when the sultan came to the throne. The collection was begun in the 19th century and ranges from the earliest period of Islam, under the Omayyad caliphate (661–750), through to modern times.

Each room concentrates on a different chronological period or geographical area of the Islamic world, with detailed explanations in both Turkish and English. The museum is particularly renowned for its collection of rugs. These range from 13th-century Seljuk fragments to the palatial Persian silks that cover the walls from floor to ceiling in the palace's great hall.

On the ground floor, an ethnographic section focuses on the lifestyles of different Turkish peoples, particularly the nomads of central and eastern Anatolia. The exhibits include recreations of a round felt *yurt* (Turkic nomadic tent) and a traditional brown tent.

Recreated yurt interior, Museum of Turkish and Islamic Arts

of the congregation of Haghia Sophia (see pp72–5) when it was used as a mosque. With the women's entrance at one end of the building and the men's at the other, their absolute symmetry makes them perhaps the most handsome baths in the city. The men's section of the baths faces Haghia Sophia and has a fine colonnaded portico.

Each end of the baths starts with a *camekan*, a massive domed hall which would originally have been centred on a fountain. Next is a small *soğukluk*, or intermediate room, which opens into a *hararet*, or steam room. The hexagonal massage slab in each *hararet*, the *göbek taşı*, is inlaid with coloured marbles, indicating that the baths are of imperial origin.

The baths functioned as a public bathhouse for more than 350 years until 1910. After their closure, they continued to be used for various purposes, including as a coal and fuel store and as a government-run carpet shop. The baths are currently closed while they undergo renovations to restore them to their original state. When the baths reopen, they are due to operate as public baths once more.

Blue Mosque ❻

Sultan Ahmet Camii

The blue mosque, which takes its name from the mainly blue İznik tilework *(see p161)* decorating its interior, is one of the most famous religious buildings in the world. Serene at any time, it is at its most magical when floodlit at night, its minarets circled by keening seagulls. Sultan Ahmet I *(see p33)* commissioned the mosque during a period of declining Ottoman fortunes, and it was built between 1609–16 by Mehmet Ağa, the imperial architect. The splendour of the plans provoked great hostility at the time, especially because a mosque with six minarets was considered a sacrilegious attempt to rival the architecture of Mecca itself.

A 19th-century engraving showing the Blue Mosque viewed from the Hippodrome *(see p80)*

Thick piers support the weight of the dome.

Mihrab

The loge *(see p39)* accommodated the sultan and his entourage during mosque services.

The Imperial Pavilion

Minbar
The 17th-century minbar is intricately carved in white marble. It is used by the imam during prayers on Friday (see pp38–9).

Prayer hall

Exit for tourists

Müezzin mahfili *(see p38)*

Entrance to courtyard

★ İznik Tiles
No cost was spared in the decoration of the mosque. The tiles were made at the peak of tile production in İznik (see p161).

STAR FEATURES

★ İznik Tiles

★ Inside of the Dome

★ View of the Domes

★ **Inside of the Dome**
Mesmeric designs, employing flowing arabesques, are painted onto the interior of the mosque's domes and semidomes. The windows which pierce the domes no longer have their original 17th-century stained glass.

VISITORS' CHECKLIST

Meydanı 21, Sultanahmet. **Map** 3 E5 (5 E5). *Tel* (0212) 458 07 76. Sultanahmet. 8:30am–noon, 1:45–4:30pm daily. prayer times. **Son et Lumière** May–Sep: daily after dusk (see the board on Mimar Mehmet Ağa Caddesi).

★ **View of the Domes**
The graceful cascade of domes and semidomes makes a striking sight when viewed from the courtyard below.

Over 250 windows allow light to flood into the mosque.

Entrance

Ablutions Fountain
The hexagonal şadırvan is now purely ornamental since ritual ablutions are no longer carried out at this fountain.

Each minaret has two or three balconies.

Exit to Hippodrome

Washing the Feet
The Muslim's ritual ablutions conclude with the washing of the feet (see p39). Taps outside the mosque are used by the faithful for this purpose.

The courtyard covers the same area as the prayer hall, balancing the whole building.

Egyptian Obelisk and the Column of Constantine Porphyrogenitus

Hippodrome ❽
At Meydanı

Sultanahmet. **Map** 3 E4 (5 D4).
🚋 *Sultanahmet.*

Little is left of the gigantic stadium which once stood at the heart of the Byzantine city of Constantinople *(see pp22–3)*. It was originally laid out by Emperor Septimus Severus during his rebuilding of the city in the 3rd century AD *(see p19)*. Emperor Constantine *(see p20)* enlarged the Hippodrome and connected its *kathisma*, or royal box, to the nearby Great Palace *(see pp82–3)*. It is thought that the stadium held up to 100,000 people. The site is now an elongated public garden, At Meydanı, Cavalry Square. There are, however, enough remains of the Hippodrome to get a sense of its scale and importance.

The road running around the square almost directly follows the line of the chariot racing

Relief carved on the base of the Egyptian Obelisk

track. You can also make out some of the arches of the *sphendone* (the curved end of the Hippodrome) by walking a few steps down İbret Sokağı. Constantine adorned the *spina*, the central line of the stadium, with obelisks and columns from Ancient Egypt and Greece. Conspicuous by its absence is the column which once stood on the spot where the tourist information office is now located. This was topped by four bronze horses which were pillaged during the Fourth Crusade *(see p24)* and taken to St Mark's in Venice. Three ancient monuments remain, however. The **Egyptian Obelisk**, which was built in 1500 BC, stood outside Luxor until Constantine had it brought to his city. This carved monument is probably only one third of its original height. Next to it is the **Serpentine Column**, believed to date from 479 BC, which was shipped here from Delphi.

Another obelisk still standing, but of unknown date, is usually referred to as the **Column of Constantine Porphyrogenitus**, after the emperor who restored it in the 10th century AD. Its dilapidated state owes much to the young Janissaries *(see p127)* who routinely scaled it as a test of their bravery.

The only other structure in the Hippodrome is a domed fountain which commemorates the visit of Kaiser Wilhelm II to Istanbul in 1898.

The Hippodrome was the scene of one of the bloodiest events in Istanbul's history. In 532 a brawl between rival chariot-racing teams developed into the Nika Revolt, during which much of the city was destroyed. The end of the revolt came when an army of mercenaries, under the command of Justinian's general Belisarius, massacred an estimated 30,000 people trapped in the Hippodrome.

Marmara University Museum of the Republic ❾
Cumhuriyet Müzesi

Sultanahmet. **Map** 3 D5 (5 D5).
🚋 *Sultanahmet.* ⏱ 10am–6pm Tue–Sun.

This fine art collection run by Marmara University is comprised of works by more than 85 artists, both from Turkey and around the world. The museum was initiated in 1973 as an etching exhibition held to celebrate 50 years of Turkey as a Republic. Today, print paintings, calligraphy and other traditional Turkish art forms have been added to the collection.

Cistern of 1001 Columns ❿
Binbirdirek Sarnıcı

İmran Okten Sok 4, Sultanahmet.
Map 3 D4 (5 D4). **Tel** *(0212)*
518 10 01. 🚋 Çemberlitaş.
⏱ 9am–6pm daily.

This cistern, dating back to the 4th century AD, is the second largest underground Byzantine cistern in Istanbul after the Basilica Cistern *(see p76)*. Spanning an area of

CEREMONIES IN THE HIPPODROME

Beginning with the inauguration of Constantinople on 11th May 330 *(see p20)*, the Hippodrome formed the stage for the city's greatest public events for the next 1,300 years. The Byzantines' most popular pastime was watching chariot racing in the stadium. Even after the Hippodrome fell into ruins following the Ottoman conquest of Istanbul *(see p26)*, it continued to be used for great public occasions. This 16th-century illustration depicts Murat III watching the 52-day-long festivities staged for the circumcision of his son Mehmet. All the guilds of Istanbul paraded before the Sultan displaying their crafts.

Sultan Murat III

Palace of İbrahim Paşa (Museum of Turkish and Islamic Arts, see p77)

Column of Constantine Porphyrogenitus

Serpentine Column

Egyptian Obelisk

---

64 m (210 ft) by 56 m (185 ft), the herring-bone brick roof vaults are held up by 264 marble columns – the 1,001 columns of its name is poetic exaggeration. Until not long ago, the cistern was filled with rubble and only explored by adventurous visitors, but it has been transformed into an atmospheric shopping complex specializing in jewellery, carpets and tiles and other merchandise inspired by Ottoman culture.

Tomb of Sultan Mahmut II ⓫
Mahmut II Türbesi

Divanyolu Cad, Çemberlitaş.
Map 3 D4 (4 C3). 🚊 Çemberlitaş.
⏰ 9:30am–4:30pm daily.

This large octagonal mausoleum is in the Empire style (modelled on Roman architecture), made popular by Napoleon. It was built in 1838, the year before Sultan Mahmut II's death and is shared by sultans Mahmut II, Abdül Aziz and Abdül Hamit II *(see pp32–3)*. Within, Corinthian pilasters divide up walls which groan with symbols of prosperity and victory. The huge tomb dominates a cemetery that has beautiful headstones, a fountain and, at the far end, a good café.

Constantine's Column ⓬
Çemberlitaş

Yeniçeriler Cad, Çemberlitaş.
Map 3 D4 (4 C3). 🚊 Çemberlitaş.
Çemberlitaş Baths Vezirhani Cad 8. **Tel** (0212) 511 25 35. ⏰ 6am–midnight daily.

A survivor of both storm and fire, this 35-m (115-ft) high column was constructed in AD 330 as part of the celebrations to inaugurate the new Byzantine capital *(see p20)*. It once dominated the magnificent Forum of Constantine *(see p23)*.

Made of porphyry brought from Heliopolis in Egypt, it was originally surmounted by a Corinthian capital bearing a statue of Emperor Constantine dressed as Apollo. This was brought down in a storm in 1106. Although what is left is relatively unimpressive, it has been carefully preserved. In the year 416 the 10 stone drums making up the column were reinforced with metal rings. These were renewed in 1701 by Sultan Mustafa III, and consequently the column is

Constantine's Column

known as Çemberlitaş (the Hooped Column) in Turkish. In English it is sometimes referred to as the Burnt Column because it was damaged by several fires, especially one in 1779 which decimated the Grand Bazaar *(see pp98–9)*.

A variety of fantastical holy relics were supposedly entombed in the base of the column, which has since been encased in stone to strengthen it. These included the axe which Noah used to build the ark, Mary Magdalen's flask of anointing oil, and remains of the loaves of bread with which Christ fed the multitude.

Next to Constantine's Column, on the corner of Divanyolu Caddesi, stand the Çemberlitaş Baths. This splendid *hamam* complex *(see p67)* was commissioned by Nur Banu, wife of Sultan Selim II, and built in 1584 to a plan by the great Sinan *(see p91)*. Although the original women's section no longer survives, the baths still have separate facilities for men and women. The staff are used to foreign visitors, so this is a good place for your first experience of a Turkish bath.

Sokollu Mehmet Paşa Mosque ⓭

Sokollu Mehmet Paşa Camii

Şehit Çeşmesi Sok, Sultanahmet.
Map 3 D5 (4 C5). 🚇 *Çemberlitaş or Sultanahmet.* ⭘ *daily.*

Built by the architect Sinan *(see p91)* in 1571–2, this mosque was commissioned by Sokollu Mehmet Paşa, grand vizier to Selim II *(see p32)*. The simplicity of Sinan's design solution for the mosque's sloping site has been widely admired. A steep entrance stairway leads up to the mosque courtyard from the street, passing beneath the teaching hall of its *medrese (see p38)*, which still functions as a college. Only the tiled lunettes above the windows in the portico give a hint of the jewelled mosque interior to come.

Inside, the far wall around the carved mihrab is entirely covered in İznik tiles *(see p161)* of a sumptuous green-blue hue. This tile panel, designed specifically for the space, is complemented by six stained-glass windows. The "hat" of the *minbar* is covered with the same tiles. Most of the mosque's other walls are of plain stone, but they are enlivened by a few more tile panels. Set into the wall over the entrance there is a small piece of greenish stone which is supposedly from the Kaaba, the holy stone at the centre of Mecca.

The Byzantine Church of SS Sergius and Bacchus, now a mosque

SS Sergius and Bacchus' Church ⓮

Küçük Ayasofya Camii

Küçük Ayasofya Cad. **Map** 3 D5 (4 C5). 🚇 *Çemberlitaş or Sultanahmet.* ⭘ *daily.* ♿

Commonly referred to as "Little Haghia Sophia", this church was built in 527, a few years before its namesake *(see pp72–5)*. It too was founded by Emperor Justinian *(see p20)*, together with his empress, Theodora, at the beginning of his long reign. Ingenious and highly decorative, the church gives a somewhat higgledy-piggledy impression both inside and out and is one of the most charming of all the city's architectural treasures.

Inside, an irregular octagon of columns on two floors supports a broad central dome composed of 16 vaults. The

RECONSTRUCTION OF THE GREAT PALACE

In Byzantine times, present-day Sultanahmet was the site of the Great Palace, which, in its heyday, had no equal in Europe and dazzled medieval visitors with its opulence. This great complex of buildings – including royal apartments, state rooms, churches, courtyards and gardens – extended over a sloping, terraced site from the Hippodrome to the imperial harbour on the shore of the Sea of Marmara. The palace was built in stages, beginning under Constantine in the 4th century. It was enlarged by Justinian following the fire caused by the Nika Revolt in 532 *(see p80)*. Later emperors, especially the 9th-century Basil I *(see p21)*, extended it further. After several hundred years of occupation, it was finally abandoned in the second half of the 13th century in favour of Blachernae Palace *(see p117)*.

The Mese was a colonnaded street lined with shops and statuary.

Hippodrome (see p80)

Hormisdas Palace

Church of SS Peter and Paul

Church of SS Sergius and Bacchus

Interior of the 16th-century Sokollu Mehmet Paşa Mosque

mosaic decoration which once adorned some of the walls has long since crumbled away. However, the green and red marble columns, the delicate tracery of the capitals and the carved frieze running above the columns are original features of the church.

The inscription on this frieze, in boldly carved Greek script, mentions the founders of the church and St Sergius, but not St Bacchus. The two saints were Roman centurions who converted to Christianity and were martyred. Justinian credited them with saving his life when, as a young man, he was implicated in a plot to kill his uncle, Justin I. The saints supposedly appeared to Justin in a dream and told him to release his nephew.

The Church of SS Sergius and Bacchus was built between two important edifices to which it was connected, the Palace of Hormisdas and the Church of SS Peter and Paul, but has outlived them both. After the conquest of Istanbul in 1453 *(see p26)* it was converted into a mosque.

Bucoleon Palace **⑮**
Bukoleon Sarayı

Kennedy Cad, Sultanahmet.
Map 3 E5. 🚇 *Sultanahmet.*

Finding the site of what remains of the Great Palace of the Byzantine emperors requires precision. It is not advisable to visit the ruins alone as they are usually inhabited by tramps.

Take the path under the railway from the Church of SS Sergius and Bacchus, turn left and walk beside Kennedy Caddesi, the main road along the shore of the Sea of Marmara for about 400 m (450 yards). This will bring you to a stretch of the ancient sea walls, constructed to protect the city from a naval assault. Within these walls you will find a creeper-clad section of stonework pierced by three vast windows framed in

marble. This is all that now survives of the Bucoleon Palace, a maritime residence that formed part of the sprawling Great Palace. The waters of a small private harbour lapped right up to the palace and a private flight of steps led down in to the water, allowing the emperor to board imperial caïques. The ruined tower just east of the palace was a lighthouse, called the Pharos, in Byzantine times.

Wall of Bucoleon Palace, the only part of the Byzantine Great Palace still standing

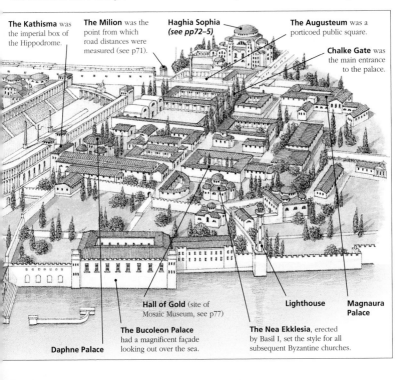

The Kathisma was the imperial box of the Hippodrome.

The Milion was the point from which road distances were measured (see p71).

Haghia Sophia *(see pp72–5)*

The Augusteum was a porticoed public square.

Chalke Gate was the main entrance to the palace.

Daphne Palace

The Bucoleon Palace had a magnificent façade looking out over the sea.

Hall of Gold (site of Mosaic Museum, see p77)

The Nea Ekklesia, erected by Basil I, set the style for all subsequent Byzantine churches.

Lighthouse

Magnaura Palace

THE BAZAAR QUARTER

Trade has always been important in a city straddling the continents of Asia and Europe. Nowhere is this more evident than in the warren of streets lying between the Grand Bazaar and Galata Bridge. Everywhere, goods tumble out of shops onto the pavement. Look through any of the archways in between shops and you will discover hidden courtyards or hans *(see p96)* containing feverishly

Window from Nuruosmaniye Mosque

industrious workshops. With its seemingly limitless range of goods, the labyrinthine Grand Bazaar is at the centre of all this commercial activity. The Spice Bazaar is equally colourful but smaller and more manageable.

Up on the hill, next to the university, is Süleymaniye Mosque, a glorious expression of 16th-century Ottoman culture. It is just one of numerous beautiful mosques in this area.

SIGHTS AT A GLANCE

Mosques and Churches
Atik Ali Paşa Mosque ⑳
Bodrum Mosque ⑫
Church of St Theodore ⑥
Kalenderhane Mosque ⑩
Mahmut Paşa Mosque ㉒
New Mosque ①
Nuruosmaniye Mosque ㉑
Prince's Mosque ⑨
Rüstem Paşa Mosque ③
Süleymaniye Mosque pp90–91 ⑤
Tulip Mosque ⑪

Bazaars, Hans and Shops
Book Bazaar ⑯
Grand Bazaar pp98–9 ⑱
Spice Bazaar ②
Valide Hanı ⑰
Vefa Bozacısı ⑧

Museums and Monuments
Forum of Theodosius ⑬
Museum of Calligraphy ⑭
Valens Aqueduct ⑦

Squares and Courtyards
Beyazıt Square ⑮
Çorlulu Ali Paşa Courtyard ⑲

Waterways
Golden Horn ④

KEY

▨	Street-by-Street map *See pp86–7*
⛴	Ferry boarding point
🚉	Tram stop
🚌	Main bus stop
C	Mosque

GETTING AROUND
Trams from Sultanahmet run down Yeniçeriler Caddesi, and stop outside the Grand Bazaar. Ferries from various destinations dock at Eminönü, opposite the Spice Bazaar.

◁ **The inside of the Grand Bazaar, always thronging with bargain-hunters**

Street-by-Street: Around the Spice Bazaar

The narrow streets around the Spice Bazaar encapsulate the spirit of old Istanbul. From here buses, taxis and trams head off across the Galata Bridge and into the interior of the city. The blast of ships' horns signals the departure of ferries from Eminönü to Asian Istanbul. It is the quarter's shops and markets, though, that are the focus of attention for the eager shoppers who crowd the Spice Bazaar and the streets around it, sometimes breaking for a leisurely tea beneath the trees in its courtyard. Across the way, and entirely aloof from the bustle, rise the domes of the New Mosque. On one of the commercial alleyways which radiate out from the mosque, an inconspicuous doorway leads up stairs to the terrace of the serene, tile-covered Rüstem Paşa Mosque.

Nargile on sale near the Spice Bazaar

★ **Rüstem Paşa Mosque**
The interior of this secluded mosque is a brilliant pattern-book made of İznik tiles (see p161) *of the finest quality* ❸

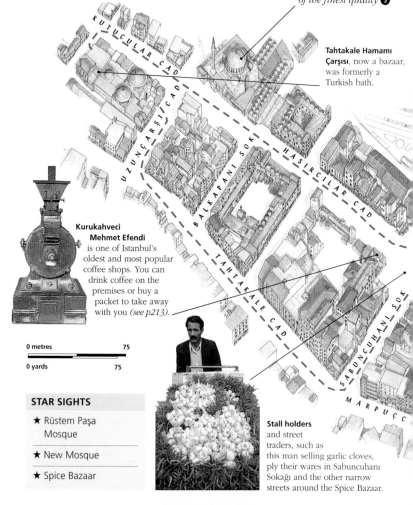

Tahtakale Hamamı Çarşısı, now a bazaar, was formerly a Turkish bath.

Kurukahveci Mehmet Efendi is one of Istanbul's oldest and most popular coffee shops. You can drink coffee on the premises or buy a packet to take away with you *(see p213)*.

0 metres   75

0 yards   75

STAR SIGHTS

★ Rüstem Paşa Mosque

★ New Mosque

★ Spice Bazaar

Stall holders and street traders, such as this man selling garlic cloves, ply their wares in Sabuncuhanı Sokağı and the other narrow streets around the Spice Bazaar.

Eminönü is the port from which ferries depart to many destinations *(see p242)* and for trips along the Bosphorus *(see pp144–9)*. It bustles with activity as traders compete to sell drinks and snacks.

LOCATOR MAP
See Street Finder map 2

Galata Bridge

The royal pavilion, a suite of beautifully tiled private rooms, is linked by a passage to the sultan's loge inside the New Mosque.

Eminönü sea bus boarding point

Eminönü bus terminal

REŞADİYE CAD

İS CAD

Eminönü tram stop

CAMİ MEYDANI SOK

Tea Gardens

★ **New Mosque**
This mosque, which dominates the Eminönü waterfront, was completed in the 17th century by the mother of Sultan Mehmet IV (see p33) ❶

K PAZARI SOK

YENİ CAMİ CAD

Mausoleum of Turhan Hatice Valide Sultan, mother of Mehmet IV

Pet market and garden centre

D

KEY

– – – Suggested route

★ **Spice Bazaar**
This market was built in 1660 as part of the New Mosque complex, and it has always been associated with the sale of spices, though today there is much more on offer ❷

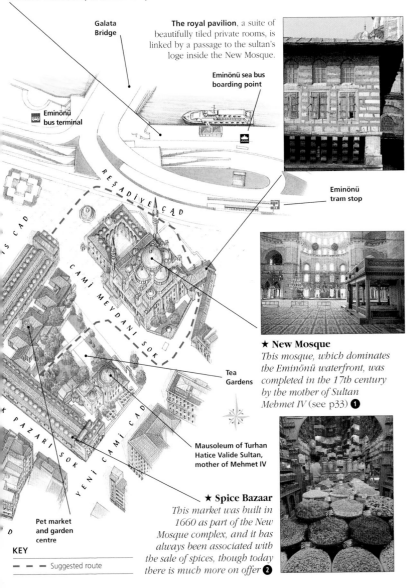

New Mosque ❶
Yeni Cami

Yeni Cami Meydanı, Eminönü.
Map 3 D2. 🚊 Eminönü. ⬜ daily.

Situated at the southern end of Galata Bridge, the New Mosque is one of the most prominent mosques in the city. It dates from the time when a few women from the harem became powerful enough to dictate the policies of the Ottoman sultans *(see p27)*. The mosque was started in 1597 by Safiye, mother of Mehmet III, but building was suspended on the sultan's death as his mother then lost her position. It was not completed until 1663, after Turhan Hadice, mother of Mehmet IV, had taken up the project.

Though the mosque was built after the classical period of Ottoman architecture, it shares many traits with earlier imperial foundations, including a monumental courtyard. The mosque once had a hospital, school and public baths.

The turquoise, blue and white floral tiles decorating the interior are from İznik *(see p161)* and date from the mid-17th century, though by this time the quality of the tiles produced there was already in decline. More striking are the tiled lunettes and bold Koranic frieze decorating the porch between the courtyard and the prayer hall.

At the far left-hand corner of the upper gallery is the sultan's loge *(see p39)*, which is linked to his personal suite of rooms *(see p87)*.

A selection of nuts and seeds for sale in the Spice Bazaar

Spice Bazaar ❷
Mısır Çarşısı

Cami Meydanı Sok. **Map** 3 D2 (4 C1).
🚊 Eminönü. ⬜ 8am–7pm Mon–Sat.

This cavernous, L-shaped market was built in the early 17th century as an extension of the New Mosque complex. Its revenues once helped maintain the mosque's philanthropic institutions.

In Turkish the market is named the Mısır Çarşısı – the Egyptian Bazaar – because it was built with money paid as duty on Egyptian imports. In English it is usually known as the Spice Bazaar. From medieval times spices were a vital and expensive part of cooking and they became the market's main produce. The bazaar came to specialize in spices from the orient, taking advantage of Istanbul's site on the trade route between the East (where most spices were grown) and Europe.

Stalls in the bazaar stock spices, herbs and other foods such as honey, nuts, sweetmeats and *pastirma* (cured beef). Today's expensive Eastern commodity, caviar, is also available, the best variety being Iranian.

Nowadays an eclectic range of other items can be found in the Spice Bazaar, including everything from household goods, toys and clothes to exotic aphrodisiacs. The square between the two arms of the bazaar is full of commercial activity, with cafés, and stalls selling plants and pets.

Floral İznik tiles adorning the interior of Rüstem Paşa Mosque

Rüstem Paşa Mosque ❸
Rüstem Paşa Camii

Hasıcılar Cad, Eminönü.
Map 3 D2. 🚊 Eminönü. ⬜ daily.

Raised above the busy shops and warehouses around the Spice Bazaar, this mosque was built in 1561 by the great architect Sinan *(see p91)* for Rüstem Paşa, son-in-law of and grand vizier to Süleyman I *(see p26)*. Rents from the businesses in the bazaar were intended to pay for the upkeep of the mosque.

The staggering wealth of its decoration says something about the amount of money that the corrupt Rüstem managed to salt away during his career. Most of the interior is covered in İznik tiles of the very highest quality.

The New Mosque, a prominent feature on the Eminönü waterfront

The four piers are adorned with tiles of one design but the rest of the prayer hall is a riot of different patterns, from abstract to floral. Some of the finest tiles can be found on the galleries. All in all, there is no other mosque in the city adorned with such a magnificent blanket of tiles.

The mosque is also notable for its numerous windows: it was built with as many as the structure would allow.

Golden Horn ❹
Haliç

Map 3 D2. 🚇 *Eminönü.*
🚌 *55T, 99A.*

Often described as the world's greatest natural harbour, the Golden Horn is a flooded river valley which flows southwest into the Bosphorus. The estuary attracted settlers to its shores in the 7th century BC and later enabled Constantinople to become a rich and powerful port. According to legend, the Byzantines threw so many valuables into it during the Ottoman conquest *(see p26)*, that the waters glistened with gold. Today, however, belying its name, the Golden Horn has become polluted by the numerous nearby factories.

For hundreds of years the city's trade was conducted by ships that off-loaded their goods into warehouses lining the Golden Horn. Nowadays, though, the great container

ships coming to Istanbul use ports on the Sea of Marmara. Spanning the mouth of the Horn is the Galata Bridge, which joins Eminönü to Galata. The bridge, built in 1992, opens in the middle to allow access for tall ships. It is a good place from which to appreciate the complex geography of the city and admire the minaret-filled skyline.

The functional Halic Bridge replaced the raffish charm of a pontoon bridge. The Old Galata Bridge has been reconstructed just south of the Rahmi Koç Museum *(see p127)*. There is another bridge, Unkapanı (also known as Atatürk), between these, and a fourth, New Galata Bridge, further up the Horn near the end of the city walls. Between Sütlüce and Eyüp, the da Vinci pedestrian bridge, soon to be finished, will be another addition.

Süleymaniye Mosque ❺
See pp90–91.

Church of St Theodore ❻
Kilise Camii

Vefa Cad, Cami Sok, Vefa.
Map 2 B2. 🚌 *28, 61B, 87.*

Apart from its delightfully dishevelled ancient exterior, very little else remains of the former Byzantine Church of St Theodore. The elaborate

church was built in the 12th–14th centuries, the last great era of Byzantine construction. It was converted into a mosque following the Ottoman conquest of the city in 1453 *(see p26)*.

One feature that is still evident in the south dome in its outer porch is a 14th-century mosaic of the Virgin Mary surrounded by the Prophets. The fluted minaret makes a sympathetic addition.

The 4th-century Valens Aqueduct crossing Atatürk Bulvarı

Valens Aqueduct ❼
Bozdoğan Kemeri

Atatürk Bulvarı, Saraçhane.
Map 2 A3. 🚇 *Laleli.* 🚌 *28, 61B, 87.*

Emperor Valens built this mighty aqueduct, supported by two imposing rows of arches, in the late 4th century AD. Part of the elaborate water system feeding the palaces and fountains of the Byzantine capital, it brought water from the Belgrade Forest *(see p158)* and mountains over 200 km (125 miles) away to a vast cistern which stood in the vicinity of what is now Beyazıt Square *(see p94)*.

The aqueduct supplied the city's water until the late 19th century, when it was made obsolete by a modern water distribution network. The original open channels, however, had by this stage already been replaced first by clay pipes and then by iron ones. The structure was repaired many times during its history, latterly by sultans Mustafa II (1695–1703) and Ahmet III *(see p25)*. It was originally 1,000 m (3,300 ft) long, of which 625 m (2,050 ft) remain.

Fisherman on the modern Galata Bridge spanning the Golden Horn

Süleymaniye Mosque ❺

Süleymaniye Camii

Istanbul's most important mosque is both a tribute to its architect, the great Sinan, and a fitting memorial to its founder, Süleyman the Magnificent *(see p26)*. It was built above the Golden Horn in the grounds of the old palace, Eski Saray *(see p94)*, between 1550–57. Like the city's other imperial mosques, the Süleymaniye Mosque was not only a place of worship, but also a charitable foundation, or *külliye (see p38)*. The mosque is surrounded by its former hospital, soup kitchen, schools, caravanserai and bath house. This complex provided a welfare system which fed over 1,000 of the city's poor – Muslims, Christians and Jews alike – every day.

Courtyard
The ancient columns that surround the courtyard are said to have come originally from the kathisma, the Byzantine royal box in the Hippodrome (see p80).

Muvakkithane Gateway
The main courtyard entrance (now closed) contained the rooms of the mosque astronomer, who determined prayer times.

Minaret

Tomb of Sinan

The caravanserai provided lodging and food for travellers and their animals.

İmaret Gate

Café in a sunken garden

İmaret
The kitchen – now a restaurant, Dârüzziyafe (see p200) – fed the city's poor as well as the mosque staff and their families. The size of the millstone in its courtyard gives an idea of the amount of grain needed to feed everyone.

★ Mosque Interior

A sense of soaring space and calm strikes you as you enter the mosque. The effect is enhanced by the fact that the height of the dome from the floor is exactly double its diameter.

The Tomb of **Roxelana** contains Süleyman's beloved wife *(see p76).*

Entrance

Graveyard

★ Tomb of Süleyman

Ceramic stars said to be set with emeralds sparkle above the coffins of Süleyman, his daughter Mihrimah and two of his successors, Süleyman II and Ahmet II.

These marble benches were used to support coffins before burial.

"Addicts Alley" is so called because the cafés here once sold opium and hashish as well as coffee and tea.

The medreses *(see p38)* to the south of the mosque house a library containing 110,000 manuscripts.

Former hospital and asylum

SINAN, THE IMPERIAL ARCHITECT

Like many of his eminent contemporaries, Koca Mimar Sinan (c.1491–1588) was brought from Anatolia to Istanbul in the *devşirme*, the annual roundup of talented Christian youths, and educated at one of the elite palace schools. He became a military engineer but won the eye of Süleyman I, who made him chief imperial architect in 1538. With the far-sighted patronage of the sultan, Sinan – the closest Turkey gets to a Renaissance architect – created masterpieces which demonstrated his master's status as the most magnificent of monarchs. Sinan died aged 97, having built 131 mosques and 200 other buildings.

Bust of the great architect Sinan

STAR FEATURES

★ Mosque Interior

★ Tomb of Süleyman

Vefa Bozacısı ❽

Katip Çelebi Cad 104/1, Vefa. **Map** 2
B2. **Tel** (0212) 519 49 22. 🚌 61B,
90. ⬭ 8am–midnight daily.

With its wood-and-tile
interior and glittering
glass-mosaic columns, this
unusual shop and bar has
changed little since the 1930s.
It was founded in 1876 to sell
boza, a popular winter drink
made from bulgur (cracked
wheat, *see p197*). In summer
a slightly fermented grape
juice known as *şıra* is sold.
The shop's main trade throughout the whole year, however,
is in wine vinegar.

Inside the shop you will
see a glass from which Kemal
Atatürk *(see p31)* drank *boza*
in 1937, enshrined in a display
beneath a glass dome.

**Bottles of *boza*, a wheat-based drink, lining
the interior of Vefa Bozacısı**

Prince's Mosque ❾
Şehzade Camii

Şehzade Başı Cad 70, Saraçhane.
Map 2 B3. 🚇 Laleli. ⬭ daily.
Tombs ⬭ 9am–5pm Tue–Sun.

This mosque complex was
erected by Süleyman the
Magnificent *(see p26)* in
memory of his eldest son by
Roxelana *(see p76)*, Şehzade
(Prince) Mehmet, who died of
smallpox at the age of 21. The
building was Sinan's *(see p91)*
first major imperial commission
and was completed in 1548.
The architect used a delightful
decorative style in designing
this mosque before abandon-
ing it in favour of the classical
austerity of his later work.
The mosque is approached

**Dome of the Prince's Mosque,
Sinan's first imperial mosque**

through an elegant porticoed
inner courtyard, while the
other institutions making up
the mosque complex, including a *medrese (see p38)*, are
enclosed within an
outer courtyard.

The interior of the
mosque is unusual and
was something of an
experiment in that it
is symmetrical, having
a semidome on each
of its four sides.

The three tombs
located to the rear of
the mosque, belonging
to Şehzade Mehmet
himself and grand vi-
ziers İbrahim Paşa and
Rüstem Paşa *(see p88)*,
are the finest in the
city. Each has beauti-
ful İznik tiles *(see
p161)* and lustrous original
stained glass. That of Şehzade
Mehmet also boasts the finest
painted dome in Istanbul.

On Fridays you will notice
a crowd of women flocking
to another tomb within the

complex, that of Helvacı
Baba, as they have done for
over 400 years. Helvacı Baba
is said to miraculously cure
crippled children, solve fertil-
ity problems and find husbands
or accommodation for those
who beseech him.

Kalenderhane Mosque ❿
Kalenderhane Camii

16 Mart Şehitleri Cad, Saraçhane.
Map 2 B3. 🚇 Üniversite.
⬭ prayer times only.

Sitting in the lee of the
Valens Aqueduct *(see p89)*,
on the site where a Roman
bath once stood, is this Byzantine church with a chequered
history. It was built and rebuilt several times between
the 6th and 12th centuries,
before finally being converted
into a mosque shortly after
the conquest in 1453 *(see
p26)*. The mosque is named
after the Kalender brotherhood
of dervishes which used the
church as its headquarters for
some years after the conquest.

The building has the cruci-
form layout characteristic of
Byzantine churches of the
period. Some of the decoration remaining from its last
incarnation, as the Church
of Theotokos Kyriotissa (her
Ladyship Mary, Mother of
God), also survives in the
prayer hall with its marble
panelling and in the fragments of fresco in the narthex
(entrance hall). A series of
frescoes depicting the life of
St Francis of Assisi were removed in the 1970s and are
no longer on public view.

A shaft of light illuminating the interior of Kalenderhane Mosque

The Baroque Tulip Mosque, housing a marketplace in its basement

Tulip Mosque ⑪
Lâleli Camii

Ordu Cad, Lâleli. **Map** 2 B4.
🚇 *Lâleli.* ⬭ *prayer times only.*

Built in 1759–63, this mosque complex is the best example in the city of the Baroque style, of which its architect, Mehmet Tahir Ağa, was the greatest exponent. Inside the mosque, a variety of gaudy, coloured marble covers all of its surfaces.

More fascinating is the area underneath the main body of the mosque. This is a great hall supported on eight piers, with a fountain in the middle. The hall is now used as a subterranean marketplace, packed with Eastern Europeans and Central Asians haggling over items of clothing.

The nearby Büyük Taş Hanı *(see p96)*, or Big Stone Han, is likely to have been part of the mosque's original complex but now houses a number of leather shops and a restaurant. To get to it turn left outside the mosque into Fethi Bey Caddesi and then take the second left into Çukur Çeşme Sokağı. The main courtyard of the han is at the end of a long passage situated off this lane.

Bodrum Mosque ⑫
Bodrum Camii

Sait Efendi Sok, Laleli. **Map** 2 A4.
🚇 *Laleli.* ⬭ *prayer times only.*

Narrow courses of brick forming the outside walls, and a window-pierced dome, betray the early origins of this mosque as a Byzantine church. It was built in the early 10th century by co-Emperor Romanus I Lacapenus (919–44) as part of the Monastery of Myrelaion and adjoined a small palace. The palace was later converted into a nunnery where the emperor's widow, Theophano, lived out her final years. She was eventually buried in a sanctuary chapel beneath the church, which is closed to the public.

In the late 15th century the church was converted into a mosque by Mesih Paşa, a descendant of the Palaeologus family, the last dynasty to rule Byzantium. The building was gutted by fire several times and nothing remains of its internal decoration. Today it is still a working mosque and is accessed via a stairway which leads up to a raised piazza filled with coat stalls.

Forum of Theodosius ⑬

Ordu Cad, Beyazıt. **Map** 2 C4 (4 A3).
🚇 *Üniversite or Beyazıt.*

Constantinople *(see p20)* was built around several large public squares or forums. The largest of them stood on the site of present-day Beyazıt Square. It was originally known as the Forum Tauri (the Forum of the Bull) because of the huge bronze bull in the middle of it in which sacrificial animals, and sometimes even criminals, were roasted.

After Theodosius the Great enlarged it in the late 4th century, the forum took his name. Relics of the triumphal arch and other structures can be found lying and stacked on either side of the tram tracks along Ordu Caddesi. The huge columns, decorated with a motif reminiscent of a peacock's tail, are particularly striking. Once the forum had become derelict, these columns were reused all over the city. Some can be seen in the Basilica Cistern *(see p76)*. Other fragments from the forum were built into Beyazıt Hamamı, a Turkish bath *(see p67)* further west down Ordu Caddesi, now a bazaar.

Peacock feather design on a column from the Forum of Theodosius

Museum of Calligraphy **14**

Türk Vakıf Hat Sanatları Müzesi

Beyazıt Meydanı, Beyazıt. **Map** 2 C4 (4 A3). **Tel** *(0212) 527 58 51.* Üniversite. 9am–4pm Tue–Sat. with assistance.

The pretty courtyard in which this museum has been installed was once a *medrese (see p38)* of Beyazıt Mosque, situated on the other side of the square.

Its changing displays are taken from the massive archive belonging to the Turkish Calligraphy Foundation. As well as some beautiful manuscripts, including some dating back to the 13th century, there are examples of calligraphy on stone and glass. There is also an exhibition of tools used in calligraphy. One of the cells in the *medrese* now contains a waxwork tableau of a master calligrapher with his pupils.

Beyazıt Tower, within the wooded grounds of Istanbul University

Beyazıt Square **15**

Beyazıt Meydanı

Ordu Cad, Beyazıt. **Map** 2 C4 (4 A3). Beyazıt.

Always filled with crowds of people and huge flocks of pigeons, Beyazıt Square is the most vibrant space in the old part of the city. Throughout the week the square is the venue for a flea market, where everything from carpets *(see pp218–19)* and Central Asian silks to general bric-a-brac can be purchased. When

The fortress-like entrance to Istanbul University, Beyazıt Square

you have tired of rummaging, there are several cafés.

On the northern side of the square is the Moorish-style gateway leading into Istanbul University. The university's main building dates from the 19th century and once served as the Ministry of War. Within the wooded grounds rises Beyazıt Tower. This marble fire-watching station was built in 1828 on the site of Eski Saray, the palace first inhabited by Mehmet the Conqueror *(see p26)* after Byzantium fell to the Ottomans. Two original timber towers were destroyed by fire. At one time, you could climb to the top of the tower but it is now closed to the public.

On the square's eastern side is Beyazıt Mosque, which was commissioned by Beyazıt II and completed in 1506. It is the oldest surviving imperial mosque in the city. Behind the impressive outer portal is a harmonious courtyard with an elegant domed fountain at its centre. Around the courtyard are columns made of granite and green and red Egyptian porphyry, and a pavement of multicoloured marble. The layout of the mosque's interior, with its central dome and surrounding semi-domes, is heavily inspired by the design of Haghia Sophia *(see pp72–5).*

Book Bazaar **16**

Sahaflar Çarşısı

Sahaflar Çarşısı Sok, Beyazıt. **Map** 2 C4 (4 A3). Üniversite. 8am–8pm daily.

This charming booksellers' courtyard, on the site of the Byzantine book and paper market, can be entered either from Beyazıt Square or from inside the Grand Bazaar *(see pp98–9).* Racks are laden with all sorts of books, from tourist guides to academic tomes.

During the early Ottoman period *(see pp25–7),* printed books were seen as a corrupting European influence and were banned in Turkey. As a result the bazaar only sold manuscripts. Then on 31 January 1729 İbrahim Müteferrika (1674–1745) produced the first printed book in the Turkish language, an Arabic dictionary. His bust stands in the centre of the market today. Note that book prices are fixed and cannot be haggled over.

Customers browsing in the Book Bazaar

The Art of Ottoman Calligraphy

Calligraphy is one of the noblest of Islamic arts. Its skills were handed down from master to apprentice, with the aim of the pupil being to replicate perfectly the hand of his master. In Ottoman Turkey, calligraphy was used to ornament firmans (imperial decrees) as well as poetry and copies of the Koran. However, many examples are also to be found on buildings, carved in wood and applied to architectural ceramics. The art of the calligrapher in all cases was to go as far as possible in beautifying the writing without altering the sense of the text. It was particularly important that the text of the Koran should be accurately transcribed. With the text of a firman, made to impress as much as to be read, the calligrapher could afford to add more flourishes.

The great calligraphers *of the Ottoman period were Şeyh Hamdullah (1436–1520), whose work is seen in this Koran, Hafiz Osman (1642–98) and Ahmet Karahisari (d.1556). Their pupils also achieved great renown.*

Floral decorations

Ornamental loops

The sultan's tuğra *was his personal monogram, used in place of his signature. It would either be drawn by a calligrapher or engraved on a wooden block and then stamped on documents. The tuğra incorporated the sultan's name and title, his patronymic and wishes for his success or victory – all highly stylized. This is the tuğra of Selim II (1566– 74).*

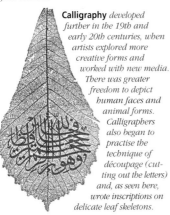

Calligraphy *developed further in the 19th and early 20th centuries, when artists explored more creative forms and worked with new media. There was greater freedom to depict human faces and animal forms. Calligraphers also began to practise the technique of découpage (cutting out the letters) and, as seen here, wrote inscriptions on delicate leaf skeletons.*

The later sultans *were taught calligraphy as part of their education and became skilled artists. This panel, from the 19th century, is by Mahmut II (1808–39).*

Breathing techniques *were probably practised by some calligraphers in order to achieve the steadiness of hand required for their craft.*

Burnisher

Knife for cutting pen nib

The calligrapher's tools *and materials included a burnisher, usually made of agate, which was used to prepare the paper. A knife was used to slit the reed nib of the pen before writing.*

Valide Han

Valide Hanı

Junction of Tarakçılar Sok and Çakmakçılar Yokuşu, Beyazıt. **Map** 2 C3 (4 B2). 🚋 Beyazıt, then 10 mins walk. ⬜ 9:30am–5pm Mon–Sat.

If the Grand Bazaar (see pp98–9) seems large, it is sobering to realize that it is only the covered part of an huge area of seething commercial activity which reaches all the way to the Golden Horn (see p89). As in the Grand Bazaar, most manufacturing and trade takes place in hans, courtyards hidden away from the street behind shaded gateways.

The largest han in Istanbul is Valide Han. It was built in 1651 by Kösem, the mother of Sultan Mehmet IV. You enter it from Çakmakçılar Yokuşu through a massive portal. After passing through an irregularly shaped forecourt, you come out into a large courtyard centring on a Shiite mosque. This was built when the han became the centre of Persian trade in the city. Today, the han throbs to the rhythm of hundreds of weaving looms.

A short walk further down Çakmakçılar Yokuşu is Büyük Yeni Han, hidden behind another impressive doorway. This Baroque han, built in

Carpet shops in Çorlulu Ali Paşa Courtyard

1764, has three arcaded levels. The entrance is on the top level, where distinctive bird cages are among the wares.

In the labyrinth of narrow streets around these hans, artisans are grouped according to their wares: on Bakırcılar Caddesi, for instance, you will find metal workers, while the craftsmen of Uzunçarşı Caddesi make wooden items.

Grand Bazaar

See pp98–9.

HANS OF ISTANBUL

The innumerable hans that dot the centre of Istanbul originally provided temporary accommodation for travellers, their pack animals and their wares. The typical han was built as part of a mosque complex (see pp38–9). It consists of two- or three-storey buildings around a courtyard. This is entered via a large gateway which can be secured by a heavy wooden door at night. When vans and lorries replaced horses and mules, the city's hans lost their original function and most of them were converted into warrens of small factories

Café in Büyük Taş Han, near the Tulip Mosque (see p93)

and workshops. These working hans are frequently in bad repair, but in them you can still sense the entrepreneurial, oriental atmosphere of bygone Istanbul.

Çorlulu Ali Paşa Courtyard

Çorlulu Ali Paşa Külliyesi

Yeniçeriler Cad, Beyazıt. **Map** 4 B3. 🚋 Beyazıt. ⬜ daily.

Like many others in the city, the medrese (see p38) of this mosque complex outside the Grand Bazaar has become the setting for a tranquil outdoor café. It was built for Çorlulu Ali Paşa, son-in-law of Mustafa II, who served as grand vizier under Ahmet III (see p27). Ahmet later exiled him to the island of Lésvos and had him executed there in 1711. Some years later his family smuggled his head back to Istanbul and interred it in the tomb built for him.

The complex is entered from Yeniçeriler Caddesi by two alleyways. Several carpet shops now inhabit the medrese and rugs are hung and spread all around, waiting for prospective buyers. The carpet shops share the medrese with a kahve, a traditional café (see p208), which is popular with locals and students from the nearby university. It advertises itself irresistibly as the "Traditional Mystic Water Pipe and Erenler Tea Garden". Here you can sit and drink tea, and perhaps smoke a nargile (bubble pipe), while deciding which carpet to buy (see pp218–19).

Situated across Bıleycıler Sokak, an alleyway off Çorlulu Ali Paşa Courtyard, is the Koca Sinan Paşa tomb complex, the courtyard of which is another tea garden. The charming *medrese*, mausoleum and *sebil* (a fountain where water was handed out to passers-by) were built in 1593 by Davut Ağa, who succeeded Sinan (*see p91*) as chief architect of the empire. The tomb of Koca Sinan Paşa, grand vizier under Murat III and Mehmet III, is a striking 16-sided structure.

Just off the other side of Yeniçeriler Caddesi is Gedik Paşa Hamamı, thought to be the oldest working Turkish baths (*see p67*) in the city. It was built around 1475 for Gedik Ahmet Paşa, grand vizier under Mehmet the Conqueror (*see p26*).

The dome and minaret of the mosque of Atik Ali Paşa, dating from 1496

Atik Ali Paşa Mosque ⑳

Atik Ali Paşa Camii

Yeniçeriler Cad, Beyazıt. **Map** 3 D4 (4 C3). 🚋 Çemberlitaş. 🚌 61B. ⬜ *daily.* ⊘

Secreted behind walls in the area south of the Grand Bazaar, this is one of the oldest mosques in the city. It was built in 1496 during the reign of Beyazıt II, the successor of Mehmet the Conqueror, by his eunuch grand vizier, Atik Ali Paşa. The mosque stands in a small garden. It is a simple rectangular structure entered through a deep stone porch. In an unusual touch, its mihrab

is contained in a kind of apse. The other buildings which formed part of the mosque complex – its kitchen (*imaret*), *medrese* and Sufi monastery (*tekke*) – have all but disappeared during the widening of the busy Yeniçeriler Caddesi.

Nuruosmaniye Mosque ㉑

Nuruosmaniye Camii

Vezirhanı Cad, Beyazıt. **Map** 3 D4 (4 C3). 🚋 Çemberlitaş. 🚌 61B. ⬜ *daily.* ⊘

Nuruosmaniye Caddesi, a street lined with carpet and antique shops, leads to the gateway of the mosque from which it gets its name. Mahmut I began the mosque in 1748, and it was finished by his brother, Osman III. It was the first in the city to exhibit the exaggerated traits of the Baroque, as seen in its massive cornices. Its most striking features, however, are the enormous unconcealed arches supporting the dome, each pierced by a mass of windows.

Light floods into the plain square prayer hall, allowing you to see the finely carved wooden calligraphic frieze which runs around the walls above the gallery.

On the other side of the mosque complex is the Nuruosmaniye Gate. This leads into Kalpakçılar Caddesi, the Grand Bazaar's street of jewellery shops (*see p212*).

The tomb of Mahmut Paşa, behind the mosque named after him

Mahmut Paşa Mosque ㉒

Mahmut Paşa Camii

Vezirhanı Cad, Beyazıt. **Map** 3 D3 (4 C3). 🚋 Çemberlitaş. 🚌 61B. ⬜ *daily.* ⊘

Built in 1462, just nine years after Istanbul's conquest by the Ottomans, this was the first large mosque to be erected within the city walls. Unfortunately, it has been over-restored and much of its original charm lost.

The mosque was funded by Mahmut Paşa, a Byzantine aristocrat who converted to Islam and became grand vizier under Mehmet the Conqueror. In 1474 his disastrous military leadership incurred the sultan's fury, and he was executed. His tomb, behind the mosque, is unique in Istanbul for its Moorish style of decoration, with small tiles in blue, black, turquoise and green set in swirling geometric patterns.

Rows of windows illuminating the prayer hall of Nuruosmaniye Mosque

Grand Bazaar ⑱

Kapalı Çarşı

Nothing can prepare you for the Grand Bazaar. This labyrinth of streets covered by painted vaults is lined with thousands of booth-like shops, whose wares spill out to tempt you and whose shopkeepers are relentless in their quest for a sale. The bazaar was established by Mehmet II shortly after his conquest of the city in 1453 *(see p26)*. It can be entered by several gate-ways, two of the most useful being Çarşıkapı Gate (from Beyazıt tram stop) and Nuruosmaniye Gate (from Nuruosmaniye Mosque). It is easy to get lost in the bazaar in spite of the signposting. Most of the bazaar's goods were once manufactured and traded behind the scenes in a large area made up of secluded courtyards called hans *(see p96)*.

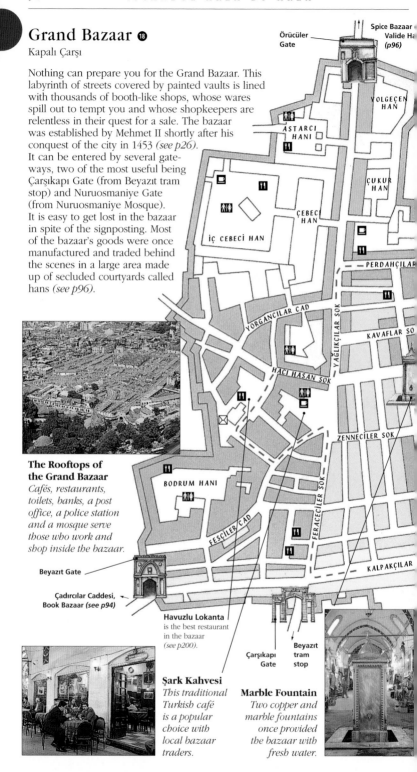

Örücüler Gate

Spice Bazaar Valide Ha (p96)

YOLGEÇEN HAN

ASTARCI HANI

ÇUKUR HAN

ÇEBECİ HAN

İÇ CEBECİ HAN

PERDAHÇILAR

YORGANCILAR CAD

YAĞLIKÇILAR SOK

KAVAFLAR SO

HACI HASAN SOK

ZENNECİLER SOK

FERACECİLER SOK

The Rooftops of the Grand Bazaar
Cafés, restaurants, toilets, banks, a post office, a police station and a mosque serve those who work and shop inside the bazaar.

BODRUM HANI

FESÇİLER CAD

Beyazıt Gate

Çadırcılar Caddesi, Book Bazaar *(see p94)*

KALPAKÇILAR

Havuzlu Lokanta
is the best restaurant in the bazaar *(see p200)*.

Çarşıkapı Gate

Beyazıt tram stop

Şark Kahvesi
This traditional Turkish café is a popular choice with local bazaar traders.

Marble Fountain
Two copper and marble fountains once provided the bazaar with fresh water.

Zincirli Han
This is one of the prettiest hans in the bazaar. Here a piece of jewellery can be made to your own choice of design.

VISITORS' CHECKLIST

Çarşıkapı Cad, Beyazıt. **Map** 2 C4 (4 B3). ▮ Beyazıt (for Çarşıkapı Gate), Çemberlitaş (for Nuruosmaniye Gate). ▮ 61B. ○ 8:30am–7pm Mon–Sat.

The İç Bedesten is the oldest part of the bazaar. Once a locked warehouse, it also served as a place where jewellers could make and sell their wares.

The Oriental Kiosk was built as a coffee house in the 17th century and is now a jewellery shop.

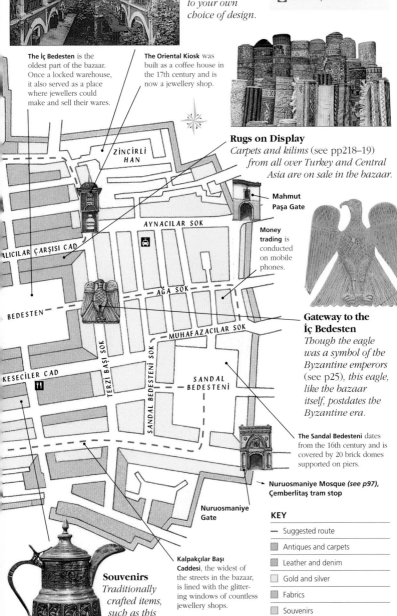

Rugs on Display
Carpets and kilims (see pp218–19) from all over Turkey and Central Asia are on sale in the bazaar.

Mahmut Paşa Gate

Money trading is conducted on mobile phones.

ZİNCİRLİ HAN

AYNACILAR SOK

ALICILAR ÇARŞISI CAD

AĞA SOK

BEDESTEN

MUHAFAZACILAR SOK

TERZİ BAŞI SOK

SANDAL BEDESTENİ SOK

KESECİLER CAD

SANDAL BEDESTENİ

Gateway to the İç Bedesten
Though the eagle was a symbol of the Byzantine emperors (see p25), this eagle, like the bazaar itself, postdates the Byzantine era.

The Sandal Bedesteni dates from the 16th century and is covered by 20 brick domes supported on piers.

Nuruosmaniye Mosque *(see p97)*, Çemberlitaş tram stop

Nuruosmaniye Gate

KEY

— Suggested route

▮ Antiques and carpets

▮ Leather and denim

▯ Gold and silver

▮ Fabrics

▮ Souvenirs

▯ Household goods and workshops

▮ Boundary of the bazaar

Souvenirs
Traditionally crafted items, such as this brass coffee pot, are for sale in the bazaar.

Kalpakçılar Başı Caddesi, the widest of the streets in the bazaar, is lined with the glittering windows of countless jewellery shops.

0 metres 40

0 yards 40

BEYOĞLU

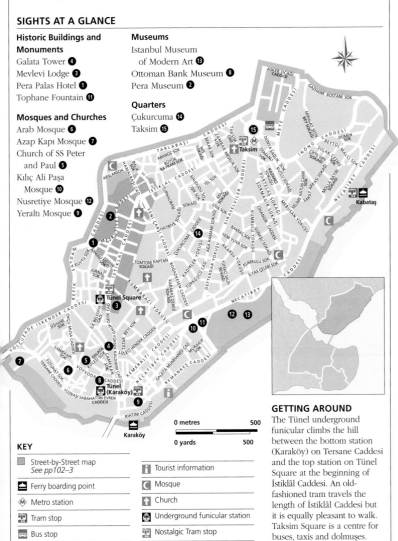

For centuries Beyoğlu, a steep hill north of the Golden Horn, was home to the city's foreign residents. First to arrive here were the Genoese. As a reward for their help in the reconquest of the city from the Latins in 1261 *(see p24)*, they were given the Galata area, which is now dominated by the Galata Tower. During the Ottoman period, Jews from

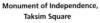

Monument of Independence, Taksim Square

Spain, Arabs, Greeks and Armenians settled in communities here. From the 16th century the great European powers established embassies in the area to further their own interests within the lucrative territories of the Ottoman Empire. The district has not changed much in character over the centuries and is still a thriving commercial quarter today.

SIGHTS AT A GLANCE

Historic Buildings and Monuments
Galata Tower **4**
Mevlevi Lodge **3**
Pera Palas Hotel **1**
Tophane Fountain **11**

Mosques and Churches
Arab Mosque **6**
Azap Kapı Mosque **7**
Church of SS Peter and Paul **5**
Kılıç Ali Paşa Mosque **10**
Nusretiye Mosque **12**
Yeraltı Mosque **9**

Museums
Istanbul Museum of Modern Art **13**
Ottoman Bank Museum **8**
Pera Museum **2**

Quarters
Çukurcuma **14**
Taksim **15**

GETTING AROUND

The Tünel underground funicular climbs the hill between the bottom station (Karaköy) on Tersane Caddesi and the top station on Tünel Square at the beginning of İstiklâl Caddesi. An old-fashioned tram travels the length of İstiklâl Caddesi but it is equally pleasant to walk. Taksim Square is a centre for buses, taxis and dolmuşes.

KEY

- ▢ Street-by-Street map *See pp102–3*
- Ferry boarding point
- Ⓜ Metro station
- Tram stop
- Bus stop
- ℹ Tourist information
- Ⓒ Mosque
- ✝ Church
- Underground funicular station
- Nostalgic Tram stop

◁ **The Galata Tower and backstreets of Beyoğlu, rising up from the Golden Horn**

Street-by-Street: İstiklâl Caddesi

Crest on top of the Russian Consulate gate The pedestrianized İstiklal Caddesi is Beyoğlu's main street. Once known as the Grande Rue de Pera, it is lined by late 19th-century apartment blocks and European embassy buildings whose grandiose gates and façades belie their use as mere consulates since Ankara became the Turkish capital in 1923 *(see p31)*. Hidden from view stand the churches which used to serve the foreign communities of Pera (as this area was formerly called), some still buzzing with worshippers, others just quiet echoes of a bygone era. The once seedy backstreets of Beyoğlu, off İstiklâl Caddesi, are now filled with trendy jazz bars, shops selling handcrafted jewellery, furniture and the like. Crowds are also drawn by the area's cinemas and numerous stylish restaurants. Be aware that the street numbers on İstiklal Caddesi are in the process of being changed.

★ Pera Palas Hotel
This hotel is an atmospheric period piece. Many famous guests, including Agatha Christie, Ernest Hemingway and Alfred Hitchcock have stayed here since it opened in 1892 ❶

St Mary Draperis is a Franciscan church dating from 1789. This small statue of the Virgin stands above the entrance from the street. The vaulted interior of the church is colourfully decorated. An icon of the Virgin, said to perform miracles, hangs over the altar.

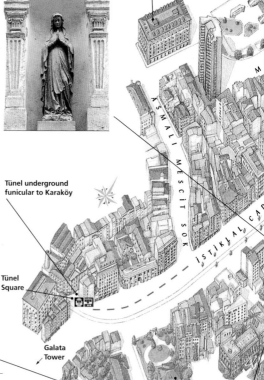

★ Mevlevi Lodge
A peaceful garden surrounds this small museum of the Mevlevi Sufi sect (see p104). On the last Sunday of every month visitors can see dervishes perform their famous swirling dance ❸

Tünel underground funicular to Karaköy

Tünel Square

Galata Tower

Russian Consulate

Swedish Consulate

KEY

– – – Suggested route

| 0 metres | 75 |
| 0 yards | 75 |

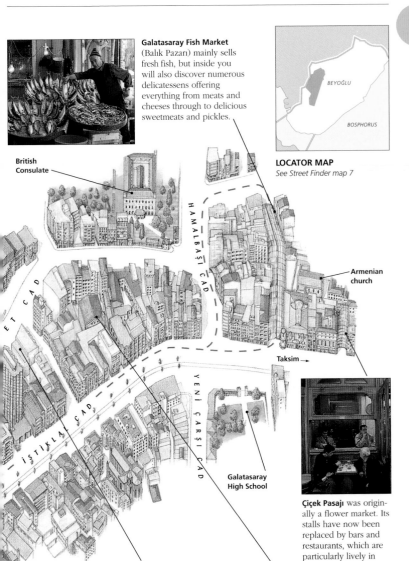

Galatasaray Fish Market
(Balık Pazarı) mainly sells
fresh fish, but inside you
will also discover numerous
delicatessens offering
everything from meats and
cheeses through to delicious
sweetmeats and pickles.

LOCATOR MAP
See Street Finder map 7

BEYOĞLU

BOSPHORUS

British
Consulate

HAMALBAŞI CAD

ET CAD

İSTIKLAL CAD

YENİ ÇARŞI CAD

Armenian
church

Taksim →

Galatasaray
High School

Dutch
Consulate

Çiçek Pasajı was originally a flower market. Its
stalls have now been
replaced by bars and
restaurants, which are
particularly lively in
the evenings.

Pera Museum
*Oriental paintings,
Anatolian weights and
measures and Kütahya
tiles and ceramics are
part of the collection* ❷

STAR SIGHTS

★ Pera Palas Hotel

★ Mevlevi Lodge

The Church of the Panaghia
serves the now much reduced
Greek Orthodox population
of Beyoğlu. Dedicated to the
Virgin Mary, it contains this
beautiful classical iconostasis.

The elegant Grand Orient bar in the Pera Palas Hotel

Pera Palas Hotel ❶
Pera Palas Oteli

Meşrutiyet Cad 98–100, Tepebaşı.
Map 7 D5. **Tel** (0212) 251 45 60.
🚇 Tünel. ♿ by arrangement.
📷 by appointment only.
www.perapalas.com

The Pera Palas *(see p189)* has attained a legendary status. Relying on the hazy mystique of yesteryear, it has changed little since it opened in 1892, mainly to cater for travellers on the Orient Express *(see p66)*. It still evokes images of uniformed porters and exotic onward destinations such as Baghdad. The Grand Orient bar serves cocktails beneath its original chandeliers, while the patisserie attracts customers with its irresistible cakes and genteel ambience.

Former guests who have contributed to the hotel's reputation include Mata Hari, Greta Garbo, Jackie Onassis, Sarah Bernhardt, Josephine Baker and Atatürk *(see p31)*, whose favourite room is now a museum. A room used by the writer Agatha Christie can be visited on request.

SUFISM AND THE WHIRLING DERVISHES

Sufism is the mystical branch of Islam *(see pp38–9)*. The name comes from *suf*, the Arabic for wool, for Sufis were originally associated with poverty and self-denial, and often wore rough woollen clothes next to the skin. Sufis aspire to a personal experience of the divine. This takes the form of meditative rituals, involving recitation, dance and music, to bring the practitioner into direct, ecstatic communion with Allah. There are several sects of Sufis, the most famous of which are the Mevlevi, better known as the Whirling Dervishes on account of their ritual spinning dance.

Painting of the Whirling Dervishes (1837) at the Mevlevi Lodge

Pera Museum ❷
Pera Müzesi

Meşrutiyet Cad 141, Tepebaşı.
Map 7 D4. **Tel** (0212) 334 99 00.
🚇 Tünel. 🚌 From Taksim Square down Tarlabaşı. ⏰ 10am–7pm Tue–Sat, noon–6pm Sun. ⬤ 1 Jan, first day of Religious Holidays. ♿ 📷 (disabled visitors enter free). 🖥 🏛
www.peramuzesi.org.tr

The Pera Museum was opened in June 2005 by the Suna and İnan Kıraç Foundation, with the aim of providing a cultural centre. It is housed in a historic building, formerly the Hotel Bristol. Notable collections include Ottoman weights and measures, over 400 examples of 18th-century Kütahya tiles and ceramics, and the Suna and İnan Kıraç Foundation's exhibition of Orientalist art. This collection brings together works by European artists inspired by the Ottoman world from the 17th century to the early 19th century. It also covers the last two centuries of the Ottoman Empire and provides an insight into upper class lives, customs and dress. The Pera also provides spaces for modern art exhibitions.

Mevlevi Lodge ❸
Mevlevi Tekkesi

Galip Dede Cad 15, Beyoğlu. **Map** 7 D5. **Tel** (0212) 245 41 41. 🚇 Tünel. ⏰ 9am–4pm Wed–Mon. 📷

Although Sufism was banned by Atatürk in 1924, this monastery has survived as the Divan Edebiyatı Müzesi, a museum of *divan* literature (classical Ottoman poetry). The monastery belonged to the most famous sect of Sufis, who were known as the Whirling Dervishes. The original dervishes were disciples of the mystical poet and

The peaceful courtyard of the Mevlevi Lodge

great Sufi master "Mevlana" (Our Leader) Jelaleddin Rumi, who died in Konya, in central Anatolia in 1273.

Tucked away off a street named after one of the great poets of the sect, Galip Dede, the museum centres on an 18th-century lodge, within which is a beautiful octagonal wooden dance floor. Here, for the benefit of visitors, the *sema* (ritual dance) is performed by a group of latter-day Sufi devotees on the last Sunday of every month. At 3pm a dozen or so dancers unfurl their great circular skirts to whirl round the room in an extraordinary state of ecstatic meditation, accompanied by haunting music.

Around the dance floor are glass cases containing a small exhibition of artifacts belonging to the sect, including hats, clothing, manuscripts, photographs and musical instruments. Outside, in the calm, terraced garden, stand the ornate tombstones of ordinary sect members and prominent sheikhs (leaders).

Galata Tower **4**

Galata Kulesi

Büyük Hendek Sok, Beyoğlu.
Map 3 D1. **Tel** *(0212) 293 81 80.*
🚇 *Tünel.* ⏰ *9am–7pm daily.*
Restaurant & show
⏰ *8pm–midnight daily.*
www.galatatower.net

The most recognizable feature on the Golden Horn, the Galata Tower is 60-m

Doorway into the main courtyard of the Church of SS Peter and Paul

(196-ft) high and topped by a conical tower. Its origins date from the 6th century when it was used to monitor shipping. After the conquest of Istanbul in 1453, the Ottomans turned it into a prison and naval depot. In the 18th century, aviation pioneer, Hezarfen Ahmet Çelebi, attached wings to his arms and "flew" from the tower to Üsküdar. The building was subsequently used as a fire watchtower.

The tower has been renovated and on the ninth floor there is a restaurant with nightly shows of folk music and belly dancing. The unmissable view from the top encompasses the city's skyline and beyond as far as Princes' Islands *(see p159)*.

Church of SS Peter and Paul **5**

Sen Piyer Kilisesi

Galata Kulesi Sok 44, Karaköy.
Map 3 D1. **Tel** *(0212) 249 23 85.*
🚇 *Tünel.* ⏰ *7am–5pm Mon–Sat & 10:30am–noon Sun.*

When their original church was requisitioned as a mosque (to become the nearby Arab Mosque) in the early 16th century, the Dominican brothers of Galata moved to this site, just below the Galata Tower. The present building, dating from 1841, was built by the Fossati brothers, architects of Italian-Swiss origin who also worked on the restoration of Haghia Sophia *(see pp72–5)*. The church's rear wall is built into a section of Galata's old Genoese ramparts.

According to Ottoman regulations, the main façade of the building could not be directly on a road, so the church is reached through a courtyard, the entrance to which is via a tiny door on the street. Ring the bell to gain admittance.

The church is built in the style of a basilica, with four side altars. The cupola over the choir is sky blue, studded with gold stars. Mass is said here in Italian every morning.

Arab Mosque **6**

Arap Camii

Kalyon Sok 1, Galata. **Map** 3 D1.
🚇 *Tünel.* ⏰ *prayer times only.*

The Arabs after whom this mosque was named were Moorish refugees from Spain. Many settled in Galata after their expulsion from Andalusia following the fall of Granada in 1492. The church of SS Paul and Dominic, built in the first half of the 14th century by Dominican monks, was given to the settlers for use as a mosque. It is an unusual building for Istanbul: a vast, strikingly rectangular Gothic church with a tall square belfry which now acts as a minaret. The building has been restored several times, but of all the converted churches in the city it makes the least convincing mosque.

The distinctive Galata Tower, as seen from across the Golden Horn

Azap Kapı Mosque, built by the great architect Sinan

Azap Kapı Mosque ⑦
Azap Kapı Camii

Tersane Cad, Azapkapı. **Map** 2 C1. 🚇 *Tünel.* 🚌 *46H, 61B.* ◯ *prayer times only.*

Delightful though they are, this little mosque complex and fountain are somewhat overshadowed by the stream of traffic thundering over the adjacent Atatürk Bridge. The trees surrounding the mosque, however, help to screen it from the noise. It was built in 1577–8 by Sinan (see p91) for Grand Vizier Sokollu Mehmet Paşa and is considered to be one of Sinan's more attractive mosques. Unusually, the entrance is up a flight of internal steps.

Ottoman Bank Museum ⑧
Osmanlı Bankası Müzesi

Bankalar Cad 35–37, Karaköy. **Map** 3 D1. **Tel** (0212) 334 22 70. 🚇 *Tünel.* 🚌 *25E, 56.* ◯ *10am–6pm daily.* 🎟 🖥 🚻 🚫
www.obmuseum.com

The Ottoman Bank Museum has the most interesting collection of state archives in Turkey. Exhibits include Ottoman banknotes, promissory notes from officials at the imperial palace and photos of the Empire's ornately crafted branches.

Outstanding are the 6,000 photographs of the bank's employees – a unique social registry.

Yeraltı Mosque ⑨
Yeraltı Camii

Karantina Sok, Karaköy. **Map** 3 E1. 🚇 *Tünel.* ◯ *daily.*

This mosque, literally "the underground mosque", contains the shrines of two Muslim saints, Abu Sufyan and Amiri Wahibi, who died during the first Arab siege of the city in the 7th century (see p21). It was the discovery of their bodies in the cellar of an ancient Byzantine fortification in 1640 that led to the creation of first a shrine on the site and later, in 1757, a mosque.

The tombs of the saints are behind grilles at the end of a low, dark prayer hall, the roof of which is supported by a forest of pillars.

Kılıç Ali Paşa Mosque ⑩
Kılıç Ali Paşa Camii

Necatibey Cad, Tophane. **Map** 7 E5. 🚌 *25E, 56.* 🚋 *Tophane.* ◯ *daily.*

This mosque was built in 1580 by Sinan, who was by then in his 90s. The church of Haghia Sophia (see pp72–5) provided the architect with his inspiration. İznik tiles adorn the mihrab and there is a delightful deep porch before the main door. Above the entrance portal is an inscription giving the date when the mosque was established.

Kılıç Ali Paşa, who commissioned the mosque, had a colorful life. Born in Italy, he was captured by Muslim pirates

Detail of a carved panel on Tophane Fountain

Koranic inscription in İznik tiles at the Kılıç Ali Paşa Mosque

and later converted to Islam in the service of Süleyman the Magnificent (1520–66). He served as a naval commander under three sultans and after retiring asked Murat III (see p27) where to build his mosque. The sultan is said to have replied "in the admiral's domain, the sea". Taking him at his word, Kılıç Ali Paşa reclaimed part of the Bosphorus for his complex.

Tophane Fountain ⑪
Tophane Çeşmesi

Tophane İskele Cad, Tophane. **Map** 7 E5. 🚌 *25E, 56.* 🚋 *Tophane.*

Beside Kılıç Ali Paşa Mosque stands a beautiful but abandoned Baroque fountain, built in 1732 by Mahmut I. With its elegant roof and dome, it resembles the fountain of Ahmet III (see p60). Each of the four walls is entirely covered in low-relief floral carving, which would once have been gaily painted.

The name, meaning "cannon foundry fountain", comes from the brick and stone foundry building on the hill nearby. Established in 1453 by Mehmet the Conqueror (see p26) and rebuilt several times, the foundry no longer produces weapons but is still owned by the military.

Nusretiye Mosque ⑫
Nusretiye Camii

Necatibey Cad, Tophane. **Map** 7 E5. 🚌 *25E, 56.* ◯ *daily.*

The baroque "Mosque of Victory" was built in the 1820s by Kirkor Balyan (see p128), who went on to found a dynasty of architects. This ornate building seems more like a large palace

The window-filled dome and arches of Nusretiye Mosque

pavilion than a mosque, with its decorative outbuildings and marble terrace.

Commissioned by Mahmut II to commemorate his abolition of the Janissary corps in 1826 (see p30), it faces the Selimiye Barracks (see p132), across the Bosphorus, which housed the New Army that replaced the Janissaries. The Empire-style swags and embellishments celebrate the sultan's victory. The marble panel of calligraphy around the interior of the mosque is particularly fine, as is the pair of sebils (kiosks for serving drinks) outside.

Istanbul Museum of Modern Art ⓭
İstanbul Modern Sanat Müzesi

Meclis-i Mebusan Cad, Liman İşletmeleri Sahası, Antrepo 4, Karaköy. **Map** 7 F5. **Tel** (0212) 334 73 00. 🚋 Tophane. 🚌 56. ⊙ 10am–6pm Tue–Sun. 📷 ♿ 📧 🖌 www.istanbulmodern.org

The Istanbul Modern, a new building perched on the Golden Horn, opened in 2005 as the most upbeat and thoroughly contemporary museum in Turkey. It houses both permanent collections and temporary exhibitions, providing a showcase for many of the eccentric and talented personalities who have shaped modern art in Turkey from the early 20th

century to the present day. Many of the works are from the private collection of the Ecacıbaşı family, who founded the museum. Exhibits include abstract art, landscapes and watercolours as well as a sculpture garden and a stunning display of black and white photography.

Çukurcuma ⓮

Map 7 E4.
🚇 Taksim.

Suzani textiles (see p212) on sale in Çukurcuma

This charming old quarter of Beyoğlu, radiating from a neighbourhood mosque on Çukurcuma Caddesi, has become an important centre for Istanbul's furnishings and antiques trades. The old warehouses and houses in this district have been converted into shops and showrooms, where modern upholstery materials are piled up in carved marble basins and antique cabinets. It is worth browsing here to discover hidden treasures, ranging from valuable paintings and prints and 19th-century Ottoman embroidery to 1950s biscuit boxes.

Taksim ⓯

Map 7 E3. 🚋 Taksim. 🚇 Taksim.
Taksim Art Gallery Cumhuriyet Caddesi Gezi Dükkanları 26, Taksim. **Tel** (0212) 245 20 68. ⊙ 10am–7pm Mon–Sat. ● Jun–Sep.

Centring on the vast Taksim Square (Taksim Meydanı), the Taksim area is the hub of activity in modern Beyoğlu. Taksim means "water distribution centre"; from the early 1700s, it was from this site that water from the Belgrade Forest (see p158) was distributed throughout the city. The original stone reservoir, built in 1732 by Mahmut I, still stands at the top of İstiklâl Caddesi.

In the southwest of the square is the 1928 Monument of Independence, by the Italian artist Canonica. It shows Atatürk (see pp30–31) and the other founding fathers of the modern Turkish Republic.

Further up is the modern building of the **Taksim Art Gallery**. As well as temporary exhibitions, the gallery has a permanent display of Istanbul landscapes by some of Turkey's most important 20th-century painters.

Flower sellers in Taksim Square

GREATER ISTANBUL

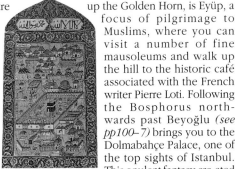

Tiles depicting Mecca, Cezri Kasım Paşa Mosque, Eyüp

Away from the city centre there are many sights which repay the journey to visit them. Greater Istanbul has been divided into five areas shown on the map below; each also has its own map to help you get around. Closest to the centre are the mosques and churches of Fatih, Fener and Balat: most conspicuously the gigantic Fatih Mosque. Across the Golden Horn *(see p89)* from Balat are two sights worth seeing: Aynalı Kavak Palace and a fascinating industrial museum. The Theodosian Walls, stretching from the Golden Horn to the Sea of Marmara, are one of the city's most impressive monuments. Along these walls stand sev-eral ancient palaces and churches: particularly interesting is the Church of St Saviour in Chora, with its stunning Byzantine mosaics. Beyond the walls,

up the Golden Horn, is Eyüp, a focus of pilgrimage to Muslims, where you can visit a number of fine mausoleums and walk up the hill to the historic café associated with the French writer Pierre Loti. Following the Bosphorus north-wards past Beyoğlu *(see pp100–7)* brings you to the Dolmabahçe Palace, one of the top sights of Istanbul. This opulent fantasy cre-ated in the 19th century by Sultan Abdül Mecit I requires a lengthy visit. Beyond it is peaceful Yıldız Park containing yet more beautiful palaces and pavilions. Not all visitors to Istanbul make it to the Asian side, but if you have half a day to spare it is only a short ferry trip from Eminönü *(see pp 242–3)*. Its attractions include some splendid mosques, a handsome railway station and a small museum dedicated to Florence Nightingale.

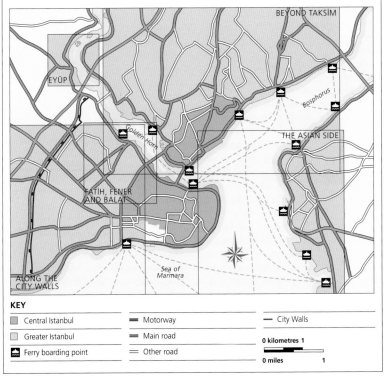

KEY

▦ Central Istanbul	— City Walls
▢ Greater Istanbul	**0 kilometres** 1
⛴ Ferry boarding point	**0 miles** 1
▭ Motorway	
▭ Main road	
▭ Other road	

◁ **Fountain in the grounds of the sumptuous Dolmabahçe Palace**

Fatih, Fener and Balat

A visit to these neighbourhoods is a reminder that for centuries after the Muslim conquest *(see p26)*, Jews and Christians made up around 40 per cent of Istanbul's population. Balat was home to Greek-speaking Jews from the Byzantine era onwards; Sephardic Jews from Spain joined them in the 15th century. Fener became a Greek enclave in the early 16th century and many wealthy residents rose to positions of prominence in the Ottoman Empire. Hilltop Fatih is linked to the city's radical Islamic tradition and you will see far more devout Muslims here than anywhere else in Istanbul. All three areas are residential, their maze of streets the preserve of washing lines and children playing.

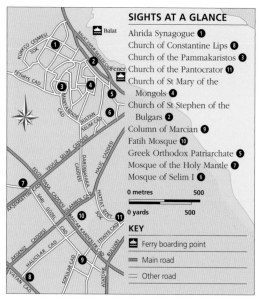

SIGHTS AT A GLANCE

Ahrida Synagogue ❶
Church of Constantine Lips ❽
Church of the Pammakaristos ❸
Church of the Pantocrator ⓫
Church of St Mary of the Mongols ❹
Church of St Stephen of the Bulgars ❷
Column of Marcian ❾
Fatih Mosque ❿
Greek Orthodox Patriarchate ❺
Mosque of the Holy Mantle ❼
Mosque of Selim I ❻

| 0 metres | 500 |
| 0 yards | 500 |

KEY

⛴ Ferry boarding point
▬ Main road
— Other road

Ahrida Synagogue ❶

Ahrida Sinagogu

Gevgili Sok, Balat. **Map** 1 C1. 🚌 *55T, 99A.* ⬜ *by appointment.* 📷

The name of Istanbul's oldest and most beautiful synagogue is a corruption of Ohrid, a town in Macedonia from which its early congregation came. It was founded before the Muslim conquest of the city in 1453 and, with a capacity for up to 500 worshippers, has been in constant use ever since. However, tourists can only visit by prior arrangement with a guided tour company *(see p228)*. The synagogue's painted walls and ceilings, dating from the late 17th century, have been restored to their Baroque glory. Pride of place, however, goes to the central Holy Ark, covered in rich tapestries, which contains rare holy scrolls.

During an explosion of fervour that swept the city's Jewish population in the 17th century, the religious leader Shabbetai Zevi (1629–76), a self-proclaimed messiah, started preaching at this synagogue. He was banished from the city and later converted to Islam. However, a significant number of Jews held that Zevi's conversion was a subterfuge and his followers, the Sabbatians, exist to this day.

Church of St Stephen of the Bulgars ❷

Bulgar Kilisesi

Mürsel Paşa Cad 85, Balat.
Map 1 C1. 🚌 *55T, 99A.* ⬜ *Balat.*
⬜ *9am–5pm daily.*

Astonishingly, this entire church was cast in iron, even the internal columns and galleries. It was created in Vienna in 1871, shipped all the way to the Golden Horn *(see p89)* and assembled on its shore. The church was needed for the Bulgarian community who had broken away from the authority of the Greek Orthodox Patriarchate just up the hill. Today, it is still used by this community, who keep the marble tombs of the first Bulgarian patriarchs permanently decorated with flowers. The church stands in a pretty little park that is dotted with trees and flowering shrubs and which runs down to the edge of the Golden Horn.

The Church of St Stephen of the Bulgars, wholly made of iron

Church of the Pammakaristos ❸

Fethiye Camii

Fethiye Cad, Draman. **Map** 1 C2. 🚌 *90, 90B.* ⬜ *prayer times only.* 📷

This Byzantine church is one of the hidden secrets of Istanbul. It is rarely visited despite the important role it has played in the history of the city and its breathtaking series of mosaics. For over

Byzantine façade of the Church of the Pammakaristos

100 years after the Ottoman conquest it housed the Greek Orthodox Patriarchate, but was converted into a mosque in the late 16th century by Murat III *(see p32)*. He named it the Mosque of Victory to commemorate his conquests of Georgia and Azerbaijan.

The charming exterior is obviously Byzantine, with its alternating stone and brick courses and finely carved marble details. The main body of the building is the working mosque, while the extra-ordinary mosaics are in a side chapel. This now operates as a museum and officially you need to get permission in advance from Haghia Sophia *(see pp72–5)* to see it. However, the caretaker, if around, may simply let you in.

Dating from the 14th century, the great Byzantine renaissance *(see p25)*, the mosaics show holy figures isolated in a sea of gold, a reflection of the heavens. From the centre of the main dome, Christ Pantocrator ("the All-Powerful"), surrounded by the Old Testament prophets, stares solemnly down. In the apse another figure of Christ, seated on a jewel-encrusted throne, gives his benediction. On either side are portraits of the Virgin Mary and John the Baptist beseeching Christ. They are overlooked by the four archangels, while the side apses are filled with other saintly figures.

Church of St Mary of the Mongols ④
Kanlı Kilise

Tevkii Cafer Mektebi Sok, Fener. **Map** 1 C2. **Tel** *(0212) 521 71 39.* ▦ *55T, 99A.* ○ *by appointment.*

Consecrated in the late 13th century, the Church of St Mary of the Mongols is the only Greek Orthodox church in Istanbul to have remained continuously in the hands of the Greek community since the Byzantine era. Its immunity from conversion into a mosque was

Detail on Church of St Mary of the Mongols

decreed in an order signed by Mehmet the Conqueror *(see p26)*. A copy of this is kept by the church to this day.

The church gets its name from the woman who founded it, Maria Palaeologina, an illegitimate Byzantine princess who was married off to a Mongol khan, Abagu, and lived piously with him in Persia for 15 years. On her husband's assassination, she returned to Constantinople, built this church and lived out her days in it as a nun.

A beautiful Byzantine mosaic which depicts Theotokos Pammakaristos ("the All-Joyous Mother of God") is the church's greatest treasure.

Greek Orthodox Patriarchate ⑤
Ortodoks Patrikhanesi

Sadrazam Ali Paşa Cad 35, Fener. *Tel (0212) 525 54 16.* ▦ *55T, 99A.* ○ *9am–5pm daily.* ▣

This walled complex has been the seat of the patriarch of the Greek Orthodox Church since the early 17th century. Though nominally head of the whole church, the patriarch is now shepherd to a diminishing flock in and around Istanbul.

As you walk up the steps to enter the Patriarchate through a side door you will see that the main door has been welded shut. This was done in memory of Patriarch Gregory V, who was hanged here for treason in 1821 after encouraging the Greeks to overthrow Ottoman rule at the start of the Greek War of Independence (1821–32). Antagonism between the Turkish and Greek communities worsened with the Greek occupation of parts of Turkey in the 1920s *(see p31)*. There were anti-Greek riots in 1955, and in the mid-1960s many Greek residents were expelled. Today the clergy here is protected by a metal detector at the entrance.

The Patriarchate centres on the basilica-style Church of St George, which dates back to 1720. Yet the church contains much older relics and furniture. The patriarch's throne, the high structure to the right of the nave, is thought to be Byzantine, while the pulpit on the left is adorned with fine Middle Eastern wooden inlay and Orthodox icons.

The ornate, gilded interior of the Church of St George in the Greek Orthodox Patriarchate

İznik tile panel capping a window in the Mosque of Selim I

Mosque of Selim I ❻

Selim I Camii

Yavuz Selim Cad, Fener. **Map** 1 C2. 🚌 55T, 90, 90B, 99A. ⬜ daily.

This much-admired mosque is also known locally as Yavuz Sultan Mosque: Yavuz, "the Grim", being the nickname the infamous Selim acquired (see p26). It is idyllic in a rather off-beat way, which seems at odds with the barbaric reputation of the sultan.

The mosque, built between 1522 and 1529, sits alone on a hill beside a sunken parking lot, once the Byzantine Cistern of Aspar. Sadly it is rarely visited and has an air of neglect, yet the mosque's courtyard gives an insight into concept of paradise in Islam. At the centre of this lovely garden is an octagonal, domed fountain, surrounded by trees filled with chirruping birds.

The windows set into the porticoes in the courtyard are capped by early İznik tiles (see p161). These were made by the *cuerda seca* technique, in which each colour is separated during the firing process, thus affording the patterns greater definition.

Similar tiles lend decorative effect to the simple prayer hall, with its fine mosque furniture (see pp38–9) and original painted woodwork.

Mosque of the Holy Mantle ❼

Hırka-i Şerif Camii

Keçeciler Cad, Karagümrük. **Map** 1 B3. 🚌 28, 87, 90, 91. ⬜ daily.

Built in the Empire Style in 1851, this mosque was designed to house a cloak (hırka) in the imperial collection which once belonged to and was worn by the Prophet Mohammed. This resides in a sanctuary directly behind the mihrab. The mosque's minarets are in the form of Classical columns, and its balconies styled like Corinthian capitals. The interior of the octagonal prayer hall, meanwhile, has a plethora of decorative marble. Abdül Mecit I, the mosque's patron, was jointly responsible for the design of its calligraphic frieze.

Knocker, Mosque of the Holy Mantle

Church of Constantine Lips ❽

Fenari İsa Camii

Vatan Cad, Fatih. **Map** 1 B4. 🚌 90B. ⬜ daily.

This 10th-century monastic church, dedicated to the Immaculate Mother of God, was founded by Constantine Lips Dungarios, a commander of the Byzantine fleet. Following the Byzantine reconquest

Byzantine brickwork exterior of the Church of Constantine Lips

of the city in 1261 (see p24), Empress Theodora, wife of Michael VIII Palaeologus (see pp24–5), added a second church. She also commissioned a funerary chapel, where she and her sons were buried.

This unusual history has given the structure its present rambling appearance. In an idiosyncratic touch, there are also four tiny chapels perched on the roof around the main dome. Another highlight is the building's eastern exterior wall. This is decorated with a *tour de force* of brick friezes, of the kind that are a hallmark of Byzantine churches of this period. When the church was converted into a mosque in 1496, it adopted the name Fenari İsa, or the Lamp of Jesus. This was in honour of İsa (Turkish for Jesus), the leader of a Sufi brotherhood (see p104) who worshipped here at that time. Inside the mosque, which is still in use today, there are some well-restored capitals and decorated cornices.

Column of Marcian ❾

Kız Taşı

Kıztaşı Cad, Saraçhane. **Map** 1 C4 (2 A3). 🚌 28, 87, 90, 91.

Standing in a little square, this 5th-century Byzantine column was once surmounted by a statue of the Emperor Marcian (AD 450–57). On its base you can still see a pair of Nikes, Greek winged goddesses of victory, holding an inscribed medallion.

Interestingly, the column's Turkish name translates as the Maiden's Column, suggesting that it was mistaken for the famous Column of Venus. According to legend, this column was said to sway at the passing of an impure maid. It originally stood nearby and is thought to have been employed as one of the largest columns in the Süleymaniye Mosque (see pp90–91).

Chandelier hanging in the light and airy interior of Fatih Mosque

Fatih Mosque ❿
Fatih Camii

Macar Kardeşler Cad, Fatih. **Map** 1 C3. 🚌 *28, 87, 90, 91.* 🔓 *daily.*

A spacious outer courtyard surrounds this vast Baroque mosque, which is the third major structure on this site. The first was the Church of the Holy Apostles (*see p23*), the burial place of most of the Byzantine emperors. When Mehmet the Conqueror (*see p26*) came to construct a mosque here, the church's crumbling remains provided a symbolic location. But the first Fatih Mosque collapsed in an earthquake in 1766, and most of what you see today was the work of Mehmet Tahir Ağa, the chief imperial architect under Mustafa III. Many of the buildings he constructed around the prayer hall, including eight Koranic colleges (*medreses*) and a hospice, still stand.

The only parts of Mehmet the Conqueror's mosque to have survived are the three porticoes of the courtyard, the ablutions fountain, the

main gate into the prayer hall and, inside, the mihrab. Two exquisite forms of 15th-century decoration can be seen over the windows in the porticoes: İznik tiles made using the *cuerda seca* technique and lunettes adorned with calligraphic marble inlay.

Inside the prayer hall, stencilled patterns decorate the domes, while the lower level of the walls is revetted with yet more tiles – although these are inferior to those used in the porticoes.

The tomb of Mehmet the Conqueror stands behind the prayer hall, near that of his consort Gülbahar. His sarcophagus and turban are both appropriately large. It is a place of enormous gravity, always busy with supplicants.

If you pay a visit to the mosque on a Wednesday, you will also see the weekly market (*see p214*) which turns the streets around it into a circus of commerce. From tables piled high with fruit and vegetables to lorries loaded with unspun wool, this is a real spectacle, even if you don't buy anything.

Church of the Pantocrator ⓫
Zeyrek Camii

İbadethane Sok, Küçükpazar. **Map** 2 B2. 🚌 *28, 61B, 87.* 🔓 *prayer times daily.* ♿

Empress Irene, the wife of John II Comnenus (*see p19*), founded the Church of the Pantocrator ("Christ the Almighty") during the 12th century. This hulk of Byzantine masonry was once the centrepiece of one of the city's most important religious foundations, the Monastery of the Pantocrator. As well as a monastery and church, the complex included a hospice for the elderly, an asylum and a hospital. In this respect it prefigured the social welfare system provided by the great imperial mosque complexes that the Ottomans later built in the city (*see p38*).

The church, now a mosque, boasts a magnificent figurative marble floor. It is composed of three interlinked chapels. The one with the highest dome was built by Empress Irene. Emperor John II added another as a mortuary chapel when Irene died in 1124, and he later filled the area between with a third apsed chapel. The rest of the Comnenus dynasty and many of the Palaeologus imperial family were interred within these chapels.

Shortly after the Muslim conquest in 1453 (*see p26*), the building was converted into a mosque. A caretaker may let you in outside prayer times in the afternoons.

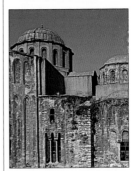

Church of the Pantocrator, built by Empress Irene in the 12th century

Along the City Walls

Istanbul's land walls are one of the most impressive remains of the city's Byzantine past. Pierced by monumental gates and strengthened by towers, they encompass the city centre in a great arc, stretching all the way from Yedikule, on the Sea of Marmara, to Ayvansaray, on the Golden Horn *(see p89)*. The suburbs that lie adjacent to the walls, particularly Edirnekapı and Topkapı, are mainly working-class, residential districts, interspersed with areas of wasteland which are unsafe to explore alone. Dotted around these suburbs, however, are important remnants of the city's past, particularly the Byzantine period. The outstanding sight here is the Church of St Saviour in Chora *(see pp118–19)*, with its beautifully preserved mosaics and frescoes.

Silivrikapı, one of the gateways through the Theodosian Walls

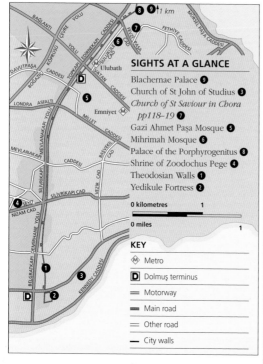

SIGHTS AT A GLANCE

Blachernae Palace **9**
Church of St John of Studius **3**
Church of St Saviour in Chora
pp118–19 **7**
Gazi Ahmet Paşa Mosque **5**
Mihrimah Mosque **6**
Palace of the Porphyrogenitus **8**
Shrine of Zoodochus Pege **4**
Theodosian Walls **1**
Yedikule Fortress **2**

0 kilometres   1

0 miles   1

KEY

Ⓜ Metro

Ⓓ Dolmuş terminus

═══ Motorway

▬▬ Main road

══ Other road

▬ City walls

The walls were built between AD 412–22, during the reign of Theodosius II (408–50). In 447 an earthquake destroyed 54 of the towers but these were immediately rebuilt, under threat of the advancing Attila the Hun. Subsequently the walls resisted sieges by Arabs, Bulgarians, Russians and Turks. Even the determined armies of the Fourth Crusade *(see p24)* only managed to storm the ramparts along the Golden Horn, while the land walls stood firm.

Mehmet the Conqueror finally breached the walls in May 1453 *(see p26)*. Successive Ottoman sultans then kept the walls in good repair until the end of the 17th century.

Large stretches of the walls, particularly around Belgratkapı (Belgrade Gate) have been rebuilt. Byzantine scholars have criticized the restoration for insensitive use of modern building materials, but the new sections do give you an idea of how the walls used to look. Many, although not all, of the gateways are still in good repair. Mehmet the Conqueror directed his heaviest cannon at the St Romanus and Charsius gates. Under the Ottomans, the former became known as Topkapı, the Gate

Theodosian Walls **1**
Teodos II Surları

From Yedikule to Ayvansaray.
Map 1 A1. 🚃 *Topkapı, Ulubatlı.*

With its 11 fortified gates and 192 towers, this great chain of double walls sealed Constantinople's landward side against invasion for more than a thousand years. Extending for a distance of 6.5 km (4 miles) from the Sea of Marmara to the Golden Horn, the walls are built in layers of red tile alternating with limestone blocks. Different sections can be reached by metro, tram, train or bus; but to see their whole length you will need to take a taxi or dolmuş *(see p238)* along the main road that runs outside them.

Carving of the Byzantine eagle over Yedikule Gate

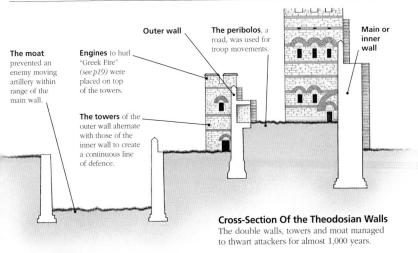

Outer wall

The peribolos, a road, was used for troop movements.

Main or inner wall

The moat prevented an enemy moving artillery within range of the main wall.

Engines to hurl "Greek Fire" *(see p19)* were placed on top of the towers.

The towers of the outer wall alternate with those of the inner wall to create a continuous line of defence.

Cross-Section Of the Theodosian Walls
The double walls, towers and moat managed to thwart attackers for almost 1,000 years.

of the Cannon (not to be confused with Topkapı Palace, *see pp54–9*). Unfortunately, a section of walls close to this gate was demolished in the 1950s to make way for a road, Millet Caddesi. The Charsius Gate (now called Edirnekapı), Silivrikapı, Yeni Mevlanakapı and other original gates still give access to the city. The Yedikule Gate (which stands beside the fortress of the same name) has an imperial Byzantine eagle *(see p25)* carved above its main archway.

Yedikule Fortress ❷
Yedikule Müzesi

Kule Meydanı 4, Yedikule.
Tel *(0212) 585 89 33.* 🚌 *31, 80, 93T.*
🕐 *9:30am–5pm Thu–Tue.*

Yedikule, the "Fortress of the Seven Towers", is built on to the southern section of the Theodosian Walls. Its seven towers are connected by thick walls to make a five-sided fortification. One of the sides, with four towers spaced along it, is formed by a stretch of the land walls themselves.

The fortress as it is today incorporates both Byzantine and Ottoman features. The two stout, square marble towers built into the land walls once flanked the Golden Gate (now blocked up), the triumphal entrance into medieval Byzantium *(see p22)* built by Theodosius II. Imperial

processions would enter the city through this gate to mark the investiture of a new emperor or in celebration of a successful military campaign. When it was first built, the gate was covered in gold plate and the façade decorated with sculptures, including a statue of a winged Victory, four bronze elephants and an image of Emperor Theodosius himself.

In the 15th century, Mehmet the Conqueror added the three tall, round towers that are not part of the land walls, and the connecting curtain walls, to complete the fortress.

After viewing the castle from the outside, you can enter through a doorway in the northeastern wall. The tower immediately to your left as you enter is known as the *yazılı kule*, "the tower with inscriptions". This was used

as a prison for foreign envoys and others who fell foul of the sultan. These hapless individuals carved their names, dates and other details on the walls and some of these inscriptions are still visible.

Executions were carried out in Yedikule Castle, in the northern of the two towers flanking the Golden Gate. Among those executed here was the 17-year-old Osman II *(see p33)*. In 1622 he was dragged to Yedikule by his own Janissaries *(see p127)*, after four years of misrule, which included, it is alleged, using his own pages as targets for archery practice.

The walkway around the ramparts is accessible via a steep flight of stone steps. It offers good views of the land walls and nearby suburbs, and also of the cemeteries.

Aerial view of Yedikule Fortress with the Sea of Marmara behind

Church of St John of Studius ❸

İmrahor Camii

İmam Aşir Sok, Yedikule. 🚌 80, 80B, 80T. 🚇 Yedikule.

Istanbul's oldest surviving church, St John of Studius, is now a mere shell consisting only of its outer walls. However, you can still get an idea of the original beauty of what was once part of an important Byzantine institution.

The church was completed in AD 463 by Studius, a Roman patrician who served as consul during the reign of Emperor Marcian (450–57). Originally connected to the most powerful monastery in the Byzantine Empire, in the late 8th century it was a spiritual and intellectual centre under the rule of Abbot Theodore, who was buried in the church's garden. The abbot is venerated today in the Greek Orthodox Church as St Theodore.

Until its removal by the soldiers of the Fourth Crusade (see p24), the most sacred relic housed in the church was the head of St John the Baptist. The emperor would visit the church each year for the Beheading of the Baptist feast on 29 August.

In the 15th century the church housed a university and was converted into a mosque. The building was abandoned in 1894 when it was severely damaged by an earthquake.

The church is a perfect basilica, with a single apse at the east end, preceded by a narthex and a courtyard. It has a magnificent entrance portal, with carved Corinthian capitals and a sculpted architrave and cornice. Inside, it is empty, apart from a colonnade of six columns of verdigris.

Ruins of the Church of St John of Studius

The Shrine of Zoodochus Pege, founded on a sacred spring

Shrine of Zoodochus Pege ❹

Balıklı Kilise

Seyit Nizam Cad 3, Silivrikapı. **Tel** (0212) 582 30 81. 🚇 Seyitnizam. 🚌 93T. 🕐 8am–4pm daily.

The Fountain of Zoodochus Pege ("Life-Giving Spring") is built over Istanbul's most famous sacred spring, which is believed to have miraculous powers. The fish swimming in it are supposed to have arrived though a miracle which occurred shortly before the fall of Constantinople (see p26). They are said to have leapt into the spring from a monk's frying pan on hearing him declare that a Turkish invasion of Constantinople was as likely as fish coming back to life.

The spring was probably the site of an ancient sanctuary of Artemis. Later, with the arrival of Christianity, a church was built around it, which was dedicated to the Virgin Mary. The spring was popular throughout the Byzantine era, especially on Ascension Day, when the emperor would visit it. The church was destroyed and rebuilt many times over the years by various Byzantine emperors, but the present one dates from 1833. The inner courtyard is filled with tombs of bishops and patriarchs of the Greek Orthodox Church.

Gazi Ahmet Paşa Mosque ❺

Gazi Ahmet Paşa Camii

Undeğirmeni Sok, Fatma Sultan. 🕐 Prayer times only. 🚇 Ulubatlı. 🚌 Topkapı. 🚌 93T.

One of the most worthwhile detours along the city walls is the Gazi Ahmet Paşa Mosque, also known as Kara Ahmet Paşa. This lovely building, with its peaceful leafy courtyard and graceful proportions, is one of Sinan's (see p91) lesser known achievements. He built it in 1554 for Kara Ahmet Paşa, a grand vizier of Süleyman the Magnificent (see p26).

The courtyard is surrounded by the cells of a *medrese* and a *dershane*, or main classroom. Attractive apple-green and yellow İznik tiles (see p161) grace the porch, while blue-and-white ones are found on the east wall of the prayer hall. These tiles date from the mid-16th

Tilework over *medrese* doorway at Kara Ahmet Paşa Mosque

century. Of the three galleries, the wooden ceiling under the west one is elaborately painted in red, blue, gold and black.

Outside the city walls, nearby, is tiny Takkeci İbrahim Ağa Mosque, which dates from 1592. Wooden-domed, it has some particularly fine İznik tile panels.

Mihrimah Mosque ❻

Mihrimah Camii

Sulukule Cad, Edirnekapı. **Map** 1 A2. 🚌 28, 87, 91. 🕐 daily.

An imposing monument located just inside the city walls, the Mihrimah Mosque complex was built by Sinan between 1562 and 1565. Mihrimah, the daughter of Süleyman the Magnificent *(see p26)*, was then the recently widowed wife of Rüstem Paşa, a grand vizier who gave his name to the tiled mosque near the Spice Bazaar *(see pp88–9)*.

This mosque rests on a platform, occupying the highest point in the city. Its profile is visible from far away on the Bosphorus and also when approaching Istanbul from Edirne *(see pp154–7)*.

The building is square in shape, with four strong turrets at its corners, and is surmounted by a 37-m (121-ft) high dome. The single minaret is tall and slender, so much so that it has twice been destroyed by earthquakes. On the second occasion, in 1894, the minaret crashed through the roof of the mosque. The 20th-century stencilling on the inside of the prayer hall was added following this accident.

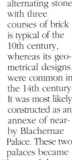

Stained-glass window in the Mihrimah Mosque

The interior is illuminated by numerous windows, some of which have stained glass. The supporting arches of the sultan's loge *(see p39)* have been skilfully painted to resemble green-and-white marble. The carved marble *minbar* is also impressive.

Church of St Saviour in Chora ❼

See pp118–19.

Palace of the Porphyrogenitus ❽
Tekfur Sarayı

Şişehane Cad, Edirnekapı. **Map** 1 B1.
Tel *(0212) 522 175.* 🚌 *87, 90, 126.*
🔲 *daily.*

Only glimpses of the former grandeur of the Palace of the Porphyrogenitus (Sovereign) during its years as an imperial residence are discernible from the sketchy remains. Its one

extant hall, now open to the elements, does, however, have an attractive three-storey façade in typically Byzantine style. This is decorated in red brick and white marble, with arched doorways at ground level and two rows of windows overlooking a courtyard.

The palace, also known as Tekfur Palace Museum, dates from the late Byzantine era and is the only surviving palace from this period. Its exact age is debatable since the technique of alternating stone with three courses of brick is typical of the 10th century, whereas its geometrical designs were common in the 14th century. It was most likely constructed as an annexe of nearby Blachernae Palace. These two palaces became the main residences of the imperial sovereigns in the last two centuries before the fall of Byzantium in 1453 *(see p26)*.

During the reign of Ahmet III (1703–30, *see p27*) the last remaining İznik potters *(see p161)* moved to the palace. However, by this time their skills were in decline and the tiles made here never acquired the excellence of

those created at the height of production in İznik. Cezri Kasım Paşa Mosque in Eyüp *(see p121)* has some fine examples of these tiles.

Blachernae Palace ❾
Anemas Zindanları

İvaz Ağa Cad, Ayvansaray.
🚌 *55T, 99A.*

As the city walls approach the Golden Horn you come to the scant remains of Blachernae Palace. These consist of a tower in the city wall, known as the Prison of Anemas, a terrace to the east (the present site of the İvaz Efendi Mosque), and another tower to the south of the terrace, known as the Tower of Isaac Angelus.

The origins of the palace date as far back as AD 500, when it was an occasional residence for imperial visitors to the shrine of Blachernae. It was the great Comnenus emperors *(see p21)* who rebuilt the structure in the 12th century, transforming it into a magnificent palace.

The remains of the marble decoration and wall frescoes in the Anemas tower indicate that this was probably an imperial residence. Although you can walk around the site, you will be unable to gain access into the towers unless the caretaker is there.

Brick and marble façade in the Palace of the Porphyrogenitus

Church of St Saviour in Chora ❼
Kariye Müzesi

Some of the very finest Byzantine mosaics and frescoes can be found in the Church of St Saviour in Chora. Little is known of the early history of the church, although its name "in Chora", which means "in the country", suggests that the church originally stood in a rural setting.

Scene from the Life of the Virgin

The present church dates from the 11th century. Between 1315–21 it was remodelled and the mosaics and frescoes added by Theodore Metochites, a theologian, philosopher and one of the elite Byzantine officials of his day.

View of St Saviour in Chora

THE GENEALOGY OF CHRIST

Theodore Metochites, who restored St Saviour, wrote that his mission was to relate how "the Lord himself became a mortal on our behalf". He takes the *Genealogy of Christ* as his starting point: the mosaics in the two domes of the inner narthex portray 66 of Christ's forebears.

The crown of the southern dome is occupied by a figure of Christ. In the dome's flutes are two rows of his ancestors: Adam to Jacob ranged above the 12 sons of Jacob. In the northern dome, there is a central image of the Virgin and Child with the kings of the House of David in the upper row and lesser ancestors of Christ in the lower row.

Mosaic showing Christ and his ancestors, in the southern dome of the inner narthex

THE LIFE OF THE VIRGIN

All but one of the 20 mosaics in the inner narthex depicting the *Life of the Virgin* are well preserved. This cycle is based mainly on the apocryphal Gospel of St James, written in the 2nd century, which gives an account of the Virgin's life. This was popular in the Middle Ages and was a rich source of material for ecclesiastical artists.

Among the events shown are the first seven steps of the Virgin, the Virgin entrusted to Joseph and the Virgin receiving bread from an angel.

THE INFANCY OF CHRIST

Scenes from the *Infancy of Christ*, based largely on the New Testament, occupy the semicircular panels of the outer narthex. They begin on

GUIDE TO THE MOSAICS AND FRESCOES

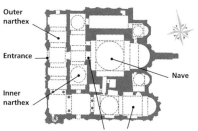

Outer narthex

Entrance

Inner narthex

Nave

Entrance to nave   Pareeclesion

Outer narthex looking east

KEY

- ☐ The Genealogy of Christ
- ☐ The Life of the Virgin
- ☐ The Infancy of Christ
- ☐ Christ's Ministry
- ☐ Other Mosaics
- ☐ The Frescoes

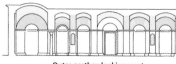

Outer narthex looking west

the north wall of the outer narthex with a scene of Joseph being visited by an angel in a dream. Subsequent panels include Mary and Joseph's *Journey to Bethlehem*, their *Enrolment for Taxation*, the *Nativity of Christ* and, finally, Herod ordering the *Massacre of the Innocents*.

The *Enrolment for Taxation*

CHRIST'S MINISTRY

While many of the mosaics in this series are badly damaged, some beautiful panels remain. The cycle occupies the vaults of the seven bays of the outer narthex and some of the south bay of the inner narthex. The most striking mosaic is the portrayal of Christ's temptation in the wilderness, in the second bay of the outer narthex.

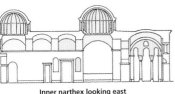

Theodore Metochites presents St Saviour in Chora to Christ

OTHER MOSAICS

There are three panels in the nave of the church, one of which, above the main door from the inner narthex, illustrates the *Dormition of the Virgin*. This mosaic, protected by a marble frame, is the best

preserved in the church. The Virgin is depicted laid out on a bier, watched over by the Apostles, with Christ seated behind. Other devotional panels in the two narthexes include one, on the east wall of the south bay of the inner narthex, of the *Deësis*, depicting Christ with the Virgin Mary and unusually, without St John. Another, in the inner narthex over the door into the nave, is of Theodore Metochites himself, shown wearing a large turban, and humbly presenting the restored church as an offering to Christ.

THE FRESCOES

The frescoes in the parecclesion are thought to have been painted just after the mosaics were completed, probably in around 1320. The

VISITORS' CHECKLIST

Kariye Camii Sok, Edirnekapı.
Map 1 B1. **Tel** *(0212) 631 92 41.* 🚌 *28, 86 or 90, then 5 minutes' walk.* ⏰ *9am–4pm Thu–Tue.* ▨ 🎫

most engaging of the frescoes – which reflect the purpose of the parecclesion as a place of burial – is the *Anastasis*, in the semidome above the apse. In it, the central figure of Christ, the vanquisher of death, is shown dragging Adam and Eve out of their tombs. Under Christ's feet are the gates of hell, while Satan lies before him. The fresco in the vault overhead depicts *The Last Judgment*, with the souls of the saved on the right and those of the damned to the left.

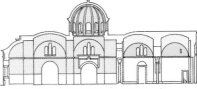

Figure of Christ from the *Anastasis* fresco in the parecclesion

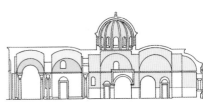

Inner narthex looking east

Pareclesion and outer narthex looking south

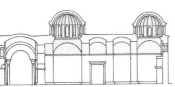

Inner narthex looking west

Pareclesion and outer narthex looking north

Eyüp

As the burial place of Eyüp Ensari, the standard bearer of the Prophet Mohammed, the village of Eyüp is a place of pilgrimage for Muslims from all over the world. Its sacrosanct status has kept it a peaceful place of contemplation, far removed from the squalid effects of industrialization elsewhere on the Golden Horn (see p89). The wealthy elite established mosques and street fountains in the village but, above all, they chose Eyüp as a place of burial. Their grand mausoleums line the streets surrounding Eyüp Sultan Mosque, while the cypress groves in the hills above the village are filled with the gravestones of ordinary people.

Gateway to the Baroque Complex of Valide Sultan Mihrişah

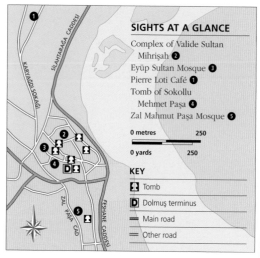

SIGHTS AT A GLANCE

Complex of Valide Sultan
Mihrişah ❷
Eyüp Sultan Mosque ❸
Pierre Loti Café ❶
Tomb of Sokollu
Mehmet Paşa ❹
Zal Mahmut Paşa Mosque ❺

0 metres   250
0 yards   250

KEY

🏛 Tomb

Ⓓ Dolmuş terminus

▬ Main road

▬ Other road

Pierre Loti Café ❶
Piyer Loti Kahvehanesi

Gümüşsuyu Karyağdı Sok 5, Eyüp.
Tel (0212) 581 26 96. 🚌 39, 55T, 99A. ◯ 8:30am–midnight daily.

This famous café stands at the top of the hill in Eyüp Cemetery, about 20 minutes' walk or short funicular ride up Karyağdı Sokağı from Eyüp Mosque, from where it commands sweeping views down over the Golden Horn. It is named after the French novelist and Turkophile Pierre Loti, who frequented a café in Eyüp – claimed to be this one – during his stay here in 1876. Loti (see p42), a French naval officer, fell in love with a married Turkish woman and wrote an autobiographical novel, *Aziyade*, about their affair. The café is prettily decked out with 19th-century furniture and the waiters wear period clothing.

The path up to the café passes by a picturesque array of tombstones, most of which date from the Ottoman era. Just before the café on the right, a few tall, uninscribed tombstones mark the graves of executioners.

Period interior of the Pierre Loti Café

Complex of Valide Sultan Mihrişah ❷
Mihrişah Valide Sultan Külliyesi

Seyit Reşat Cad. 🚌 39, 55T, 99A. ◯ 9am–6pm Tue–Sun.

Most of the northern side of the street leading from Eyüp Mosque's northern gate is occupied by the largest Baroque *külliye (see p38)* in Istanbul, although unusually it is not centred on a mosque. Built for Mihrişah, mother of Selim III *(see p33)*, the *külliye* was completed in 1791.

The complex includes the ornate marble tomb of Mihrişah and a soup kitchen, which is still in use today. There is also a beautiful grilled fountain *(sebil)*, from which an attendant once served water and refreshing drinks of sweet sherbet to passers-by.

Eyüp Sultan Mosque ❸
Eyüp Sultan Camii

Cami-i Kebir Sok. **Tel** (0212) 564 73 68. 🚌 39, 55T, 99A. ◯ daily.

Mehmet the Conqueror built the original mosque on this site in 1458, five years after his conquest of Istanbul *(see p26)*, in honour of Eyüp Ensari. That building fell into ruins, probably as a result of an earthquake, and the present mosque was completed in 1800, by Selim III *(see p33)*. The mosque's delightful inner courtyard is a garden in which two huge plane trees grow on a platform.

This platform was the setting for the Girding of the Sword of Osman, part of a sultan's inauguration from the days of Mehmet the Conqueror.

The mosque itself is predominantly covered in gleaming white marble.

Opposite the mosque is the tomb of Eyüp Ensari himself, believed to have been killed during the first Arab siege of Constantinople in the 7th century *(see p21)*. The tomb dates from the same period as the mosque and most of its decoration is in the Ottoman Baroque style. Both the outer wall of the tomb facing the mosque, and most of its interior, have an impressive covering of tiles, some of them from İznik *(see p160)*.

Zal Mahmut Paşa Mosque, as viewed from its tomb garden

Visitors at the tomb of Eyüp Ensari, Mohammed's standard bearer

Tomb of Sokollu Mehmet Paşa ❹

Sokollu Mehmet Paşa Türbesi

Cami-i Kebir Sok. 🚌 39, 55T, 99A.
🕐 9:30am–4:30pm Tue–Sun.

Grand vizier *(see p29)* Sokollu Mehmet Paşa commissioned his tomb around 1574, five years before he was assassinated by a madman in Topkapı Palace *(see pp54–7)*. Of Balkan royal blood, he started his career as falconer royal and steadily climbed the social order until he became grand vizier to Süleyman the Magnificent *(see p26)* in 1565. He held this position through the reign of Selim II *(see p27)* and into that of Murat III. The architect Sinan *(see p91)*

built this elegantly proportioned octagonal tomb. It is notable for its stained glass, some of which is original. A roofed colonnade connects the tomb to what was formerly a Koranic school.

Zal Mahmut Paşa Mosque ❺

Zal Mahmut Paşa Camii

Zal Paşa Cad. 🚌 39, 55T, 99A.
🕐 daily.

Heading south from the centre of Eyüp, it is a short walk to Zal Mahmut Paşa Mosque. The complex was built by Sinan for the man who assassinated Mustafa, the

first-born heir of Süleyman the Magnificent.

Probably erected some time in the 1560s, the mosque is notable for the lovely floral tiles around its mihrab, and for its carved marble *minbar* and *müezzin mahfili (see p38)*. Proceeding down some stone steps to the north of the mosque you will come to a garden. In it stands the large tomb of Zal Mahmut Paşa and his wife, said to have both died on the same day.

On the same street, Cezri Kasım Paşa Mosque (1515) is a small mosque with a pretty portal and a tiled mihrab. Most of the tiles were produced at the Palace of the Porphyrogenitus *(see p117)* in the first half of the 18th century.

OTTOMAN GRAVESTONES

The Ottoman graveyard was a garden of the dead, where the living happily strolled without morbid inhibitions. The gravestones within it were often lavishly symbolic: from their decoration you can tell the sex, occupation, rank and even the number of children of the deceased. As the turban was banned in 1829 *(see p30)*, only the fez appears on men's gravestones erected after that date.

Women's *graves have a flower for each child.*

A turban's *size reflected a gentleman's status.*

This hat *indicates the grave of a member of a Sufi order.*

A fez *was worn by a paşa, or public servant (see p28).*

Beyond Taksim

The area to the north of Taksim Square *(see p107)* became fashionable in the 19th century, when sultans built palaces along the Bosphorus and in the wooded hills above it. The extravagant Dolmabahçe Palace, built by Abdül Mecit I *(see p30)*, started the trend. High-ranking court officials soon followed, and the area achieved a glamour that it retains to this day. Two other sights worth seeing are on the northern shore of the Golden Horn. Aynalı Kavak Palace is the last surviving trace of a grand palace built by Ahmet III *(see p27)*, while the Rahmi Koç Museum, in nearby Hasköy, is an interesting industrial museum. Hasköy became a royal park in the 15th century and later supported fruit orchards, before dockyards brought industrialization to the area in the 19th century.

Ortaköy's fashionable waterfront square and ferry landing

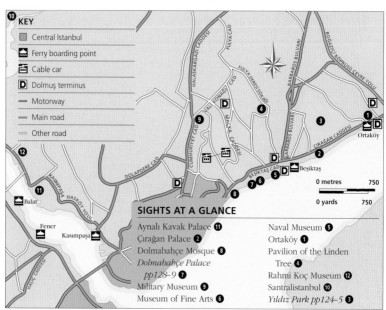

KEY

■	Central Istanbul
⛴	Ferry boarding point
🚠	Cable car
D	Dolmuş terminus
—	Motorway
—	Main road
—	Other road

SIGHTS AT A GLANCE

Aynalı Kavak Palace ⑪
Çırağan Palace ②
Dolmabahçe Mosque ⑧
Dolmabahçe Palace pp128–9 ⑦
Military Museum ⑨
Museum of Fine Arts ⑥
Naval Museum ⑤
Ortaköy ①
Pavilion of the Linden Tree ④
Rahmi Koç Museum ⑫
Santralistanbul ⑩
Yıldız Park pp124–5 ③

Cobbled Ortaköy side street lined with cafés and shops

Ortaköy ①

Map 9 F3. ⛴ *25E, 40.*

Crouched at the foot of Bosphorus Bridge *(see p138)*, the suburb of Ortaköy has retained a village feel. Life centres on İskele Meydanı, the quayside square, which used to be busy with fishermen unloading the day's catch. Nowadays, though, Ortaköy is better known for its lively Sunday market *(see p215)*, which crowds out the square and surrounding streets, and its shops selling the wares of local artisans. It is also the

location for a thriving bar and café scene, which in the summer especially is the hub of Istanbul's nightlife *(see p221)*.

Mecidiye Mosque, Ortaköy's most impressive landmark, is located on the waterfront. It was built in 1855 by Nikoğos Balyan, who was responsible for Dolmabahçe Palace *(see pp128–9)*. A simple structure, it has grace and originality, with window-filled tympanum arches and corner turrets.

Ortaköy also has a Greek Orthodox church, Haghios Phocas, and a synagogue, Etz Ahayim. The origins of both date from the Byzantine era.

Çırağan Palace ❷
Çırağan Sarayı

Dolmabahçe Cad, Beşiktaş. **Map** 9
D3. *Tel* (0212) 236 90 00. 🚌 25E,
40. **www**.ciragan-palace.com

Sultan Abdül Mecit I started
work on Çırağan Palace in
1864, but it was not com-
pleted until 1871, during the
reign of Abdül Aziz (*see p30*).
It replaced an earlier wooden
palace where torch-lit processions were held during the
Tulip Period (*see p27*).

The palace was designed
by Nikogos Balyan. At the
sultan's request he added
Arabic touches from sketches
of Moorish buildings such as
the Alhambra at Granada in
Spain. Externally this is
evidenced in the honeycomb
capitals over its windows. The
sultan entered Çırağan Palace
directly from the Bosphorus,
through the ornate ceremonial
gates along its shoreline.

Çırağan Palace had a sad,
short history as an imperial
residence. Abdül Aziz died
here in 1876, supposedly
committing suicide – although
his friends believed he had
been murdered. His successor,
Murat V (*see p33*), was imprisoned in the palace for a year
after a brief reign of only
three months. He died in the
Malta Pavilion (*see p125*)
27 years later, still a prisoner.
The palace was eventually
destroyed by fire in 1910.

**Çırağan Palace, notable for the Moorish-
style embellishments above its windows**

Baroque-style staircase at the Pavilion of the Linden Tree

It remained a burnt out shell
for many years, before being
restored in 1990 as the Çırağan
Palace Kempinski (*see p190*).

Yıldız Park ❸

See pp124–5.

Pavilion of the Linden Tree ❹
Ihlamur Kasrı

Dolmabahçe Cad, Beşiktaş. **Map** 8
B2. *Tel* (0212) 236 90 00. 🚌 26
(from Eminönü). ⬜ 9am–3pm
Tue–Wed & Fri–Sun. 🎦 🎬

This one-time residence of
sultans, dating from the early
19th century, stands in
beautiful, leafy gardens
which are planted with
magnolias and camellias,
and decorated with
ornamental fountains.
Today, the gardens are
a somewhat incongruous
reminder of the city's
Ottoman past, being
situated in the midst of
the modern suburbs of
Teşvikiye and Ihlamur.

As the pavilion's
name suggests, the
area was once a grove
of lime (linden) trees,
and the gardens are all
that remain of what
was previously a vast
wooded park. This
park was a favourite
retreat and hunting
ground of the Ottoman
sultans. In the early

19th century, Abdül Mecit I
(*see p30*) often came here and
stayed in the original pavilion
on this site. That building was
so unassuming that the French
poet Alphonse de Lamartine
(1790–1869) expressed great
surprise that a sultan should
have entertained him in a
humble cottage, with a gar-
dener working in plain view
through the windows.

In 1857 Abdül Mecit chose
Nikogos Balyan, who had by
then finished Dolmabahçe
Palace with his father, to
design another residence
here. Two separate pavilions
were built, the grander of
which is the Ceremonial
Pavilion, or Mabeyn Köşkü,
used by the sultan and his
guests. The Entourage
Pavilion, or Maiyet Köşkü, a
short distance away, was
reserved for the sultan's
retinue, including the women
of the harem. Both buildings
are open to visitors – the
Entourage Pavilion is currently
a café and bookshop.

The pavilions are constructed
mainly of sandstone and
marble. Their façades are in
the Baroque style, with
double stairways, many
decorative embellishments
and hardly a single straight
line to be seen. The ornate
interiors of the buildings
reflect 19th-century Ottoman
taste, incorporating a mixture
of European styles. With their
mirrors, lavish furnishings and
gilded details, they are similar
to but less ostentatious than
those of Dolmabahçe Palace.

Yıldız Park ❸

Yıldız Parkı

Fountain, Yıldız
Palace Theatre

Yıldız Park was originally laid out as the garden of the first Çırağan Palace (see p123). It later formed the grounds of Yıldız Palace, an assortment of buildings from different eras now enclosed behind a wall and entered separately from Ihlamur-Yıldız Caddesi. Further pavilions dot Yıldız Park, which, with its many ancient trees and exotic shrubs, is a favourite spot for family picnics. The whole park is situated on a steep hill and, as it is a fairly long climb, you may prefer to take a taxi up to the Şale Pavilion and walk back down past the other sights.

Bridge over the lake in the
grounds of Yıldız Palace

Yıldız Palace

The palace is a collection of pavilions and villas built in the 19th and 20th centuries. Many of them are the work of the eccentric Sultan Abdül Hamit II (1876–1909, see p33), who made it his principal residence as he feared a sea-borne attack on Dolmabahçe Palace (see pp128–9).

The main building in the entrance courtyard is the **State Apartments** (Büyük Mabeyn), dating from the reign of Sultan Selim III (1789–1807, see p33), but not presently open to the public. Around the corner, the **City Museum** (Şehir Müzesi) has a display of Yıldız porcelain. The Italianate building opposite it is the former armoury, or Silahhane. Next door to the City Museum is the **Yıldız Palace Museum**, housed in what was once the Marangozhane, Abdül Hamit's carpentry workshop. This has a changing collection of art and objects from the palace.

A monumental arch leads from the first courtyard to the harem section of the palace.

The Italianate Silahhane, the former armoury of Yıldız Palace

On the left beside the arch is a pretty greenhouse, the Limonluk Serası (Lemon House).

Further on, **Yıldız Palace Theatre** is now a museum. It was completed in 1889 by Abdül Hamit, who encouraged all forms of Western art. The decor of the theatre's restored interior is mainly blue and gold. The stars on the domed ceiling are a reference to the name of the palace: *yıldız* means "star" in Turkish.

Abdül Hamit sat alone in a box over the entrance. Since no one was allowed to sit with his back to the sultan, the stalls were not used. Backstage, the former dressing rooms are given over to displays on the theatre, including costumes and playbills.

The lake in the palace grounds is shaped like Abdül Hamit's *tuğra (see p95)*. A menagerie was kept on the islands in the lake where 30 keepers tended tigers, lions, giraffes and zebras.

Salon in the lavish Şale Pavilion

Şale Pavilion

The single most impressive building in the park, the Şale Pavilion (Şale Köşkü) was among those erected by Abdül Hamit II. Although its façade appears as a whole, it was in fact built in three stages.

The first, left-hand section of the buildling was designed to resemble a Swiss chalet. It probably dates from the 1870s. Winston Churchill, Charles de Gaulle and Nicolae Ceauşescu have all stayed in its rooms.

The second section was added in 1889, to accommodate Kaiser Wilhelm II on the first ever state visit of a foreign monarch to the Ottoman capital. The 14-room suite includes a dining room known as the Mother-of-Pearl Salon (Sedefli Salon) after the delicate inlay that covers almost all of its surfaces.

The third section was also built for a visit by Kaiser Wilhelm II, this time in 1898. Its reception chamber is the grandest room in the whole pavilion. The vast silk Hereke carpet *(see p218)* covering its floor was painstakingly hand-knotted by 60 weavers.

Malta and Çadır Pavilions

These two lovely pavilions were built in the reign of Abdül Aziz (1861–76, *see p30*). Both formerly served as prisons but are now open as cafés. Malta Pavilion, also a

restaurant, has a superb view and on Sunday is a haunt for locals wanting to relax and read the newspapers.

Midhat Paşa, reformist and architect of the constitution, was among those imprisoned in Çadır Pavilion, for instigating the murder of Abdül Aziz. Meanwhile, Murat V and his mother were locked away in Malta Pavilion for 27 years after a brief incarceration in Çırağan Palace *(see p123)*.

Façade of Çadır Pavilion, which has now been refurbished as a café

Imperial Porcelain Factory

In 1895 this factory opened to feed the demand of the upper classes for European-style ceramics to decorate their homes. The unusual building was designed to look like a stylized European medieval castle, complete with turrets and portcullis windows.

The original sugar bowls, vases and plates produced here depict idealized scenes of the Bosphorus and other local beauty spots; they can be seen in museums and palaces all over Istanbul. The factory is normally not open to visitors but the mass-produced china of today is on sale in its shop.

Park entrance

PALANGA CADDESİ

rial Porcelain Factory

...GAN CADDESİ

| 0 metres | 250 |
| 0 yards | 250 |

KEY

▦ Buildings of palace

— Park wall/Palace wall

🅿 Parking

Naval Museum ❺
Deniz Müzesi

Hayrettin Paşa İskelesi Sok, Beşiktaş.
Map 8 B4. **Tel** (0212) 261 00 40.
🚌 25E, 28, 40, 56. 🕐 9am–noon,
1:30–5:30pm Wed–Sun. 📷 📹

This museum is located next
to the ferry landing in
Beşiktaş. One building, the
Caïques Gallery, is devoted to
huge imperial rowing boats,
or caïques (some of them
manned by replica oarsmen),
dating from the 17th century.
The largest of these, at 40 m
(130 ft), was used by Mehmet
IV and powered by 144 oarsmen. The rowing boats used
by Atatürk (see p30) look tiny
in comparison: it
is remarkable to
think that he
entertained
heads of
state in
them. The
exhibits in
the neigh-
bouring main
museum include
oil paintings of
various military
scenes, ship
figureheads, naval uniforms,
and objects from, and
paintings of, Atatürk's yacht,
the Savarona.

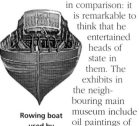
**Rowing boat
used by
Atatürk**

Museum of Fine Arts ❻
Resim ve Heykel Müzesi

Hayrettin Paşa İskelesi Sok,
Beşiktaş. **Map** 8 B4. **Tel** (0212)
261 42 98. 🚌 25E, 28, 40, 56.
🕐 noon–4pm Wed–Sun.

This building adjacent to
Dolmabahçe Palace (see
pp128–9) houses a fine
collection of 19th- and
20th-century paintings and
sculpture. In the 1800s, the
westernization of the Ottoman
Empire (see pp30–31) led
artists such as Osman Hamdi
Bey (1842–1910, see p62) to
experiment with Western-style
painting. While their styles
rely heavily on European art
forms, the subject matter of
their work gives a glimpse
into the oriental history of the
city. Look out for Woman
with Mimosas, Portrait of a

Woman with Mimosas by Osman
Hamdi Bey, Museum of Fine Arts

Young Girl and Man with a
Yellow Robe, all by Osman
Hamdi Bey, Sultan Ahmet
Mosque by Ahmet Ziya
Akbulut (1869–1938), and
Âşık, a statue of a poet by
İsa Behzat (1867–1944).

Dolmabahçe Palace ❼

See pp128–9.

Dolmabahçe Mosque ❽
Dolmabahçe Camii

Meclis-i Mebusan Cad, Kabataş.
Map 8 A5. 🚋 Kabataş. 🚌 25E, 40.
🕐 daily.

Completed at the same time as
Dolmabahçe Palace, in 1853,
the mosque standing beside it
was also built by the wealthy
Balyan family. Its slim minarets
were constructed in the form
of Corinthian columns, while
great arching windows lighten

the interior. Inside, the
decoration includes fake
marbling and trompe l'oeil.

Military Museum ❾
Askeri Müzesi

Vali Konağı Cad, Harbiye. **Map** 7 F1.
Tel (0212) 233 27 20. 🚌 46H.
🚇 Osmanbey. 🕐 9am–5pm Wed–
Sun. **Mehter Band performances**
3–4pm Wed–Sun. 📷 📹

This impressive museum
traces the history of Turkey's
conflicts from the conquest of
Constantinople in 1453 (see
p26) through to modern warfare. The building used to be
the military academy where
Atatürk studied from 1899 to
1905. His classroom has been
preserved as it was then.
  The museum is also the main
venue for performances by the
Mehter Band, which was first
formed in the 14th-century
during the reign of Osman I
(see p25). From then until the
19th century, the band's
members were Janissaries,
who would accompany the
sultan into battle and perform
songs about Ottoman hero-
ancestors and battle victories.
  Some of the most striking
weapons on display on the
ground floor are the curved
daggers (cembiyes) carried
by foot soldiers in the 15th
century. These are decorated
with plant, flower and
geometric motifs in relief and
silver filigree. Other exhibits
include 17th-century copper
head armour for horses and
Ottoman shields made from
cane and willow covered in
silk thread.

Dolmabahçe Mosque, a landmark on the Bosphorus shoreline

Cembiyes – Ottoman curved daggers – on display in the Military Museum

A moving portrayal of trench warfare, commissioned in 1995, is included in the section concerned with the ANZAC landings of 1915 at Chunuk Bair on the Gallipoli peninsula *(see p30)*.

Upstairs, the most spectacular of all the exhibits are the tents used by sultans on their campaigns. They are made of silk and wool with embroidered decoration.

santralistanbul ⓿

Kazim Karabekir Cad 1, Eyüp. *Tel* (0212) 444 04 28. 🚌 47; also free shuttle every 20 minutes from Taksim AKM. 🕐 10am–8pm Tue–Sun. 🔴 1 Jan, first day of Religious Holidays.

Inaugurated in July 2007 and housed in the first power station built in the city during the Ottoman Period, santralistanbul is an innovative art park that includes, among other things, a centre for contemporary arts, a museum of energy, and living quarters for guest artists, architects and designers.

Aynalı Kavak Palace ⓫
Aynalı Kavak Kasrı

Kasımpaşa Cad, Hasköy. **Map** 6 A3. *Tel* (0212) 250 40 94. 🚌 47, 54. 🕐 9:30am–4pm. 🔴 Mon & Thu. 📷

Aynali Kavak Palace is the last vestige of a large Ottoman palace complex on the once lovely Golden Horn *(see p89)*. Originally it stood in extensive gardens covering an area of 7,000 sq m (75,300 sq ft). Inscriptions dated 1791 can be found all over the palace, but it is thought to have been built earlier by Ahmet III during the Tulip Period *(see p27)*, because of traces around the building of an older style of architecture.

The palace is built on a hill and as a result has two storeys on the southwest side and a single storey to the northeast. It retains some beautiful Ottoman features. These include the upper windows on the southwest façade, which are decorated with stained glass set in curvilinear stucco tracery. Particularly

striking is the composition room, which Sultan Selim III (1789–1807) is thought to have used for writing music.

The audience chamber is adorned with an inscription in gold on blue which describes the activities of Selim III while he stayed at the palace.

There is also a superb exhibition of archaic Turkish musical instruments permanently on show, in honour of Selim III, who contributed a great deal to Turkish classical music.

In summer, popular concerts of classical Turkish music are held here.

Audience chamber of Aynalı Kavak Palace on the Golden Horn

Rahmi Koç Museum ⓬
Rahmi Koç Müzesi

Hasköy Cad 27, Eyüp. *Tel* (0212) 369 66 00. 🚌 47. 🕐 10am–5pm Tue–Fri, 10am–7pm Sat, Sun. 📷

Situated in Hasköy, this old 19th-century factory, which once produced anchors and chains, now houses an eclectic collection named after its industrialist founder, Rahmi Koç. The building itself, with its four small domes, vaulted passageways and original wooden fittings is one of the museum's highlights.

The theme of the industrial age loosely connects exhibitions on aviation, transport, steam engines and scientific instruments. Exhibits range from mechanical toys and scale models of machinery to an entire recreated ship's bridge. Two fine restaurants are located on the premises.

JANISSARIES

The Janissary (New Army) corps was formed in the 14th century to serve as the sultan's elite fighting force. Its ranks were filled by *devşirme*, the levy of Christian youths brought to Istanbul to serve the sultan. A highly professional and strong army, it was instrumental in the early expansion of the Ottoman Empire and, as well as a fighting force, it acted as the sultan's personal guard. However, discipline eventually began to weaken, and by 1800 the Janissaries had become a destabilizing element in society. They mutinied and overthrew many sultans until their final demise under Mahmut II in 1826 *(see p30)*.

Janissaries depicted in a 16th-century miniature

Dolmabahçe Palace ❼
Dolmabahçe Sarayı

Sultan Abdül Mecıt *(see p33)* built Dolmabahçe Palace in 1856. As its designers he employed Karabet Balyan and his son Nikogos, members of the great family of Armenian architects who lined the Bosphorus *(see pp137–49)* with many of their creations in the 19th century. The extravagant opulence of the Dolmabahçe belies the fact that it was built when the Ottoman Empire was in decline. The sultan financed his great palace with loans from foreign banks. The palace can only be visited on a guided tour, of which two are on offer. The best tour takes you through the Selamlık (or Mabeyn-i Hümayun), the part of the palace that was reserved for men and which contains the state rooms and the enormous Ceremonial Hall. The other tour goes through the Harem, the living quarters of the sultan and his entourage. If you only want to go on one tour, visit the Selamlık.

Sèvres vase at the foot of the Crystal Staircase

★ **Crystal Staircase**
The apparent fragility of this glass staircase stunned observers when it was built. In the shape of a double horseshoe, it is made from Baccarat crystal and brass, and has a polished mahogany rail.

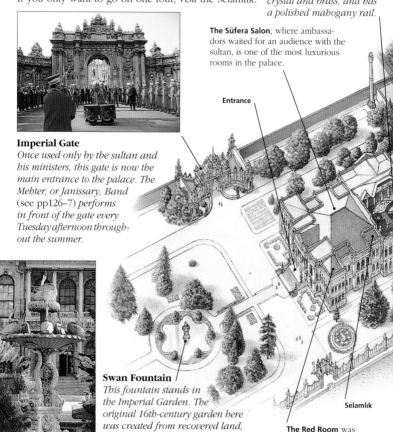

The Süfera Salon, where ambassadors waited for an audience with the sultan, is one of the most luxurious rooms in the palace.

Entrance

Imperial Gate
Once used only by the sultan and his ministers, this gate is now the main entrance to the palace. The Mehter, or Janissary, Band (see pp126–7) performs in front of the gate every Tuesday afternoon throughout the summer.

Swan Fountain
This fountain stands in the Imperial Garden. The original 16th-century garden here was created from recovered land, hence the palace's name, Dolmabahçe, meaning "Filled-in Garden".

Selamlık

The Red Room was used by the sultan to receive ambassadors.

★ **Ceremonial Hall**
This magnificent domed hall was designed to hold 2,500 people. Its chandelier, reputedly the heaviest in the world, was bought in England.

VISITORS' CHECKLIST

Dolmabahçe Cad, Beşiktaş.
Map 8 B4. **Tel** (0212) 236 90 00.
25E, 40. ◯ 9am–4pm (last adm) Tue, Wed & Fri–Sun (Oct–Feb: last adm 3pm).
⬤ the first day of religious festivals.

Blue Salon
On religious feast days the sultan's mother would receive his wives and favourites in the Harem's principal room.

The Zülvecheyn, or Panorama Room

Harem

The Rose-coloured salon was the assembly room of the Harem.

Reception room of the sultan's mother

Main shore gate

Sultan Abdül Aziz's bedroom had to accommodate a huge bed built especially for the 150-kg (23-stone) amateur wrestler.

Atatürk's Bedroom
Atatürk (see pp30–31) died in this room at 9:05am on 10 November 1938. All the clocks in the palace, such as this one near the crystal staircase, are stopped at this time.

★ **Main Bathroom**
The walls of this bathroom are revetted in finest Egyptian alabaster, while the taps are solid silver. The brass-framed bathroom windows afford stunning views across the Bosphorus.

STAR FEATURES

★ Crystal Staircase

★ Ceremonial Hall

★ Main Bathroom

The Asian Side

The Asian side of Istanbul comprises the two major suburbs of Üsküdar and Kadıköy, which date from the 7th century BC *(see p19)*. Üsküdar (once known as Scutari after the 12th-century Scutarion Palace which was located opposite Leander's Tower) was the starting point of Byzantine trade routes through Asia. It retained its importance in the Ottoman period and today is renowned for its many classical mosques.

A number of residential districts radiate from Üsküdar and Kadıköy. Moda is a pleasant leafy suburb famous for its ice cream, while there is a lighthouse and an attractive park at Fenerbahçe. From there it is a short walk up to Bağdat Caddesi, one of Istanbul's best-known shopping streets *(see p204)*.

Leander's Tower, on its own small island

SIGHTS AT A GLANCE

Atik Valide Mosque ❺
Big Pine Hill ❿
Haydarpaşa Station ❾
İskele Mosque ❸
Karaca Ahmet Cemetery ❼
Leander's Tower ❶
Selimiye Barracks ❽
Şemsi Paşa Mosque ❷
Tiled Mosque ❻
Yeni Valide Mosque ❹

0 kilometres   1

0 miles   1

KEY

⛴ Ferry boarding point

🚉 Railway station

D Dolmuş terminus

━━ Motorway

━━ Main road

━ Other road

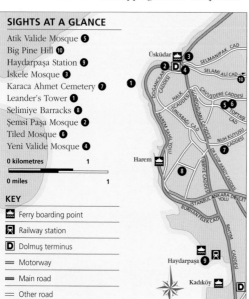

Leander's Tower ❶

Kız Kulesi

Üsküdar. **Map** 10 A3. **Tel** (0216) 342 47 47. ⛴ *Üsküdar.* **www**.kizkulesi.com.tr

Located offshore from Üsküdar, the tiny, white Leander's Tower is a well-known Bosphorus landmark. The islet on which this 18th-century tower stands was the site of a 12th-century Byzantine fortress built by Manuel I Comnenus. The tower has served as a quarantine centre during a cholera outbreak, a

lighthouse, a customs control point and a maritime toll gate. It is now a restaurant and nightclub *(see p206)*.

The tower is known in Turkish as the "Maiden's Tower" after a legendary princess, said to have been confined here after a prophet foretold that she would die from a snakebite. The snake duly appeared from a basket of figs and struck the fatal blow. The English name of the tower derives from the Greek myth of Leander, who swam the Hellespont (the modern-day Dardanelles, *see p170*) to see his lover Hero.

Şemsi Paşa Mosque ❷

Şemsi Paşa Camii

Sahil Yolu, Üsküdar. **Map** 10 A2. ⛴ *Üsküdar.* ◯ *daily.*

This is one of the smallest mosques to be commissioned by a grand vizier *(see p29)*. Its miniature dimensions combined with its picturesque waterfront location make it one of the most attractive mosques in the city.

Şemsi Ahmet Paşa succeeded Sokollu Mehmet Paşa *(see p82)* as grand vizier, and may have been involved in his murder. Sinan *(see p91)* built this mosque for him in 1580.

The garden, which overlooks the Bosphorus, is surrounded on two sides by the *medrese (see p38)*, with the mosque on the third side and the sea wall on the fourth. The mosque itself is unusual in that the tomb of Şemsi Ahmet is joined to the main building, divided from the interior by a grille.

Şemsi Paşa Mosque, built by Sinan for Grand Vizier Şemsi Ahmet Paşa

İskele Mosque ❸
İskele Camii

Hakimiyeti Milliye Cad, Üsküdar.
Map 10 B2. 🚢 *Üsküdar.* ◯ *daily.*

One of Üsküdar's most prominent landmarks, the İskele Mosque (also known as Mihrimah Sultan Mosque), takes its name from the ferry landing where it stands. A massive structure on a raised platform, it was built by Sinan between 1547 and 1548 for Mihrimah Sultan, favourite daughter of Süleyman the Magnificent and wife of Grand Vizier Rüstem Paşa *(see p88).*

Without space to build a courtyard, Sinan constructed a large protruding roof which extends to cover the *şadırvan* (ablutions fountain) in front of the mosque. The porch and interior are rather gloomy as a result. This raised portico is an excellent place from which to look down on the main square below, in which stands the Baroque Fountain of Ahmet III, built in 1726.

The *mektep* (Koranic school) over the gate of Yeni Valide Mosque

Fountain set into the platform below the İskele Mosque

Yeni Valide Mosque ❹
Yeni Valide Camii

Hakimiyeti Milliye Cad, Üsküdar.
Map 10 B2. 🚢 *Üsküdar.* ◯ *daily.*

Across the main square from İskele Mosque, the Yeni Valide Mosque, or New Mosque of the Sultan's Mother, was built by Ahmet III between 1708 and 1710 to honour his mother, Gülnuş Emetullah. The complex is entered through a large gateway, with the *mektep* (Koranic school) built above it. This leads into a spacious courtyard. The buildings in the complex date from an important turning point in Ottoman architecture. The mosque is in the classical style, yet there are Baroque embellishments on the tomb of the Valide Sultan, the neighbouring *sebil* (kiosk from which drinks were served) and the *şadırvan*.

Atik Valide Mosque ❺
Atik Valide Camii

Çinili Camii Sok, Üsküdar. **Map** 10 C3. 🚌 *12C (from Üsküdar).* ◯ *prayer times only.*

The Atik Valide Mosque, set on the hill above Üsküdar, was one of the most extensive mosque complexes in Istanbul. The name translates as the Old Mosque of the Sultan's Mother, as the mosque was built for Nur Banu, the Venetian-born wife of Selim II ("the Sot") and the mother of Murat III. She was the first of the sultans' mothers to rule the Ottoman Empire from the harem *(see p27).*

Dome in the entrance to Atik Valide Mosque

Sinan completed the mosque, which was his last major work, in 1583. It has a wide shallow dome which rests on five semidomes, with a flat arch over the entrance portal.

The interior is surrounded on three sides by galleries, the undersides of which retain the rich black, red and gold stencilling typical of the period. The *mihrab* apse is almost completely covered with panels of fine İznik tiles *(see p161),* while the mihrab itself and the *minbar* are both made of beautifully carved marble. Side aisles were added to the north and south in the 17th century, while the grilles and architectural trompe l'oeil paintings on the royal loge in the western gallery date from the 18th century.

Outside, a door in the north wall of the courtyard leads down a flight of stairs to the *medrese,* where the *dershane* (classroom) projects out over the narrow street below, supported by an arch. Of the other buildings in the complex, the *şifahane* (hospital) is the only one which has been restored and is open to the public. Located just to the east of the mosque, it consists of 40 cells around a courtyard and was in use well into the 20th century.

Women attending an Islamic class in the Tiled Mosque

Tiled Mosque ⑥
Çinili Camii

Çinili Camii Sok, Üsküdar. **Map** 10
C3. 🚌 *Üsküdar, then 20 mins walk.*
◻ *prayer times only.*

This pretty little mosque
is best known for the fine
tiles from which it takes its
name. It dates from 1640
and is noticeably smaller than
other royal foundations of the
17th century. This is partly
because by the middle of the
century much of Istanbul's
prime land had already been
built on, and the size of the
plot did not allow for a larger
building. There was also a
trend away from endowing
yet more enormous mosque
complexes in the city.

The mosque was founded
by Mahpeyker Kösem Sultan.
As the wife of Sultan Ahmet I
(see p33), and mother of
sultans Murat IV and İbrahim
the Mad, she wielded great
influence. Indeed, she was
one of the last of the powerful
harem women *(see p27)*.

In the courtyard is a massive,
roofed ablutions fountain. The
adjacent *medrese (see p38)*,
however, is tiny. The façade
and interior of the mosque are
covered with İznik tiles *(see
p161)* in turquoise, white, grey
and a range of blues. There
are none of the red and green
pigments associated with the
heyday of İznik tile production, but the designs are still
exquisite. Even the conical
cap of the marble *minbar* is
tiled, and the carving on the
minbar itself is picked out in
green, red and gold paint.

The mosque's Turkish bath is
on Çinili Hamam Sokağı. It has
been renovated and is used
by local residents.

Karacaahmet Cemetery ⑦
Karacaahmet Mezarlığı

Nuh Kuyusu Cad, Selimiye. **Map** 10
C4. 🚌 *12.* ◻ *daily.* **Tomb** ◻ *daily.*

Sprawling over a large area,
this cemetery is a pleasant
place in which to stroll among
old cypress trees and look at
ancient tombstones. The
earliest dated stone is from
1521, although the cemetery
itself, one of the largest in
Turkey, is thought to date
from 1338.

The carvings on
each tombstone
tell a story
(see p121). A
man's tomb is
indicated by a
fez or a turban.
The style of the
turban denotes
the status of the
deceased.
Women's stones
are adorned with
carved flowers,
hats and shawls.

Crimean War memorial in the British War Cemetery

Standing on the corner of
Gündoğumu Caddesi and Nuh
Kuyusu Caddesi is the tomb
of Karaca Ahmet himself.
This warrior died fighting in
the Turkish conquest of the
Byzantine towns of Chryso-
polis and Chalcedon (Üsküdar
and Kadıköy) in the mid-14th
century. The tomb and monument to his favourite horse
date from the 19th century.

Selimiye Barracks ⑧
Selimiye Kışlası

Çeşme-i Kebir Cad, Selimiye.
Map 10 B5. **Tel** *(0216) 343 73
10.* 🚊 *Harem.* 🚌 *12.*
◻ *9am–5pm Sat.*

The Selimiye Barracks were
originally built by Selim III
in 1799 to house his New
Army, with which he hoped
to replace the Janissaries *(see
p127)*. He failed in his attempt,
and was deposed and killed
in a Janissary insurrection in
1807–8 *(see p30)*. The barracks
burnt down shortly afterwards.
The present building, which
dominates the skyline of the
Asian shore, was started by
Mahmut II in 1828, after he
had finally dis-
banded the
Janissary corps.
Abdül Mecit I
added three more
wings between
1842 and 1853.
The barracks
were used as a
military hospital
during the
Crimean War
(1853–6). They
became famously
associated with
Florence Nightin-
gale, who lived and worked
in the northeast tower from
1854. The rooms she
occupied are now a museum,
and are the only part of the
barracks open to the public.
They contain their original
furniture and the lamp from
which she gained the epitaph
"Lady of the Lamp". Visits
must be arranged in advance
by faxing 0216 333 10 09.

Visitor praying at the tomb of the warrior Karaca Ahmet

Haydarpaşa Station, terminus for trains arriving from Anatolia

Big Pine Hill ❿
Büyük Çamlıca

Çamlıca. 🚌 11F, KÇ1; then 30 mins walk. **Park** ◯ 9am–11pm daily.

On a clear day the view from the top of this hill takes in the Princes' Islands, the Sea of Marmara, the Golden Horn and Beyoğlu, and the Bosphorus as far as the Black Sea. It is even possible to see snow-capped Mount Uludağ near Bursa (see p169) to the south. Big Pine Hill, 4 km (2.5 miles) east of Üsküdar, is the highest point in Istanbul, at 261 m (856 ft) above sea level. Even the forest of radio and TV masts further down the slopes of the hill does not obscure the view.

The park at the summit, which was created by the Turkish Touring and Automobile Club (see p181) in 1980, is laid out with gardens, marble kiosks and two 18th-century-style cafés.

Neighbouring Küçük Çamlıca (Little Pine Hill), located to the south, is rather less cultivated and consequently attracts fewer tourists to its little tea garden. It is another lovely place for a stroll, again with beautiful views.

Two other sites near the barracks – the Selimiye Mosque and the British War Cemetery – are both worth seeing. Built in 1804, the mosque is in a peaceful, if somewhat neglected, garden courtyard. The interior is filled with light from tiers of windows set in high arches. It is simply decorated with a classically painted dome and grey marble *minbar*. The royal pavilion in the northwest corner of the compound is flanked by graceful arches.

The British War Cemetery is a short walk south, on Burhan Felek Caddesi. It contains the graves of men who died in the Crimean War, in World War I at Gallipoli (see p170) and in World War II in the Middle East. There is no sign outside and opening hours vary, but the caretaker will usually be there to let you in.

Haydarpaşa Station ❾
Haydarpaşa Garı

Haydarpaşa İstasyon Cad, Haydarpaşa. **Tel** (0216) 336 04 75 or 336 20 63. 🚆 Haydarpaşa or Kadıköy. ◯ daily.

The waterfront location and grandeur of Haydarpaşa Station, together with the neighbouring tiled jetty, make it an impressive point of arrival or departure in Istanbul. The first Anatolian railway line, which was built in 1873, ran from here to İznik (see p160). The extension of this railway was a major part of Abdül Hamit II's drive to modernize the Ottoman Empire. Lacking sufficient funds to continue the project, he applied for help to his German ally, Kaiser Wilhelm II. The Deutsche Bank agreed to invest in the construction and operation of the railway. In 1898 German engineers were contracted to build the new railway lines running across Anatolia and beyond into the far reaches of the Ottoman Empire. At the same time a number of stations were built. Haydarpaşa, the grandest of these, was completed in 1908. Trains run from Haydarpaşa into the rest of Asia.

FLORENCE NIGHTINGALE

A 19th-century painting of Florence Nightingale in Selimiye Barracks

The British nurse Florence Nightingale (1820–1910) was a tireless campaigner for hospital, military and social reform. During the Crimean War, in which Britain and France fought on the Ottoman side against the Russian Empire, she organized a party of 38 British nurses. They took charge of medical services at the Selimiye Barracks in Scutari (Üsküdar) in 1854. By the time she returned to Britain in 1856, at the end of the war, the mortality rate in the barracks had decreased from 20 to 2 percent, and the fundamental principles of modern nursing had been established. On her return home, Florence Nightingale opened a training school for nurses.

BEYOND
ISTANBUL

THE BOSPHORUS

If the noise and bustle of the city get too much, nothing can beat a trip up the Bosphorus (*see pp144–9*), the straits separating Europe and Asia, which join the Black Sea and the Sea of Marmara. The easiest way to travel is by boat. An alternative is to explore the sights along the shores at your own pace. For much of their length the shores are lined with handsome buildings: wooden waterside villas known as yalıs, graceful mosques and opulent 19th-century palaces. The grander residences along the

Faik and Bekir Bey Yalı, Yeniköy

Bosphorus have waterfront entrances. These date from the days when wooden caïques, boats powered by a strong team of oarsmen, were a popular form of transport along the straits among the city's wealthier inhabitants. Interspersed between the monumental architecture are former fishing villages, where you will find some of Istanbul's finest clubs and restaurants. The Bosphorus is especially popular in summer, when the cool breezes off the water provide welcome relief from the heat of the city.

SIGHTS AT A GLANCE

Museums and Palaces
Aşiyan Museum ⑤
Beylerbeyi Palace ②
Khedive's Palace ⑪
Küçüksu Palace ④
Maslak Pavilion ⑩
Sadberk Hanım Museum ⑬
Sakıp Sabancı Museum ⑨

Towns and Villages
Bebek ③
Beykoz ⑫
Kanlıca ⑦
Rumeli Kavağı ⑭

Historic Buildings
Bosphorus Bridge ①
Fortress of Europe ⑥

Parks
Emirgan Park ⑧

KEY

▢ Central Istanbul

▢ Greater Istanbul

⛴ Ferry stops on Bosphorus trip

— Motorway

— Main road

0 kilometres   5

0 miles   5

THE BOSPHORUS TRIP

This vital navigational channel is 30 km (19 miles) long and varies between 700 m (2,300 ft) and 3.6 km (2 miles) wide. The trip has been divided into three stages, indicated by the boxes on this map.

Black Sea

Kilyos

Rumeli Feneri

See pp148–9

D016

D020

O-2 (E80)

O-1(E5)

O-3

See pp146–7

O-2 (E80)

D020

D100

O-4 (E80)

See pp144–9

Sea of Marmara

◁ **Anadolu Hisarı, the Fortress of Asia, on the Asian shore of the Bosphorus**

The Bosphorus suspension bridge between Ortaköy and Beylerbeyi

Bosphorus Bridge ❶
Boğaziçi Köprüsü

Ortaköy and Beylerbeyi. **Map** 9 F2.
🚌 40, 200, 202 (double deckers from Taksim).

Spanning the Bosphorus between the districts of Ortaköy and Beylerbeyi, this was the first bridge to be built across the straits that divide Istanbul. Construction began in February 1970 and finished on 29 October 1973, the 50th anniversary of the inauguration of the Turkish Republic (see p31). It is the world's ninth longest suspension bridge, at a length of 1,074 m (3,524 ft), and it reaches 64 m (210 ft) above water level.

Beylerbeyi Palace ❷
Beylerbeyi Sarayı

Beylerbeyi Cad, Asian side.
Tel (0216) 321 93 20. 🚌 15 (from Üsküdar). 🚢 from Üsküdar.
🕐 9:30am–5pm Tue, Wed & Fri–Sun (Oct–Apr until 4pm). 🎦 📷

Designed in the Baroque style by Sarkis Balyan, Beylerbeyi Palace seems fairly restrained compared to the excesses of the earlier Dolmabahçe (see pp128–9) or Küçüksu (see p140) palaces. It was built for Sultan Abdül Aziz (see p30) in 1861 as a summer residence and a place to entertain visiting heads of state. Empress Eugénie of France visited Beylerbeyi on her way to the opening of the Suez Canal in 1869 and had her face slapped by the sultan's mother for daring to enter the palace on the arm of Abdül Aziz. Other regal visitors to the palace included the Duke and Duchess of Windsor.

The palace looks its most attractive from the Bosphorus, from where its two bathing pavilions – one for the harem and the other for the *selamlık* (the men's quarters) – can best be seen.

The most attractive room is the reception hall, which has a pool and fountain. Running water was popular in Ottoman houses for its pleasant sound and cooling effect in the heat. Egyptian straw matting is used on the floor as a form of insulation. The crystal chandeliers are mostly Bohemian and the carpets (see pp218–19)

Ornate landing at the top of the stairs in Beylerbeyi Palace

are from Hereke. Despite her initial reception, Empress Eugénie of France was so delighted by the elegance of the palace that she had a copy of the window in the guest room made for her bedroom in Tuileries Palace, in Paris.

Bebek ❸

European side. 🚌 25E, 40.

Bebek is one of the most fashionable villages along the Bosphorus. It is famous for its marzipan (*badem ezmesi, see p213*), and for the cafés which line its waterfront. It was once a favourite location for summer residences and palaces of Ottoman aristocrats, and at the end of the 19th century, caïques (see p126) of merrymakers would set off on moonlit cruises from the bay, accompanied by a boat of musicians. The women in the party would trail pieces of velvet or satin edged with silver fishes in the water behind them while the musicians played to the revellers.

Detail of the gate of the Egyptian Consulate, Bebek

One of the hosts of these parties was the mother of the last Khedive of Egypt (see p29), Abbas Hilmi II. Built in the late 19th century, the only remaining monumental architecture in Bebek is the Egyptian Consulate, which, like the Khedive's Palace (see p142), was commissioned by Abbas Hilmi II. The steep, mansard roof of this yalı is reminiscent of 19th-century northern French architecture. There are lighter Art Nouveau touches including the railings draped in wrought-iron vines and a rising sun between the two turrets, symbolizing the beginning of the new century.

The khedive used the yalı as a summer palace until he was deposed by the British in 1914. From then on to the present day it has been used as the Egyptian Consulate.

Yalıs on the Bosphorus

At the end of the 17th century, *paşas*, grand viziers and other distinguished citizens of Ottoman Istanbul began to build themselves elegant villas – yalıs – along the shores of the Bosphorus. These served as summer residences, and the styles employed reflected their owners' prestige. Since then,

Old yalı at Kandilli, Asian side

the yalıs that have been built have become larger and more elaborate, adopting Baroque, Art Nouveau and modern styles of architecture. Most of them still conform to a traditional plan, making maximum use of the waterfront and, inside, having a large sitting room surrounded by bedrooms.

Köprülü Amcazade Hüseyin Paşa Yalı (see p147), *near Anadolu Hisarı, was built in 1699 and is the oldest building on the shores of the Bosphorus. Early yalıs, like this one, were built at the water's edge, but in later years they were constructed a little way inland.*

A cumba, or bay window, projects over the water.

Traditional wooden yalıs were normally painted rust red, a colour known as "Ottoman rose".

Later yalıs, built from the 18th century, were painted in pastel shades.

A bracket supports the projecting upstairs rooms.

Fethi Ahmet Paşa Yalı (see p145), *or Mocan Yalı, at Kuzguncuk, was built in the late 18th century. Among visitors were the composer Franz Liszt and the architect Le Corbusier. Famous as the "Pink Yalı", after its boldly decorated exterior, the house is almost invisible from the land.*

Baroque influence is clearly visible in the ornately carved balcony.

Ethem Pertev Yalı (see p147), *at Kanlıca, is a prime example of the so-called "cosmopolitan period" of yali building, between 1867 and 1908. It has a boat house below and combines intricate wood carving, a later development, with the more traditional features of a yalı.*

Boat house under the yali

The Egyptian Consulate (see p146) *at Bebek clearly shows the influence of Art Nouveau, with its wrought iron railings worked into a leaf design. It was commissioned by the Khedive of Egypt (see p138) in around 1900.*

French-style mansard roof

Ornamental details were inspired by Austrian Art Nouveau designs.

A narrow quay often separates 19th-century yalıs from the shore.

Küçüksu Palace ❹
Küçüksu Kasrı

Küçüksu Sahili–Anadoluhisari Beykoz, Asian side. *Tel (0216) 332 02 37.* 🚌 *15 (from Üsküdar) or 101 (from Beşiktaş).* 🕐 *9:30am–5pm Tue, Wed, Fri–Sun (Oct–Apr until 4pm).*

Marble-fronted Küçüksu Palace has one of the prettiest façades on the shores of the Bosphorus. Particularly attractive is the curving double staircase which leads up to its main waterside entrance.

Sultan Abdül Mecit I *(see p30)* employed court architect Nikogos Balyan *(see p128)* to build this palace to accommodate his entourage on their visits to the Sweet Waters of Asia. This was the romantic name European visitors gave to the Küçüksu and Göksu rivers. For centuries the Ottoman nobility liked to indulge in picnics in the meadows between the streams.

On the completion of Küçüksu Palace in 1856, the sultan complained that it was too plain and demanded more ornamentation, including his monogram engraved on the façade. Later, in the reign of Abdül Aziz *(see p30)*, the façade was further embellished, with the result that it is hard to follow the lines of the original architecture.

The room arrangement is typically Ottoman, with a large central salon opening on to four corner rooms on each floor. The interior decor was carried out by Séchan, the decorator of the Paris Opera, soon after the palace was finished. The carpets are fine examples from Hereke *(see pp218–19)* and the chandeliers Bohemian crystal.

Küçüksu Palace, an ornate Bosphorus residence built in 1856

On the shore near Küçüksu Palace is the picturesque, turreted Fountain of the Valide Sultan Mihrişah. Dating from 1796, it is in the Baroque style.

Kıbrıslı Yali, just south of the palace, was built in 1760. At over 60 m (200 ft), its brilliant white façade is the longest of any yalı *(see p139)* along the Bosphorus. A little further south again is Kırmızı Yalı, the Red Yalı, which is so called for its distinctive crimson colour and was built for one of Sultan Mahmut II's gardens in the 1830s.

Aşiyan Museum ❺
Aşiyan Müzesi

Aşiyan Yolu, Bebek, Asian side. *Tel (0212) 263 69 86.* 🚌 *25E, 40.* 🕐 *9am–4pm Tue–Sat.*

Aşiyan, or bird's nest, is the former home of Tevfik Fikret (1867–1915), a teacher, utopian visionary and one of Turkey's leading poets. The wooden mansion, built by Fikret himself in 1906, is an attractive example of Turkish vernacular architecture. The views from its upper-storey balcony are stunning.

On show are the poet's possessions and *Sis* (Fog), a painting by Caliph Abdül Mecit (1922–24), inspired by Fikret's poem of that name.

Fortress of Europe ❻
Rumeli Hisarı

Yahya Kemal Cad, European side. *Tel (0212) 263 53 05.* 🚌 *25E, 40.* 🕐 *9:30am–4:30pm Thu–Tue.* 📷

This fortress was built by Mehmet the Conqueror in 1452 as his first step in the conquest of Constantinople *(see p26)*. Situated at the narrowest point of the Bosphorus, the fortress controlled a major Byzantine supply route. Across the straits is Anadolu Hisarı, or the Fortress of Asia, which was built in the 14th century by Beyazıt I.

The Fortress of Europe's layout was planned by Mehmet himself. While his grand vizier *(see p29)* and two other viziers were each responsible for the building of one of the three great towers, the sultan took charge of the walls. In the spirit of competition which evolved, the fortress was completed in four months.

The Fortress of Europe, built by Mehmet the Conqueror to enable him to capture Constantinople

The new fortress was soon nicknamed Boğazkesen – meaning "Throat-cutter" or "Strait-cutter". It was garrisoned by a force of Janissaries (see p127). These troops trained their cannons on the straits to prevent the passage of foreign ships. After they had sunk a Venetian vessel, this approach to Constantinople was cut off. Following the conquest of the city, the fortress lost its importance as a military base and was used as a prison, particularly for out-of-favour foreign envoys and prisoners-of-war.

The structure was restored in 1953. Open-air theatre performances are now staged here during the Istanbul Music and Dance Festival (see p45).

Café serving the yoghurt for which Kanlıca is famous

Kanlıca ❼

Asian side. 🚌 15, 101.

A delicious, creamy type of yoghurt is Kanlıca's best known asset. The İskender Paşa Mosque, overlooking the village square, is a minor work by Sinan (see p91), built for Sultan Süleyman's vizier İskender Paşa in 1559–60. There have been changes to the original building: the wooden dome has been replaced by a flat roof, and the porch was added later.

There are a number of yalıs in and around Kanlıca, including the Köprülü Amcazade Hüseyin Paşa Yalı (see p139), the oldest surviving Bosphorus yalı, just south of the village. This was built in 1698 by Mustafa II's grand vizier Hüseyin Paşa, the fourth grand vizier from the Köprülü family. The Treaty of

Karlowitz, in which the Ottomans acknowledged the loss of territory to Austria, Venice, Poland and Russia, was signed here in 1699 (see p27). All that remains of the yalı, which is not open to visitors, is a T-shaped salon, its dome only saved by wooden props.

Emirgan Park ❽
Emirgan Parkı

Emirgan Sahil Yolu, European side. **Tel** (0212) 277 57 82. 🚌 25E, 40. ⭕ 7am–10.30pm daily. 🚗 for vehicles.

Emirgan Park is the location of some famous tulip gardens, which are at their finest for the annual Tulip Festival in April (see p44). Tulips originally grew wild on the Asian steppes and were first propagated in large quantities in Holland. They were later reintroduced to Turkey by Mehmet IV (1648–87). The reign of his son Ahmet III is known as the Tulip Period (see p27) because of his fascination with the flowers.

In the late 19th century Sultan Abdül Aziz gave the park to the Egyptian Khedive (see p29), İsmail Paşa, and its three pavilions date from that era. They are known by their colours. The Sarı Köşk (Yellow Pavilion), built in the style of a Swiss chalet, suffered fire damage in 1954 and was rebuilt in concrete with a façade resembling the original. The Beyaz Köşk (White Pavilion) is a Neo-Classical style mansion, while the Pembe Köşk

Pembe Köşk in Emirgan Park

(Pink Pavilion) is in the style of a traditional Ottoman house. All three are now cafés.

Sakıp Sabancı Museum ❾
Sakıp Sabancı Müzesi

İstinye Cad 22, Emirgan 34467. **Tel** (0212) 229 55 18. 🚌 40, 41 from Taksim Sq; any bus to İstinye or Sarıyer. ⭕ 10am–5pm Tue, Thu, Fri; 10am–7pm Wed & Sat; noon–5pm Sun. ⬤ 1 Jan, 1st day of religious hols. 🎫 🚗 ♿ 🖥 🛍 www.muze. sabanciuniv.edu

With a superb view over the Bosphorus, the Sakıp Sabancı Museum is also known as the Horse Mansion (Atlı Köşk). Exhibitions comprise over 400 years of Ottoman calligraphy and other Koranic and secular art treasures. The collection of paintings is exquisite, with works by Ottoman court painters and European artists enthralled with Turkey.

BIRDS OF THE BOSPHORUS

In September and October, thousands of white storks and birds of prey fly over the Bosphorus on their way from their breeding grounds in eastern Europe to wintering regions in Africa. Large birds usually prefer to cross narrow straits like the Bosphorus rather than fly over an expanse of open water such as the Mediterranean. Among birds of prey on this route you can see the lesser spotted eagle and the honey buzzard. The birds also cross the straits in spring on their way to Europe but, before the breeding season, they are fewer in number.

The white stork, which migrates over the straits

Hot-house plants in the conservatory at Maslak Pavilions

Maslak Pavilions ⑩
Maslak Kasırları

Büyükdere Cad, Maslak. **Tel** (0212) 276 10 22. ▨ 40S (from Taksim). ☐ 9:30am–5pm Tue, Wed & Fri–Sun (Nov–Feb until 4pm).

This small group of buildings was a royal hunting lodge and country residence, much prized for its glorious views. The pavilions were built in the early and mid-19th century, when the focus of Istanbul court life moved away from Topkapı Palace (see pp54–9), in the centre of the city, to the sultans' lavish estates along the shore of the Bosphorus. The buildings are thought to date mainly from the reign of Abdül Aziz (1861–76). He gave Maslak to his son Abdül Hamit in the hope that the crown prince would then stop sailing at Tarabya (see p148), which his father regarded as unsafe.

The four main buildings are less ornate than other 19th-century pavilions in Istanbul. This is possibly due to the austere character of Abdül Hamit. He personally crafted the balustrades of the beautiful central staircase in the Kasr-ı Hümayun (the Pavilion of the Sultan) during his stay here. His initials in Western script – AH – can also be seen in the headpieces over the mirrors. The pavilion's lounge retains an Oriental feel, with a low sofa and a central coal-burning brazier.

Behind the small but elegant Mabeyn-i Hümayun (the Private Apartments) is a large conservatory full of camellias, ferns and banana plants. Nearby, at the edge of the forest stands a tiny octagonal folly with an ornate balcony called the Çadır Köşkü, or Tent Pavilion, which now serves as a bookshop. The Paşalar Dairesi (the Apartments of the Paşa) are located at the other side of the complex.

Khedive's Palace ⑪
Hidiv Kasrı

Hidiv Kasrı Yolu 32, Çubuklu. **Tel** (0216) 413 96 44. ▨ 15, 15A, 15P (from Üsküdar) or 221 (from Taksim), then 5 mins' walk from Kanlıca. ☐ 9am–11pm daily (May–Oct: to 10:30pm). ▣

Built in 1907 by the last khedive (the hereditary viceroy of Egypt, see p29), Abbas Hilmi II, this summer palace is one of the most striking buildings of its era in Istanbul. Its tower is an imposing landmark for those travelling up the Bosphorus.

The Italian architect Delfo Seminati based the design of the palace on an Italianate villa, throwing in Art Nouveau and Ottoman elements. Most impressive of all is the round entrance hall. This is entered through Art Nouveau glass doors and features a stained-glass skylight above a central fountain surrounded by eight pairs of elegant columns.

Renovated by the Turkish Touring Club (TTOK, see p245), the palace is now a luxury restaurant (see p206).

Beykoz ⑫

Asian shore. ▨ 15 (from Üsküdar) or 221 (from Taksim).

Beykoz is famous for its walnuts (beykoz means "prince's walnut") and for the glass produced here in the 1800s. The distinctive, mainly opaque, Beykoz glass (see p213), with its rich colours and

JASON AND THE SYMPLEGADES

The upper Bosphorus features in the Greek myth of Jason's search for the Golden Fleece. The Argonauts, Jason's crew, helped a local king, Phineus, by ridding him of the harpies (female demons) sent by Zeus to torment him. In return, the king advised them on how to tackle the Symplegades, two rocks at the mouth of the Bosphorus which were reputed to clash together, making passage impossible. His advice was to send a dove in advance of the ship; if it went through safely, so would the ship. This the Argonauts duly did, and the rocks clipped the dove's tail feathers. The Argo then went through with only some damage to its stern.

Jason and the Argonauts making their way through the Symplegades

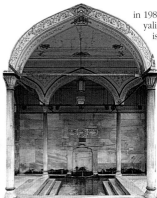

Fountain in the village square at Beykoz

graceful designs, can be seen in museums all over Turkey. Nowadays, the village's main attraction is its fish restaurants, which serve excellent turbot.

A fine fountain stands in the central square. Built on the orders of Sultan Mahmut I *(see p33)*, it is called the İshak Ağa Çeşmesi, after the customs inspector who commissioned it in 1780. It has a large domed and colonnaded loggia, and 10 conduits spouting a constant stream of water.

Industrialization, mainly bottling and leather factories, has taken its toll, and only a few buildings hint at the village's former splendour. An attractive 19th-century waterside mansion, Halil Ethem Yalı, interestingly combines Neo-Classical and Neo-Baroque styles. It stands on İbrahim Kelle Caddesi, south of the ferry landing.

Sadberk Hanım Museum 🔞
Sadberk Hanım Müzesi

Piyasa Cad 27–29, Büyükdere.
Tel *(0212) 242 38 13.* 🚌 *25E.*
🕐 *10am–6pm Thu–Tue.* 🎦 🚫
www.sadberkhanimmuzesi.org.tr

Occupying two archetypal wooden Bosphorus yalis *(see p139)*, the Sadberk Hanım Museum was the first private museum to open in Turkey,

in 1981. The larger of these yalis, the Azaryan Yali, is the former summer house of the wealthy Koç family. A four-storey mansion, it was built in 1911 and, like many buildings of the time, was inspired by European architecture. The distinctive criss-crossed wooden slats on its façade distinguish it from the neighbouring buildings. It contains some fine ethnographic artifacts collected by Sadberk Hanım, wife of the industrialist Vehbi Koç, to whom the museum is dedicated. She found many of them in the Grand Bazaar *(see pp98–9)* and in Istanbul's other markets. A number of exhibits are laid out in tableaux depicting 19th-century Ottoman society. These include a henna party, at which the groom's female relatives would apply henna to the hands of his bride; and a circumcision bed, with a young boy dressed in traditional costume. Also worth seeking out in this section is a display of infinitely delicate *oya*, Turkish embroideries. These remarkably life-like pieces imitate garlands of flowers, such as carnations, roses, hyacinths and lilies and were used to fringe scarves and petticoats. Some of the examples on show were made in palace harems in

Attic vase, Sadberk Hanım Museum

the 18th century. The neighbouring building is called the Sevgi Gönül Wing. Also dating from the early 20th century, it was bought to house the archaeological collection of Hüseyin Kocabaş, a friend of the Koç family. Displays are ordered chronologically, ranging from the late Neolithic period (5400 BC) to the Ottoman era. Exhibits are changed from time to time, but typically include Assyrian cuneiform tablets dating from the second millennium BC, Phrygian metalwork and Greek pottery from the late Geometric Period (750– 680 BC). Among other items are Byzantine reliquary and pendent crosses, and a selection of Roman gold jewellery.

Rumeli Kavağı 🔢

European shore. 🚌 *25A (from Beşiktaş).* 🚢 Rumeli Kavağı.

This pretty village has a broad selection of restaurants specializing in fish and fried mussels. They are clustered around the harbour from where there are views of the wild, rocky shores on the approach to the Black Sea. On the hill above Rumeli Kavağı are the scant remains of a castle, İmros Kalesi, built by Manuel I Comnenus *(see p21)* in the 12th century to guard his customs point.

Further up the Bosphorus, the shore road leads from Rumeli Kavağı to Altın Kum beach. This small strip of sand backed by restaurants is popular with local people.

The fishing village of Rumeli Kavağı, on the upper Bosphorus

The Bosphorus Trip

Ceremonial gate, Çırağan Palace

One of the great pleasures of a visit to Istanbul is a cruise up the Bosphorus. You can go on a pre-arranged guided tour or take one of the small boats that tout for passengers at Eminönü. But there is no better way to travel than on the official trip run by Istanbul Sea Bus Company (İDO, *see pp242–3*), which is described on the following pages. The İDO Bosphorus Cruise makes a round-trip to the upper Bosphorus two or three times daily, stopping at six piers along the way. You can return to Eminönü on the same boat or make your way back by bus, dolmuş or taxi. A 2-hour cruise also departs daily from Eminönü and Üsküdar.

LOCATOR MAP

Dolmabahçe Palace
This opulent 19th-century palace (see pp128–9) has a series of ornate gates along the waterfront. These were used by the sultan to enter the palace from his imperial barge.

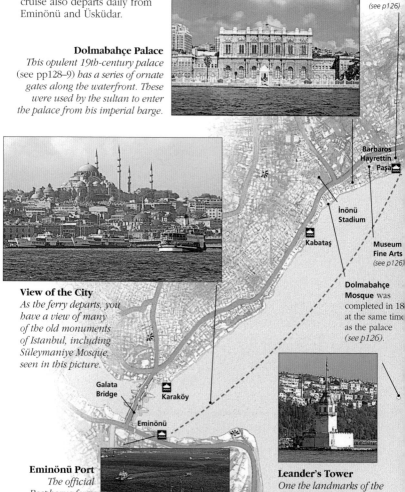

Naval Museum (see p126)

Barbaros Hayrettin Paşa

İnönü Stadium

Kabataş

Museum Fine Arts (see p126)

Dolmabahçe Mosque was completed in 18 at the same time as the palace (see p126).

View of the City
As the ferry departs, you have a view of many of the old monuments of Istanbul, including Süleymaniye Mosque, seen in this picture.

Galata Bridge **Karaköy**

Eminönü

Eminönü Port
The official Bosphorus ferry departs from Istanbul's busiest ferry terminal.

Leander's Tower
One the landmarks of the city, this white tower stands prominently in mid-channel, a short way off the Asian shore (see p130).

VISITORS' CHECKLIST

Eminönü Pier 3 (Boğaz Hattı). **Map** 3 D2. ***Tel*** *(0212) 522 00 45.* *Eminönü.* *daily: May–Sep, 10:30am & 1:30pm; Oct–Apr, 10:30am. Round trip takes 6 hours.* *Tickets should be purchased at the departure pier.* **www**.ido.com.tr

See pages 146–7
Arnavutköy
Kuleli Military School has a pretty wooden mosque beside it.
Galatasaray Island is a public pool and bar/restaurant.
Çengelköy
Sadullah Paşa Yalı, built in the 1783, is painted red-brown, as are many old yalıs *(see p139)*.
Beylerbeyi
Ortaköy
(see p122)
Yıldız Park
(see pp124–5)
Bosphorus Bridge
(see p138)
Çırağan Palace dates from 1874, but had to be rebuilt after a devastating fire in 1910. It is now a luxury hotel *(see p123)*.
Kuzguncuk
Fethi Ahmet Paşa Yalı
(see p139)
İskele Mosque
(see p131)
küdar
0 metres 750
0 yards 750
KEY
Motorway
Main road
Other road
Built-up area
Ferry boarding point
Route of Bosphorus trip
Yalı (see p139)
Viewpoint

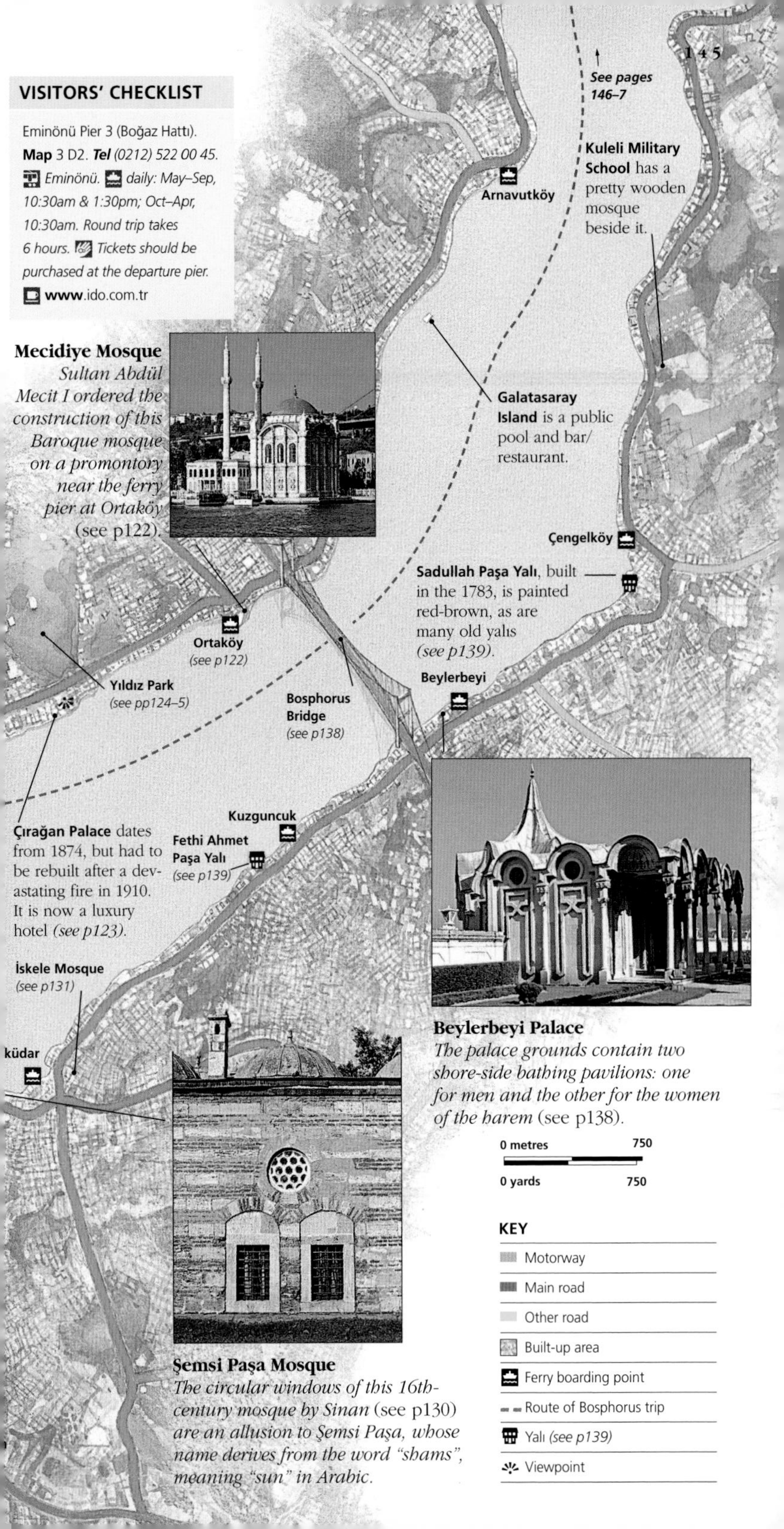

Mecidiye Mosque
Sultan Abdül Mecit I ordered the construction of this Baroque mosque on a promontory near the ferry pier at Ortaköy (see p122).

Beylerbeyi Palace
The palace grounds contain two shore-side bathing pavilions: one for men and the other for the women of the harem (see p138).

Şemsi Paşa Mosque
The circular windows of this 16th-century mosque by Sinan (see p130) *are an allusion to Şemsi Paşa, whose name derives from the word "shams", meaning "sun" in Arabic.*

The Middle Bosphorus

Fountain at Küçüksu

North of Arnavutköy, the outskirts of Istanbul give way to attractive towns and villages, such as Bebek with its bars and cafés. The Bosphorus flows fast and deep as the channel reaches its narrowest point – 700 m (2,300 ft) across – on the approach to the Fatih Sultan Mehmet bridge. It was at this point that the Persian emperor Darius and his army crossed the Bosphorus on a pontoon bridge in 512 BC, on their way to fight the Greeks. Two famous old fortresses face each other across the water near here. Several elegant yalıs are also found in this part of the strait, particularly in the region known to Europeans as the Sweet Waters of Asia.

LOCATOR MAP

İstinye Bay
This huge natural bay, the largest inlet on the Bosphorus, has been used as a dock for centuries. There is a fish market along the quay every morning.

Emirgan Park
Situated above the pretty village of Emirgan, this park is famous for its tulips in spring (see p44). The grounds contain pleasant cafés and pavilions (see p141).

The Bosphorus University, one of the most prestigious in Turkey, enjoys spectacular views. Almost all teaching here is in English.

Bebek
(see p138)

Egyptian Consulate
(see p138)

Kan

Fortress of Europe
Situated at the narrowest point on the Bosphorus, this fortress (see p140) was built by Mehmet II in 1452, as a prelude to his invasion of Constantinople (see p26).

Arnavutköy

See pages 144–5

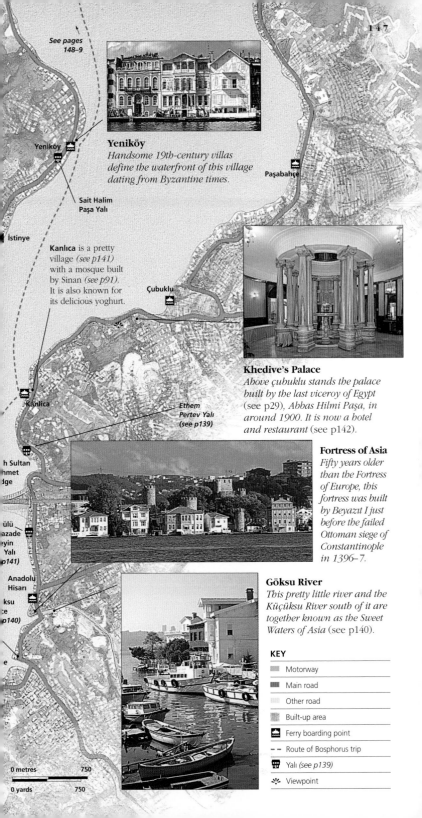

See pages
148–9

Yeniköy

*Handsome 19th-century villas
define the waterfront of this village
dating from Byzantine times.*

Yeniköy

Paşabahçe

Sait Halim
Paşa Yalı

İstinye

Kanlıca is a pretty
village *(see p141)*
with a mosque built
by Sinan *(see p91)*.
It is also known for
its delicious yoghurt.

Çubuklu

Kanlıca

Ethem
Pertev Yalı
(see p139)

Khedive's Palace

*Above çubuklu stands the palace
built by the last viceroy of Egypt
(see p29), Abbas Hilmi Paşa, in
around 1900. It is now a hotel
and restaurant (see p142).*

h Sultan
hmet
dge

Fortress of Asia

*Fifty years older
than the Fortress
of Europe, this
fortress was built
by Beyazıt I just
before the failed
Ottoman siege of
Constantinople
in 1396–7.*

ülü
azade
eyin
Yalı
p141)

Anadolu
Hisarı

ksu
e
p140)

e

Göksu River

*This pretty little river and the
Küçüksu River south of it are
together known as the Sweet
Waters of Asia (see p140).*

KEY

▦	Motorway
▦	Main road
▦	Other road
▦	Built-up area
⛴	Ferry boarding point
– –	Route of Bosphorus trip
⊞	Yalı *(see p139)*
☆	Viewpoint

0 metres	750
0 yards	750

The Upper Bosphorus

Black Sea mussels

In the 19th century ambassadors to Turkey built their summer retreats between Tarabya and Büyükdere, on the European side of the Bosphorus. As the hills fall more steeply towards the shore along the upper reaches of the straits, the built-up area peters out. There is time to explore and take lunch at Anadolu Kavağı on the Asian side before the boat returns to Eminönü. You can also catch a bus or dolmuş back to the city. The Bosphorus itself continues for 8 km (5 miles) or so to meet the Black Sea, but the land on both sides of this stretch is now under military control.

LOCATOR MAP

Sadberk Hanım Museum
This museum, housed in two wooden yalıs, has variety of interesting exhibits. These include antiquities from Greece and Rome, and Ottoman craftwork (see p143).

Sarıyer

Büyükdere

Tarabya Bay
The small village set within a lovely bay first attracted wealthy Greeks in the 18th century. The bay still thrives as an exclusive resort with up-market fish restaurants.

Huber Köş
is a 19th-century yalı own by the gove ment.

FISHING ON THE BOSPHORUS

A multitude of fishing vessels ply the waters of the Bosphorus, ranging from large trawlers returning from the Black Sea to tiny rowing boats from which a line is cast into the water. On a trip up the Bosphorus you often see seine nets spread out in circles, suspended from floats on the surface. The

Fishing boats at Sarıyer, the main fishing port on the Bosphorus

main types of fish caught are mackerel, mullet, *hamsi* (similar to anchovy, *see p194*) and sardine. Much of the fish caught is sold at Istanbul's principal fish market in Kumkapı.

Rumeli Kavağı
This village is the most northerly ferry stop on the European side (see p143). From here the Bosphorus widens out to meet the Black Sea.

Anadolu Kavağı
A short climb from this village – the last stop on the trip – brings you to a ruined 14th-century Byzantine fortress, the Genoese Castle, from which there are great views over the straits.

Beykoz
Beykoz is the largest fishing village along the Asian shore. Close to its village square, which has this fountain dating from 1746, are several fish restaurants which are very popular in summer (see p142).

KEY	
▬▬▬	Main road
	Other road
	Built-up area
⛴	Ferry boarding point
– –	Route of Bosphorus trip
⛩	Yalı *(see p139)*
☀	Viewpoint

0 metres   750
0 yards   750

Halil Ethem Yalı *(see p143)*

See pages 146–7

EXCURSIONS FROM ISTANBUL

*S*tanding at a natural crossroads, Istanbul makes a good base for excursions into the neighbouring areas of Thrace and Anatolia – European and Asian Turkey respectively. Whether you want to see great Islamic architecture, immerse yourself in a busy bazaar, relax on an island or catch a glimpse of Turkey's rich birdlife, you will find a choice of destinations within easy reach of the city.

On public holidays and weekends nearby resorts become crowded with Istanbul residents taking a break from the noisy city. For longer breaks, they head for the Mediterranean or Aegean, so summer is a good time to explore the Marmara and western Black Sea regions while they are quiet.

The country around Istanbul varies immensely from lush forests to open plains and, beyond them, impressive mountains. The Belgrade Forest is one of the closest green areas to the city if you want a short break. The Princes' Islands, where the pine forests and monasteries can be toured by a pleasant ride in a horse-and-carriage, are also just a short boat trip away from the city.

Window, Selímiye Mosque, Edirne

Further away, through rolling fields of bright yellow sunflowers, is Edirne, the former Ottoman capital. The town stands on a site first settled in the 7th century BC. It is visited today for its fine mosques, especially the Selimiye.

South of the Sea of Marmara is the pretty spa town of Bursa, originally a Greek city which was founded in 183 BC. The first Ottoman capital, it has some fine architecture.

Near the mouth of the straits of the Dardanelles (which link the Sea of Marmara to the Aegean) lie the ruins of the legendary city of Troy, dating from as early as 3600 BC. North of the Dardanelles are cemeteries commemorating the battles which were fought over the Gallipoli peninsula during World War I.

Boats in Burgaz Harbour on the Princes' Islands, a short ferry ride from Istanbul

◁ The Green Tomb of Mehmet I in Bursa, one of the city's best-known landmarks

Exploring Beyond Istanbul

Within a radius of 250 km (150 miles) of Istanbul there are many destinations worth visiting. To the northwest is Edirne, an attractive riverside town and the location of several fine mosques. South of Istanbul is Bursa, which lies at the foot of Uludağ, a mountain famed for its skiing. Closer to Istanbul are the Black Sea resorts of Şile, Polonezköy and Kilyos, and the Princes' Islands, which are easily reached by ferry. The war cemeteries of the Dardanelles and the site of ancient Troy require a longer trip.

The 15th-century Beyazıt II Mosque in Edirne

Burgas

BULGAR

Lalapaşa

Khaskovo

Süloğlu

Demirköy

Kırklareli

Yıldız L

EDİRNE ❶

0·3   Hasköy

Pınarhisar

Havsa

Karacaoğlan

Vize

GREECE

Babaeski

Lüleburgaz

Uzunköprü

Büyükkarıştıran   100

Meriç

Hayrabolu

Muratlı

Çorlu

Ergene Irmağı

Küplü

Hamidiye

550

Susuzmüsellim

Banarlı

İpsala

Paşayiğit

Malkara

İnecik   110

Tekirdağ

Keşan

Alexandroúpoli

Karahisar

Ballı

Kumbağ

Enez

İsiklar Dağı

Mecidiye

Şarköy

Marmara   *Marmar*

MAR
ISLA ❷

Saros Körfezi

Bolayır

Avşa

550

Gelibolu

Çanakkale Boğazı (Dardanelles)

Erde

Lâpseki

Gökçeada

Eceabat   200

Gallipoli Peninsula

Canakkale

Biga

200   BIRD PARAD
NATIONAL PA

Kus

THE ❸
DARDANELLES

555

Cape Helles

Çan

Göner

TROY ❹

210

Gönen Çayı

Bozcaada

550

Ezine

555

AEGEAN
SEA

Balık

Edremit   230

İvrindi

Ayvacık

Edremit Körfezi

Burhaniye

Savaştepe

550

Ayvalık

İzmir

KEY

═══ Motorway

─── Main road

┄┄┄ Minor road

━━━ Scenic route

╍╍╍ Main railway

─── Minor railway

▓▓▓ International border

0 kilometres   25

0 miles   25

For additional map symbols *see back flap*

SIGHTS AT A GLANCE

Belgrade Forest **3**
Bird Paradise National Park **11**
Bursa pp162–8 **9**
The Dardanelles **13**
Edirne pp154–7 **1**
İznik **8**
Kilyos **2**
Marmara Islands **12**
Polonezköy **5**
Princes' Islands **6**
Şile **4**
Termal **7**
Troy **14**
Uludağ National Park **10**

View over the picturesque city of Bursa

BLACK SEA

Karacaköy

Durusu **KİLYOS 2**

Bahçeköy   Sarıyer   **ŞİLE 4**
BELGRADE   Beykoz
Çatalca **FOREST 3**   **5** **POLONEZKÖY**   Kandıra

Büyük
Çekmece   **İSTANBUL**
Küçük
Çekmece

PRINCES' 6
ISLANDS   Gebze   İzmit   Adapazarı

armara Denizi   Yalova   Gölcük   Ankara
(a of Marmara)

Armutlu   **7 TERMAL**   Geyve

Gemlik   *İznik Gölü* **8 İZNİK**   *Sakarya Nehri*

Mudanya
Karacabey   Yenişehir   Bilecik

Ulubat   **9**
Gölü   **BURSA**   Cumalıkızık   İnegöl

Mustafakemalpaşa   **10**
ULUDAĞ
NATIONAL PARK

Susurluk

Kepsut

TTING AROUND

e road network around
nbul is steadily improving,
1 modern, cheap and efficient
ches *(see p244)* will get you to
st places. Ferries and sea buses
e p244) cross the Sea of
rmara to ports on its southern
re and reach both the Princes'
1 Marmara Islands.

One of the main ski runs in Uludağ National Park

Edirne ❶

Standing on the river Tunca near the border with Greece, Edirne is a provincial university town which is home to one of Turkey's star attractions, the Selimiye Mosque *(see pp156–7)*. As this huge monument attests, Edirne was historically of great importance. It dates back to AD 125, when the Roman Emperor Hadrian joined two small towns to form Hadrianopolis, or Adrianople. For nearly a century, from when Murat I *(see p25)* took the city in 1361 until Constantinople was conquered in 1453 *(see p26)*, Edirne was the Ottoman capital. The town has one other claim to fame – the annual grease wrestling championships in June.

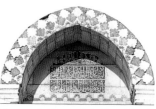
Entrance arch, Mosque of the Three Balconies

of the commonest afflictions. The colonnaded inner mosque courtyard, unlike most later examples, covers three times the area of the mosque itself. Inside, the weight of the impressive dome is supported on sweeping pendentives.

◖ Mosque of the Three Balconies
Üç Şerefeli Camii
Hükümet Cad. ◯ *daily.* ⬛
Until the fall of Constantinople, this was the grandest building in the early Ottoman state. It was finished in 1447 and takes its name from the three balconies adorning its southeast minaret, at the time the tallest in existence. In an unusual touch, the other three minarets of the mosque are each of a different design and height. Unlike its predecessors in

Bursa *(see pp162–8)*, the mosque has an open courtyard, setting a precedent for the great imperial mosques of Istanbul. The plan of its interior was also innovative. With minimal obstructions, the mihrab and *minbar* can both be seen from almost every corner of the prayer hall. Like the minarets, the dome, too, was the largest of its time.

◖ Old Mosque
Eski Cami
Talat Paşa Asfaltı. ◯ *daily.* ⬛
The oldest of Edirne's major mosques, this is a smaller version of the Great Mosque in Bursa *(see p164)*. The eldest son of Beyazıt I *(see p32)*, Süleyman, began the mosque in 1403, but it was his youngest son, Mehmet I, who completed it in 1414.

A perfect square, the mosque is divided by four massive piers into nine domed sections. On either side of the prayer hall entrance there are massive Arabic inscriptions proclaiming "Allah" and "Mohammed".

Entrance to Beyazıt II Mosque viewed from its inner courtyard

◖ Beyazıt II Mosque
Beyazıt II Külliyesi
Yeniimaret Mah, Beyazıt Cad.
◯ *daily.* **Health Museum** *Tel* (0284) 212 09 22. ◯ *9:30am–5:30pm daily.* ⬛ ♿
Beyazıt II Mosque stands in a peaceful location on the northern bank of the Tunca River, 1.5 km (1 mile) from the town centre. It was built in 1484–8, soon after Beyazıt II *(see p32)* succeeded Mehmet the Conqueror *(see p26)* as sultan.

The mosque and its courtyards are open to the public. Of the surrounding buildings in the complex, the old hospital, which incorporated an asylum, has been converted into the **Health Museum**. Disturbed patients were treated in the asylum – a model of its time – with water, colour and flower therapies. The Turkish writer Evliya Çelebi (1611–84) reported that singers and instrumentalists would play soothing music here three times a week. Overuse of hashish was one

---

GREASE WRESTLING

The Kırkpınar Grease Wrestling Championships take place annually in July, on the island of Sarayiçi in the Tunca River. The event is famed throughout Turkey and accompanied by a week-long carnival. Before competing, the wrestlers dress

Grease wrestlers parading before they fight

in knee-length leather shorts *(kispet)* and grease themselves from head to foot in diluted olive oil. The master of ceremonies, the *cazgır*, then invites the competitors to take part in a high-stepping, arm-flinging parade across the field, accompanied by music played on a deep-toned drum *(davul)* and a single-reed oboe *(zurna)*. Wrestling bouts can last up to two hours and involve long periods of frozen, silent concentration interspersed by attempts to throw down the opponent.

🏛 Rüstem Paşa Caravanserai

Rüstem Paşa Kervansarayı
İki Kapılı Han Cad 57.
Tel *(0284) 212 6119.*

Sinan *(see p91)* designed this caravanserai for Süleyman's most powerful grand vizier, Rüstem Paşa *(see p88)*, in 1560–61. It was constructed in two distinct parts. The larger courtyard, or han *(see p96)*, which is now the Rüstem Paşa Kervansaray Hotel *(see p191)*, was built for the merchants of Edirne, while the smaller courtyard, now a student hostel, was an inn for other travellers.

A short walk away, on the other side of Saraçlar Caddesi, is the Semiz Ali Paşa Bazaar, where Edirne's merchants still sell their wares. This is another work of Sinan, dating from 1589. It consists of a long, narrow street of vaulted shops.

🏛 Museum of Turkish and Islamic Arts

Türk ve İslam Eserleri Müzesi
Kadir Paşa Mektep Sok. **Tel** *(0284) 225 16 25.* ◯ 9am–noon, 1:30–5pm Tue–Sun. ◙

Edirne's small collection of Turkish and Islamic works of art is attractively located in the *medrese* of the Selimiye Mosque *(see pp156–7)*.

The museum's first room is devoted to the local sport of grease wrestling. It includes enlarged reproductions of miniatures depicting 600 years of the sport. These show the wrestling stars resplendent in their leather shorts, their skin glistening with olive oil.

Other objects on display include the original doors of the Beyazıt II Mosque. There are also military exhibits. Among them are some beautiful 18th-century Ottoman shields, with woven silk exteriors, and paintings of military subjects.

The tranquil 15th-century Muradiye Mosque

🅲 Muradiye Mosque

Muradiye Camii
Küçükpazar Cad. ◯ *prayer times only.* ⬛

This mosque was built as a *zaviye* (dervish hospice) in 1421 by Murat II *(see p32)*, who dreamt that the great dervish leader Jelaleddin Rumi *(see p104)* asked him to build one in Edirne. Only later was it converted into a mosque. Its interior is notable for its massive inscriptions, similar to those in the Old Mosque, and for some fine early 15th-century İznik tiles *(see p161)*.

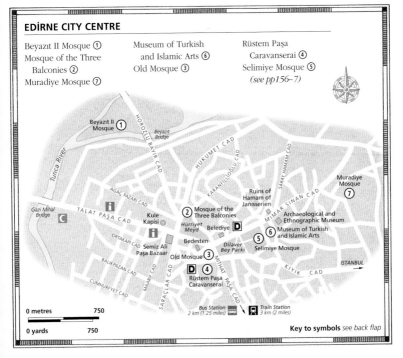

EDİRNE CITY CENTRE

Tunca River · HOROZLU BAYIR CAD · Beyazıt II Mosque ① · *Beyazıt Bridge* · HUKUMET CAD · KARANFİLLİOĞLU CAD · SARAY HAMAM CAD · Muradiye Mosque ⑦ · AGAÇ PAZARI CAD · *Gazi Mihal Bridge* · TALAT PAŞA CAD · Kule Kapısı · Mosque of the Three Balconies ② · *Hürriyet Meyd* · Belediye 🅳 · Ruins of Hamam of Janisserien · MİMAR SİNAN CAD · Archaeological and Ethnographic Museum · Museum of Turkish and Islamic Arts ⑥ · ORTAKAPI CAD · Semiz Ali Paşa Bazaar · Bedesten · *Dilaver Bey Parkı* · Selimiye Mosque ⑤ · BALIKPAZAN CAD · MARİF CAD · SARAÇLAR CAD · Old Mosque ③ · 🅳 ④ · Rüstem Paşa Caravanserai · MİTHAT PAŞA CAD · KIYIK CAD · **ISTANBUL** · CUMHURFYET CAD

Bus Station 2 km (1.25 miles) · Train Station 3 km (2 miles)

0 metres 750
0 yards 750

Key to symbols *see back flap*

Edirne: Selimiye Mosque

Selimiye Camii

The Selimiye is the greatest of all the Ottoman mosque complexes, the apogee of an art form and the culmination of a lifetime's ambition for its architect, Sinan *(see p91)*. Built on a slight hill, the mosque is a prominent landmark. Its complex includes a *medrese (see p38)*, now housing the Museum of Turkish and Islamic Arts *(see p155)*, a school and the Kavaflar Arasta, a covered bazaar.

Selim II *(see p27)* commissioned the mosque. It was begun in 1569 and completed in 1575, a year after his death. The dome was Sinan's proudest achievement. In his memoirs, he wrote: "With the help of Allah and the favour of Sultan Selim Khan, I have succeeded in building a cupola six cubits wider and four cubits deeper than that of Haghia Sophia". In fact, the dome is of a diameter comparable to and slightly shallower than that of the building *(see pp72–5)* Sinan had so longed to surpass.

★ Minarets
The mosque's four slender minarets tower to a height of 84 m (275 ft). Each one has three balconies. The two northern minarets contain three intertwining staircases, each one leading to a differ-ent balcony.

Ablutions Fountain
Intricate, pierced carving decorates the top of the 16-sided open şadırvan (ablutions fountain), which stands in the centre of the courtyard. The absence of a canopy helps to retain the uncluttered aspect of the courtyard.

STAR FEATURES

- ★ Minarets
- ★ Dome
- ★ Minbar

The columns supporting the arches of the courtyard are made of old marble, plundered from Byzantine architecture.

Courtyard Portals
Alternating red and honey-coloured slabs of stone were used to build the striking arches above the courtyard portals. This echoes the decoration of the magnificent arches running around the mosque courtyard itself.

★ Dome
The dome masterfully dominates the entire interior of the mosque. Not even the florid paintwork – the original 16th-century decoration underwent restoration in the 19th century – detracts from its effect.

VISITORS' CHECKLIST

Mimar Sinan Cad, Edirne.
Tel (0284) 213 97 35.
☐ daily. ● prayer times.

★ Minbar
Many experts claim that the Selimiye's minbar, with its conical tiled cap, is the finest in Turkey. Its lace-like side panels are exquisitely carved.

Mihrab, cut from Marmara marble

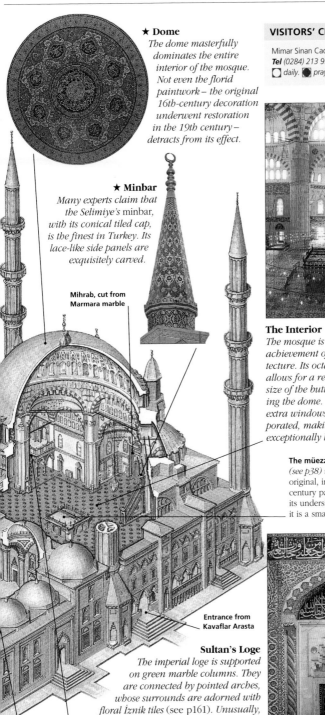

The Interior
The mosque is the supreme achievement of Islamic architecture. Its octagonal plan allows for a reduction in the size of the buttresses supporting the dome. This permitted extra windows to be incorporated, making the mosque exceptionally light inside.

The müezzin mahfili
(see p38) still retains original, intricate 16th-century paintwork on its underside. Beneath it is a small fountain.

Entrance from Kavaflar Arasta

Sultan's Loge
The imperial loge is supported on green marble columns. They are connected by pointed arches, whose surrounds are adorned with floral İznik tiles (see p161). Unusually, its ornately decorated mihrab contains a shuttered window, which opened on to countryside when the mosque was first built.

Main entrance

Kilyos ②

27 km (17 miles) N of Istanbul.
🏛 *1,665.* 🅳 *from Sarıyer.*

Kilyos, on the shore of the Black Sea, is the closest seaside resort to Istanbul and very popular. It has a long, sandy beach and temptingly clear water, but visitors should not swim here in the absence of a lifeguard because there are dangerous currents beneath the calm surface.

A 14th-century Genoese castle perches on a cliff top overlooking the town but it is not open to visitors. The three ruined towers on the left of the main approach road into the village were formerly water control towers. They were part of the system that once brought water here from the Belgrade Forest.

Belgrade Forest ③
Belgrad Ormanı

20 km (12 miles) N of Istanbul.
🚌 *42, 40S from Taksim to Çayırbaşı, then 42 to Bahçeköy.* **Park Tel** *(0212) 226 23 35.* ☐ *May–Sep 6am–9pm daily; Oct–Apr 7am–7:30pm.* 📷 ♿

One of the most popular escapes from the city, the Belgrade Forest is the only sizeable piece of woodland in the immediate vicinity of Istanbul. The forest is made up of pines, oaks, beeches, chestnuts and poplars, beneath which a profusion of wild flowers grow in spring. Within it is a huge woodland park, best visited during the week, since it attracts hordes of picnickers at weekends. The main entrance to the park is near the village of Bahçeköy and the popular Neşetsuyu picnic area is a half-hour stroll from this gate.

The park's other attractions are the relics of the dams, reservoirs and aqueducts used for over 1,000 years to transport spring water in to Istanbul. The

Büyük Bent, a Byzantine dam and reservoir in the Belgrade Forest

oldest structure, Büyük Bent (Great Reservoir), dates back to the early Byzantine era. It is a pleasant half-hour walk from Neşetsuyu picnic area. Meanwhile, the Sultan Mahmut Dam, outside the park's gate, is a fine curve of marble which dates from 1839.

Eğri Kemer (Crooked Aqueduct) and Uzun Kemer (Long Aqueduct) are on the 016 road between Levent and Kısırmandıra and are best reached by taxi. Both have impressive rows of arches. The former probably dates from the 12th century, while Sinan *(see p91)* built the latter for Süleyman the Magnificent *(see p26)*.

Şile ④

72 km (45 miles) NE of Istanbul.
🏛 *25,372.* 🚌 *from Üsküdar.*

The quintessential Black Sea holiday village of Şile has a number of fine, sandy beaches and a black-and-white striped cliff-top lighthouse.

The village of Şile, a holiday resort and centre for cotton production

In antiquity, the village, then known as Kalpe, was a port used by ships sailing east from the Bosphorus.

Şile's lighthouse, the largest in Turkey, was built by the French for Sultan Abdül Aziz *(see p30)* in 1858–9; it can be visited after dusk. Apart from tourism, the main industry is now the production of a coarse cotton which is made into clothing and sold in shops along Üsküdar Caddesi.

Polonezköy ⑤

25 km (16 miles) NE of Istanbul.
🏛 *500.* 🚌 *221 from Taksim to Beykoz, then dolmuş.*

Polonezköy was originally called Adampol, after the Polish Prince Adam Czartoryski who bought prime arable land here in 1842 for Polish emigrants settling in Turkey. Soon after, in 1853, the Poles formed a band of Cossack soldiers to fight for Abdül Mecit I *(see p30)* in the Crimea. After this he granted them the land as a tax-free haven.

Polonezköy's rustic charm is now big business, and a number of health spas and villas have sprung up. A couple of restaurants *(see p207)* still serve the pork for which the town was once famous.

The surrounding beech forest, which offers pleasant walks, has now been protected from further development. As part of this scheme, the locals have even waived their rights to collect firewood.

Princes' Islands ❻

Adalar

12 km (7 miles) SE of Istanbul.
🏛 16,171. 🚢 8–10 crossings daily
from Kabatas to Büyükada.
ℹ️ (0216) 382 70 71.

The pine-forested Princes'
Islands provide a welcome
break from the bustle of the
city and are just a short ferry
ride southeast from Istanbul.
Most ferries call in turn at the
four largest of the nine islands:
Kınalıada, Burgazada, Heybeliada and finally Büyükada.

Easily visited on a day
trip, the islands take their
name from a royal
palace built by Justin II
on Büyükada, then
known as Prinkipo
(Island of the Prince)
in 569. During the
Byzantine era the
islands became in-
famous as a place of
exile. Members of the
royal family and public
figures were often
banished to the
monasteries here.

In the latter half of
the 19th century, with the
inauguration of a steamboat
service from Istanbul, several
wealthy ex-patriates settled on
the islands. Among these was
Leon Trotsky. From 1929–33
he lived at 55 Çankaya
Caddesi, one of the finest
mansions on Büyükada.

Büyükada, the largest island,
attracts the most visitors with
its sandy beaches and *fin-de-
siècle* elegance. Its 19th-century
atmosphere is enhanced by

**Door to the
Monastery of
St George**

the omnipresence of horse-
drawn phaetons. These quaint
carriages are the only form of
public transport on Büyükada
(and Heybeliada) since
motorized transport is banned.
At the top of Büyükada's
wooded southern hill, in a
clearing, stands the Monastery
of St George. It is a 20th-
century structure, built on
Byzantine foundations.

To the left of the ferry pier
on Heybeliada, the second
largest island, is the imposing
former Naval High School
(Deniz Harp Okulu), built
in 1942. The island's
northern hill is the
stunning location of
the Greek Orthodox
School of Theology
(built in 1841). The
school is now closed
but its library, famous
among Orthodox
scholars, is still open.
The island also has a
pleasant beach on its
south coast at Çam
Limanı Köyü.

The smaller
islands of Kınalıada
and Burgazada are less
developed and are peaceful
places to stop off for a meal.

Termal ❼

38 km (24 miles) SE of Istanbul. 🏛
5,018. 🚢 from Kabataş to Yalova. ℹ️
Termal-Yalova, (0226) 675 74 00.

This small spa buried deep
in a wooded valley has been
patronized by ruling elites
since the Roman era. Termal is

**Ornamental fountain at Atatürk's
former house at Termal**

12 km (7 miles) from the port
of Yalova. Its popularity was
revived by Sultan Abdül Hamit
II *(see p33)* in the early 20th
century, when he refurbished
the **Yalova Termal Baths**, now
part of the Ministry of Health
complex of five baths and
four hotels. Facilities include
Turkish baths *(see p67)*, a
sauna and a swimming pool.

Atatürk enjoyed taking the
waters here. The small chalet-
style house he built at the
bottom of the valley, now the
Atatürk Museum, preserves
some of his possessions.

🛁 **Yalova Termal Baths**
Termal. **Tel** (0226) 675 74 00.
⬜ 8am–10pm daily.

🏛 **Atatürk Museum**
Atatürk Köşkü, Termal. **Tel** (0226)
675 70 28. ⬜ May–Oct 9am–5pm
Tue, Wed, Fri–Sun; Nov–Apr
9:30am–4pm.

The harbour of Burgazada, one of the relaxed and picturesque Princes' Islands near Istanbul

İznik ❽

87 km (54 miles) SE of Istanbul.
🏛 20,100. 🚌 Yeni Mahalle,
Yakup Sok, (0224) 757 25 83.
ℹ️ Belediye Hizmet Binası,
Kılıçaslan Cad 97, (0224) 757 10
10. 🛒 Wed. 🎪 İznik Fair (5–10
Oct); Liberation Day (28 Nov).

A charming lakeside town,
İznik gives little clue
now of its former glory as, at
one point, the capital of the
Byzantine Empire. Its most important legacy dates, however,
from the 16th century, when
its kilns produced the finest
ceramics ever to be made in
the Ottoman world.

The town first reached
prominence in AD 325, when
it was known as Nicaea. In
that year Constantine (see
p20) chose it as the location
of the first Ecumenical Council
of the Christian Church. At
this meeting, the Nicene Creed,
a statement of doctrine on the
nature of Christ in relation to
God, was formulated.

The Seljuks (see p21) took
Nicaea in 1081 and renamed
it İznik. It was wrested back
from them in 1097 by the First
Crusade on behalf of Emperor
Alexius I Comnenus. After the
capture of
Constantinople in
1204 (see p26), the
city was capital of
the 'Empire of
Nicaea', a remain-
ing fragment of
the Byzantine
Empire, for half
a century. In
1331, Orhan
Gazi (see p32)
captured İznik

Grand domed portico fronting the Archaeological Museum

and incorporated it into the
Ottoman Empire. İznik still
retains its original layout.
Surrounded by the **city walls**,
its two main streets are in the
form of a cross, with minor
streets running out from them
on a grid plan. The walls still
more or less delineate the
town's boundaries. They were
built by the Greek Lysimachus,
then ruler of the
town, in 300
BC, but they
were frequently
repaired by
both the
Byzantines
and later the
Ottomans. They
cover a total of
3 km (2 miles)
in circumference
and are punc-
tuated by huge gateways. The
main one of these, Istanbul
Gate (İstanbul Kapısı), is at
the city's northern limit. It is
decorated with a carved relief
of fighting horsemen and is
flanked by Byzantine towers.

**Istanbul Gate from within
the city walls**

One of the town's oldest
surviving monuments, the
ruined church of **Haghia
Sophia Museum**, stands at the

intersection of the main
streets, Atatürk Caddesi and
Kılıçaslan Caddesi. The
current building was erected
after an earthquake in 1065.
The remains of a fine mosaic
floor, and also of a Deësis, a
fresco that depicts Christ, the
Virgin and John the Baptist,
are protected from damage
behind glass screens. Just off
the eastern end
of Kılıçaslan Cad-
desi, the 14th-
century **Green
Mosque** (Yeşil
Cami) is named
after the tiles
covering its
minaret. Unfor-
tunately, the
originals have
been replaced
by modern
copies of an inferior quality.

Opposite the mosque, the
Kitchen of Lady Nilüfer
(Nilüfer Hatun İmareti), one
of İznik's loveliest buildings,
now houses the town's
Archaeological Museum. This
imaret was set up in 1388 by
Nilüfer Hatun, wife of Orhan
Gazi, and also served as a
hospice for wandering
dervishes. Entered through a
spacious five-domed portico,
the central domed area is
flanked by two further domed
rooms. The museum has displays of Roman antiquities
and glass as well as some
recently discovered examples
of Seljuk and Ottoman tiles.

🕌 **Haghia Sophia Museum**
Müze Cad. **Tel** (0224) 757 10 27.
🕐 8am–noon, 1–5pm Tue–Sun.

🕌 **Green Mosque**
Müze Sok. 🕐 daily (after prayer).

🏛 **Archaeological Museum**
Müze Sok. **Tel** (0224) 757 10 27.
🕐 by appointment.

Green Mosque, İznik, named after the green tiles adorning its minaret

İznik Ceramics

Towards the end of the 15th century, the town of İznik began to produce large quantities of ceramic bowls, jars and, later, tiles for the many palaces and mosques of Istanbul. Drawing on local deposits of fine clay and inspired by imported Chinese ceramics, the work of the craftsmen of İznik soon excelled both technically and aesthetically. İznik pottery is made from hard, white "fritware", which is

16th-century İznik mosque lamp

akin to porcelain. This style of pottery was invented in Egypt in around the 12th century. It is covered by a bright, white slip (a creamy mixture of clay and water) and a transparent glaze. Early İznik pottery is brilliant blue and white. Later, other colours, especially a vivid red, were added. The potteries of İznik reached their height in the late 16th and early 17th centuries but shortly after fell into decline.

Chinese porcelain, *which was imported into Turkey from the 14th century and of which there is a large collection in Topkapı Palace (see pp54–9), often inspired the designs used for İznik pottery. During the 16th century, İznik potters produced imitations of pieces of Chinese porcelain such as this copy of a Ming dish.*

Rock and wave border pattern

Cobalt blue and white *was the striking combination of colours used in early İznik pottery (produced between c.1470–1520). The designs used were a mixture of Chinese and Arabesque, as seen on this tiled panel on the wall of the Circumcision Chamber in Topkapı Palace. Floral patterns and animal motifs were both popular at this time.*

Damascus ware *was the name erroneously given to ceramics produced at İznik during the first half of the 16th century. They had fantastic floral designs in the new colours of turquoise, sage green and manganese. When such tiles were discovered at Damascus, the similar İznik pots were wrongly assumed to have been made there.*

Armenian bole, *an iron-rich red colour, began to be used in around 1550, as seen in this 16th-century tankard. New, realistic tulip and other floral designs were also introduced, and İznik ware enjoyed its heyday, which lasted until around 1630.*

Wall tiles *were not made in any quantity until the reign of Süleyman the Magnificent (1520–66). Süleyman used İznik tiles to refurbish the Dome of the Rock in Jerusalem.*
Some of the best examples are seen in Istanbul's mosques, notably in the Süleymaniye (see pp90–91), Rüstem Paşa Mosque (pp88–9) and, here, in this example from the Blue Mosque (pp78–9).

Miniature depicting potters

Bursa

Basin, Museum of Turkish and Islamic Arts

Bursa extends in a swathe along the northern foothills of Mount Uludağ *(see p169)*. A settlement known as Prusa was reputedly established here in the 3rd century BC by Prusias I of Bithynia. However, it was the Romans who first spotted the potential of Bursa's mineral springs: today there are an estimated 3,000 baths in the city. In 1326 Bursa became the first capital of the Ottoman Empire, following its capture by Osman Gazi *(see p25)*.

View over the rooftops of the city of Bursa

Today Bursa is a provincial capital whose status as one of Turkey's foremost centres of commerce and industry is evident in its broad boulevards and busy shops and bazaars. Apart from the central market area *(see pp164–5)*, the most frequented sightseeing area is Yeşil, on the eastern side of the Gök River, where the Green Mosque and Green Tomb are the main attractions.

🗝 Yıldırım Beyazıt Mosque
Yıldırım Beyazıt Camii
Yıldırım Cad. ☐ *daily.*
This mosque is named after Beyazıt I *(see p32)*, whose nickname was "Yıldırım", meaning "thunderbolt". This referred to the speed with which he reacted to his enemies. Built in 1389, just after Beyazıt became sultan, the mosque at first doubled as a lodge for Sufi dervishes *(see p104)*. It has a lovely portico with five domed bays.

Inside, the interior court (a covered "courtyard" in Bursa mosques, which prefigures the open courtyards preferred by later Ottoman architects) and prayer hall are divided by an impressive arch. This rises from two mihrab-like niches. The walls of the prayer hall itself are adorned with several bold and attractive pieces of calligraphic design *(see p95)*.

🗝 Green Tomb
Yeşil Türbe
Yeşil Cad. ☐ *daily.* 💶 *donation.*
The tomb of Mehmet I *(see p30)*, which stands elevated above the mosque among tall cypress trees, is one of the city's most prominent landmarks. It was built between 1414 and 1421. The tomb is much closer to the Seljuk *(see p21)* style of architecture than Classical Ottoman. Its exterior is covered in green tiles, although these are mainly 19th-century replacements for the original faïence. However, a few older tiles survive around the entrance portal.

The interior, entered through a pair of superbly carved wooden doors, is simply dazzling. The space is small and the ornamentation, covering a relatively large surface area, is breathtaking in its depth of colour and detail. The mihrab has especially intricate tile panels, including a representation of a mosque lamp hanging from a gold chain between two candles.

The sultan's magnificent sarcophagus is covered in exquisite tiles and adorned by a long Koranic inscription. Nearby sarcophagi contain the remains of his sons, daughters and nursemaid.

🗝 Green Mosque
Yeşil Cami
Yeşil Cad. ☐ *daily.*
Bursa's most famous monument was commissioned by Mehmet I in 1412, but it remained unfinished at his death in 1421 and still lacks a portico. Nevertheless, it is the finest Ottoman mosque built before the conquest of Constantinople *(see p26)*.

The main portal is tall and elegant, with an intricately carved canopy. It opens into the entrance hall. Beyond this is an interior court, with a carved fountain at its centre. A flight of three steps leads up from here into the prayer hall. On either side of the steps are niches where worshippers once left their shoes *(see p39)*. Above the entrance to the court is the sultan's loge, resplendent in richly patterned tiles created using the *cuerda seca* technique. They are in beautiful greens, blues and yellows, with threads of gold which were added after firing.

The Green Tomb and Green Mosque, Bursa's most distinctive monuments

The tiling of the prayer hall was carried out by Ali İbn İlyas Ali, who learnt his art in Samarkand. It was the first time that tiles were used extensively in an Ottoman mosque and set a precedent for the later widespread use of İznik tiles *(see p161)*. The tiles covering the walls of the prayer hall, which is well lit by floor-level windows, are simple, green and hexagonal. Against this plain backdrop, the effect of the mihrab is especially glorious. Predominantly turquoise, deep blue

and white, with touches of gold, the mihrab's tiles depict flowers, leaves, arabesques and geometric patterns. The mosque's exterior was also once clad in tiles, but they have since disappeared.

🏛 Museum of Turkish and Islamic Arts

Türk ve İslam Eserleri Müzesi
Yeşil Cad. **Tel** (0224) 327 76 79.
⏰ 10am–5pm Tue–Sun. 🎫
This museum is housed in a fine Ottoman building, the former *medrese (see p38)* of the Green Mosque. A

VISITORS' CHECKLIST

90 km (60 miles) S of İstanbul.
🚌 1,995,000. ✈ 20 km (12 miles) NW. 🚌 Kıbrıs Şehitler Cad, (0224) 261 54 00. D Atatürk Cad; Osman Gazi Cad.
ℹ Ulucami Parkı, Orhangazi Altgeçidi, No. 1 (0224) 220 18 48. 🎭 Textiles Fair (mid-Apr); Bursa Festival (12 Jun–12 Jul).

colonnade surrounds its courtyard on three sides and the cells leading off from it, formerly used by the students, are now exhibition galleries. At the far end of the courtyard is the large, domed hall which was originally the main classroom.

Exhibits dating from the 12th–20th centuries include Seljuk and Ottoman ceramics, elaborately decorated Korans and costumes ranging from linen dervish robes to ornate wedding gowns. A display on Turkish baths *(see p67)* features embroidered towels and exotic high-heeled silver bath clogs. There is also a recreated setting of a traditional circumcision room, complete with a four-poster bed.

Façade of the Museum of Turkish and Islamic Arts

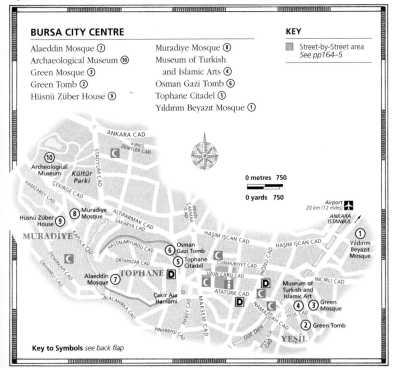

BURSA CITY CENTRE

Alaeddin Mosque ⑦
Archaeological Museum ⑩
Green Mosque ③
Green Tomb ②
Hüsnü Züber House ⑨
Muradiye Mosque ⑧
Museum of Turkish
and Islamic Arts ④
Osman Gazi Tomb ⑥
Tophane Citadel ⑤
Yıldırım Beyazıt Mosque ①

KEY

⬜ Street-by-Street area
See pp164–5

0 metres 750
0 yards 750

Key to Symbols *see back flap*

Bursa: The Market Area

Bursa's central market area is a warren of streets and ancient Ottoman courtyards (hans). The area is still central to Bursa's commercial activity and is a good place to experience the life of the city. Here too you can buy the local fabrics for which the town is famous, particularly handmade lace, towelling and silk. The silkworm was introduced to the Byzantine Empire in the 6th century and there is still a brisk trade in silk cocoons carried out in Koza Han all year round. Among the many other items on sale today are the lovely hand-painted, camel-skin Karagöz puppets *(see p168).*

★ Covered Bazaar
The great bazaar, built by Mehmet I in the 15th century, consists of a long hall with domed bays, adjoining by a high, vaulted hall. The Bedesten is home to jewellers' shops.

★ The Great Mosque
A three-tiered ablutions fountain stands beneath the central dome of this monumental mosque, which was erected in 1396–9.

Şengül Hamamı Turkish baths

FEVZI ÇAKMAK CAD

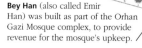

Bey Han (also called Emir Han) was built as part of the Orhan Gazi Mosque complex, to provide revenue for the mosque's upkeep.

Cafés

KOZA PARK

ATATÜRK CAD

The Bey Hamamı
(1339) is the oldest Turkish baths building in the world. It now houses workshops.

Koza Park
The gardens in front of Koza Han, with their fountains, benches and shaded café tables, are a popular meeting place for locals and visitors throughout the day.

★ Koza Han
This is the most attractive and fascinating building in the market area. Since it was built in 1491 by Beyazıt II, it has been central to the silk trade.

Geyve Han is also known as İvaz Paşa Han.

Fidan Han dates from around 1470, when it was built by a grand vizier of Mehmet the Conqueror.

İçkoza Han

Flower Market
The numerous bunches of flowers for sale in the streets around the town hall make a picturesque sight in the midst of Bursa's bustling market area.

BORSA SOK

UZUN ÇARŞI CAD

ÇÖMLEK SOK

BELEDIYE CAD

| 0 metres | 40 |
| 0 yards | 40 |

STAR SIGHTS

★ Great Mosque

★ Covered Bazaar

★ Koza Han

The Belediye, Bursa's town hall, is a Swiss chalet-style, half-timbered building that forms a surprising landmark in the centre of the town.

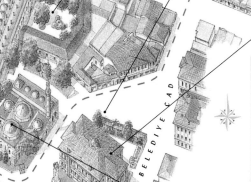

Orhan Gazi Mosque
Built in 1339, just 13 years after the Ottoman conquest of Bursa, this mosque is the oldest of the city's imperial mosques.

KEY

– – – Suggested route

Bursa: Tophane and Muradiye

The clocktower in Tophane

Tophane, the most ancient part of Bursa, is distinguished by its clocktower which stands on top of a hill. This area was formerly the site of the citadel and is bounded by what remains of the original Byzantine walls. It is also known as Hisar, which means "fortress" in Turkish. If you continue westwards for 2 km (1mile), crossing the Cılımboz River, you come to the historic district of Muradiye. The 15th-century Muradiye Mosque, from which this suburb takes its name, is one of the most impressive royal mosque and tomb complexes in the city.

Exploring Tophane

Tophane's northern limit is marked by the best preserved section of the citadel walls, built on to an outcrop of rock. At the top is a pleasant park filled with cafés, which also contains the imposing clocktower and the tombs of the founders of the Ottoman dynasty. From here you can look down on the lower part of Tophane, where archetypal Ottoman houses still line many of the twisting streets. Pınarbaşı Kapısı, at Tophane's southern point, is the gate through which Orhan Gazi entered Bursa in 1326 *(see p25)*.

⛩ Tophane Citadel

Hisar
Osman Gazi Cad. ◯ *daily.* ♿
The citadel walls can be viewed from a set of steps which lead uphill from the intersection of Cemal Nadir Caddesi and Atatürk Caddesi. These steps end at the tea gardens above. The citadel fell into Turkish hands when

Orhan Gazi's troops broke through its walls. Later, he built a wooden palace inside the citadel and had the old Byzantine ramparts refortified. The walls had until this era delimited the entire circumference of the ancient city. However, Orhan began to encourage Bursa's expansion and developed the present-day commercial heart of the city further to the east.

South of Hastalaryurdu Caddesi is an area notable for its old Ottoman houses *(see p61)*. Most of these have overhanging upper storeys. They consist of a timber frame filled in with adobe and plastered over, then painted in bright colours. Kaleiçi Sokağı, which can be reached down Karadut Sokağı from Hastalaryurdu Caddesi, is one of the best streets of such houses.

⬛ Tombs of Osman and Orhan Gazi

Osman & Orhan Gazi Türbeleri
Ulu Cami Cad. ◯ *daily.* 📷 *donation.*
Osman Gazi began the process of Ottoman expansion in the 13th century *(see p25)* and attempted to capture Bursa. But it was his son, Orhan, who took the city just before his father died. Orhan brought his father's body to be buried in the baptistry of a converted church and he himself was later buried in the nave. The tombs that can be seen today date from 1868. They were rebuilt after the destruction of the church and the original tombs in an earthquake in 1855. Fragments of the church's mosaic floor survive inside the tomb of Orhan Gazi.

Tomb of Osman Gazi, the first great Ottoman leader

⬛ Alaeddin Mosque

Alaeddin Camii
Alaeddin Mahallesi. ◯ *prayer times only.* 🚫
Further exploration in the Tophane area reveals the Alaeddin Mosque, the oldest in Bursa, built within 10 years of the city's conquest. It is in the form of a simple domed square, fronted by a portico of four Byzantine columns with capitals. The mosque was commissioned by Alaeddin Bey, brother of and vizier *(see p39)* to Orhan Gazi.

Exploring Muradiye

Muradiye is a leafy, largely residential district. Close to the Muradiye Mosque are the Hüsnü Züber House and the Ottoman House, two fine examples of traditional Turkish homes. To the north is a park, among the attractions of which are a boating lake and the Archaeological Museum.

⬛ Muradiye Mosque

Muradiye Külliyesi
Murat II Cad. ◯ *daily.* 📷 *donation.*
This mosque complex was built by Murat II, father of Mehmet the Conqueror *(see p26)*, in the early 15th century. The mosque itself is preceded by a graceful domed portico.

Popular café in the park above the ancient citadel walls in Tophane

Octagonal tomb of Mustafa in the grounds of Muradiye Mosque

Its wooden door is finely carved and the interior decorated with early İznik tiles *(see p161)*. The *medrese*, beside the mosque, now serves as a dispensary. It is a perfectly square building, with cells surrounding a central garden courtyard. Its *dershane*, or main classroom, is richly tiled and adorned with an ornate brickwork façade.

The mosque garden, with its cypresses, well-tended flower beds and fountains, is one of Bursa's most tranquil retreats. Murat II was the last Ottoman sultan to be buried in Bursa and his mausoleum, standing in the garden beside the mosque and *medrese*, was completed in 1437. His earth-filled sarcophagus lies beneath an opening in the roof. The eaves above the tomb's 16th-century porch still retain their original painted decoration.

There are 11 other tombs in the garden, several of which were built for murdered princes. One such is the tomb of Mustafa, a son of Süleyman the Magnificent, who was disposed of to clear the way for his younger brother, Selim II, "the Sot" *(see p76)*. According to an inscription, Selim had the octagonal mausoleum built for his brother. The interior is decorated with some particularly beautiful İznik tile panels depicting carnations, tulips and hyacinths. The tiles date from the best İznik period, the late 16th century.

🏛 Hüsnü Züber House

Hüsnü Züber Evi, Yaşayan Müze Uzunyol Sok 3, Muradiye. **Tel** (0224) 221 35 42. ◻ 10am–midday, 1–5pm Tue–Sun. 🎫 🔲 **Ottoman House Tel** (0224) 285 48 13. ◻ 10am–5pm Tue–Sun.

Among the numerous well-preserved houses in the Muradiye district is the Hüsnü Züber House. This 150-year-old mansion has been opened as a museum by its present owner, the artist Hüsnü Züber. It was originally a guest house for visiting dignitaries, later becoming the Russian Consulate and, most recently, a private residence.

The house is an interesting example of vernacular architecture. The upper storey projects over the street in the traditional manner

Muradiye Mosque, constructed by Murat II

of Ottoman houses *(see p63)*. Overlooking the interior courtyard, which has rooms arranged around it on three sides, there is a loggia. Originally this would have been open, but it is now glazed. Meanwhile, inside the house, the decorative wooden ceilings (some with hand-painted borders) are particularly attractive.

Hüsnü Züber's private collection of carved wooden objects is now displayed here. These include spoons, musical instruments and even farming utensils. They are all decorated with Anatolian motifs by a unique technique of engraving by burning known as pyrogravure.

The 18th-century **Ottoman House** (Osmanlı Evi) stands on the square in front of the Muradiye Mosque. The upper storey of this fine house is adorned with elaborately patterned brickwork. Shutters and grilles hide the windows.

Hüsnü Züber House, dating from the mid-19th century

🏛 Archaeological Museum

Arkeoloji Müzesi
Kültür Parkı. **Tel** (0224) 234 49 18. ◻ 10am–5pm Tue–Sun. 🎫
Finds dating from the third millennium BC up to the Ottoman conquest of Bursa are collected in this museum. In the first hall there are clasps, vessels and an inscription from the Phrygian period. Other exhibits include Roman and Hellenistic jewellery and ceramics, a number of Roman statues of Cybele, goddess of nature, and a Roman bronze of the god Apollo with strange, lifelike eyes. There are also displays of Byzantine religious objects and coins.

Bursa: Çekirge

With a name which translates literally as "Realm of the Crickets", Çekirge still earns Bursa the tag of yeşil, or "green", by which it is known in Turkey. This leafy western spa suburb of the city has attracted visitors to its mineral springs since Roman times. In the 6th century the Emperor Justinian *(see p20)* built a bathhouse here and his wife Theodora later arrived with a retinue of 4,000. Çekirge is also the location of most of the city's finest hotels and the area's hillside setting affords some spectacular views.

Çekirge's Old Spa, dating back to the 14th-century reign of Murat I

New Spa

Yeni Kaplıca
Mudanya Yolu 6. **Tel** (0224) 236 69 68.
☐ daily 5am–midnight.
Despite their name, the New Spa baths have a substantial pedigree. They were rebuilt in 1522 by Rüstem Paşa, grand vizier *(see p29)* to Süleyman the Magnificent *(see p26)*. The sultan is said to have ordered their rebuilding in gratitude after his recovery from gout when bathing in the Byzantine baths that stood on this site.

The central pool is surrounded with bays adorned with beautiful but damaged İznik tiles *(see p161)*. They are not open to women. Within the same complex, however, there are two other baths: the modern Kaynarca baths which is for women and the Karamustafa baths for couples.

🏨 Çelik Palas Hotel

Çelik Palas Otel
Çekirge Cad 79.
Tel (0224) 233 38 00.
This five-star hotel stands on one of Bursa's main thoroughfares. Built in 1933, it is the city's oldest, most prestigious spa hotel. Atatürk *(see pp30–31)* frequented its baths. Open to both sexes, their centrepiece is an attractive circular pool in a domed marble room.

🛁 Old Spa

Eski Kaplıca
Hotel Kervansaray, Çekirge Meydanı, Kervansaray. **Tel** (0224) 233 93 00.
☐ 8am–10:30pm daily.
The Old Spa baths were established by Murat I in the late 14th century and renovated in 1512, during the reign of Beyazıt II. Remnants of an earlier building, said to date from the reign of Emperor Justinian *(see p20)*, are also visible. These include some Byzantine columns and capitals in the *hararet* (steam room) of the men's section *(see p67)*. You enter the baths through the new Kervansaray Termal Hotel. Spring water, said to cure skin diseases and rheumatism, bubbles into the central pool of both the men's and women's sections at 45 °C (113 °F). The women's baths are not as old or grand, but are still the most attractive women-only ones in Bursa.

🟥 Murat I Hüdavendigar Mosque

Murat I Hüdavendigar Camii
I. Murat Cad, Çekirge. ☐ daily.
Bursa's most unusual mosque was built for Murat I, self-styled Hüdavendigar, meaning "Creator of the Universe", in 1385. It is unlike any other mosque in the Ottoman world: its prayer hall is on the ground floor, with the *medrese* built around a second storey.

The façade looks more like that of a palace than a mosque, with a five-arched portico surmounted by a colonnade. This colonnade in turn has five sets of double-arched windows divided by Byzantine columns. Inside, the domed court and prayer hall rise through both storeys. The upper storey colonnade leads to the cells of the *medrese*. On this level, passageways lead around both sides of the mosque to a mysterious room, located over the mihrab, whose original purpose is unknown.

KARAGÖZ SHADOW PUPPETS

Suspended above Çekirge Caddesi is an imposing monument to the town's two famous scapegoats, Karagöz and Hacıvat. According to legend, these local clowns were executed in the 14th century for distracting their fellow workers while building the Orhan Gazi Mosque *(see p165)*. It is said that Sultan Orhan *(see p32)* created a shadow play about them in remorse.

In fact, shadow puppet theatre arrived in Turkey later and is thought to have originated in Southeast Asia. Selim I is reported to have brought it back to Istanbul after his Egyptian campaign in 1517. The camel-skin puppets are 35–40 cm (14–16 in) high, brightly dyed and oiled to aid translucency. They are still made today and can be purchased in an antique shop in the Bedesten run by Şinasi Çelikkol, who also occasionally puts on shows.

Cadi, a witch in the Karagöz puppet shows

Uludağ National Park, a popular ski resort in winter

Uludağ National Park ❿
Uludağ Milli Parkı

100 km (60 miles) S of Istanbul. *Tel* (0224) 283 21 97. 🚡 *Teleferik to Sarıalan, then dolmuş.* ⭘ *daily.* 🅿 *only for vehicles.*

One of a number of Turkish mountains to claim the title of Mount Olympus, Uludağ was believed by the Bithynians (of northwest Asia Minor) to be the home of the gods. In the Byzantine era, it was home to several monastic orders. After the Ottoman conquest of Bursa, Muslim dervishes *(see p104)* moved into their abandoned monasteries. Nowadays, however, no traces of Uludağ's former religious communities remain.

A visit to Uludağ National Park is especially enjoyable in spring or summer, when its alpine heights are relatively cool and it becomes a popular picnic area. The park includes 27,000 acres (67,000 hectares) of woodland. As you ascend, the deciduous beech, oak and hazel gradually give way to juniper and aspen, and finally to dwarf junipers. In spring, hyacinths and crocuses blanket the wooded slopes.

In winter, Uludağ is transformed into Turkey's most fashionable ski resort. The industry centres on the Oteller region, which has good alpine-style hotels.

Osman Gazi *(see p25)* is supposed to have founded seven villages for his seven sons and their brides in the Bursa region. **Cumalıkızık**, on the lower slopes of Uludağ, is the most perfectly preserved of the five surviving villages and is now registered as a national monument. Among its houses are many 750-year-old semi-timbered buildings. The village can be reached by minibus from Bursa.

Bird Paradise National Park ⓫
Kuşcenneti Milli Parkı

115 km (70 miles) SW of Istanbul. *Tel* (0266) 735 54 22. 🅳 *from Bandırma.* ⭘ *8am–8pm daily.* ♿

An estimated 255 species of birds visit Bird Paradise National Park at the edge of Kuş Gölü, the lake formerly known as Manyas Gölü. Located on the great migratory paths between Europe and Asia, the park is a happy combination of plant cover, reed beds and a lake that supports at least 20 species of fish.

At the entrance to the park, there is a small museum with displays about various birds.

Spoonbill wading in the lake at Bird Paradise National Park

Binoculars are provided at the desk and visitors make their way to an observation tower.

Two main groups of birds visit the lake: those that come here to breed (March–July), and those which pass by during migration, either heading south (November) or north (April–May). Among the numerous different birds that breed around the lake are the endangered Dalmatian pelican, the great crested grebe, cormorants, herons, bitterns and spoonbills. The migratory birds, which can be seen in spring and autumn, include storks, cranes, pelicans and birds of prey such as sparrowhawks and spotted eagles.

Sandy beach on Avşa, the most popular of the Marmara Islands

Marmara Islands ⓬
Marmara Adaları

120 km (75 miles) SW of Istanbul. 🚢 *from Yenikapı.* 🛈 *Neyire Sıtkı Cad 31/3, Erdek, (0266) 835 11 69.*

This beautiful archipelago in the Sea of Marmara is a popular destination with Turkish holiday-makers, particularly with residents of Istanbul.

The loveliest of the islands is Avşa, whose sandy beaches and regular summer ferry service make it popular with Turks and, increasingly, foreign tourists. The ferry arrives at Türkeli on the west coast. Transport to the most popular beach, at Maviköy, is by a tractor-pulled train.

Marmara, the largest island, has one beach, north of Marmara village at Çınarlı. It is famous for producing the prized Proconnesian marble.

The Dardanelles ⑬

Çanakkale Boğazı

200 km (125 miles) SW of Istanbul.
🚢 Çanakkale–Eceabat car ferry.
🚌 Çanakkale. 🛈 Çanakkale İskele
Meydanı 27, (0286) 217 11 87.

Named after Dardanus, an ancient king of Çanakkale, the Dardanelles are the straits that link the Aegean Sea to the Sea of Marmara, and which separate European Turkey from Asia. Some 40 km (25 miles) long and narrowing to little more than a kilometre (half a mile) wide, they are steeped in legend and have been of strategic importance for thousands of years. In modern times they are probably best known as the setting for a disastrous Allied campaign during World War I.

The classical name for this channel of water was the Hellespont. According to legend, the Greek goddess Helle fell into the straits from the back of a golden winged ram. In another tale, the lovelorn Leander swam nightly across the Hellespont to meet his lover, Hero, until one night he drowned. The English Romantic poet Byron swam across the straits in 1810, in emulation of Leander, and remarked on the hazardous nature of the currents.

Çanakkale, the old town at the mouth of the Dardanelles, has two museums. The **Military and Naval Museum** is a short walk from the ferry docks. Its collection includes a pocket watch that saved the

**The Çanakkale Şehitleri Memorial,
honouring the Turkish dead**

LOCATOR MAP

Anzac Cove ③
Çanakkale ⑥
Cape Helles ⑦
Chunuk Bair ②
Kabatepe Visitors'
  Centre ④
National Park Information
  Centre ⑤
Suvla Bay ①

KEY

☐ Area of war memorials

▬ Road

--- Ferry route

AEGEAN SEA

GALLIPOLI PENNINSULA

DARDANELLES

life of Atatürk (see pp30–31) when he was hit by shrapnel. The **Archaeological Museum**, south of the town centre, has exhibits from ancient Troy.

To the west is the beautiful **Gallipoli** (Gelibolu) **Peninsula**. Part of this land is a national park, with an information centre near Eceabat. The peninsula, which is now quite tranquil, was the scene of horrific battles that took place in 1915. The objectives of the Allied forces' invasion of Gallipoli were to capture Istanbul, force Turkey into submission and open a strategic supply route to Russia. The campaign began on 25 April 1915 with the landings of British and French troops at **Cape Helles**, and the Anzacs (Australian and New Zealand forces) at what they thought was the beach at Kabatepe. But currents had swept the Anzac force about 1.5 km (1mile) to the north, to a place now known as **Anzac Cove**, near Arı Burnu. Here they were faced with unknown and tough terrain, including a cliff.

The Turks managed to retain the high ground of **Chunuk Bair**. The battle here lasted three days, during which 28,000 men were

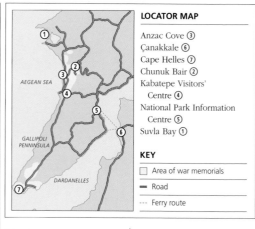

**Mehmetçik Memorial
near Anzac Cove**

killed. When the Allied forces failed to make headway, more British troops landed at **Suvla Bay** on 6 August. This new offensive might have been successful, but Allied intelligence continually underestimated the Turks and the difficult ground. The terrible slaughter of deadlocked trench warfare continued until the Allies were finally evacuated on 19 December. More than 500,000 Allied and Turkish troops lost their lives and the whole peninsula is scattered with battlefield sites and war memorials.

The best place to begin a tour of the war memorials and cemeteries is at the **Kabatepe Visitors' Centre**, which houses a small collection of memorabilia including weapons, uniforms and soldiers' poignant letters home. North of here, near Anzac Cove, are several cemeteries and monuments. Chunuk Bair, now a peaceful pine grove above the beaches, has a memorial to the New Zealanders who died and some reconstructed Turkish trenches. The British Memorial is at Cape Helles, on the peninsula's tip. Further east along the coast stand both the French Memorial and the vast Çanakkale Şehitleri Memorial to the Turks who died defending Gallipoli.

🏛 **Military Museum**
Çimenlik Kalesi, Çanakkale.
Tel (0286) 213 17 30. ◯ 9am–noon, 1:30– 5:30pm Tue, Wed & Fri–Sun. 🖼

🏛 **Archaeological Museum**
Atatürk Cad, Çanakkale. **Tel** (0286) 217 67 40. ◯ 8:30am–5:30pm. 🖼

🛈 **National Park Information Centre**
Near Eceabat. **Tel** (0286) 814 11 28. ◯ 9am–6pm Mon–Fri.
Park ◯ daily. 🖼

🛈 **Kabatepe Visitors' Centre**
Near Kabatepe. **Tel** (0286) 814 12 97. ◯ 9am–6pm daily. 🖼

Troy ⑭
Truva

350 km (220 miles) SW of Istanbul.
🚌 from Çanakkale. 🛈 Çanakkale İskele Meydanı 27, (0286) 217 11 87. ◯ 8am–7pm daily (Nov–Apr: until 5pm). 🖼

Model of the legendary wooden horse at Troy

In Homer's epic poem, the *Iliad*, the city of Troy is besieged by the Greeks for ten years. For centuries Troy was assumed by many to be as mythical as Achilles, Hector and the other heroes in the tale. But a handful of 19th-century archaeologists were convinced that Homer had based his story on the events that happened to a real city and that traces of it could be found by searching near the Dardanelles. In 1865 British Consul Frank Calvert began investigating some ruins in Hisarlık. This interested the German archaeologist Heinrich Schliemann who soon found evidence of an ancient city resembling the layout of Homer's Troy. Over the last hundred years most historians have come to accept that this city must at least have inspired Homer, and was possibly even called Troy and besieged at the time specified in the story.

The settlement mound in fact has nine distinct levels (labelled Troy I–IX) representing 3,000 years of habitation. Sadly, the remains are sparse, and it takes some imagination to evoke an image of a city. Many structures were made of mud bricks and obviously levelled before new settlements were built on top.

The city Homer refers to is probably Troy VI (1800–1250 BC), while the Greek and Roman levels, when the city was known as Ilion, are Troy VIII (700–300 BC) and Troy IX (300 BC–AD 1) respectively.

What has survived includes a defence wall, palaces and houses from various periods, two sanctuaries (probably 8th century BC) and a Roman theatre. The grandest dwelling is the Pillar House, near the southern gate. Some believe this is the Palace of King Priam mentioned in the *Iliad*.

More conspicuous is a re-creation of the wooden horse, inside which a small group of the Greeks supposedly hid. There is also a visitors' centre with a video and a scale model of the site.

SCHLIEMANN'S SEARCH FOR ANCIENT TROY

Heinrich Schliemann used a fortune amassed in business to realize his life-long dream of discovering ancient Troy. He began excavating some likely sites in the 1860s and started on the ruins at Hisarlık in 1870. An amateur, Schliemann drove a great trench through the mound, destroying some walls in his haste. He soon claimed to have found Troy, though he knew not all his findings pointed to this. His greatest find – a hoard of gold and silver jewellery that he smuggled to Germany, calling it "Priam's Treasure" *(see p64)* – pre-dates Homer's Troy by 1,000 years. Some of the treasure disappeared after World War II only to reappear spectacularly in Moscow in August 1994.

Schliemann's wife wearing some of the excavated treasure

THREE GUIDED WALKS

With its frenetic atmosphere, traditional cafés at almost every corner and historic sights from centuries of different rulers, Istanbul is a wonderful city for walkers.

On the following five pages are routes for three walks that take you through three different areas of Istanbul. They will take you past many of the most interesting sights. The areas covered range from the old Greek and Jewish neighbourhoods of Balat and Fener, where historic synagogues can still be seen amid traditional tripe shops, to the wonderful aromas of coffee, spices and fresh fish permeating

the air in the Galata region of the city. For a little more elegance, a stroll along İstiklâl Caddesi will confirm why this area of Istanbul has the reputation for celebrating its European side, rather than Asian, while the Istanbul Modern Art Museum *(see p107)* is the finest venue in the city for contemporary art. All the walks are intended to be done at a leisurely pace, and there are plenty of suggestions for refreshment stops along each route. In addition to these walks, each of the four areas of Istanbul described in the *Area-by-Area* section of this book has a walk on its *Street-by-Street* map.

**Istanbul Modern
Art Museum sign**

CHOOSING A WALK

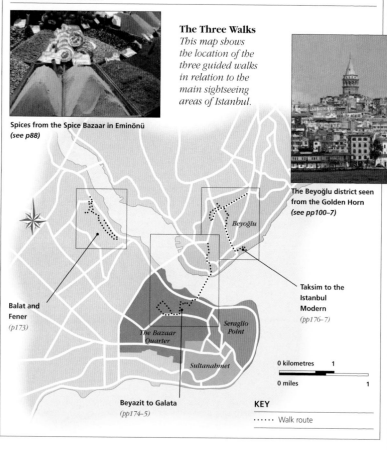

**Spices from the Spice Bazaar in Eminönü
(see p88)**

The Three Walks
*This map shows
the location of the
three guided walks
in relation to the
main sightseeing
areas of Istanbul.*

The Beyoğlu district seen
from the Golden Horn
(see pp100–7)

Beyoğlu

**Taksim to the
Istanbul
Modern**
(pp176–7)

**Balat and
Fener**
(p173)

*Seraglio
Point*

*The Bazaar
Quarter*

Sultanahmet

0 kilometres   1

0 miles   1

Beyazit to Galata
(pp174–5)

KEY

······ Walk route

A 45-Minute Walk in Balat and Fener

The Balat and Fener neighbourhoods epitomize the cultural diversity and tolerance that was the hallmark of the Ottomans. Fener was predominantly a Greek area, while Balat was Jewish, and this walk guides you around the ancient churches, synagogues, Turkish baths and mosques in the atmospheric back streets. They may have seen better days, but a rejuvenation scheme is putting life back into this picturesque locality.

> **TIPS FOR WALKERS**
>
> **Starting point:** Ahrida Synagogue.
> **Length:** 1.5 km (1 mile).
> **Getting there:** From Eminönü bus terminus, take No 99 or any bus displaying Eyüp or Ayvansaray. Ask the driver to let you off at Balat. There are also ferry points at Fener and Balat.
> **Stopping-off points:** Hotel Daphnis ⑬ is a good spot to stop for a meal.

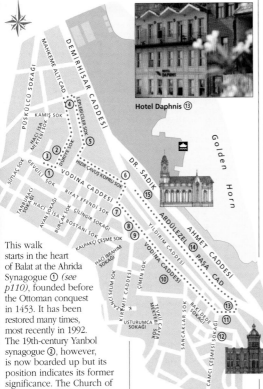

Hotel Daphnis ⑬

This walk starts in the heart of Balat at the Ahrida Synagogue ① (see p110), founded before the Ottoman conquest in 1453. It has been restored many times, most recently in 1992. The 19th-century Yanbol synagogue ②, however, is now boarded up but its position indicates its former significance. The Church of Holy Angels ③ dates from Byzantine times. Below it flows a sacred spring and every 14 September supplicants of all religions gather here to pray for cures from their ailments.

Walk to Leblebiciler Sokak and on the right at No. 51 is Merkez şekerci ④, a sweet shop since the 1870s. Further along is Agora ⑤, Istanbul's oldest tavern (meyhane). Turn left on Hızır Çavuş Köprü Sokak and continue down this road until you reach

KEY

• • • Walk route

⚓ Ferry boarding point

Köfteci Arnavut ⑥. This traditional meatball restaurant has been serving its loyal customers since 1947.

Turn right and then left on to Vodina Caddesi and on your right is Tahtalı Minare Hamam ⑦, one of the oldest Turkish baths in the city, dating from the 1500s. Note the boiler room chimney on the roof. A short distance further on your right is Tahtalı Minare Mosque ⑧, built by Fatih Sultan Mehmet II in 1458. Next door is the Tomb

of Hazreti Hüseyin Sadık ⑨, who was buried as a *gazi* (warrior of the faith) in the 1450s. Continue down the road and you will be able to see the cross of Aya Yorgi Metokhi Church ⑩ (no public access) above its high wall.

At the end of the road turn left and on the right is the Greek Orthodox Patriarchate ⑪ (see p111), seat of the Greek church since 1601. Look at the red-brick building on the ramparts above. This is the Fener Greek Boys High School ⑫, established in Byzantine times. On the left is the Hotel Daphnis ⑬. Turn left onto Abdülezel Paşa Caddesi and the stone building on your right is the Women's Library ⑭, the city's sole female-only information centre. Further up is the Church of St Stephen of the Bulgars ⑮ (see p110). From here the Fener ferry point will take you back to the city centre.

Back streets of the Balat district

A 90-Minute Walk from Taksim Square to the Istanbul Modern Art Museum

It was in the Pera district that Constantinople's cosmopolitan population lived and worked in the 19th century, where the embassies and palatial residences mirrored the lifestyle of Topkapı Palace, on the opposite side of the Golden Horn. Once known as the "Paris of the East", life centred on the main street of Pera, today's İstiklâl Caddesi. Even today the Avrupa Pasajı and Balık Pazar markets seem wistfully unchanged, especially when contrasted with the remarkable Pera Museum and the sophisticated Istanbul Modern Art Museum.

A Çiçek Pasajı restaurant ④

Avrupa Pasajı bazaar ⑥

Along İstiklâl Caddesi

Begin the walk in Taksim Square ① at the Independence Monument, completed by Pietro Canonica in 1928, that depicts Atatürk with his political contemporaries. Before following the vintage tram line down İstiklâl Caddesi, have a look at the octagonal stone tower, known as the Maksem ②, on the corner of Taksim Caddesi. Dating from 1832, it was once used as a reservoir – you can still see carved bird houses and remains of a fountain. It now houses an art gallery. On your right is the French Cultural Centre, while on the left, further down at No. 127 is a traditional sweet shop, Hacı Bekir, dating from 1777. Saray Muhallebicisi ③ is perfect for a coffee and one of the renowned pastries.

Market shopping

Pass Yeşilçam Sokak, the home of Turkish cinema, and at Şarabi Wine House, turn into the former flower

market, Çiçek Pasajı ④, built by Italian architect Michel Capello in 1856, and now filled with restaurants. At Stop Restaurant, veer left then right on Şahne Sokak, which forms the backbone of the Fish Market, or Balık Pazar ⑤.

Return along Sahne Sokak and stroll down the arcaded Hall of Mirrors, or Avrupa Pasajı ⑥ on the right. The Neo-Renaissance interior, with marble floors and classical statues, was once lit by gas lamps and mirrors amplified the light.

Turn right and then left onto Meşrutiyet Caddesi and follow the road around to the left with the British Consulate General ⑦ on your right. Follow this street down, past TRT (Turkish Radio and Television) and the celebrated but now faded Grand Hotel de Londres until

you reach the exquisite Pera Museum ⑧ (once the Bristol Hotel), where the philanthropic Koç family exhibits their art collection and Turkish tiles.

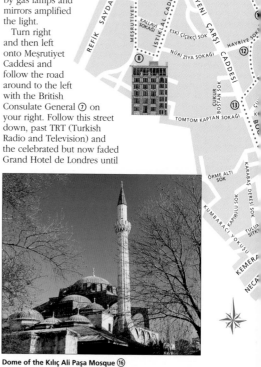

Dome of the Kılıç Ali Paşa Mosque ⑯

Historic buildings

Walk through the Odakule Arkade and turn left on to İstiklâl Caddesi. Opposite the Galatasary High School is the Old Beyoğlu Post Office ⑨. A campaign to keep it open was unsuccessful and the Baroque marble building was closed in 1998. Originally a wealthy merchant's residence, it still has an ornamental fountain in the penthouse.

Take the second right onto Tornacıbaşı Sokak,

Istanbul Modern Art Museum ⑳

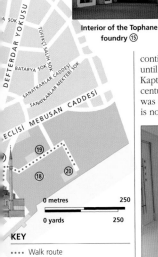

Interior of the Tophane foundry ⑮

which takes you past the Greek Orthodox school, Zografyon ⑩ on the left. In front of you is Galatasaray Hamamı ⑪, Turkish baths built in 1481 and in use ever since.

Take the steep cobbled street that descends beside the Turkish baths, Çapanoğlu Sokak, which becomes a staircase at the bottom. Turn right onto Harbiye Sokak and you will reach French Street, or Fransız Sokağı ⑫ on the left, where an elegant French ambience meets classy Beyoğlu. Enjoy lunch or a glass of wine at one of the French-style cafés.

Refreshed, continue along French Street and at the end turn right onto Boğazkesen Caddesi and continue left down the hill until you reach Tomtom Kaptan Mosque ⑬. The 17th-century fountain here, which was once a grand landmark, is now sadly neglected.

TIPS FOR WALKERS

Starting point: Taksim Square.
Length: 2.5 km (1.5 miles).
Getting there: From Sultanahmet, take the tramway to Karaköy, from where you can ride the Tünel funicular train to Tünel Square at the southern end of İstiklâl Caddesi in Beyoğlu. Travel up İstiklâl Caddesi by nostalgic tram to Taksim Square.
Stopping-off points: The fish market on Sahne Sokak has lots of cheerful eateries. French Street is ideal for an elegant drink.

Shopping and museums

Çukurcuma Caddesi and Tomtom Kaptan Sokak intersect here and both have curio shops such as Tüterler ⑭ at No. 186. At the bottom of this street on the corner of Defterdar Yokuşu is the Tophane ⑮, once an Ottoman cannon foundry.

Cross Necatibey Caddesi over the tramline to the 16th-century Kılıç Ali Paşa Mosque ⑯ *(see p106)*, one of the last masterpieces of architect Mimar Sinan. Opposite is the Tophane fountain ⑰ *(see p106)* built in 1732, which now bestows locally bottled drinking water. From here you can also see the Baroque Clock Tower ⑱.

Continue left along Salı Pazarı ⑲ with its shops, restaurants and *narghile* (pipe) smokers. A sign directs you to the Istanbul Modern Art Museum ⑳ *(see p107)*, with its collection of contemporary Turkish art.

To get back to the city centre, catch the west-bound tram which takes you directly back to Sultanahmet over the Galata Bridge.

TAKSIM MEYDANI ①

Taksim Ⓜ

İSTİKLÂL CADDESİ ②

KEY

•••• Walk route

Ⓜ Metro

0 metres 250
0 yards 250

Pera Museum ⑧

A 90-Minute Walk from Beyazit to Galata

Istanbul is a seductive mix of ancient and modern, religious and secular, and this walk will give you a flavour of both. Starting at Beyazit Tower in the city's historic quarter, the route takes you through narrow shopping streets brimming with energy, over the Galata Bridge with its stunning views of the Bosphorus, to the Beyoğlu district and trendy Tünel area, where the shops, bars and cafés lend Istanbul its chic reputation.

Striking façade of Sülemaniye Mosque

Mimar Sinan architecture

Start at Sami Onar Cadessi, from where you can see the striking Beyazit Tower ①, also visible from much of the surrounding area. It was built in 1828 as a fire watch and stands in the grounds of Istanbul University ②, which once served as the Ministry of War and whose huge, ornamental gates are a worthy photographic subject in

TIPS FOR WALKERS

Starting point: Beyazit Tower.
Length: 1 km (0.5 miles).
Getting there: Get off at Beyazit on the tramway that runs from Zeytinburnu near the airport to Eminönü, or take either the T4 or 61B bus, both of which run from Taksim to Sultanahmet.
Stopping off points: You are never far from a café or bar in Istanbul, but the obvious halfway stopping off point is at one of the numerous cafés or bars on Galata Bridge. The Tünel district also has plenty of elegant taverns (meyhanes) and restaurants if you want to end your walk with a leisurely lunch or dinner or ponder over a glass of wine.

themselves. Take a right up Prof Siddik Sokak past the stunning Sülemaniye Mosque ③ (*see pp90–91*). This breathtaking structure was completed in 1557 by the architect Mimar Sinan (*see p91*). Keep going until you reach Sifahane Sokak. Turn right into the street and, if you are feeling peckish or thirsty, you can make a pit stop at historic Dârüzziyafe restaurant ④, with its 16th-century detailing, housed in the former soup kitchens of the Sülemaniye Mosque (*see p201*).

Turn right on to Mimar Sinan Caddesi and at the bottom of the street, on the corner in front of you, is the tomb of the architect Mimar Sinan ⑤ – a poignant tribute to the great man even if its design is a little humble compared to his own creations.

Coffee and spices

Turn left onto Ismetiye Caddesi and then left again on to Uzunçarsi Caddesi. Walk to the end of the street until you reach bustling Tahtakale Caddesi, where you can jostle with the locals who come here to shop for bargains on everything from electronic goods to clothing. On the right is the Tahtakale Hamami Çarsisi ⑥, a 500-year-old Turkish bathhouse that has been renovated and turned into a shopping centre. There is also a lovely café under the domed roof where you can stop to refuel.

Turn down any of the side streets to the left and you will come to Hasircilar Caddesi ⑦, famed for its spice shops, coffee stalls and delis. Walk towards the end of the street, turn left on to Tahmis Caddesi

and you will reach Kurukahreci Mehmet Efendi ⑧, a traditional coffee shop, opened in 1871, famous for its range of blends.

Galata Bridge

Walk to Galata Bridge ⑨ for fantastic views of the city. You can either stroll across the top and watch the many amateur fishermen suspending their rods into

Fishermen hoping for a catch on Galata Bridge

Coffee machine, Kurukahveci Mehmet Efendi ⑧

KEY

• • • Walk route

🚋 Funicular stop

0 metres	250
0 yards	250

the water below in hope of a catch, or go down the steps and walk along the lower deck, where there are a number of cafés, bars and restaurants. After a leisurely moment spent taking in the breathtaking views of the Bosphorus below, continue to the bustling and aromatic Karaköy fish market ⑩, where you can buy some of the freshest, cheapest fish Istanbul has to offer.

Judaism to Islam

Walk up Harraççi Ali Sokak until you reach the Jewish Museum ⑪ on Karaköy Meydani. This 17th-century museum, once a synagogue, now contains a fascinating collection of old photographs, documents and religious objects relating to the city's Jewish population.

From here, walk up Camekan Sokak to the Gothic-looking Beyoğlu Hospital ⑫, built in 1904 as a British naval hospital. Continue until you come to the Galata Tower ⑬ *(see p105)* in Galata Square, the focal point of the district. The 360° viewing deck at the top of the tower gives the perfect vantage point from which to see almost the entire city laid out before you.

Now turn right and left on to Yüsek Kaldirim Caddesi ⑭, a steep cobblestone street lined with music shops selling just about every conceivable musical instrument you can think of,

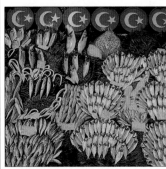

Fresh fish at the Karaköy fish market

both traditional and hi-tech. Tucked away off to the right on Galip Dede Caddesi is the Mevlevi Monastery ⑮ *(see p104)*, once home to the Whirling Dervishes.

Chic Tünel

At the top of the street, at Tünel Square, you have the option to catch the underground funicular ⑯ back down to Karaköy. The one-stop subway was opened in 1876 and is the third-oldest underground system in the world after London and New York. However do not miss the opportunity to experience this fashionable neighbourhood. Just opposite the funicular is Tünel Geçidi, an open-air passage lined with Ottoman buildings, most of which have now been turned into apartments with shops and cafés at ground level. For a refreshing iced coffee in sumptuous Viennese-style surroundings, pop into the KV restaurant ⑰, before making your way to ARtrium ⑱ to pick up some high-class antiques.

To get back to the city centre, from Tünel square you can take a 10-minute tram ride back to the Sultanahmet district. Alternatively you can head to the ferry port of Kasımpaşa and take a ferry to the Haliç Hatti stop across the water.

TRAVELLERS' NEEDS

WHERE TO STAY

Whether you feel like staying in an Ottoman palace, taking a room in a restored mansion or traditional wooden house, or even spending a night in a converted prison, you will find the hotel of your choice in Istanbul. Following a recent boom in tourism, the city's hotels and guesthouses now cater for every taste, as well as all budgets. Hotels tend to be clustered around Istanbul's main sightseeing areas. Sultanahmet contains many of the city's historic hotels, guesthouses and

Doorman at Hilton (p190)

new boutique hotels. Beyoğlu, across the Golden Horn, is a good place to look for three- and four-star hotels, including the grand old hotels of the 19th century. The hotels listed on pages 184–91 have been chosen from the best the city can offer across all price ranges. Each hotel is given a brief description and details are provided about the facilities available. Also check the website www.istanbulhotels.com on the Internet. Information on other types of accommodation is on page 183.

CHOOSING A HOTEL

Many hotels in Istanbul are rated by the Ministry of Culture and Tourism according to a star system. They range from comfortable but basic one-star hotels to five-star luxury hotels. Other types of accommodation licensed by the Ministry are the converted buildings known as Special Licence hotels. A further category is the accommodation licensed by the Greater Istanbul Municipality. These hotels provide perfectly reasonable facilities, but with less stringent standards.

Accommodation is available in most central areas of the city. The Sultanahmet district is conveniently situated within walking distance of most of the city's major sights. Many of the Special Licence hotels in this area are tucked away on residential side streets. There are guesthouses along Divanyolu Caddesi, the main through road, and on the

The luxurious Four Seasons Hotel, formerly a prison (see p187)

Lounge of the Ceylan Intercontinental Hotel in Taksim (see p189)

slopes leading down to the Sea of Marmara. There are also middle-range hotels in central Sultanahmet.

A short tram ride west from Sultanahmet are the Beyazıt, Laleli and Aksaray districts, which are packed with one-, two- and three-star hotels. The cheaper hotels here are used mostly by Central Asian and Russian traders, while many of the three-star hotels cater for package tour groups.

Beyoğlu and Taksim, the old European centre of Istanbul, are within easy reach of the best sights in the city. Both have innumerable cheap hotels that are comfortable and dependable, as well as international chain hotels.

The Asian side of Istanbul is a mainly residential area but also contains some hotels. There are also hotels in Kadıköy, which are used more by Turks than foreigners and tourists.

LUXURY HOTELS

There has been a rapid growth in the number of luxury hotels in the city, and most international chains are now represented in Istanbul. Almost all five-star hotels boast spectacular Marmara or Bosphorus views, and between them they have some of the best international restaurants in the city. All the major hotels have swimming pools and health clubs. Many of them also have Turkish baths. Conference facilities are provided, and many hotels have extensive entertainment facilities. Most can also arrange tours of Istanbul and nearby places through local companies. All hotels must provide sections or floors where smoking is forbidden. They also provide facilities for disabled visitors, arrange special activities for children (see p182) and have wireless Internet in all rooms.

◁ **Freshly fried fish sandwiches being prepared on a boat in Eminönü (see p208)**

SPECIAL LICENCE HOTELS

A number of the city's old buildings have been renovated and transformed into hotels. However, due to the nature of the buildings in which they are housed, some of these hotels cannot provide facilities such as lifts. They belong to a separate category, the Special Licence hotel, and are under private management.

The Special Licence hotels constitute some of Istanbul's most interesting and attractive hotels. They are often located in the residential streets of historic areas, and range from small, modestly priced traditional wooden houses to luxury Ottoman mansions. Special Licence hotels, whether large or small, are generally of a high standard. The authentic period decor of many of them gives even the larger ones a cosy atmosphere. A number of Special Licence hotels exist only as a result of the strenuous efforts of the Turkish Touring and Automobile Club (the TTOK, *see p245*). Led by its former crusading director, Çelik Gülersoy, it has successfully preserved the Ottoman

Latticed window of a Special Licence hotel

atmosphere of parts of the city by saving old buildings from demolition and restoring them. Its work can be seen particularly in the Special Licence hotels of Soğukçeşme Sokağı *(see p61)*. Increasingly, many of the city's boutique-style hotels are choosing not to apply for official ratings or stars. This does not, however, imply any lack of standards or amenities. In fact, these establishments are contributing to the continually rising standards of accommodation in the city. All have their own websites where you can take a virtual tour, compare prices and facilities, and make a booking.

CHEAPER HOTELS

Istanbul has plenty of cheap, comfortable accommodation which meets the standards of the Turkish Ministry of Culture and Tourism. When choosing a cheaper hotel, however, do not base your decision on the façade or lobby, which may look brand new.

One-star hotels provide the most basic facilities, but often have rooms with a private shower and toilet. Two- and three-star hotels have more comfortable rooms and usually a café or bar. Many three-star hotels offer rooms with a TV and mini-bar.

Guesthouses vary in terms of facilities. Most provide bed-linen and towels, and the better ones will have rooms with ensuite bathrooms. All should have communal cooking

Hotel roof terrace overlooking Sultanahmet

facilities. While cheaper hotels usually have central heating they are unlikely to have air conditioning, but an electric fan may be provided. Some small hotels may not provide hot water 24 hours a day.

WHAT TO EXPECT

All hotels listed in this book are comfortable and welcoming. Front desk staff usually speak English, and will be able to give information on sights and travel.

Hotel rooms in Istanbul generally have two single beds, and enough space to add a third one if need be. If you want a double bed you should make this clear when booking or checking in.

Most hotels with three or more storeys will have a lift. There may not be a lift in a Special Licence hotel, however, because of the problems of installing one in an older building. Facilities for wheelchair users are increasingly found in hotels.

Noise can be a problem even in some smart hotels, so in busy areas choose a room that doesn't face on to a main street. If you are not satisfied with your room, you can always ask for another.

Breakfast *(see p194)* is included in the price of the room and typically consists of a generous open buffet, including cold meats, fruits, cereals and yoghurt. Many larger hotels have restaurants that serve à la carte meals. Upmarket hotels have at least one dining room serving evening meals, but some of the smaller, cheaper hotels do not. It is a good idea to check when booking and confirm by email or fax.

Yeşil Ev *(see p187)*, a Special Licence hotel

Reception desk at the Istanbul Hilton *(see p190)*

PRICES AND DISCOUNTS

Hotel prices are quoted in euros and Turkish Lira (TL) and sometimes in US dollars. Prices are per room not per person. All prices usually include breakfast, and tax. Apart from top-class hotels, which have standard prices that do not change throughout the year, tariffs differ according to the season. The busy season, when hotel prices tend to be at their highest, is from April to the end of October. During the brief Christmas and New Year period, the higher summer tariffs are applied. There are no single rooms, but all hotels offer a single room rate of slightly more than half the price of a double room.

It is always worth attempting to bargain with hotels, but do not expect to get a discount. For longer stays of a week or more you may be able to get a reduction. Some hotels also offer discounts for Internet bookings, cash payments, or out-of-season stays. However, do not expect a room with any kind of a view if you have got it at a discount.

BOOKING A ROOM

While you will always be able to find a room of a reasonable standard, it is advisable to book in advance for the best hotels or those of your choice during the busy season. You can book any hotel listed in this guide directly, by telephone, fax and e-mail. Many hotels also have their own website registration forms. You may be asked to give your credit card details, which will guarantee your reservation. If you cannot find a place in any of the hotels that fall in your preferred price range, try one of the established travel companies based in Istanbul, such as **Gazella Travel Designer**, **Meptur**, **Plan Tours** *(see p228)* or **Vip Tourism**. If you arrive without having reserved a room, the tourist information offices *(see p229)* in the airport, Sirkeci Station, Sultanahmet Square or Karaköy International Maritime Terminal will help you find a hotel, but they will not make a reservation for you.

Lounge area of the Empress Zoe *(see p185)*

CHECKING OUT AND PAYING

Guests are expected to check out by midday, but hotels will usually keep luggage for collection later. All hotels accept the major credit cards, as well as Turkish lira and other currencies. VAT is always included in the room price. It is usual to leave a few dollars, or its equivalent, in the room for the cleaner, and to give a tip to the receptionist to be divided among the staff. Phone calls and mini-bar drinks can add to the size of your bill.

CHILDREN

Children up to six years old are often not charged for rooms, and pay 50% until 12 years old. It is possible to negotiate a discount for older children who share a room with their parents. Most hotels also have cots for babies.

Some hotels arrange special entertainment for children. The Swissôtel *(see p190)* offers a weekend package.

HOSTELS

For those on a tight budget, Istanbul has a number of inexpensive hostels, mostly in the Sultanahmet area. A popular hostel in Istanbul is the **Sultan Hostel**. This hostel is right in the heart of the Sultanahmet district on Akbıyık Caddesi, close to Haghia Sophia, Topkapı Palace and the Grand Bazaar. The hostel's mission is to provide accommodation that is comfortable, stylish,

Double room in the Special Licence Kariye Hotel *(see p189)*

Guests at a youth hostel in Istanbul

convenient and affordable, which is great for younger and more independent travellers on a restricted budget. It offers a variety of dormitory rooms with 6, 18 and 26 beds, as well as single, double and triple rooms, which are less crowded. The Sultan is a member of the International Youth Hostel Federation (IYHF) and offers a discount for members. The hostel has a wealth of facilities, including a common room and library, a barbecue area, security lockers, a 24-hour reception, a luggage store and free Internet access. There is also a travel agent who can help guests with travel arrangements and a currency exchange. On the same street, the **Orient Hostel** is a modern youth hostel with excellent facilities, including a rooftop café, a bar and a safe. In the evening, a programme of entertainment, including belly dancing, is offered.

The tour operator Gençtur (see p229) is also affiliated to the IYHF and can provide detailed information on additional hostels in the city.

CAMPING

Camping and caravanning in Turkey have steadily gained popularity in recent years. There is an ever-increasing variety of excellent camping places with self-catering facilities open in the summer season, which lasts from May until October. **Londra Kamping** is open throughout the year. It has washing and cooking facilities, a fast-food restaurant, bar, pool table and football pitch. As well as providing camping facilities, it also has two-room bungalows for rent. On the Black Sea

coast but situated to the east of the Bosphorus is another equally attractive and popular camp site, the **Kumbaba Moteli**, which is situated 1.2 miles (2 km) outside the resort of Şile (see p158). This site is open between May and September, and the amenities it has to offer include hot showers and cooking facilities.

For further details, contact the **Turkish Camping and Caravanning Association**, which is helpful and informative. The association also has a website with comprehensive listings of sites throughout the country.

View over Dolmabahçe Mosque from the Swissôtel (see p190)

SELF-CATERING

Istanbul has a number of apartment hotels located near various central business and residential districts, providing fully furnished apartments for those who prefer more homely surroundings. The **Akmerkez Residence Apart Hotel**, which is mostly used by business-men, is in the upmarket Akmerkez shopping mall in Etiler (see p211). Its luxuriously decorated flats have air-conditioning and all domestic appliances. The **Entes Apart Hotel** has compact modern apartments.

Global real estate franchises like **Century 21** and **Remax** can assist in finding long- or short-term rental accommodation.

DIRECTORY

TRAVEL AGENTS

Gazella Travel Designer
Cumhuriyet Cad Babil Sok 2, Elemdağ.
Tel (0212) 233 15 98.
www.gazella.com

Meptur
Büyükdere Cad 26, Mecidiyeköy.
Tel (0212) 275 02 50.
www.meptur.com.tr

Vip Tourism
Tel (0212) 241 65 14.
www.viptourism.com.tr

YOUTH HOSTELS

Orient Hostel
Akbıyık Cad 13, Sultanahmet.
Map 3 E5 (5 E5).
Tel (0212) 517 94 93.
www.orienthostel.com

Sultan Hostel
Akbıyık Cad 21, Sultanahmet.
Map 3 E5 (5 E5).
Tel (0212) 516 92 60.
www.sultanhostel.com

CAMPING

Kumbaba Moteli
Şile. *Tel* (0216) 711 50 38.
Fax (0216) 711 48 51.

Londra Kamping
Londra Asfaltı, Bakırköy.
Tel (0212) 560 42 00.
Fax (0212) 559 34 38.

Turkish Camping and Caravanning Association
Feliz Sok, 52 Kartaltepe Mah, Bakırköy.
Tel (0212) 662 46 15.
www.kampkaravan.org

SELF-CATERING

Akmerkez Residence
Akmerkez Shopping & Business Centre, Etiler.
Tel (0212) 282 01 20.
www.akmerkez.com.tr

Century 21
Topçular Kışla Cad 5, Rami-Eyüp.
Tel (0212) 493 26 00.
www.century21.com.tr

Entes Apart Hotel
İpek Sok 19, Taksim. **Map** 7 E4.
Tel (0212) 293 22 08.
www.entesapart.com

Remax
Tel (0212) 232 48 20.
www.remax.com.tr

Choosing a Hotel

The hotels in this guide have been selected across a wide range for their good value, facilities and location. These listings highlight some of the factors that may influence your choice. Hotels are listed by area, beginning with Seraglio Point. All the entries are alphabetical within each price category.

PRICE CATEGORIES
For a standard double room per night, inclusive of breakfast, service charges and any additional taxes.

ⓢ under US$100
ⓢⓢ US$100–$150
ⓢⓢⓢ US$150–$200
ⓢⓢⓢⓢ US$200–$300
ⓢⓢⓢⓢⓢ Over US$300

SERAGLIO POINT

Ayasofya Konakları   ⓢⓢⓢ

Soğukçeşme Sokak, Sultanahmet, 34122 **Tel** *(0212) 513 36 60* **Fax** *(0212) 513 43 93* **Rooms** 64 **Map** 3 E4 (5 F3)

Nine restored wooden houses comprise this charming accommodation on the cobbled street behind Haghia Sophia. They have beautiful names such as Jasmine, Honeysuckle and Rose and are painted in pastel colours. The rooms are elegant and decorated with antiques. Booking is essential. **www.ayasofyapensions.com**

Kybele Hotel   ⓢⓢⓢ

Yeribatan Caddesi 35, 34410 **Tel** *(0212) 511 77 66* **Fax** *(0212) 513 43 93* **Rooms** 16   **Map** 3 E4 (5 E3)

This tiny, multi-storied hotel is located in the heart of the tourist area. The antiques and craft items of every description create a homely and friendly atmosphere. A wonderful breakfast is served in the garden in summer and in one of the ornate rooms in winter. The Kybele is a firm favourite with many visitors. **www.kybelehotel.com**

SULTANAHMET

Antea   ⓢ

Piyerloti Caddesi 21, Çemberlitaş, 34400 **Tel** *(0212) 638 11 21* **Fax** *(0212) 517 79 49* **Rooms** 42   **Map** 3 D4 (4 C4)

The Antea is a peaceful hotel on a side street off the main tourist area of Sultanahmet. Like its neighbours, this is a restored building. Rooms are modern and attractively furnished. The restaurant serves Turkish and international dishes. A perfect place to relax after a day of sightseeing and shopping. **www.anteahotel.com**

Apricot   ⓢ

Amiraltafdil Sok 18, Sultanahmet, 34122 **Tel** *(0212) 638 16 58* **Fax** *(0212) 458 35 74* **Rooms** 6   **Map** 3 E5 (5 E5)

This is such a pretty little hotel and it has been restored to a far better state than the original Ottoman building. It boasts comfortable beds, well-furnished rooms and polished hard-wood floors. Internet access and many other amenities are also available. Meals (except breakfast) are served by arrangement. **www.apricothotel.com**

Hotel Mina   ⓢ

Piyerloti Caddesi, Dostluk Urdu Sokak 6, Sultanahmet, 34122 **Tel** *(0212) 458 28 00* **Rooms** 46   **Map** 3 D4 (4 C4)

Hotel Mina is tucked away in the backstreets protected from the hustle of the main tourist area. The owners are very welcoming and friendly. Rooms are comfortable and well furnished, although they are not too ornate or fussy. This is a comfortable base within walking distance of all the main attractions of Sultanahmet. **www.minahotel.com.tr**

Hotel Sultanahmet   ⓢ

Divanyolu Cad 20, Sultanahmet, 34122 **Tel** *(0212) 527 02 39* **Fax** *(0212) 512 11 33* **Rooms** 20   **Map** 3 D4 (5 D5)

A well-located budget hotel close to all the sights. It has few frills but is clean and neat, and adequately furnished. There is a pretty terrace with a decent view and evening meals and snacks are served here. The hotel is well run and staff are always hospitable. **www.hotelsultanahmet.com**

Orient Hostel   ⓢ

Akbıyık Caddesi 13, Sultanahmet, 34400 **Tel** *(0212) 517 94 93* **Fax** *(0212) 518 38 94* **Rooms** 15 **Map** 3 E5 (5 E5)

This is the cheapest and most cheerful place to stay in Sultanahmet making it the proverbial backpackers' paradise. Rooms are sparse and many resemble a dormitory with three or four beds. Forget about chandeliers and en suite bathrooms, but there is always hot water and other weary, friendly wanderers. **www.orienthostel.com**

Şebnem   ⓢ

Adliye Sokak 1, Sultanahmet, 34122 **Tel** *(0212) 517 66 23* **Fax** *(0212) 638 10 56* **Rooms** 15   **Map** 3 E4 (5 F4)

This small but welcoming guesthouse, is more like a doll's house. It has pretty, colourful rooms and serviceable wooden furniture. There is a panoramic roof terrace where you can look out at the main buildings of Sultanahmet and across the Bosphorus and Sea of Marmara. **www.sebnemhotel.net**

Key to Symbols *see back cover flap*

Sidera

🏃📧　　　　　　Ⓢ

Kadirga Meydani, Dönüş Sok 14, Sultanahmet **Tel** *(0212) 638 34 60* **Fax** *(0212) 518 72 62* **Rooms** *18* **Map** *2 C5 (4 B5)*

A converted 19th-century wooden house, the Sidera is painted a distinctive green and is more like a family home. Although small, it offers adequate facilities. Rooms can be a bit dark but the location, on a narrow street lined with other Ottoman-style wooden houses, is part of its nostalgic charm. **www.hotelsiderapalace.com**

Ararat

🏃📧　　　　　　ⓈⓈ

Torun Sokak 3, Sultanahmet, 34122 **Tel** *(0212) 458 20 31* **Fax** *(0212) 518 52 41* **Rooms** *12* 　　**Map** *3 E5 (5 E5)*

An unusual and highly individualistic family-run hotel. Each room has its own theme with one-of-a-kind decor. The owner is always available to offer advice and to attend to details. The hotel is close to the Blue Mosque and has splendid views across the Sea of Marmara from the top floor terrace. **www.ararathotel.com**

Aziyade

🍽♨🏃📧　　　　ⓈⓈ

Piyerloti Caddesi 62, Çemberlitaş, 34490 **Tel** *(0212) 638 22 00* **Fax** *(0212) 518 50 65* **Rooms** *105* **Map** *3 D4 (4 B4)*

Aziyade has some lovely features that one might expect to find at a more luxurious level. The small swimming pool on the roof is unique in the area. Rooms are elegant and tastefully decorated. The café is reminiscent of the Fruit Room in the Harem at Topkapı Palace *(see p58)*. **www.aziyadehotel.com**

Dersaadet

📺🏃📧🅿　　　　ⓈⓈ

Küçük Ayasofya Caddesi, Kapıağası Sokak 5, 34122 **Tel** *(0212) 458 07 60/61* **Rooms** *17* 　　**Map** *3 E5 (5 D5)*

This impeccable hotel is a local pioneer in renovation. It has been authentically designed and furnished by traditional artisans. Small details abound and the owner is always around to ensure your stay is memorable. The sumptuous Sultan's Penthouse suite has wonderful views from the balcony. **www.hoteldersaadet.com**

Empress Zoe

📺🍽🏃📧　　　　ⓈⓈ

Akbıyık Cad, Adliye Sokak 10, 34122 **Tel** *(0212) 518 25 04* **Fax** *(0212) 518 56 99* **Rooms** *25* 　　**Map** *3 E4 (5 F4)*

It is claimed that Empress Zoe actually lived here. The two buildings have been restored to an exceptionally high standard of taste and design with an abundance of spacious suites. The garden is idyllic and contains the remains of a bath house built in 1483. **www.emzoe.com**

Historia

🏃📧　　　　　　ⓈⓈ

Amiral Tafdil Sokak 23, 34122 **Tel** *(0212) 517 74 72* **Fax** *(0212) 516 81 69* **Rooms** *27* 　　**Map** *3 E5 (5 F5)*

This attractive wooden hotel has wonderful sea views from the rooftop terrace. Most rooms tend to be quite basic, but they are well decorated and comfortable. Several also have balconies that overlook the back garden. The breakfast patio is secluded and shaded. **www.historiahotel.com**

Hotel Nena

📺🍽🏃📧　　　　ⓈⓈ

Binbirdirek Mahallesi, Klodfarer Caddesi 8–10, 34122 **Tel** *(0212) 516 52 64* **Rooms** *29* 　　**Map** *3 D4 (5 D4)*

Hotel Nena has a Byzantine atmosphere and is richly decorated and very comfortable. Some rooms have balconies with classic sea and mosque vistas. The beautiful conservatory basks in sun and has wrought-iron and glass furniture as well as flourishing tropical greenery. **www.istanbulhotelnena.com**

Nomade

🍽🏃📧　　　　　ⓈⓈ

Ticarethane Sokak 15, Çağaloğlu, 34122 **Tel** *(0212) 513 81 72* **Fax** *(0212) 513 24 04* **Rooms** *16* **Map** *3 E4 (5 D3)*

One of the oldest houses in this area, the Nomade has undergone a wonderful and extensive renovation. The owners have added appealing designer touches to the individually designed bedrooms and bathrooms. Meals and afternoon drinks are served on the rooftop terrace. **www.hotelnomade.com**

Sarı Konak

🏃📧　　　　　　ⓈⓈ

Mimar Mehmet Ağa Caddesi 42–46, Sultanahmet, 34122 **Tel** *(0212) 638 62 58* **Rooms** *17* 　　**Map** *3 E5 (5 E5)*

Sarı means "yellow" in Turkish and this delightful wooden house is easily identifiable by its distinctive hue. It has a charming patio, marble fountain and latticed balconies. Rooms are tastefully decorated and the suites have high-speed Internet access. **www.istanbulhotelsarikonak.com**

Sarnıç

🏃📧🅿　　　　　ⓈⓈ

Küçük Ayasofya Caddesi 26, 34122 **Tel** *(0212) 518 23 23* **Fax** *(0212) 518 24 14* **Rooms** *21* 　　**Map** *3 D5 (5 D5)*

Sarnıç is a clean and tidy place with a homely feel. It is painted a soft pink colour and the building is surrounded by others of the same history and heritage. It has well decorated rooms and a rooftop restaurant and bar area. Useful extras include a laundry service, baby-sitting and valet parking. **www.sarnichotel.com**

Spectra Hotel

📺🏃📧　　　　　ⓈⓈ

Şehit Mehmetpaşa Yok 2, Sultanahmet, 34122 **Tel** *(0212) 516 35 46* **Rooms** *19* 　　**Map** *3 D5 (5 D5)*

One of the assets of this hotel is the owner, a retired archaeologist, who is a source of wisdom on many aspects of local life. The rooms are comfortable and well-appointed. Breakfast is served on the terrace with grand views of the Blue Mosque. Guests have free Internet access. The Spectra is handy to all central sights. **www.hotelspectra.com**

Alzer

📺🍽🏃📧　　　　ⓈⓈⓈ

At Meydanı 72, Sultanahmet, 34122 **Tel** *(0212) 516 62 62/63* **Fax** *(0212) 516 00 00* **Rooms** *22* **Map** *3 D4 (5 D4)*

This renovated town house with beautifully appointed and furnished rooms has plenty of definitive touches. In the summer tables are available at street level, but the greatest attraction is the roof restaurant. A cheerful bijou hotel with attentive service. **www.alzerhotel.com**

Avicenna

Amiral Tafdil Sokak 31–33, 34122 **Tel** *(0212) 517 05 50-54* **Fax** *(0212) 516 65 55* **Rooms** *50*   **Map** *3 E5 (5 E5)*

Occupying two handsomely renovated Ottoman buildings, this conveniently located mid-range hotel has luxurious interior furnishings, including rich textiles, carpets and traditional wooden floors. Try to reserve rooms on the attic floors for panoramic sea views. **www.avicennahotel.com**

Citadel

Kennedy Caddesi, Sahil Yolu 32, Ahırkapı, 34122 **Tel** *(0212) 516 23 13* **Rooms** *31*   **Map** *3 E5 (5 F5)*

Now under the umbrella of the Best Western Group, the dusty pink Citadel Hotel occupies a large stone building under the city walls. Rooms are small but pleasantly furnished with all the essentials. Some rooms look directly onto the sea. **www.citadelhotel.com**

Hotel Alp Guest House

Akbıyık Caddesi, Adliye Sokak 4, Sultanahmet, 34122 **Tel** *(0212) 517 70 67* **Rooms** *14*   **Map** *3 E4 (5 F4)*

There are wonderful views from the roof terrace of this hotel hidden away behind the Blue Mosque. It is known as a friendly place to stay with excellent service. The hotel has been extensively renovated to a high standard, with traditional furnishings in the bedrooms. **www.alpguesthouse.com**

İbrahim Paşa

Terzihane Sokak 5, Sultanahmet, 34122 **Tel** *(0212) 518 03 94* **Fax** *(0212) 518 44 57* **Rooms** *16* **Map** *3 D4 (5 D4)*

This charming stone-built hotel is located opposite the Museum of Turkish and Islamic Arts *(see p77)*. Rooms are individually furnished and, along with the rooftop terrace, are stylish and unique. The decor successfully blends Art Deco with traditional Turkish influences. **www.ibrahimpasha.com**

Mavi Ev

Dalbastı Sokak 14, Sultanahmet, 34122 **Tel** *(0212) 638 90 10* **Fax** *(0212) 638 90 17* **Rooms** *27* **Map** *3 E5 (5 E5)*

Under the same polished management as the Pudding Shop, this is a distinctive Wedgwood blue *konak* (wooden mansion) restored in period style in the heart of Sultanahmet. It is peaceful and has a leafy garden and acclaimed rooftop restaurant. The views over the Sea of Marmara are magnificent. **www.bluehouse.com.tr**

Pierre Loti

Piyerloti Caddesi 5, Çemberlitaş, 34122 **Tel** *(0212) 518 57 00* **Fax** *(0212) 516 18 86* **Rooms** *38* **Map** *3 D4 (4 C4)*

Named after a Romantic novelist who lived in Istanbul, this was one of the first hotels in the area to be renovated to a high standard. It is in the thick of things on the main road but the summer garden and glassed-in café give you a fine view of the world going by. Rooms are small but wonderfully comfortable. **www.pierrelotihotel.com**

Side Hotel and Pension

Utangaç Sokak 20, Sultanahmet, 34122 **Tel** *(0212) 517 66 23* **Fax** *(0212) 638 10 56* **Rooms** *36*   **Map** *3 E4*

This family run establishment combines a pension for budget-conscious guests and also a ritzier hotel. Pension prices are cheaper and facilities are fewer, with no air conditioning in rooms. The hotel is comfortable and some rooms have private Jacuzzis available as an extra. **www.sidehotel.com**

Valide Sultan Konağı

Kutlugün Sokak 1, Sultanahmet, 34122 **Tel** *(0212) 638 06 00* **Fax** *(0212) 638 07 05* **Rooms** *17* **Map** *3 E4 (5 F4)*

A long-term favourite with visitors to Istanbul, the Valide Sultan's proximity to the Topkapı Palace is an advantage. It has kept up appearances, like its palatial neighbour. The rooms have been individually decorated and, although small, are comfortable. There is a glorious summer terrace with good views. **www.hotelvalidesultan.com**

Armada

Ahır Kapı Sokak 24, Sultanahmet, 34122 **Tel** *(0212) 455 44 55* **Fax** *(0212) 455 44 99* **Rooms** *110* **Map** *3 E5 (5 E5)*

Possibly one of Istanbul's best kept secrets, this hotel is dignified and yet immensely friendly. The rooms are elegantly decorated in soothing colours and the restaurant is highly recommended. There is great live music and regular tango evenings are held here. **www.armadahotel.com.tr**

Hotel Sultanahmet Palace

Torun Sokak 19, Sultanahmet, 34122 **Tel** *(0212) 458 04 60* **Fax** *(0212) 518 62 24* **Rooms** *36*   **Map** *3 E5 (5 E5)*

This is the ideal place to spoil yourself. Less authentically refurbished than some other establishments, it is, nevertheless, a refined hotel that deserves its palace title. The domes of the Blue Mosque rise right beside you. The garden is perfect and the service is subtle and polished. **www.sultanahmetpalace.com**

Kalyon

Sahil Yolu, Cankurtaran, 34122 **Tel** *(0212) 517 44 00* **Fax** *(0212) 638 11 11* **Rooms** *112*   **Map** *3 E5 (5 F5)*

The Kalyon is not just a tourist hotel; locals use it and it is a first-rate business hotel. Its position away from the centre of Sultanahmet means that it is quiet and it faces directly onto the Sea of Marmara. Rooms are beautifully furnished to a superb standard. The restaurant is one of the most underrated in the city. **www.kalyon.com**

Seven Hills

Tevkifhane Sokak 8/A, Sultanahmet, 34122 **Tel** *(0212) 516 94 97* **Fax** *(0212) 517 10 85* **Rooms** *20*   **Map** *3 E5 (5 D5)*

This is a hotel that goes out of its way to ensure your stay exceeds expectations. Rooms are beautifully decorated and suites are spacious with private Jacuzzis and fitness facilities in each room. Incredible views along with a first-class restaurant *(see p198)* are found on the terrace. **www.hotelsevenhills.com**

Yeşil Ev

⬜ 🍴 🧍 📧 $$$$$

Kabasakal Sokak 5, Sultanahmet, 34122 **Tel** *(0212) 517 67 85* **Fax** *(0212) 517 67 80* **Rooms** *19* **Map** *3 E4 (5 E4)*

Yeşil Ev (Green House) is a local landmark that typifies the spirit of Ottoman luxury. Rooms are furnished with antiques, one even has its own Turkish bath, and the service is impeccable. There is a secluded garden and an outstanding restaurant. **www.yesilev.com.tr**

Eresin Crown

⬜ 🍴 🏊 🧍 🍴 📧 🅿️ $$$$$

Küçük Ayasofya Caddesi 40, Sultanahmet, 34122 **Tel** *(0212) 639 44 28* **Rooms** *60*   **Map** *3 D5 (5 D5)*

This highly rated, luxury hotel stands on the site of what was once the Great Palace *(see p82)*. Some of the extraordinary Byzantine treasures and heritage mosaics unearthed here are on display in the hotel's own museum. There are several bars and dining options. The Eresin Crown is in a class of its own. **www.eresincrown.com.tr**

Four Seasons

⬜ 🍴 🏊 🧍 🍴 📧 $$$$$

Tevkifhane Sokak 1, Sultanahmet, 34110 **Tel** *(0212) 638 82 00* **Fax** *(0212) 638 82 10* **Rooms** *65* **Map** *3 E4 (5 F4)*

Built as a prison for dissident writers in 1917, the Four Seasons has been restored to a Neo-Classical haven of luxury. Every room has a theme that blends Turkish traditions with contemporary comfort. It is ideally situated a short distance from the main Sultanahmet sights. **www.fourseasons.com/istanbul**

THE BAZAAR QUARTER

Antik Hotel

🍴 🧍 📧 $$$

Ordu Cad, Darphane Sok 10, Beyazıt, 34130 **Tel** *(0212) 638 58 58* **Fax** *(0212) 638 58 65* **Rooms** *96* **Map** *2 C4 (4 A3)*

This comfortable hotel built around a 1,500-year-old water cistern, has fine views over the Sea of Marmara. It also has an acclaimed pub, wine bar and unusual restaurant. The cistern itself has been converted into a subterranean night club. The Antik is a swinging and lively hotel that makes all ages feel at home. **www.antikhotel.com**

Bulvar Palas

⬜ 🍴 🏊 🧍 🍴 📧 $$$

Atatürk Bul 152, Saraçhane, 34470 **Tel** *(0212) 528 58 81* **Fax** *(0212) 528 60 81* **Rooms** *70*   **Map** *2 A3*

A makeover has given this cheerful hotel a pleasant atmosphere. The beauty treatment and fitness centre complement the hairdressing salon and Turkish bath. The decor is traditional, but it is an excellent hotel at a fair price. The large restaurant serves some good Turkish dishes. **www.hotelbulvarpalas.com**

President

⬜ 🍴 🧍 📧 $$$

Tiyatro Caddesi 25, Beyazıt, 34126 **Tel** *(0212) 516 69 80* **Fax** *(0212) 516 69 98* **Rooms** *204*   **Map** *2 C4 (4 A4)*

Part of the Best Western chain, the President has an excellent reputation. It is located in the heart of the city with well appointed rooms and good service. Wireless Internet is available in the reception area and in many rooms. The Turkish nights and belly-dancing evenings are legendary. **www.thepresidenthotel.com**

BEYOĞLU

Galata Residence Camondo Apart Hotel

🍴 $

Felek Sokak 2, Beyoğlu, 34420 **Tel** *(0212) 292 48 41* **Fax** *(0212) 244 23 23* **Rooms** *15*   **Map** *7 D5*

Set in a 19th-century mansion that was once owned by the famous Camondo banking family, these fully equipped apartments are large and comfortable, if a bit dated. They are centrally located, but off the main tourist trail. There is a Greek restaurant upstairs and an onsite bar too. **www.galataresidence.com**

Hotel the Pera Hill

⬜ 🧍 📧 $

Meşrutiyet Caddesi 95, Beyoğlu, 34430 **Tel** *(0212) 245 66 06* **Fax** *(0212) 245 66 42* **Rooms** *35*   **Map** *7 D4*

In the cultural heart of Beyoğlu and housed in a solid stone building this hotel was once the Libyan consulate. It is a modest but hugely comfortable establishment and well known as an ideally situated budget hotel. Rooms are plain but are kept meticulously clean. **www.hoteltheperahill.com**

La Casa di Maria Pia

$

Yeni Çarşi Caddesi 37, Galatasaray, 34425 **Tel** *(0541) 624 54 62* **Rooms** *6*   **Map** *7 D4*

Tucked away on a quiet side street behind a colourful doorway adorned with hanging plants, these comfortable furnished apartments allow up to five people per unit to live like locals in the old bohemian area of Pera. There are plenty of local grocery shops and restaurants nearby. The friendly owner is on hand in the downstairs apartment.

Galata Antique Hotel

🧍 📧 $$

Meşrutiyet Caddesi 119, Tünel, 34430 **Tel** *(0212) 245 59 44* **Fax** *(0212) 245 59 47* **Rooms** *23*   **Map** *7 D5*

This small, family-run boutique hotel is located in an Ottoman-French mansion designed by the famous architect Alexandre Vallaury. It has a lot of character and is in an excellent location for exploring Beyoğlu, although some rooms can be noisy. Helpful staff can arrange day trips and tours. **www.galataantiquehotel.com**

Hotel La Villa
$$$

Topçu Caddesi 12, Taksim, 80090 **Tel** *(0212) 256 56 26/27* **Fax** *(0212) 297 53 28* **Rooms** *28*   **Map** *7 E3*

La Villa is a small, low-cost but attractive hotel in the shadow of many prestigious neighbours. It has all the things one would expect from a modern hotel, including Internet access and 24-hour room service. The hotel arranges day trips and Turkish evenings for guests. **www.boutiquehotellavilla.com**

Hotel Villa Zurich
$$$

Akarsu Yokuşu 44/6, Cihangir, 34437 **Tel** *(0212) 293 06 04* **Fax** *(0212) 249 02 32* **Rooms** *42*   **Map** *7 E5*

In the heart of the popular Cihangir neighbourhood, an area filled with cafés, galleries, restaurants and antique shops, Villa Zurich offers spacious, well-furnished rooms with free Internet access. Breakfast is served with a Bosphorus view on the terrace, which becomes a lively bar at night. **www.hotelvillazurich.com**

House Hotel Galatasaray
$$$

Bostanbasi Caddesi 19, Çukurcuma, 34440 **Tel** *(0212) 244 34 00* **Fax** *(0212) 245 23 07* **Rooms** *20*   **Map** *7 E4*

Set amid the picturesque, winding streets of Çukurcuma, one of Istanbul's top districts for antique shops, this hotel offers stylish, luxurious rooms at reasonable prices. The 1890s building has been lovingly restored by the people behind the popular House Café restaurants *(see p205)*. **www.thehouse-hotels.com**

Santa Ottoman Boutique Hotel
$$$

Zambak Sokak 1, Taksim, 34500 **Tel** *(0212) 252 28 78* **Fax** *(0212) 252 28 89* **Rooms** *18*   **Map** *7 E3*

Comfortable, refurbished rooms and friendly, eager-to-please staff make this boutique hotel a welcoming oasis in the middle of the Taksim Square action (some rooms can be noisy at night on weekends). Its La Boheme Cafe serves French, Turkish and other dishes in a brasserie-inspired atmosphere. **www.santaottomanboutiquehotel.com**

Seminal
$$$

Şehit Muhtar Caddesi 25, Taksim, 80090 **Tel** *(0212) 297 34 34* **Fax** *(0212) 297 28 18* **Rooms** *88*   **Map** *7 E3*

This is an agreeable place to stay with friendly staff, and sights and shops nearby. There is a small fitness room, a room for disabled guests and also a fine swimming pool. The ten rooms all have sea views. This is an established hotel with a good reputation. **www.seminalotel.com**

Suite Home Cihangir
$$$

Pürtelaş Sokak 12, Taksim, 34433 **Tel** *(0212) 243 31 01* **Fax** *(0212) 243 29 05* **Rooms** *13*   **Map** *7 E4*

With two Taksim locations, one of which is right on bustling İstiklâl Caddesi, these spacious condo units make a suitable home away from home. Rooms have wireless Internet and guests staying in either building can use the sauna and fitness facilities at Suite Home Cihangir. Parking is available for an extra fee. **www.istanbulsuite.com**

Taxim Hill
$$$

Sıraselviler Caddesi 5, Taksim, 80090 **Tel** *(0212) 334 85 00* **Fax** *(0212) 334 85 98* **Rooms** *58*   **Map** *7 E4*

A distinctive landmark on the corner of Taksim's main square, the Hill is a great place to stay with excellent business facilities, Jacuzzis and a well-equipped health club. Rooms are attractively decorated and comfortable, and some have a view over the Bosphorus. **www.taximhill.com.tr**

Lamartine
$$$

Lamartin Caddesi 25, Taksim, 80090 **Tel** *(0212) 254 62 70* **Fax** *(0212) 256 27 76* **Rooms** *67*   **Map** *7 E5*

Named after the French poet who once visited Istanbul, Lamartine is close to all the sights in Taksim, shopping outlets and a short walk to the lively cultural district of Beyoğlu. The hotel offers a consistently reliable standard of comfort at an affordable price. **www.lamartinehotel.com**

Tomtom Suites
$$$$

Tomtom Kaptan Sokak 18, Beyoğlu, 34413 **Tel** *(0212) 292 49 49* **Fax** *(0212) 292 42 30* **Rooms** *20*   **Map** *7 D5*

Set inside a beautiful historical building on a quiet street, this hidden gem draws high marks for the excellent service given by helpful staff, its modern, well-appointed rooms and the wonderful terrace views. Some rooms have Jacuzzi tubs and balconies. There's a top-notch restaurant and a terrace bar. **www.tomtomsuites.com**

Central Palace
$$$$

Lamartin Caddesi 18, Taksim, 34437 **Tel** *(0212) 313 40 40* **Fax** *(0212) 313 40 39* **Rooms** *54*   **Map** *7 E3*

Late Ottoman style is combined with modern luxuries at this eminent hotel. The rooms are luxurious and supremely comfortable, and there is an excellent healthfood restaurant. No alcohol is sold or served but you can bring your own to rooms. The Central Palace is highly recommended. **www.thecentralpalace.com**

Germir Palas
$$$$

Cumhuriyet Caddesi 7, Taksim, 34437 **Tel** *(0212) 361 11 10* **Fax** *(0212) 361 10 70* **Rooms** *49*   **Map** *7 E3*

It is easy to miss the entrance to this mid-town gem on the main street. The lobby and bars are plush, and the rooms are well decorated with interesting textiles. The terrace restaurant is great in summer, with fine views over the Bosphorous. The street-level Vanilla Café is very stylish. **www.germirpalas.com**

Marmara Pera
$$$$

Meşrutiyet Caddesi, Tepebaşı, 34437 **Tel** *(0212) 251 46 46* **Fax** *(0212) 249 80 33* **Rooms** *200*   **Map** *7 D5*

This luxury hotel provides every service you could ever need and 360-degree views of the city. Excellent for business travellers, with wireless Internet access available in every room. There is an interesting mural in the lobby, along with plenty of seating. **www.themarmarahotels.com**

Key to Price Guide *see p184* **Key to Symbols** *see back cover flap*

Witt Istanbul Suites
⬛⬛ $$$$

Defterdar Yokuşu 26, Cihangir, 34433 **Tel** *(0212) 393 79 00* **Fax** *(0212) 310 24 94* **Rooms** *15*   **Map** *7 E5*

The luxury suites here are large, well-appointed and equipped with kitchenettes. Some have terraces and sea views. The location is quiet but close to Tophane tram stop, which offers easy access to the sights of Sultanahmet. The heart of the Cihangir neighbourhood is a short walk away. Free parking nearby. **www.wittistanbul.com**

Ceylan Intercontinental
⬛⬛⬛⬛⬛⬛⬛ $$$$$

Asker Ocağı Caddesi 1, Taksim, 34435 **Tel** *(0212) 368 44 44* **Fax** *(0212) 368 44 99* **Rooms** *390*   **Map** *7 F3*

This is one of the top hotels in Istanbul with first-class facilities for groups, visitors and business travellers. High-profile guests welcome the security barriers at the exit and entrance. The tea lounge is an afternoon tradition and harp music is played here. The lively City Lights bar is innovative. **www.interconti.com.tr**

Marmara Taksim
⬛⬛⬛⬛⬛⬛⬛ $$$$$

Taksim Meydanı, Taksim, 34437 **Tel** *(212) 251 46 96* **Fax** *(0212) 244 05 09* **Rooms** *458*   **Map** *7 E4*

The rooms here are extremely comfortable and beautifully decorated. The staff are always helpful and happy. The Panorama restaurant on the roof is a prestigious eating spot, while the trendy Kitchenette café on the ground floor is one of Istanbul's favourite meeting places. **www.themarmarahotels.com**

Pera Palas
⬛⬛⬛⬛⬛ $$$$$

Meşrutiyet Caddesi 52, Tepebaşı, 34430 **Tel** *(0212) 222 80 90* **Fax** *(0212) 222 81 79* **Rooms** *145*   **Map** *7 D5*

A legendary Istanbul landmark *(see p104)*, this hotel caters to the famous. Agatha Christie stayed here and her room has been maintained exactly as it was. Luxury can be found elsewhere but if mystery and history appeal, you will love the atmosphere and original trappings. **www.perapalace.com**

GREATER ISTANBUL

Hush Hostel
⬛ $

Miralay Nazım Sokak 20, Kadıköy, 34710 **Tel** *(0216) 330 91 88* **Rooms** *13*

This trendy hostel in a renovated Ottoman house offers a fun place to stay on a small budget. There's a choice of dormitory or private rooms, and guests can make use of the relaxing garden, kitchen and lounge with TV, DVD player and musical instruments. There is an onsite art gallery and plenty to do nearby. **www.hushhostelistanbul.com**

Büyük Ada Princess
⬛⬛⬛⬛ $$

23 Nisan Caddesi, Büyük Ada **Tel** *(0216) 382 16 28* **Fax** *(0216) 382 19 49* **Rooms** *24*

Established in 1895, the Princess is an elegant Neo-Classical stone building in the town square on the largest of the Princes' Islands. Rooms are comfortable and some have balconies overlooking the sea. There is an outdoor swimming pool and children's playground. The atmosphere is relaxing and appealing. **www.buyukadaprincess.com**

Polka Country Hotel
⬛⬛⬛⬛ $$

Cumhuriyet Yolu 20, Polonezköy, 81650 **Tel** *(0216) 432 32 20* **Fax** *(0216) 432 32 21* **Rooms** *15*

This stone and timber lodge is brimming with atmosphere. The town and surrounding area are untouched by development. Settled by Polish migrants in the 19th century, the area gets extremely busy on the weekends but guests can walk, bike, picnic, hike, or just sit and play chess. **www.polkahotel.com**

Taşhan
⬛⬛⬛⬛⬛ $$

Taşhan Caddesi 57, Bakırköy, 34142 **Tel** *(0212) 543 65 75* **Fax** *(0212) 561 09 88* **Rooms** *40*

Once a mediocre hotel snuggled in a leafy residential area, the Taşhan is now a Best Western hotel. Refreshingly remote from city lights, it is a short walk from Ataköy Marina, the Galleria shopping centre *(see p220)*, and a ten-minute journey to the airport. This is a friendly, efficient hotel. **www.tashanhotel.com.tr**

Güneş
⬛⬛⬛⬛⬛⬛ $$$

Nadide Caddesi, Günay Sokak 1, Merter, 34173 **Tel** *(0212) 483 30 30* **Fax** *(0212) 483 30 45* **Rooms** *130*

This hotel is situated in a quiet residential suburb, but it is only 10 km (6 miles) from the airport and is an established and popular executive hotel. The tramway to the central sights is a five-minute walk away. Book online for discounted prices. **www.guneshotel.com.tr**

Kariye
⬛⬛⬛⬛ $$$

Kariye Camii Sokak 6, Edirnekapı, 34240 **Tel** *(0212) 635 79 97* **Fax** *(0212) 521 66 31* **Rooms** *27*   **Map** *1 B1*

Situated in the shadow of the Church of St Saviour in Chora *(see pp118–19)*, the Kariye is a wooden *konak* (mansion) renovated in the style of the early 1900s. The rooms feature polished wooden floors and latticed windows. The Asitane restaurant *(see p204)* is famous for its rare Ottoman recipes. **www.kariyeotel.com**

Splendid Palace
⬛⬛⬛⬛ $$$

23 Nisan Caddesi 53, Büyük Ada, 81330 **Tel** *(0216) 382 69 50* **Fax** *(0216) 382 67 75* **Rooms** *70*

The Splendid Palace was opened in 1908. Though influenced somewhat by Art Nouveau, it clearly displays a fusion of East and West architectural designs with a bright inner courtyard encircled with rooms, and pillars around the courtyard. The silver domes and red shutters add a festive touch to the hotel.

Village Park Country Resort

🔲 ⏸ ♨ 👥 ☰ 🅿️ $$$

Ayazma Mahallesi 19, Ishaklı Köyü, Beykoz, Asian side, 81680 **Tel** *(0216) 434 59 31* **Fax** *(0216) 434 54 15* **Rooms** *20*

This is a haven of peace and tranquility for those who do not want to be in the city. Weekend packages are available as well as country pursuits such as horse riding. Dogs are welcome and kennels are provided. A restaurant, several bars and a popular picnic area make this a sought-after retreat. **www.villagepark.com.tr**

Barceló Eresin Topkapı

🔲 ⏸ ♨ 👥 📺 ☰ 🅿️ $$$$

Millet Caddesi 186, Topkapı, 34093 **Tel** *(0212) 631 12 12* **Fax** *(0212) 631 37 02* **Rooms** *231*

Not related to or near Topkapı Palace, the Barceló was once the Eresin Hotel. It is a huge stone edifice situated away from the main hotel quarter. It is run by a Spanish conglomerate and is efficiently grand, with an excellent restaurant. Public transport is convenient and most sights are a short distance away. **www.barcelo.com**

Bentley Hotel

🔲 ⏸ 👥 📺 ☰ $$$$

Halaskargazi Caddesi 75, Harbiye, 34367 **Tel** *(0212) 291 77 30* **Fax** *(0212) 291 77 40* **Rooms** *50*   **Map** *7 F1*

The Bentley is a reliable provider of luxury and style in the heart of the city. Many beautifully furnished suites are available and the guest list of the glamorous and famous is impressive. The fusion cuisine restaurant and stylish bar have won accolades. **www.bentley-hotel.com**

Çınar

🔲 ⏸ ♨ 👥 📺 ☰ 🅿️ $$$$

Şevketiye Mahallesi, Fener Mevkii, Yeşilköy 34149 **Tel** *(0212) 663 29 00* **Fax** *(0212) 663 29 21* **Rooms** *220*

The Çınar borders the Sea of Marmara, so try to get a room facing the sea. It has wonderful restaurants and bars, and the outdoor pool area and terrace are great in summer. Guests can jog along the sea shore path with the locals. It is only five minutes from the airport. **www.cinarhotel.com.tr**

Hilton

🔲 ⏸ ♨ 👥 📺 ☰ 🅿️ $$$$$

Cumhuriyet Caddesi, Harbiye, 34367 **Tel** *(0212) 315 60 00* **Fax** *(0212) 240 41 65* **Rooms** *499*   **Map** *7 F2*

One of Turkey's first luxury hotels, the Hilton provides superb service and comfort. It has lovely rooms, restaurants, bars and tennis courts. Outside there is a peaceful, attractive garden, which has a pool and jogging track. It also has a world-class conference centre. **www.hilton.com**

Istanbul International Airport Hotel

🔲 ⏸ 👥 ☰ $$$$$

Atatürk Airport International Terminal, Yeşilköy, 34831 **Tel** *(0212) 465 40 30* **Fax** *(0212) 465 47 30* **Rooms** *131*

This is the first hotel within Atatürk Airport and is accessible by foot from the baggage claim area. It has everything you are likely to want, but at a cost. Nevertheless, the bars, food and excellent service exceed anything available elsewhere in the airport. **www.airporthotelistanbul.com**

Swissotel The Bosphorus

🔲 ⏸ ♨ 👥 📺 ☰ 🅿️ $$$$$

Bayıldım Caddesi 2, Maçka, 34104 **Tel** *(0212) 326 11 00* **Fax** *(0212) 326 11 22* **Rooms** *600*   **Map** *8 A4*

Run by the Raffles Group, Swissotel is the choice of many globetrotters when in Istanbul. Set within 65 acres (26 ha) of grounds and with Bosphorus vistas, it also has ten restaurants and bars, a spa and wellness centre and tennis courts. The glamorous shopping arcade will entice serious shoppers. **www.swissotel.com**

W Hotel

🔲 ⏸ 👥 📺 ☰ $$$$$

Suleyman Seba Caddesi 22, Akaretler, 34357 **Tel** *(0212) 381 21 21* **Fax** *(0212) 381 21 81* **Rooms** *160* **Map** *8 B4*

With a great location close to Nisantasi, Istanbul's trendiest shopping district, the W is housed in the historical Row Houses, erected in 1875 as accommodation for the high officers of the Ottoman Empire. Rooms are luxurious, with all mod cons and a few extra treats, such as 350 thread-count cotton blend sheets. **www.whotel.com/istanbul**

THE BOSPHORUS

Bebek

⏸ 👥 ☰ 🅿️ $$$

Cevdetpaşa Caddesi 34, Bebek, European side, 34342 **Tel** *(0212) 358 20 00* **Fax** *(0212) 263 26 36* **Rooms** *21*

This is the ultimate in sea breezes and sumptuous living, as well as dining and clubbing. The bar at Bebek has been a legend for several decades and the renovated hotel has roomy, designer rooms. The restaurant is first rate and the setting, overlooking a bay, is particularly fine. **www.bebekhotel.com.tr**

A'jia Hotel

⏸ 👥 ☰ 🅿️ $$$$$

Ahmet Rasim Paşa Yalısı, Çubuklu Caddesi 27, Kanlıca, Asian side **Tel** *(0216) 413 93 00* **Rooms** *16*

This luxury boutique hotel redefines simplicity and minimalist design. Gone are authentic Ottoman interiors or pasha's rooms; it boasts cool, calm, subdued and restful elegance. It is remote from the crowds in a district with no other hotels. Seclusion and anonymity are assured. **www.ajiahotel.com**

Sumahan on the Water

🔲 ⏸ 📺 ☰ 🅿️ $$$$$

Kuleli Caddesi 51, Çengelköy, Asian side, 34684 **Tel** *(0212) 422 80 00* **Rooms** *20*

The Sumahan sits in a stunning Bosphorus-side location on Istanbul's Asian side and provides a pampering service. This small luxury hotel has its own luxurious hamam and offers a range of spa treatments within a romantic and intimate atmosphere. A water-taxi service takes guests to central parts of the city. **www.sumahan.com**

Key to Price Guide *see p184* **Key to Symbols** *see back cover flap*

BEYOND ISTANBUL

Anzac

Saat Kulesi Meydanı 8, Çanakkale **Tel** (0286) 217 77 77 **Fax** (0286) 217 20 18 **Rooms** 27

The Anzac has become almost as legendary as its namesake (see p170). Neat, clean rooms are decorated with Gallipoli themes. There is a popular roof terrace with reasonably priced snacks. It gets very crowded during the period around 25 April, ANZAC Day. **www.anzachotel.com**

Çamlık Motel

Sahil Yolu, İznik, 16860 **Tel** (0224) 757 13 62 **Fax** (0224) 757 16 31 **Rooms** 26

The clean rooms here may offer no frills, but the lakeside setting of this motel in peaceful İznik cannot be beaten. Some rooms have balconies overlooking the lake. The hotel's restaurant, one of the few fish restaurants in town that is open out of season, serves well-prepared, reasonably priced meals. **www.iznik-camlikmotel.com**

Geçim Pansiyon

Türkeli, Avşa Ada **Tel** (0266) 896 14 93 **Fax** (0266) 896 23 45 **Rooms** 15

This is a popular family hotel and one of the better places to stay in Türkeli. Located in a peaceful neighbourhood and set back from the beach, it offers shared self-catering facilities and some well-equipped apartments. This is an excellent base from which to enjoy the delights of Avşa.

Hotel Maşukiye

Soğuksu Mahallesi, Sarmaşık Sokak 18, Maşukiye, Kartepe, Kocaeli, 41295 **Tel** (262) 354 21 74 **Rooms** 10

Maşukiye means "village of lovers" and this snug hotel inspires romance. Nestling amongst forests, lakes and mountains, this rural inn delights in every way. There are plenty of winter and summer outdoor pursuits, unique local history and splendid food and vintage wines. **www.hotelmasukiye.com**

Rüstempaşa Kervansaray

İkikapalıhan Caddesi 57, Eski Camii Yanı, Edirne, 22100 **Tel** (0284) 212 61 19 **Fax** (0284) 214 85 22 **Rooms** 75

This historic caravanserai (travel lodge) dating from the 16th century was a creation of the prolific imperial architect Sinan (see p155). It is Edirne's most venerable hostel and has thick stone walls, rows of rooms and creature comforts. In the past traders could overnight here under the sultan's protection. **www.edirnekervansarayhotel.com**

Safran

Ortapazarı Caddesi, Arka Sokak 4, Bursa, 16040 **Tel** (0224) 224 72 16 **Fax** (0224) 224 72 19 **Rooms** 10

Easily recognized by its saffron colour, this charming hotel is over 100 years old and is situated in the centre of Bursa. Its rooms are small but thoughtfully furnished. The restaurant is renowned for producing well-cooked meals and mezes and, on some evenings, there is live music. **www.safranotel.com**

İznik Çini Vakfı

Sahil Yolu Vakıf Sokak 13, İznik, 16860 **Tel & Fax** (0224) 757 60 25 **Rooms** 9

This remote guesthouse is run by the foundation that restores the traditional İznik tile-making traditions. Do not expect five-star trappings but it is peacefully artistic, reasonably comfortable and guests can always meet interesting scholarly, cultural types. It is well recommended for independent adventures.

Sığınak (The Retreat)

İbrice Limanı Yolu, Mecidiye, Keşan, 22800 **Tel** (0284) 783 43 10 **Fax** (0284) 783 43 86 **Rooms** 8

Opposite the Gallipoli Peninsula on the Gulf of Saroz is an unspoilt, largely uninhabited region of Turkey. The Retreat is remote and some minutes away from a deserted beach and coastline. Accommodation is homely with a few ethnic decorations. Guests can enjoy fresh air, splendid food and wine here. **www.siginak.com**

Acqua Verde

Kurfallı, Şile, 81740 **Tel** (0216) 721 71 43 **Fax** (0216) 721 72 33 **Rooms** 25

This tranquil, leafy backwater is located on the Ağva River at Şile. Wildlife, trees and a wilderness atmosphere make this spot enormously popular. There are bungalows and picnic areas, and their own restaurant is excellent. At weekends, city dwellers arrive in numbers. Visit mid-week if you prefer solitude. **www.acquaverde.com.tr**

Almira Hotel

Ulubatlı Hasan Bulvarı 5, Bursa, 16200 **Tel** (0224) 250 20 20 **Fax** (0224) 250 20 38 **Rooms** 235

The Almira Hotel has more than a hint of Regency, but with so many restorations to be found, this is a comforting hotel that does not shout about heritage. The rooms are large and well furnished and the lounge areas are spacious and atmospheric. There is an excellent restaurant and bars. **www.almira.com.tr**

Çirağan Palace Kempinski

Çirağan Caddesi 32, Beşiktaş, European side, 34349 **Tel** (0212) 326 46 46 **Fax** (0212) 259 66 87 **Rooms** 315

Designed to make guests feel like a sultan, the Çirağan is one of the city's leading hotels. A restored residence of the last Ottoman sultans, it retains its glory and brims with five-star opulence. It has a glorious summer terrace with the Bosphorus lapping below. **www.kempinski.com/istanbul**

RESTAURANTS, CAFÉS AND BARS

Istanbul's restaurants range from the informal *lokanta* and kebab house, which are found on almost every street corner, to the gourmet restaurants *(restoran)* of large hotels. There are a variety of international restaurants in the city offering fare from France to Japan at middle to high prices. Pages 194–7 illustrate the most typical Turkish dishes and the phrase book on pages 279–80 will help you tackle the menu. On page 197 you will find a guide to

Simit seller

drinks available. The restaurants listed on pages 198–207 have been chosen from the best that Istanbul has to offer across all price ranges, from casual eateries to award-winning restaurants. They have been recommended for their quality of food, service and value for money. A detailed description is provided with examples of signature dishes. Light meals and snacks sold by street vendors and served in cafés and bars are described on pages 208–9.

WHERE TO LOOK

Istanbul's smartest and most expensive restaurants are concentrated in the European parts of the city: along the Bosphorus in Ortaköy; in and around Taksim; in the chic shopping districts of Nişantaşı, Maçka, Bebek and Teşvikiye; and in the modern residential suburbs of Levent and Etiler, west of the Bosphorus. The best gourmet restaurants for both Western and Turkish food are usually in five-star hotels.

Beyoğlu district has the liveliest restaurants, cafés and fast-food eateries, particularly around İstiklal Caddesi *(see pp102–3)*, which cater for a young crowd.

Sultanahmet, and the neighbouring districts of Sirkeci, Eminönü and Beyazıt, are full of cheap restaurants serving the local population. There are also some stylish restaurants with modern decor in

these areas. Further afield, in areas such as Fatih, Fener, Balat and Eyüp, there are plenty of cheap restaurants, cafés and bakeries.

TYPES OF RESTAURANT

The most common type of restaurant is the traditional *lokanta*. This is an ordinary restaurant offering a variety of dishes, often listed by the entrance. Home-made dishes comprise hot meat and vegetable dishes displayed in steel containers. Other options on the menu may be *sulu yemek* (a stew) and *et* (meat – meaning grilled meat and kebabs).

Equally ubiquitous is the Turkish kebab house *(kebapçı* or *ocakbaşı)*. As well as grilled meats, almost every kebab house serves *lahmacun*, a very thin dough base with minced meat, onions and tomato sauce on top *(see p194)*.

Pierre Loti café in Eyüp *(see p120)*

Cheaper restaurants and kebab houses also serve *pide*, a flattened bread base, served with various toppings such as eggs, cheese or lamb. There are also a few specialist *pide* restaurants.

If you have had too much to drink you may welcome a tripe soup *(işkembe)*, a Turkish cure for a hangover, before going to bed. İşkembe restaurants stay open until the early hours of the morning.

The atmosphere is always informal and lively in Istanbul's innumerable fish restaurants *(balık lokantası)*. The best of these are located on the shores of the Bosphorus *(see pp205–7)* and in Kumkapı, on the Sea of Marmara, which is like one large open-air restaurant in summer. A typical fish restaurant will offer a large variety of mezes *(see p196)* before you order your main course from the day's catch. Skipjack tuna *(palamut)*, fresh sardines *(sardalya)* and sea bass *(levrek)* are the most

Poseidon, a luxury restaurant overlooking the Bosphorus *(see p206)*

Diners eating at the Konyalı Restaurant in Topkapı Palace *(see p198)*

popular fish. Also popular are Black Sea *hamsi* (a kind of anchovy), *istavrit* (bluefin) and *mezgit* (whiting). However, as fish are becoming scarcer and more expensive, farmed fish has become more widely accepted, particularly *alabalik* (trout) and a type of bream known as *çipura*. Fish is served fried or grilled and often accompanied by a large plate of salad and a bottle of rakı *(see p197)*. The majority of fish restaurants in these busy and popular areas will not accept reservations. However, if you cannot find a table at one restaurant, you will probably find one at another nearby.

International culinary experiences are encouraging local chefs to be more adventurous and innovative; the best are crafting superb, original food in a beautiful ambience. Wealthier Turks frequent the foreign restaurants found in a number of Istanbul neighbourhoods, while global icons such as Starbucks and Gloria Jean's are increasingly part of everyday life.

A *meyhane* is more like a tavern, serving alcohol and a large choice of *mezes*. They are usually more casual than some of the traditional restaurants and often attract a younger crowd. The accent is mostly on drinking and there is almost always *fasil* music and musicians who play atmospheric tunes on a zither or drum.

A selection of pastries

OPENING HOURS

Turks eat lunch between 12:30 and 2pm and have dinner around 8pm. Ordinary restaurants and kebab houses are open from about 11am to 11pm, while fish restaurants serve all day but stay open later. International restaurants have strict opening hours, usually from noon to 3:30pm and 7:30pm to midnight. *Meyhanes* will be open from 7pm until well after midnight. Most restaurants are open daily, but some are closed on either Sunday or Monday. During Ramazan *(see p47)*, when Muslims fast from sunrise to sunset, many restaurants are closed. Some only shut during daylight hours and then serve special Ramazan meals, while others, especially in religious areas such as Fatih and Eyüp, will close altogether for the whole month. In sightseeing areas, however, you will always find somewhere open.

WHAT TO EXPECT

Since July 2009 smoking has been banned in all indoor establishments, although illegal lighting up is not unheard of.

When choosing a place to eat, bear in mind that some cheaper restaurants and kebab houses do not serve alcoholic drinks. When alcohol is served, it can be expensive.

Accessibility for wheelchairs is somewhat hit or miss. Restaurants are often multi-level with family rooms on the upper floors, and ground-floor restaurants often have a step up to the entrance. Lifts are not common outside of large hotels and office buildings. Many restaurants offer options for vegetarians.

In local Turkish restaurants in conservative parts of the city and outside Istanbul, women should look for the *aile salonu* sign. This denotes an area set aside for women and children, and single women will be unwelcome in the main restaurant.

Turks are proud of their hospitality and service. Good service is always found in the upmarket restaurants, but you may find that the same standards do not always apply to the cheaper places.

SERVICE AND PAYING

The major credit cards are widely accepted, except in the cheaper restaurants, kebab houses, local *bufés* (snack kiosks) and some *lokantas*. Restaurants usually display the credit card sign or symbol at the entrance if they accept this form of payment. Value-added tax (KDV in Turkish) is always included. Some places add 10 per cent for service while others leave it to the discretion of the customer.

Delicious fried and grilled mackerel sold on Eminönü quayside *(see p208)*

The Flavours of Istanbul

The wide range of climatic zones across Turkey make it one of the few countries that can grow all its own food. Tea is cultivated in the mountains by the Black Sea and bananas in the sultry south. The Anatolian plain in between is criss-crossed by wheat fields and rich grasslands on which cattle graze, providing top quality meat and dairy produce. Fruit and vegetables flourish everywhere and fish abound in the salty seas that lap the nation's shores. Freshness is the hallmark of this varied cuisine, drawn from the many cultures that were subject to nearly five centuries of Ottoman rule.

Nar (pomegranates)

A stall in the Spice Bazaar, one of Istanbul's oldest markets

THE ANATOLIAN STEPPE

The steppe stretching from Central Asia to Anatolia is one of the oldest inhabited regions of the world. Dishes from this vast area are as varied as the different ethnic groups that live here, but are mainly traditional and simple. To fit in with a mainly nomadic way of life, food generally needed to be quick and easy to prepare. Turkey's most famous culinary staples, yogurt, flat bread and the kebab, originate in this region. The common use of fruits, such as pomegranates, figs and apricots, in Turkish savoury dishes stems from Persian influences, filtering down with the tribes that came from the north of the steppe. From the Middle East, further south, nomads introduced the occasional fiery blash of chilli. Its use was once an essential aid to preserving meat in the searing desert heat.

OTTOMAN CUISINE

It was in the vast, steamy kitchens of the Topkapı Palace that a repertoire of mouthwatering dishes to rival the celebrated cuisines of France and China grew

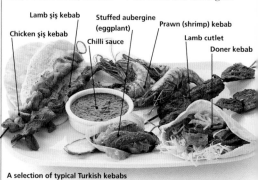

Lamb şiş kebab
Chicken şiş kebab
Stuffed aubergine (eggplant)
Chilli sauce
Prawn (shrimp) kebab
Lamb cutlet
Doner kebab

A selection of typical Turkish kebabs

LOCAL DISHES AND SPECIALITIES

Because of Istanbul's proximity to the sea, fresh fish is readily available and is a key ingredient on the city's menus. Since ancient times the Bosphorus has been known for its excellent fishing. In the winter months especially, there is a bounty of oil-rich fish, such as bluefish, bream, bonito tuna, sea bass, mullet and mackerel, waiting to be reeled in. From the Black Sea, Istanbul is also provided with a steady supply of juicy mussels and *hamsi*, a type of anchovy. Sweets are also popular and eaten throughout the day, not just after a meal. They are sold in shops, on stalls and by street vendors. Istanbul is renowned for its *baklava*, sweet pastries coated with syrup and often filled with nuts.

Turkish Delight

Midye dolmasi *Mussels are stuffed with a spiced rice mixture, steamed and served with a squirt of lemon juice.*

A splendid array of fruit, vegetables and dried goods in the Spice Bazaar

up. At the height of the Ottoman Empire, in the 16th and 17th centuries, legions of kitchen staff slaved away on the Sultan's behalf. Court cooks usually specialized in particular dishes. Some prepared soups, while others just grilled meats or fish, or dreamed up combinations of vegetables, or baked breads, or made puddings and sherbets. As Ottoman rule expanded to North Africa, the Balkans and parts of southern Russia, influences from these far-flung places crept into the Turkish imperial kitchens. Complex dishes of finely seasoned stuffed meats and vegetables, often with such fanciful names as "lady's lips", "Vizier's fingers" and the "fainting Imam", appeared. This imperial tradition lives on in many of Istanbul's

restaurants, where dishes such as *karniyarik* (halved aubergines (eggplant) stuffed with minced lamb, pine nuts and dried fruit) and *hünkar beğendili köfte* (meatballs served with a smooth purée of smoked aubergine and cheese) grace the menu.

Fresh catch from the Bosphorus on a fish stall in Karaköy

BAZAAR CULTURE

A visit to the market that spills out around Istanbul's Spice Bazaar *(see p88)* is an absolute must. A cornucopia of fine ingredients is brought here daily from farms that surround the city. Apricots, watermelons, cherries and figs sit alongside staple vegetables, such as peppers, onions, aubergines and tomatoes. Fine cuts of lamb and beef, cheeses, pickles, herbs, spices and honey-drenched pastries and puddings are also on offer.

KNOW YOUR FISH

The profusion of different species in the waters around Istanbul makes the city a paradise for fish lovers:

Barbunya Red mullet

Çupra Sea bream

Dilbaliği Sole

Hamsi Anchovy

Kalamar Squid

Kalkan Turbot

Kefal Grey mullet

Kiliç Swordfish

Levrek Sea bass

Lüfer Bluefish

Midye Mussels

Palamut Bonito tuna

Uskumru Mackerel

İmam bayildi *Aubergines, stuffed with tomatoes, garlic and onions, are baked in the oven until meltingly soft.*

Levrek pilakisi *This stew is made by simmering sea bass fillets with potatoes, carrots, tomatoes, onions and garlic.*

Kadayif *Rounds of shredded filo pastry are stuffed with nuts and doused with honey to make a sumptuous dessert.*

Mezes

As in many southern European countries, a Turkish meal begins with a selection of appetizing starters known as *mezes*, which are placed in the middle of the table for sharing. In a basic *meyhane* restaurant, you may be offered olives, cheese and slices of melon, but in a grander establishment the choice will be enormous. Mainly consisting of cold vegetables and salads of various kinds, *mezes* can also include a number of hot dishes, such as *börek* (cheese pastries), fried mussels and squid. *Mezes* are eaten with bread and traditionally washed down with *rakı* (a clear, anise-flavoured spirit).

Humus with *pide* bread

Zeytinyağli (artichokes)

Çoban salatasi (tomato, red onion and cucumber salad)

Ayşe fasulye (green beans with tomato sauce)

Melon with beyaz peynir (melon with a creamy, feta-like cheese)

Yalancı yaprak dolmasi (stuffed vine leaves)

Tarama (a dip made with cod's roe, garlic and olive oil)

TURKISH BREADS

Bread is the cornerstone of every meal in Turkey and comes in a wide range of shapes and styles. Besides *ekmek* (crusty white loaves) the other most common types of Turkish bread are *yufka* and *pide*. *Yufka*, the typical bread of nomadic communities, is made from thinly rolled sheets of dough which are cooked on a griddle, and dried to help preserve them. They can then be heated up and served to accompany any main meal as required. *Pide* is the type of flat bread that is usually served with *mezes* and kebabs in restaurants. It consists of a flattened circle or oval of dough, sometimes brushed with beaten egg and sprinkled with sesame seeds or black cumin, that is baked in an oven. It is a staple during many religious festivals. In the month of Ramadan, no meal is considered complete without *pide*. Another popular bread is *simit*, a crisp, ring-shaped savoury loaf that comes covered in sesame seeds.

A delivery of freshly baked *simit* loaves

What to Drink in Istanbul

The most common drink in Istanbul is tea *(çay)*, which is normally served black in small, tulip-shaped glasses. It is offered to you wherever you go: in shops and bazaars, and even in banks and offices. Breakfast is usually accompanied by tea, whereas small cups of strong Turkish coffee *(kahve)* are drunk mid-morning and also at the end of meals. Cold drinks include a variety of fresh fruit juices, such as orange and cherry, and refreshing syrup-based sherbets. Although Turkey does produce its own wine and beer, the most popular alcoholic drink in Istanbul is rakı, which is usually served to accompany mezes.

Fruit juice seller

SOFT DRINKS

Bottled mineral water *(su)* is sold in corner shops and served in restaurants everywhere. If you are feeling adventurous, you may like to try a glass of *ayran*, salty liquid yoghurt. *Boza*, made from bulgur wheat,

Vişne suyu   **Ayran**

is another local drink to sample *(see p92)*. There is always a variety of refreshing fruit and vegetable juices available. They include cherry juice *(vişne suyu)*, turnip juice *(şalgam suyu)* and *şıra*, a juice made from fermented grapes.

COFFEE AND TEA

Turkish coffee *(kahve)* is dark and strong and is ordered according to the amount of sugar required: *az* (little), *orta* (medium), or *çok* (a lot). You may have to ask for it especially, as some restaurants may give you instant coffee. The ubiquitous drink is tea *(çay)*. It is served with sugar but without milk, and in a small, tulip-shaped glass. Apple *(elma)*, is the most popular flavour, but there are also linden *(ıhlamur)*, rosehip *(kuşburnu)* and mint *(nane)* teas.

Traditional samovar for tea

Apple tea   **Limeflower tea**

ALCOHOLIC DRINKS

The national alcoholic drink in Turkey is rakı – "lion's milk" – a clear, anise-flavoured spirit, which turns cloudy when water is added. It is drunk with fish and mezes. The Turkish wine industry produces some good reds and whites, served in many restaurants. Doluca and Kavaklıdere are two of the leading brands. Foreign and imported wines are widely available at high prices. Turkey's own Efes Pilsen beer is widely sold. Note that alcohol is not served in some of the cheaper restaurants and kebab houses.

Rakı   **Beer**   **Red wine**   **White wine**

Turkish coffee is a very strong drink and an acquired taste for most people.

Sahlep is a hot, winter drink made from powdered orchid root.

Choosing a Restaurant

The restaurants in this guide have been selected for their good value, exceptional food, or interesting location. These listings highlight some of the factors that may influence your choice, such as whether you can opt to eat outdoors or if the venue offers live music. Entries are alphabetical within each price category.

PRICE CATEGORIES
Price categories include a three-course meal for one, and all unavoidable extras including service and tax.

$ under US$20
$$ US$20–$30
$$$ US$30–$40
$$$$ US$40–$50
$$$$$ Over US$50

SERAGLIO POINT

Sultanahmet Fish House
$$

Prof Kasim İsmail Gürkan Caddesi 14, Sultanahmet, 34110 **Tel** *(0212) 527 44 41* **Map** *3 E4*

A casual, low-key choice for good fish and meze at reasonable prices. The set lunch of fish soup, salad and the fish of the day is a particularly good deal. There is also a non-seafood choice of kebabs and casseroles. Antique lamps and colourful textiles add to the atmosphere. Alcohol is served.

Faros Restaurant
$$$

Hudavendigar Caddesi 5, Sultanahmet, 34110 **Tel** *(0212) 514 98 28* **Map** *3 E3*

The restaurant at the Faros Hotel serves well prepared Turkish food, including a good selection of dishes for vegetarians, in a friendly atmosphere that often features music and dancing. The *mahmudiye* (grilled chicken breast accompanied by rice flavoured with almonds, cinnamon, currants and honey) is a speciality. Alcohol is served.

Konyalı
$$$

Topkapı Palace, Sultanahmet, 34110 **Tel** *(0212) 513 96 96* **Map** *3 F3*

This gastronomic landmark has been in business for four decades, serving appetizing mezes, meats, salads and fish. There is an award-winning à la carte menu. Located within the Topkapı Palace, it has commanding views of the Bosphorus. Try the elegant "afternoon tea" menu. Konyalı is open for lunch only and closed on Tuesdays.

Sarnıç
$$$$

Soğukçeşme Sokak, Sultanahmet, 34110 **Tel** *(0212) 512 42 91* **Map** *3 E4 (5 F3)*

Converted from a Byzantine cistern with lofty columns and a domed ceiling, Sarnıç is dimly lit by wrought-iron chandeliers and candles and has an impressive fireplace. Piano music is often played in the evenings. The menu has variety but diners come here more for the atmosphere than the top cuisine.

SULTANAHMET

Backpackers Restaurant
$

Yeni Akbıyık Caddesi 14/1, Sultanahmet, 34400 **Tel** *(0212) 638 55 86* **Map** *3 E5 (5 E5)*

Simple, upbeat snacks are served here with the accent more on wines and beer than food. This is very much a cheerful and informal budget gathering place. People congregate to drink, eat hearty snacks, swap travel stories and plan their next journey. Backpackers is a great staging post in the budget area of Sultanahmet.

Café Camille
$

Babiali Caddesi 8, Cağaloğlu, 34110 **Tel** *(0212) 527 81 77* **Map** *3 D4 (5 D3)*

This small café, with its industrious, bustling kitchen, is the place to grab a cup of coffee or a foaming cappuccino and home-made cakes. Simple lunches with quiche, omelettes and salads are popular. They serve delicious fresh fruit juices and milk shakes. The service is brisk and friendly.

Doy-Doy
$

Şifa Hamamı Sokak 13, Sultanahmet, 34110 **Tel** *(0212) 517 15 88* **Map** *3 D5 (5 D5)*

An impressive selection of soups, kebabs, *pide* (flat bread) in abundance, colourful salads, vegetarian dishes and rich desserts is on offer here. Everything is prepared very authentically. Doy-Doy is a cheerful venue with great prices but alcohol is not served. The rooftop terrace is perfect in summer with inviting views and sea breezes.

Group Restaurant
$

Şehit Mehmet Paşa Yokuşu 4, Sultanahmet, 34110 **Tel** *(0212) 517 47 00* **Map** *3 D5 (5 D5)*

Part gift shop, part café and restaurant, this is a magnet for tourists and is always bustling. The coffee and sticky pastries are popular but more substantial fare is also served. Grills, salads and stews are on the menu and served in generous portions at reasonable prices. Alcohol is available.

Key to Symbols *see back cover flap*

Sofa Café
Mimar Mehmet Ağa Caddesi 32, Sultanahmet, 34122 **Tel** *(0212) 458 36 30* **Map** *3 E5 (5 E4)*

Casual and comfortable, Sofa Café offers a break from the hordes of tourists in Sultanahmet. It serves up straightforward Turkish fare such as *alinazik* (puréed aubergine with yoghurt and minced meat) or kebabs, helped down with a cold Efes beer or a glass of local wine.

Sultanahmet Köftecisi
Divanyolu Caddesi 12A, Sultanahmet, 34110 **Tel** *(0212) 520 05 66* **Map** *3 E4 (5 E4)*

Almost an institution in Sultanahmet, this restaurant has been going since the 1920s and turns out simple, trademark dishes such as *köfte* (meatballs), *piyaz* (beans in sauce) and *pilav* (rice). Locals crowd in here for lunch and queues mean there is no lingering.

Amedros
Hoca Rüstem Sokak 7, Sultanahmet, 34400 **Tel** *(0212) 522 83 56* **Map** *3 E4*

This Western-style bistro serves both Turkish and international fare, including Ottoman specialities such as *testi kebab* (a savoury mix of lamb and vegetables cooked inside a clay pot). The friendly service and stylish, airy interior make for an enjoyable dining experience. Alcohol is served.

Khorasani
Divanyolu Caddesi, Ticarethane Sokak 39–41, Sultanahmet, 34110 **Tel** *(0212) 519 59 59* **Map** *3 E4*

A cut above the usual kebab shop, this attractive restaurant offers dishes from the southern regions of Gaziantep and Antakya, including a reasonable number of vegetarian options. A wood fire allows for outdoor dining in the winter and there is occasional musical entertainment.

Valide Sultan Konak
Kutlugün Sokak 1, Sultanahmet, 34110 **Tel** *(0212) 638 06 00* **Map** *3 E4 (5 E4)*

The semicircular rooftop restaurant of the Valide Sultan Konağı Hotel *(see p186)* commands stunning views of the sea and historic surrounding area. Menus are well balanced with meat, vegetables, meze, kebabs and stews. The stuffed vegetables are particularly creative and taste as good as they look. They also serve seafood and pizzas.

Ahırkapı Lokanta
Armada Hotel, Ahır Kapı Sokak, Sultanahmet, 34110 **Tel** *(0212) 638 13 70* **Map** *3 F3 (5 F5)*

This restaurant has the atmosphere of a 1930s Turkish tavern and live *fasıl* music. In keeping with the decor, the cuisine is typically Turkish with a variety of delicious mezes and main dishes, such as *yoğurtlu yaprak dolması* (minced meat in vine leaves with yoghurt). The rooftop terrace boasts views over Sultanahmet.

Djazzu
İncili Çavuş Çikmazi 5–7, Sultanahmet, 34110 **Tel** *(0212) 512 22 42* **Map** *3 E4 (5 E4)*

A classy but unpretentious restaurant serving high-quality international fare crafted by a French-trained Japanese chef. This friendly establishment draws a lively mix of diners in the evenings to enjoy dishes ranging from sushi to spaghetti and kebabs. Outdoor seating in summer and a cosy fireplace in winter make Djazzu popular year-round.

Balıkçı Sabahattin
Seyt Hasankuyu Sokak 1, Sultanahmet, 34110 **Tel** *(0212) 458 18 24* **Map** *3 E3 (5 F5)*

Everything works well at this delightful fish restaurant. They have a long and delicious menu, having been in business since 1927. The fish and seafood are mouthwatering and other creative dishes include spicy squash with yoghurt. Recommended for smart service and consistently good food.

Kathisma
Yeni Akbıyık Caddesidesi 26, Sultanahmet, 34400 **Tel** *(0212) 518 97 10* **Map** *3 E5 (5 C3)*

This stylish restaurant takes its name from the Byzantine emperor's lodge which once overlooked the Hipppodrome *(see p80)*. Turkish dishes include *mücver* (fried courgettes), *fırında kuzu* (roast lamb) and some typical and delicious desserts such as *sakızlı sutlaç* (rice pudding with gum mastic).

Rumeli Café
Ticarethane Sokak 8, Sultanahmet, 34110 **Tel** *(0212) 512 00 08* **Map** *3 E4 (5 D3)*

This is a delightfully atmospheric restaurant just off the busy Divanyolu. Housed in an old printing factory, the Rumeli has a strong Greek flavour to it as well as Mediterranean aromas. Vegetarian dishes are popular and specialties include grilled lamb with various sauces. Tomatoes, herbs and yoghurt feature in many dishes.

Seasons Restaurant
Tevkifhane Sokak 1, Sultanahmet, 34110 **Tel** *(0212) 402 30 00* **Map** *3 E5*

The opulent Four Seasons Hotel *(see p187)* has a restaurant that is just as luxurious. It serves Mediterranean cuisine with some Asian influences in an attractive dining room and in the courtyard garden. Try one of the Friday evening wine tastings featuring local wines with cheeses, breads and fruit, or drop by on weekends for a lavish afternoon tea.

Giritli Restoran
Keresteci Hakkı Sokak 8, Ahır Kapı Sokak, Sultanahmet, 34122 **Tel** *(0212) 458 22 70* **Map** *3 E5 (5 F5)*

The multi-course set menu is the only option at this Cretan-style restaurant, but it offers a rich variety of hot and cold starters, as well as expertly prepared fish, served with unlimited local beer, wine or rakı (an anise-flavoured spirit). The walled garden and elegant dining room provide a setting to match the food.

BAZAAR QUARTER

Akdeniz Restaurant
Mustafa Kemalpaşa Caddesi 48, Aksaray, 36420 **Tel** *(0212) 458 13 00*   **Map** *2 A4*

This is an unassuming, mid-range *lokanta* (traditional restaurant) serving a large range of appetizers, kebabs, *lahmacun* (thin-crust crepe), *pide* (flat bread) and pizzas. The specialty is tandoor lamb. Ask for a table away from the TV screen if you prefer peace and quiet with meals. Alcohol is available.

Havuzlu
Gani Çelebi Sokak 3, Grand Bazaar, Beyazıt, 36420 **Tel** *(0212) 527 33 46*   **Map** *3 C4 (4 B3)*

Havuzlu is where you head when hunger interrupts a shopping spree. It is a small restaurant serving honest local food. Everything is cooked freshly. The soups, *dolma* (stuffed vine leaves) and different kinds of kebabs and grills are great snacks. Havuzlu means "with pool" and is named for the burbling fountain found inside.

İskender Saray
Atatürk Bulvarı 116, Aksaray, 36420 **Tel** *(0212) 520 34 04*   **Map** *2 A3*

This classic restaurant serves döner kebabs and signature dishes include *İskender kebab* (döner meat on bread with a rich sauce) and *saç kavurma* (lamb and vegetables flambéed at the table). The white table cloths and cheerful, friendly staff lend a professional touch. They do a handy takeaway service. No alcohol is served.

Karaca
Gazi Sinan Paşa Sokak, Vezir Han 1/A, Nuruosmaniye, 36420 **Tel** *(0212) 512 90 94*   **Map** *3 D4 (4 C3)*

This large restaurant is part of an authentic Ottoman caravanserai. Diners eat very well here and dishes such as *pazı dolması* (stuffed chard) and *islim kebabı* (lamb with aubergine) are hearty and filling. Save room for the calorific *kabak tatlısı* (pumpkin pudding). The clientele includes shopkeepers from the Grand Bazaar.

Özbolu Kebap House
Hoca Paşa Sokak 33, Sirkeci, 34430 **Tel** *(0212) 522 46 63*   **Map** *2 E3 (5 D2)*

In a street of budget kebaberies, this one stands out with an amazing choice of hot and cold dishes. The grills, stews, seasonal fish and puddings are hearty, fresh and delicious. Succulent and juicy kebabs are the dish of the house. The atmosphere here is cheerful. Sour cherry juice and soft drinks are available instead of alcohol.

Sefa Lokantası
Nuruosmaniye Caddesi, Cağaloğlu, 34110 **Tel** *(0212) 520 06 70*   **Map** *3 D4 (4 C3)*

Eat like the locals do at this small, no frills *"ev yemek lokantası"* (home-cooking restaurant) that is popular with shopkeepers and other workers at the nearby Grand Bazaar. Portions of freshly made stews, kebabs and vegetable dishes are generous and reasonably priced. No alcohol is served.

Borsa Lokanta
Yalı Köşkü Caddesi, Yalı Köşkü Han 60, Sirkeci, 36420 **Tel** *(0212) 511 80 79*   **Map** *3 D2 (5 D1)*

There are two eateries here, a fast-food, self-service one on the ground floor and a more formal (but still casual) one on the level above. Borsa Lokanta has many branches in Istanbul. One of their trademark recipes is *beğendili kebabı* (meat with a creamy aubergine sauce). The service is extremely competent. Alcohol is served.

Hamdi Restaurant
Kalçin Sokak 17, Eminönü, 34110 **Tel** *(0212) 528 03 90*   **Map** *3 D2 (4 C1)*

The main draw at this popular restaurant, located behind the Spice Bazaar, is the spectacular view over the Golden Horn from the upper floors. The wide variety of well-prepared kebabs and exceptionally tasty *baklava* make a delicious accompaniment to the views. Alcohol is served.

Dârüzziyafe
Şifahane Caddesi 6, Süleymaniye, 36420 **Tel** *(0212) 511 84 14 or (0212) 511 84 15*   **Map** *4 A1 (2 B2)*

The former kitchens of the Süleymaniye Mosque *(see pp90–91)* house this excellent restaurant, serving unusual and elaborate Ottoman dishes. The nourishing house soup is made with spinach, vegetables and meat. Mezes are available. For dessert, try *keşkül* (milk pudding with pistachios and almonds). It is best to reserve. No alcohol served.

BEYOĞLU

Falafel House
Şehit Muhtar Caddesi 19/1A, Beyoğlu, 34437 **Tel** *(0212) 253 77 30*   **Map** *7 E3*

Simple, cheap and well-prepared, the *falafel*, *hummus*, *tabouleh* and other Middle Eastern fare on offer at this tiny restaurant is surprisingly hard to find in Istanbul. Service is friendly and indoor seating offers the opportunity to see the chefs at work. There are also outdoor tables set amid the cobblestones. No alcohol served.

Key to Price Guide *see p198* **Key to Symbols** *see back cover flap*

Özkonak

Akarsu Yokuşu Sokak 46B, Cihangir , 34433 **Tel** *(0212) 249 13 07* **Map** *7 E5*

Istanbul's celebrity journalists, writers and fashion models flock here for the freshly cooked, honest stews, *pilavs* (rice dishes), salads and baked puddings. Some come just for the tastiest *tavuk göğsü* (milk pudding made with shredded chicken breast) in the city. This is mainly a lunch-time spot with speedy service. Alcohol is not served.

Smyrna

Akarsu Caddesi 29, Cihangir, 34430 **Tel** *(0212) 244 24 66* **Map** *7 E5*

A former antiques shop in Cihangir has been transformed into a café and restaurant. The small tables across the bar are an ideal place to enjoy a coffee while reading newspapers. Past the bar, you enter a hall with high windows. Cihangir is a district well liked by expats living in Istanbul, and many of Smyrna's customers are foreigners.

Zencefil

Kurabiye Sokak 8A, Taksim, 34430 **Tel** *(0212) 243 82 34* **Map** *7 E4*

This is one of the premier vegetarian restaurants in Istanbul. Daily specials are marked on a blackboard. Everything is fresh and wholesome and the service is skillful. Baked vegetable dishes, home-made breads, soups and herb teas do not disappoint. There are also delicious desserts available. Alcohol is served.

Ara Café

Tosbağ Sokak 8A, Galatasaray, 34433 **Tel** *(0212) 245 41 05* **Map** *7 D4*

With its large, lively patio area and charming, multi-level interior, this is a popular place for whiling away the afternoon, sipping a coffee or enjoying a salad or heartier fare. The traditional Turkish buffet breakfast is delicious. Photographs by acclaimed Turkish photographer Ara Güler adorn the walls and placemats. No alcohol is served.

Chez Vous

Cezayir Sokak 21, Galatasaray, 34430 **Tel** *(0212) 245 95 32* **Map** *7 D4*

Part of the rebirth and design revolution sweeping most of Beyoğlu, this small café (part of a restored period mansion) clings to the steep steps of trend-setting French Street. Light snacks and salads are served. The service is rushed and the table wines are expensive, but trendy Chez Vous is great for fun.

Cuppa

Yeni Yuva Sokak 22/A, Cihangir, 80090 **Tel** *(0212) 249 57 24* **Map** *7 E5*

If sightseeing around Istanbul has you craving for nourishment, head to Cuppa for a shot of wheatgrass juice. This friendly outpost can fix you up with a freshly squeezed pomegranate juice or a selection of fruit smoothies. The menu includes purported anti-ageing and cramp-beating concoctions, and a mix-and-match Turkish breakfast.

Ficcin

Kallavi Sokak 13/1, Beyoğlu, 34433 **Tel** *(0212) 293 37 86* **Map** *7 D4*

Tucked away Ficcin is a popular choice for *meyhane*-style food (and a beer or rakı) without the Nevizade crowds and craziness. The Circassian-influenced dishes put a spin on traditional meze fare, with the namesake meat pie and plump *mantı* (Turkish ravioli) especially recommended. Lively *fasıl* music drifts in from the restaurant across the street.

Gani Gani

Kudu Sokak 13, Taksim, 34433 **Tel** *(0212) 244 84 01* **Map** *7 E4*

Turkish favourites are served in traditional style at this relaxed restaurant where diners eat at low tables while luxuriating on colourful cushions. Popular dishes include *mantı* (Turkish ravioli with yoghurt sauce), *pide* (Turkish pizza) and the decadent cheese-stuffed, honey-drenched, cream-topped dessert *künefe*. No alcohol is served.

Hacı Baba

İstiklâl Caddesi 39, Taksim, 34430 **Tel** *(0212) 244 18 86* **Map** *7 E4*

This busy and popular restaurant on two floors turns out the most amazing variety of tasty, colourful dishes – over 40 different hot main meals, mezes and 25 different desserts. Try the star dish, *kuzu tandır* (slow-baked lamb). The service is polished and professional, however, the decor is somewhat drab.

Konak

İstiklâl Caddesi 153, Beyoğlu, 34433 **Tel** *(0212) 249 14 86* **Map** *7 D4*

The perfect introduction to Turkish kebab culture, Konak offers a variety of well-prepared meat dishes, from the *beyti* kebab wrapped in *lavash* (flatbread) to the *İskender* kebab drenched in yoghurt and tomato sauce. The bustling restaurant also serves good *lamacun* (flatbread topped with minced meat) and *ezme* (spicy tomato dip). No alcohol is served.

Natural Grill House

Şehit Muhtar Caddesi 30/A, Taksim, 34430 **Tel** *(0212) 238 33 61* **Map** *7 E3*

Rustic tables and talented cooking are the appeal here. Fresh salads, grilled meats and baked vegetarian dishes are well cooked and presented. Mexican steak is one of the house specialties. The Grill House is popular with locals and also guests from the nearby hotels. Several different beers are served.

Taksimoda Café

Siraselviler Caddesi 5/A, Taksim, 34430 **Tel** *(0212) 334 85 00* **Map** *7 E4*

You will find a wonderful variety of food at Taksimoda, including excellent pastries and afternoon tea cakes. It is part of the Taksim Hill hotel and makes a convenient meeting point and refreshment station. Service is frenetic, more often chaotic, but the well-prepared food compensates. Alcohol is served and there is a small bar.

11 Leblon
📋 $$$

Asmalı Mescit Sokak 7, Tünel, 34430 **Tel** *(0212) 252 86 36*
Map 7 D5

Best known for its appearance in the popular Turkish film Issız Adam, this attractive, brick-walled Tünel restaurant dishes up a well-executed international menu of meat, fish and pasta dishes that would be a draw even without the big-screen fame. There is a good wine list and dancing later in the evening.

Asır Rest
♿ 🚶 🎵 📋 $$$

Kalyoncu Kulluk Caddesi 94, Beyoğlu, 34430 **Tel** *(0212) 297 05 57*
Map 7 D4

Asır is the kind of friendly, convivial place you hope to find on holiday. The staff are friendly and attentive and the food is outstandingly good and economical. Over 50 varieties of mezes are offered amongst many innovative dishes with fish, chicken and chick peas. Typical of *meyhane* (tavern) culture, there is live *fasıl* music in the evenings.

Cezayir Restaurant
🖼 📋 $$$

Hayriye Caddesi 12, Beyoğlu, 34425 **Tel** *(212) 245 99 80*
Map 7 E4

An attractive, high-ceilinged dining room and lounge, as well as a large garden open in the summer months, provide a smart but relaxed setting for dinner and drinks. The menu features mainly modern Mediterranean cuisine with Turkish undertones and there are fixed-price options. Alcohol is served.

Galata House
🚶 🎵 $$$

Galata Kulesi Sokak 15, Galata, 34420 **Tel** *(0212) 245 18 61*
Map 7 C5

Both the location and the cuisine are unusual at this Georgian restaurant situated in a rambling old house that used to serve as the British jail in the early 1900s. The various dumpling dishes are highly recommended, and diners with a hankering for *blinis* or *borscht* will not find a better place to satisfy their craving. Alcohol is served.

Leb-i-Derya
🚶 📋 $$$

İstiklâl Caddesi, Kumbaracı Yokuşu, Kumbaracı Han 115/7, Beyoğlu, 34430 **Tel** *(0212) 293 49 89*
Map 7 D5

It is hard to beat this restaurant's marvellous view over Istanbul. Glass, wood and soft lighting are the backdrop for the abundance of appetizers and well-cooked Mediterranean-style healthy main courses, vegetable dishes and salads. There is a lively bar that attracts a dedicated happy hour crowd.

Refik
🚶 📋 $$$

Asmalı Mescit Sokak, Tünel, 34430 **Tel** *(0212) 243 28 34*
Map 7 D5

Refik is an icon of Bohemian Beyoğlu. The restaurant retains its faded plastic tablecloths and bygone era ambience. Intellectuals and media types frequent it every evening. It is an authentic *meyhane* (tavern) that favours Black Sea dishes. The mezes here are large enough for a main meal. Plenty of alcohol is served.

Yakup 2
♿ 🚶 🖼 📋 $$$

Asmalımescit Sokak 21, Tünel, 34430 **Tel** *(0212) 249 29 25*
Map 7 D5

Once the most popular restaurant amongst the journalistic and media elite, Yakup now caters more for groups and tourists. It is in the atmospheric and upbeat backstreets of Beyoğlu. The food is of a high quality with excellent salads, grills and impressive mezes. There are drinks of all sorts and many just come to enjoy this.

Zindan
🚶 📋 $$$

İstiklâl Caddesi, Emir Nevruz Sokak, Olivya Geçida 5/5A, Beyoğlu, 34430 **Tel** *(0212) 252 73 40*
Map 7 E4

Terracotta bricks and vaulted ceilings form the interior at Zindan. It is handy for Taksim and the cooking is classic Ottoman with intriguing variations. Stinging-nettle *börek* (pastry) is rare and tasty and they spruce up the meaty kebabs with fruit. Everything looks and tastes appetizing, and there are good wines.

Fischer
🚶 🎵 📋 $$$$

İnönü Caddesi 41/A, Gümüşsuyu, 34430 **Tel** *(0212) 245 25 76*
Map 7 F4

Fisher was one of the first middle European restaurants in Istanbul. The clientele has stayed loyal after decades and dishes such as borscht, schnitzel, pirogies and strudel seem as popular today as they have always been. It is a little drab, even austere, but the owners seem reluctant to renovate or change too much of a good thing.

Gitane
🚶 🖼 🎵 📋 $$$$

Firuzağa Mah, Cezayir Sokak 3 (French Street), Galatasaray, 34430 **Tel** *(0212) 245 92 63*
Map 7 D4

Gitane is owned by one of Turkey's most renowned fashion designers. The extensive menu has choices for breakfast, brunch, lunch and festive dinners and there is excellent local wine on offer. The cheese platter highlights Anatolian cheeses.

Şerif
🚶 🖼 📋 $$$$

Cumhuriyet Caddesi. 36/A Elmadağ, 34430 **Tel** *(0212) 291 99 55*
Map 7 F2

The carefully prepared menu at this very stylish up-to-the-minute café-bar cum restaurant has masterful touches. Appetizers, hamburgers and pizzas are good, and the steak, vegetable dishes, stews, fries and salads come in generous portions. Şeref has domestic wines and a well-stocked bar.

Sofyalı
♿ 🚶 🖼 📋 $$$$

Sofyalı Sokak 9, Tünel, Beyoğlu, 34430 **Tel** *(0212) 245 03 62*
Map 7 D5

Tucked away in a leafy alleyway where restaurant competition is fierce, Sofyalı has delicious home-made mezes, pretty tables and a solid reputation for skillful, professional cooking. The menu is not large but quality dominates. Try the stuffed fish. Their stuffed chard creation is also legendary. Domestic wines and other alcoholic drinks are served.

Key to Price Guide *see p198* **Key to Symbols** *see back cover flap*

Yeni Hong Kong

Dünya Sağlik Sokak 12/B, Taksim, 34430 **Tel** *(0212) 252 42 68*   **Map** *7 F4*

A taste of imperial China in the middle of Taksim, Yeni Hong Kong is easily recognized by its imposing pagoda-shaped entrance. Dragons, lanterns and rich trappings add to the decoration. The spicy Szechuan dishes, beef with hot pickles and delicious rice are good choices. Chinese beer and rice wines are available.

Asmalımescit Balıkçısı

Sofyalı Sokak 5/A, Tünel, 34430 **Tel** *(0212) 251 39 39*   **Map** *7 D5*

The pulse of Beyoğlu beats at this popular fish-only restaurant. Linen, silver service and candles add class to the stone walls and cheerful, chic atmosphere. Every kind of fresh daily catch in Istanbul is served here. Desserts are good and there is a reasonable wine list. There are monthly art exhibitions that adorn the walls.

Ayazpaşa Rus Lokantasi

Inönü Caddesi 77a, Gümüşsuyu, 34430 **Tel** *(0212) 243 48 92*   **Map** *7 F4*

This place near Taksim Square is the destination of choice for those who wish to indulge in a little "sari vodka". This was a favourite drink of the Russians who came to Istanbul during World War I, and it is served in cold carafes and small goblets. The waiters have been working here for years and will be happy to clarify anything on the menu.

Flamm

Sofyalı Sokak 12/1, Asmalımescit, 34430 **Tel** *(02120 245 76 04/05*   **Map** *7 D5*

One of the pioneer "nouveau" restaurants, Flamm is small and intimate with a casual, friendly cocktail bar. The owner came to Istanbul from Bodrum, and imported some dishes from sunny Med-side kitchens, including ingenious ways with pasta and rice. You will want to return for the excellent honest cooking and convivial ambience.

Mikla

Marmara Pera Hotel, Meşrutiyet Caddesi 167/185, Tepebaşı, Beyoğlu, 34430 **Tel** *(0212) 293 56 56*   **Map** *7 D5*

Mikla provides a magnificent dining experience – if you can get a reservation. It offers a predominantly seafood menu but unusual culinary influences mingle and the results are exquisite. There are plenty of meat dishes too. The decor is subtle and the mood dignified. There are stunning vistas from the bar at the top of the Marmara Pera Hotel.

The Panorama

Marmara Hotel, Taksim Square, Taksim, 34430 **Tel** *(0212) 251 46 96*   **Map** *7 E4*

This restaurant with fine views on the top floor of the Marmara Hotel was one of the first in the city to embrace international cuisine. It still deserves its original praise for creative cuisine. Visitors revel in the truly outstanding French and Italian food and authentic decor. Live jazz and dance music is played on weekends.

GREATER ISTANBUL

Beyti

Orman Sokak 8, Florya, 34710 **Tel** *(0212) 663 29 90*

Beyti is a 60-year-old Istanbul institution and award-winning legend when it comes to meat and kebabs. There is a vast dining area, with 12 dining rooms and secluded nooks. It is crowded here for lunch and dinner and the good service matches the unerringly excellent food. Beyti kebab is the speciality. There is a good wine selection.

Çiya Kebap

Güneşlibahçe Sokak 48/B, Kadıköy 34710 **Tel** *(0216) 336 30 13*

Turkish and foreign foodies flock to the "Çiya empire" – three restaurants on the same bustling street – for an ever-changing menu of dishes lovingly collected from all around Turkey by the owner. Unusual stews include one with meat, quince and chestnuts, and the candied walnut dessert is not to be missed. No alcohol is served.

Da Mario

Dilhayat Sokak 7, Etiler, 56730 **Tel** *(0212) 265 15 96*

This was one of Istanbul's first Italian restaurants and is still recognized for its refined and tasty cuisine. The up-market chic decor is in harmony with the contemporary cooking. Veal is especially well prepared. There are some interesting wines. Super desserts and impeccable service round it off. Reservations are advised.

Il Piccolo

Bağdat Caddesi, Ogün Sokak 2, Caddebostan, 95230 **Tel** *(0216) 369 64 43*

An established favourite that has been serving well-cooked dishes for many years and keeping up with trends. Located in an energetic shopping district on the Asian side, meals are served outdoors in summer and a live band plays on weekends. They have simple pizzas and pasta dishes with great sauces plus good wines and Italian cheeses.

Koşebaşı Ocakbaşı

Çamlık Sokak 15/3, Levent, **Tel** *(0212) 270 24 33*   **Map** *7 F1*

This internationally-acclaimed prize-winning kebab restaurant has many branches around Turkey and in Istanbul. Bright and airy with absolutely delicious kebabs in the tradition of eastern Turkey. They prepare *künefe* (a rich angel hair dessert baked with cheese) better than anybody in Istanbul.

Zeyrekhane

            ♿ ⚡ 🍴 ☰   ⑤⑤

Sinanağa Mahallesi, Ibadethane Arkası Sokak 10, Zeyrek, Fatih, 35600 **Tel** *(0212) 532 27 78*   **Map** *2 B2*

This café for tasty snacks and light meals is combined with a restaurant in a restored Ottoman building. The cool, leafy outdoor courtyard is used in summer. The main restaurant succeeds spectacularly with traditional Ottoman recipes. Alcohol is served. It is best to make a booking for an evening meal.

Akdeniz Hatay Sofrasi

            ⚡ 🍴 ☰   ⑤⑤⑤

Ahmediye Caddesi 44/A, Fatih, 34093 **Tel** *(0212) 531 33 33*   **Map** *1 B4*

This large, friendly restaurant offers delicious southeastern Turkish offerings, including juicy metre-long kebabs studded with pistachios, and succulent lamb with rice cooked inside a salt shell that is cracked at the table. The warm hummus with *pastirma* (Turkish pastrami) is also a rare treat. No alchohol served.

Cercis Murat

            ♿ 🍴 ☰   ⑤⑤⑤

Yazmacı Tahir Sokak 22, Suadiye, 34740 **Tel** *(0216) 410 92 22*

Impeccable service and presentation add to the treat of enjoying Mardin-style delicacies in Istanbul. Try the silver platter of a dozen or more salads, dips and other mezes, each with their own distinctive flavour, or the tandoori-cooked lamb. A bit of a trek for anyone staying on the European side, but reachable by ferry. Alcohol is served.

Develi

            ⚡ 🍴 ☰   ⑤⑤⑤

Gümüşyüzük Sokak 7, Samatya, Kocamustafapaşa, 35420 **Tel** *(0212) 529 08 33*

It is no exaggeration to say that you have not really eaten a kebab until you have tucked into a Develi one. Kebabs here are prepared in unusual ways and the quality keeps getting better. The service is slick and all the touches that make dining a great experience are found here. Develi easily tops the kebab charts.

Hünkar

            ♿ ⚡ 🍴 ☰   ⑤⑤⑤

Akdeniz Caddesi 21, Fatih, 35600 **Tel** *(0212) 621 64 33*   **Map** *1 C4*

This family-run restaurant has an admirable record for serving tasty Turkish food, including delightful and little known Ottoman dishes. The walls are decorated with jars of bright pickled fruits and a small fountain sits in the midst of diners. *Böreks* (stuffed pastry parcels), *köfte* (meatballs), *pilavs* (rice dishes) and salads are well prepared and served.

Sedef

            ♿ ⚡ 🍴 ☰   ⑤⑤⑤

Fevzipaşa Caddesi 19, Fatih, 35600 **Tel** *(212) 532 82 33*   **Map** *1 C3*

This is a bright and spacious restaurant that prides itself on its meat dishes. Grilled meats are the most popular but do not overlook the delicious vegetable stews. The chef does great things with hamburgers and, of course, kebabs. Children's portions are available. Like most establishments in the Fatih area, alcohol is not served.

Uludağ Et Lokantası

            ♿ ⚡ 🍴 ☰   ⑤⑤⑤

Istanbul Caddesi 12, Florya, 34710 **Tel** *(0212) 624 95 90*

One of several well respected kebaberies in Istanbul, this one also serves up its own local kebab specialty. The restaurant is on the waterfront, not far from the airport, and has space for over 1,000 guests. Come here for a typical Turkish evening and unfailingly good food. The service is smart and the wines reasonable.

Asitane

            ⚡ 🍴 🎵 ☰   ⑤⑤⑤⑤

Kariye Hotel, Kariye Camii Sokak 18, Edirnekapı, 38100 **Tel** *(0212) 635 79 97*   **Map** *1 B1*

This is an outstanding eatery specializing in Ottoman cuisine. They serve some rare and obscure recipes inspired by records found in the Topkapı Palace. Steaks, fish and creative rice dishes are also on offer. Save room for the filling desserts. Asitane is highly recommended.

Denizkızı

            ♿ ⚡ 🍴 🎵 ☰   ⑤⑤⑤⑤

Çakmaktaşı Sokak 3/5, Kumkapı, 28601 **Tel** *(0212) 518 86 59*   **Map** *2 C5*

The cobbled streets of the old fishing neighbourhood of Kumkapı are dense with fish restaurants and *meyhanes* (traditional taverns). Denizkızı (which means mermaid) is one of these in a lively district. Diners select fish from the tank and the chef will fry, grill or steam it for you with vegetables. There are tables outdoors in summer.

Doğa Balık

            ⚡ ☰   ⑤⑤⑤⑤

Akarsu Caddesi 46, Cihangir, Taksim, 34433 **Tel** *(0212) 293 91 44*   **Map** *7 E5*

This is a highly regarded fish restaurant in an attractive area. Everything is friendly and comfortable here. Mezes are freshly prepared and colourful, and there is a daily set menu available. The salads are masterful. Domestic wines are available but rakı goes best with the many fish selections.

Hacıbey

            ♿ ⚡ 🍴 ☰   ⑤⑤⑤⑤

Teşvikiye Caddesi 156/B, Teşvikiye, 80400 **Tel** *(0212) 231 71 34*   **Map** *8 A2*

A bright and modern restaurant on two floors, Hacıbey caters to shoppers and ladies who lunch in Istanbul's shopping district. Try the succulent and substantial Bursa kebab, which has butter, tomato sauce and is topped with yoghurt. All grills are done over traditional charcoal. It is great fun here but can be very loud.

La Maison

            ⚡ ☰   ⑤⑤⑤⑤

Müvezzi Caddesi 63, Beşiktaş, 82500 **Tel** *(0212) 227 42 63*   **Map** *9 D3*

This is a thoroughly reliable and no-nonsense restaurant with a studious attitude to classical French cooking, enhanced by splendid vistas over the Bosphorus to the Asian side. La Maison is just as popular for power lunches as it is for receptions and intimate dining. It is hugely popular, so a reservation is essential.

Key to Price Guide *see p198* **Key to Symbols** *see back cover flap*

Mezzaluna

🏃 📋 $$$$

Abdi İpekçi Caddesi 38/1, Nişantaşı, 80400 **Tel** *(0212) 231 31 42*   **Map** *8 A3*

Mezzaluna attracts shoppers and strollers at lunch and a serious social set in the evenings. With branches in other Turkish cities also, they cater for the upwardly mobile who crave well-cooked continental dishes. The accent is on Italian cooking and the mussels are first rate. Finish a refined meal with a potent grappa.

Café du Levant

♿ 🏃 📶 📋 $$$$$

Rahmi M. Koç Museum, Hasköy Caddesi 27, Hasköy, 69800 **Tel** *(0212) 369 66 07*

Long before others, Café du Levant initiated the trend for serving gourmet food in a museum setting. The standards have not changed over the years and this is one of the most efficient restaurants in Istanbul. It is not cheap but it is worth paying for this calibre of inspired cooking, with Turkish touches and global influences.

Halat Restaurant

♿ 🏃 📶 📋 $$$$$

Rahmi M. Koç Museum, Hasköy Caddesi 27, Hasköy, 69800 **Tel** *(0212) 369 66 16*

Halat Restaurant boasts French cooking with whimsical Mediterranean touches and flavours. The steak is a top choice and the separate dessert menu features flamboyant, highly original masterpieces. This restaurant offers memorable dining with the Golden Horn lapping below its terrace.

Şans

🏃 📋 $$$$$

Hacı Adil Caddesi 6, Aralık, Levent **Tel** *(0212) 280 38 38*

Visitors to Şans love the cozy atmosphere and restful garden. Şans, in fact, leaves nothing to chance and is an award-winning restaurant serving crisp Mediterranean dishes. The menu changes frequently but favourites such as spinach roots endure. The outstanding wine list is selected from around the world.

THE BOSPHORUS

à la Turka

🏃 📶 📋 $$

Hazine Sokak 8, Ortaköy, 34349 **Tel** *(0212) 258 79 24*   **Map** *9 F3*

Tucked away on a side street near Ortaköy mosque, à la Turka is a modest but attractive restaurant. It serves mostly classic Turkish dishes done to perfection. Particularly good are the dolma (stuffed vine leaves), and the chef uses herbs very creatively. It is recommended as a reliable favourite.

Çınaraltı

♿ 🏃 📶 $$

İskele Meydanı 44, Ortaköy, European Side **Tel** *(0212) 261 46 16*   **Map** *9 F3*

This is one of the cluster of restaurants on the picturesque waterfront in Ortaköy. Freshly prepared, colourful mezes, salads, meat and fish are all smartly served. The tables are close together and they pack in trendy customers, particularly at weekends. Try elsewhere if you are looking for a more romantic or intimate dining experience.

Abracadabra

📶 $$$

İskelenin Çapraz 50/1, Arnavutköy, 34275 **Tel** *(0212) 358 60 87*

Located in a funky, old multi-storey house along the Bosphorus in the relaxed Arnavutköy neighbourhood, this stylish restaurant offers a wide-ranging menu of fusion dishes with an emphasis on seasonal, local and organic ingredients, which is a rarity in Istanbul. Quirky desserts include curried banana mousse. Alcohol is served.

House Café

🏃 📋 $$$

Salhane Sokak 1, Ortaköy, 34349 **Tel** *(0212) 227-26 99*   **Map** *9 F3*

There are no restaurants that epitomize Istanbul's dynamic revival quite like this one. The colourful salads, snacks and main courses are excellent and the funky decor is amazing, especially the ornately carved bar and octopus chandeliers. It is a magnet for celebrities and always busy.

Pafuli

♿ 🏃 📶 📋 $$$

Kuruçeşme Caddesi 116, Kuruçeşme, European Side. **Tel** *(0212) 263 66 38*

In business for over two decades, Pafuli has indoor and outdoor tables. Fish and seafood, such as shrimp and squid, are freshly cooked and the superb Black Sea dishes are first rate. *Mıhlama* (corn bread), *hamsi* (anchovy) and cheese dishes are legendary. There is an extensive menu and wine list.

Picante

🏃 📶 📋 $$$

İskele Caddesi, Salhane Sok 2, Ortaköy, 34349 **Tel** *(0212) 236 17 35*

This hip, chic eatery serves an array of Latin American, Tex-Mex and Colombian dishes. It is particularly renowned for its delicious fajitas and potent margaritas. The original Picante opened in Bodrum in 1993; this Ortaköy branch is located in one of the neighbourhood's most beautiful buildings, and offers splendid views over the Bosphorus.

Deniz Restaurant

♿ 🏃 📶 📋 $$$$

Kefeliköy Caddesi 23, Kefeliköy, European Side **Tel** *(0212) 262 04 07*

Located on the seafront, Deniz Restaurant follows seaside trends in offering excellent fresh fish and seafood specialities. This is an ideal place to enjoy a meal by the Bosphorus (outdoors in summer) with smart, knowledgeable service. It is well patronized by locals and reservations are recommended.

Feriye

$$$$

Çırağan Caddesi 40, Ortaköy, European Side **Tel** *(0212) 227 22 16*

Map 9 E3

This smart waterfront restaurant housed in a 19th-century Ottoman building boasts a spectacular view and attentive but unobtrusive service. Grilled fish with saffron, octopus with cinnamon, and pistachio-stuffed chicken are among the specialities. There is also a decadent weekend brunch. A good selection of wines is available by the glass.

Hidiv Kasrı

$$$$

Hidiv Yolu 32, Çubuklu, Asian side **Tel** *(0216) 413 96 44*

Perched high on a hill with sweeping vistas of the straits, this former palace stands in the midst of a beautiful park. There is a large, formal restaurant that keeps up Turkish culinary traditions, while the terrace is open for buffet brunches on weekends. Come here for the view and sea breezes. No alcohol is served.

Kız Kulesi

$$$$

Leander's Tower, off Üsküdar ferry pier, Asian Side **Tel** *(0216) 342 47 47*

Map 10 A3

Located just offshore from Üsküdar on its own little islet in the Bosphorus, this old building is a self-service cafeteria during the day, and it rebounds spectacularly at night with a full-service restaurant, gourmet food and live music. Bookings for the restaurant and ferry service are advised.

Konak

$$$$

İstinye Caddesi 23-25, Emirgan, European Side **Tel** *(0212) 32 65 00/01*

This restored wooden mansion house is set on three floors on the water's edge. There is a comprehensive selection of meat, salad and international favourites, but fish is the dish of choice. There is alfresco dining under umbrellas on the breezy terrace in summer. The wines are unremarkable but the sea air and talented cooking compensate.

Kordon

$$$$

Kuleli Caddesi 51, Çengelköy, Asian Side **Tel** *(0216) 321 04 75*

This romantic restaurant is located in a smart and cleverly modernized warehouse. Seafood dishes are artistically presented and there is a fine selection of fresh fish daily. People come for the tempting food as much as for the stunning views of Istanbul's European shores. There is outdoor dining in summer.

Sardunya Fındıklı Restaurant

$$$$

Meclisi Mebusan Caddesi 22, Salıpazarı, Fındıklı, European Side **Tel** *(0212) 249 10 92*

Map 7 F4

The accent here is on regional Italian cuisine with some unusual international classics. Outdoor dining on the terrace is available in summer. The staff have a thoroughly professional attitude to their wines. A highly successful twin establishment is in Gayrettepe.

A'jia

$$$$$

A'jia Hotel, Kanlıca, Asian Side **Tel** *(0216) 413 93 53*

Remote from the urban crush, this beautiful restaurant is part of a hotel of the same name in a refurbished *yalı* on the Asian shore of the Bosphorus. The design is starkly minimalist and clinical but the food superb. Dishes draw on classic Italian recipes and new Mediterranean cooking with subtle flavours and colours. Reservations are advised.

Changa

$$$$$

Sakıp Sabancı Caddesi 22, Emirgan, European Side **Tel** *(0212) 323 09 01*

One of Istanbul's top dining experiences, Changa is located in a stunning setting at the Bosphorus-side Sakıp Sabancı Museum. Its lush garden and award-winning decor combine with a perfectly executed menu of fusion dishes, such as wasabi and salmon tortellini, and duck confit with pomegranates and raisins. Alcohol is served.

İskele Çengelköy

$$$$$

Wharf No. 10, Çengelköyü, Asian Side **Tel** *(0216) 321 55 06*

The indoor restaurant has a nautical theme but it is more fun to eat on the pretty outdoor terrace or garden in summer. The sea air and fishing village atmosphere complement the excellent fresh fish choices and seafood and everything is beautifully cooked, as expected at this popular venue. The service is polished and the wines reasonable.

Les Ambassadeurs

$$$$$

Bebek Hotel, Cevdet Paşa Caddesi 34, Bebek, European side **Tel** *(0212) 358 15 65*

Diners pay for the sea air and waterfront view but Les Ambassadeurs has a well-chosen menu and abundance of typically Turkish and international dishes. There are also a few Russian dishes on the menu and accompanying vodka. Bebek is a small village along the sea shore, so dining here is an intimate, neighbourhood experience.

Poseidon

$$$$$

Cevdetpaşa Caddesi 58, Bebek, European Side **Tel** *(0212) 287 95 31*

Poseidon boasts a dream location on a wooden terrace jutting out over the Bosphorus with geraniums and charming tables. There is an extensive Turkish and transnational menu but the staff encourage diners to order fish dishes. The fish chowder is sublime but can come with a large price tag so beware.

Süreyya

$$$$$

İstinye Caddesi 26, İstinye, European Side **Tel** *(0212) 277 58 86*

Originally established by a Russian immigrant, this restaurant is one of the premier landmarks along the Bosphorus, overlooking the pretty bay at İstinye. Its name comes from the original master chef and some of his recipes still feature on the menu. Caviar blinis, chicken Kiev and beef Stroganoff go down well with lemon vodka.

Key to Price Guide *see p198* **Key to Symbols** *see back cover flap*

Ta Nhcia

Köybaşı Caddesi 89, Yeniköy, 34430 **Tel** *(0212) 245 93 66*

This successful gourmet Greek restaurant serves dazzling Mediterranean creations that combine the best of Greek and Turkish cookery. The decor, presentation and signature touches make this a real treasure. Fish is recommended and the lamb dishes redefine gourmet tastes. There is an extensive wine list and Greek music after hours.

Urcan

Kireçburnu Caddesi 13, Tarabya, European Side **Tel** *(0212) 262 00 24*

Urcan is a neighbourly Bosphorus landmark on the European side, best known for its wonderful seafood dishes. The service is polished and the staff are always eager to please. The chef is wonderfully skilled and the creations are stylish, colourful and generous. This is a satisfying dining experience.

BEYOND ISTANBUL

Doyum Pide ve Kebap Restaurant

Cumhuriyet Meydanı 13, Çanakkale, 17100 **Tel** *(0286) 217 48 10*

Pide (flat bread) with various baked toppings and döner kebabs are very serious business here. Simple, delicious and filling foods, on which Turkey practically runs, are cooked to perfection with enormous pride and traditional skill. No alcohol is served. If you cannot actually eat here, ask them to make up a tasty takeaway.

Kebapçı İskender

Ünlü Caddesi 7, Bursa, 16020 **Tel** *(0224) 221 46 15*

A local landmark and one of the oldest kebab restaurants in Bursa, everybody comes here and all are welcomed almost like family. The restaurant is known for kebabs and they serve nothing else. Try the *patlıcan kebabı* (aubergine kebab) for the most satisfying main course. No alcohol is served.

Kitap Evi

Burç üstü 21, Tophane, Bursa, 16020 **Tel** *(0224) 225 41 60*

Kitap Evi is the ideal place to eat when in Bursa. They combine a culture centre with a reading room, bookstore and café. There are always papers to read, coffee to sip, friends to meet, and plenty of well-prepared snacks and cakes on hand when hunger strikes. The atmosphere here is great.

Yalova Liman Restaurant

Gümrük Sokak 7, Çanakkale, 17100 **Tel** *(0286) 217 10 45*

Overlooking the harbour in Çanakkale, this restaurant brims with character. It is popular with locals who come for the stews and soups for lunch and then fill the place for more formal grills, fish and steaks in the evening. Alcohol is served and they have a separate bar area below ground. Yalova Liman is recommended for great dining.

Yusuf Restaurant

Kültür Parkı içinde, Bursa, 16020 **Tel** *(0224) 234 49 54*

As with many of Bursa's restaurants, this one has been around a long time. They serve some of the city's best food and locals flock here for the tandır lamb (lamb cooked in a charcoal pit). The huge choice of mezes, grills and vegetarian food keeps the place packed. Tables spill over into the garden in summer. Alcohol is available.

Çamlık Motel

Sahil Yolu, İznik **Tel** *(0224) 757 13 62*

İznik is beautiful with lakes and mountains and wonderful undiscovered gems begging to be explored. Çamlık Motel is one gem that you may want to keep all to yourself. It is a tranquil and simple countrified retreat with a secluded garden. The local speciality, *İnegöl köfte* (meatballs) will tempt you to return.

Çanakkale Balık Restaurant

Opposite the Piri Reis fountain, Çanakkale, 17100 **Tel** *(0286) 218 04 41/42*

Located near the university campus, this is one of the premier local venues to enjoy excellent fish. The *ahtapot şiş* (octopus kebab) is one of the dining highlights. Meze choices and salads are vast but try to leave room for traditional desserts, such as quince and pumpkin compote. Alcohol is served. This is a highly recommended eatery.

Lalezar

Karaağaç Yolu, Edirne **Tel** *(0284) 213 06 00*

This is one of the most pleasant places in Edirne. It is a little way out of town but, after visiting local sights, there is nothing better than to sit here on the banks of the Meriç River and enjoy one of their fine dishes. Try to get a waterside table. Food is not exotic but the meze, kebabs and main courses are well cooked and served.

Leonardo Restaurant

Köyiçi Sokak 32, Polonezköy **Tel** *(0216) 432 30 82*

Leonardo has been going for years and seems to become ever more popular. There is a wonderful garden and also picnic areas and a small swimming pool. The food combines French and Austrian cuisine. They do a generous open buffet brunch on weekends. It gets very crowded because it is so close to the city centre.

Light Meals and Snacks

Eating on the streets is a part of life in Istanbul. You cannot go far without coming across a café, street stall or pedlar selling snacks to appease the hunger of busy passers-by. Savoury snacks like kebabs, *lahmacun, pide* and *börek (see pp192–7)* are eaten at any time of day, as are sweets and puddings. On every street corner you will find a *büfe* or *simit sarayı* (sandwich kiosk). If you want to sit down, try a traditional *kahve*, or one of the increasing number of European-style cafés in the more affluent and cosmopolitan parts of Istanbul. There are also dozens of American-style restaurants in the city, selling hamburgers, pizzas and other types of fast food.

STREET FOOD

A common sight on the streets of Istanbul is the seller of *simits* – chewy bread rings coated with sesame. The traditional *simit*-seller *(simitçi)* carries his fare on his head on a wooden tray; better-off ones push a glass-fronted cart from which they also sell *poğaça* (flaky pastry filled with cheese or mince), *su böreği* (filled layered pastry), *açma* (a fluffy *simit* shaped like a doughnut) and *çatal* (sweeter, eye-shaped *simits* without sesame seeds). They are all best eaten fresh.

During the summer street vendors sell grilled or boiled corn on the cob *(mısır)*, generously sprinkled with salt. In winter they sell roast chestnuts *(kestane)*.

Kağıt helvası, a sweet, is another summer snack. *Kağıt* means "paper", and the thin, crumbly layers of pastry filled with sugar melt in your mouth.

Street food in Ortaköy is dominated by *Kumpir,* baked potatoes smothered with every imaginable topping.

SANDWICH AND PASTRY SHOPS

Delicious sandwiches are on sale from small kiosks or *büfes,* usually near bus stops. They include inexpensive thin, toasted sandwiches *(tost)* and hot dogs *(sosisli sandviç).*

The snack bars of Ortaköy *(see p122)* specialize in pastries from southern Turkey like *gözleme* and *dürüm.* Both consist of thin layers of bread, grilled on a hot sheet of iron and stuffed with meat, cheese and vegetables. *Dürüm* bread is cooked first, then stuffed and rolled, while *gözleme* is cooked with the ingredients inside, then folded over in a triangle.

FISH

Fish sandwich sellers offer delicious grilled or fried fresh fish inside a large piece of bread. *Midye tava* (fried mussels), dressed with ground hazelnuts, garlic and oil, are also served inside bread or on a stick.

Fish and mussel sandwiches are sold at the Galatasaray Fish Market in Beyoğlu *(see p215).* Here you can also buy *midye dolma,* mussels stuffed with pine nuts, rice and currants *(see p196).* However, be vigilant when purchasing food that may have had a long street life, particularly in the summer months.

KAHVEHANES

The typical Turkish café, *kahvehane* (or *kahve),* is a male-dominated local coffee shop. The original Ottoman name, *kıraathane,* means "a place to read", but such cafés are more a place where men play backgammon and cards, puff on a nargile (bubble pipe) and drink endless cups of coffee and tea. No alcoholic drinks or food are served.

In tourist areas like Beyazıt and Sultanahmet, however, female foreigners will be welcome in *kahves* and, although they may be stared at, they will not be disturbed. **Çorlulu Ali Paşa Medresesi** *(see p96)* is a *kahve* popular with artists and students. The **Basilica Cistern Café** offers a cooling retreat in an unusual setting although you have to pay to get into the cistern *(see p76).* **Café Kafka** is frequented by academics and intellectuals. They serve delicious coffee, cake and snacks in a convivial atmosphere. In Eyüp *(see p120)* the **Pierre Loti Café** is another traditional *kahve.* Decorated with memorabilia and antique wall tiles, it serves good apple tea and claims to have been the haunt of Pierre Loti *(see p42).* **İsmail Ağa Café,** by the waterside in Kanlıca *(see p141),* is famous for delicious yoghurt.

Next to the Bebek ferry jetty *(see p138)* is **Bebek Kahvesi.** This café is a favourite with students and middle-class families who read their Sunday newspapers on the terrace while enjoying the breeze of the Bosphorus.

PATISSERIES AND PUDDING SHOPS

The best patisseries are in two Beyoğlu hotels: the Divan and Pera Palas *(see p104).* **Divan** is known for its chocolates. **Patisserie de Pera** retains its charm with period decor, classical music and tasty biscuits. It has a good selection of English teas. **İnci Patisserie** is famous for its excellent profiteroles and baklava. Despite its run-down appearance, it is always busy.

Next door to the Atatürk Cultural Centre *(see p220),* **Gezi Istanbul Café** sells hand-made confectionery such as truffles and rich torte.

Pudding shops *(muhallebici)* sell traditional sweet milk puddings *(see p195).* **Sütiş Muhallebicisi** is a long-established chain.

ICE CREAM SHOPS

Itinerant ice cream vendors are a common sight in residential districts in the summer. Turkish ice cream *(dondurma)* is thick and very sweet. It comes in milk chocolate and fruit varieties and is served in cones. One of the best places to eat ice cream is **Mado,** which has several outlets. Also try **Mini Dondurma** in Bebek.

EUROPEAN-STYLE CAFÉS

European-style cafés serving light meals such as salads, croque monsieur, omelettes and crepes are now common in Istanbul. Sweets usually include cheesecake, chocolate brownies, tiramisu and ice cream in summer.

The best are around Taksim and İstiklal Caddesi in Beyoğlu (see pp102–3). The elegant, late 19th-century **Lebon** serves savoury dishes such as vol-au-vents, as well as sumptuous Viennese cakes. **Leyla**, opposite the Tünel underground exit, is a popular meeting place for local media types.

Sultanahmet has a few chic, designer cafés. The **Lale Restaurant**, a hippie spot in the 1970s, now serves inexpensive casseroles and grilled chicken, as well as Turkish milk puddings.

Zanzibar, in the smart shopping district of Nişantaşı, is popular with a stylish young clientele. It serves dishes such as vegetable grill, Waldorf

salad and toast provençale. Also in Nişantaşı is the **Next Café**, which offers European-style cakes and pies as well as savoury dishes such as *börek*.

The area around Ortaköy (see p122), with its market, many craft shops and a good nightlife scene, is a haven of street food and light snacks.

Further up along the shores of the Bosphorus, in Rumeli Hisarı (see p140), there is an exclusive English café called **Tea Room**. Decorated in a colonial style, it serves scones and, of course, a variety of English teas.

Among a new generation of internet cafés (see p235) springing up in the city, one of the best is **Antique**.

Cafés are now beginning to open on the Asian side, too. One of the most interesting is **Kadife Chalet** near Moda. Housed in a 19th-century wooden building, it offers home-made cakes and dishes made with home-grown ingredients, as well as a range of herbal teas.

BARS

Despite the Islamic edict against alcohol, there are plenty of bars in Istanbul. The majority of the city's fashionable cafés turn into bars in the evening, signalled by a change of music from soft tunes to loud pop. It is possible just to sit with a drink, but for those who wish to have food, many serve pasta, steaks, grills and salads at the bar. Even bars that are not cafés during the day will serve snacks.

Pano Şaraphanesi is one of several historic wine houses found in the back streets of Beyoğlu which serve wine by the glass or bottle in convivial surroundings. A few hotel bars, such as **City Lights** at the Ceylan Inter-Continental Hotel (see p189), offer more elaborate dishes. Other bars, like **Zihni's**, have restaurant sections. Many bars feature live bands playing rock or jazz music. For further details see page 221.

DIRECTORY

KAHVEHANES

Bebek Kahvesi
Cevdetpaşa Cad 137,
Bebek.
Tel (0212) 257 54 02.

Café Kafka
Yeni Çarşı Cad 26/1,
Galatasaray.
Map 7 D4.
Tel (0212) 245 19 58.

Çorlulu Ali Paşa Medresesi
Yeniçeriler Cad 36,
Çemberlitaş.
Map 2 C4 (4 B3).
Tel (0212) 528 37 85.

İsmail Ağa Café
Simavi Meydanı,
Kanlıca.

Pierre Loti Café
Gümüşsuyu Karyağdı
Sok 5 (inside Eyüp
cemetary), Eyüp.
Tel (0212) 581 26 96.

PATISSERIES AND PUDDING SHOPS

Divan
Cumhuriyet Cad 2,
Elmadağ. **Map** 7 F3.
Tel (0212) 231 41 08.

Gezi Istanbul Café
İnönü Cad 5/1, Taksim.
Map 7 F4.
Tel (0212) 292 53 53.

İnci Patisserie
İstiklal Cad 124–2,
Beyoğlu. **Map** 7 E4.
Tel (0212) 243 24 12.

Patisserie de Pera
Pera Palas Hotel,
Meşrutiyet Cad 98–100,
Tepebaşı. **Map** 7 D5.
Tel (0212) 251 45 60.

Sütiş Muhallebicisi
Sıraselviler Cad 9/A,
Taksim. **Map** 7 E4.
Tel (0212) 252 82 68.

ICE CREAM SHOPS

Mado
Osmanzade Sok 26,
Ortaköy. **Map** 9 F3.
Tel (0212) 227 38 76.

Mini Dondurma
Cevdetpaşa Cad 107,
Bebek.
Tel (0212) 257 10 70.

EUROPEAN-STYLE CAFÉS

Antique
Kutlugün Sokak 51,
Sultanahmet. **Map** 3 E4.
Tel (0212) 517 67 89.

Kadife Chalet
Kadife Sok 29, Kadıköy.
Tel (0216) 347 85 96.

Lale Restaurant
Divanyolu Cad 6,
Sultanahmet.
Map 3 E4 (5 E4).
Tel (0212) 522 29 70.

Lebon
Richmond Hotel,
İstiklal Cad 445, Beyoğlu.
Map 7 D5.
Tel (0212) 252 54 60.

Leyla
Tünel Meydanı 186,
Beyoğlu. **Map** 7 D5.
Tel (0212) 245 40 28.

Next Café
Ihlamur Yolu 3–1,
Nişantaşı.
Map 7 D5.
Tel (0212) 247 80 43.

Tea Room
Yahya Kemal Cad 36A,
Rumeli Hisarı.
Tel (0212) 257 25 80.

Zanzibar
Teşvikiye Cad 43–57,
Reassürans Çarşısı No.60,
Teşvikiye. **Map** 8 A2.
Tel (0212) 233 80 46.

BARS

City Lights
Ceylan Inter-Continental
Hotel, Asker Ocağı Cad 1,
Taksim. **Map** 7 F3.
Tel (0212) 231 21 21.

Pano Şaraphanesi
Hamalbaşı Cad, Beyoğlu.
Map 7 D4.
Tel (0212) 292 66 64.

Zihni's
Muallim Naci Cad 119,
Ortaköy. **Map** 9 F2.

SHOPPING IN ISTANBUL

Istanbul's shops and markets, crowded and noisy at most times of the day and year, sell a colourful mixture of goods from all over the world. The city's most famous shopping centre is the Grand Bazaar and there are many other bazaars and markets to browse around *(see pp214–15)*. Turkey is a centre of textile production, and Istanbul has a wealth of carpet and fashion shops. If you prefer to do all your

Contemporary glass vase

shopping under one roof, head for one of the city's modern shopping malls which offer a variety of international and Turkish brand goods. Wherever you shop, be wary of imitations of famous brand products – even if they appear to be of a high standard and the salesman maintains that they are authentic. Be prepared to bargain where required: it is an important part of a shopping trip.

Brightly decorated candle lanterns in the Grand Bazaar

OPENING HOURS

Shops are open, in general, from 9am to 8pm Monday to Saturday; open-air markets from 8am onwards. Large shops and department stores open slightly later in the morning. The Grand Bazaar and Spice Bazaar open their gates at 8:30am and close at 7pm. Big shopping malls open from 10am to 10pm seven days a

week. Shops do not close for lunch, although a few small shops may close briefly at prayer times, especially for the midday prayers on Fridays. Most shops close for the religious holidays of Şeker Bayramı and Kurban Bayramı, but remain open on national holidays *(see pp44–7)*.

HOW TO PAY

Most shops that cater to tourists will be happy to accept foreign currency. If you can pay in cash, you can usually get a discount. Exchange rates are often displayed in shops and also appear in daily newspapers.

Credit cards are widely accepted (except in markets and smaller shops) and most vendors do not charge a commission. Resist any attempts to make you pay a small compensatory commission. It is not unusual to be asked to draw the money out from a bank on your card. Very few shops

now accept travellers' cheques. Cash and haggling are expected in the markets and bazaars. Start by offering half the asking price. In rural markets merchants may accept foreign currency.

VAT EXEMPTION

If you spend at least 118 TL in one shop, you can claim back VAT (known as KDV in Turkey), which is 18 per cent. More than 2,200 retail outlets display the Tax Free Shopping logo. The retailer will give you a Global Refund Cheque, which you should then present to the customs officials with your invoices and purchases for a cash refund when leaving Turkey.

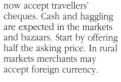

Fezes for sale a street stall

SIZES AND MEASURES

Turkey uses continental European sizes for clothes and shoes. Food and drink are sold in metric measures. This book has a conversion chart on page 227.

BUYING ANTIQUES

Before purchasing antique items, it is important to know what can and cannot be taken out of Turkey. The rule is that objects which are over 100 years old may be exported only when a certificate stating their age and granting permission to remove them from the country has been issued by the relevant

Turkish delight and boiled sweets, sold by weight at market stalls

Antiques shop in Çukurcuma

authority. Museums issue these certificates, as does the Ministry of Culture in Ankara, who will also undertake to authenticate the correct age and value of an object, if necessary. The shopkeeper from whom you bought your goods will often know which museum will be authorizing your purchases for export. In theory, a seller should already

have registered with a museum all goods for sale that are over 100 years old. In practice, sellers usually only seek permission after a particular item has been sold. In the past, antiques could be removed from Turkey without a certificate. Although this has changed, the export of antiques is not forbidden, as some believe. If the proper authorities permit your purchase to be exported, you can either take it with you or send it home, whether or not it is over 100 years old. Do take note, however, that taking antiques out of Turkey without proper permission is regarded as smuggling, and is a punishable offence.

Van cats and Kangal dogs have recently been included in this category.

HOW TO BARGAIN

In up-market shops in Istanbul, bargaining is rarely practised. However, you will probably do most of your shopping in the Grand Bazaar and the shops located in or around the old city (Sultanahmet and Beyazıt). In these places haggling is a necessity, otherwise you may be cheated. Elsewhere you can try making an offer but it may be refused.

Bazaar shopkeepers, characterized by their abrasive insistence, expect you to bargain. Always take your time and decide where to buy after visiting a few shops selling similar goods. The procedure is as follows:
• You will often be invited inside and offered a cup of tea. Feel free to accept, as this is the customary introduction to any kind of exchange and will not oblige you to buy.
• Do not feel pressurized if the shopkeeper turns the shop upside down to show you his stock – this is normal practice and most salesmen are proud of their goods.
• If you are seriously interested in any item, be brave enough to offer half the price you are asked.
• Take no notice if the shopkeeper looks offended and refuses, but raise the price slightly, aiming to pay a little more than half the original offer. If that price is really unacceptable to the owner he will stop bargaining over the item and turn your attention to other goods in the shop.

Haggling over the price of a rug

SHOPPING MALLS AND DEPARTMENT STORES

Istanbul's modern shopping malls are popular for their entertainment as well as their shopping facilities. They have multiscreen cinemas, food courts selling fast food and chic cafés, and hundreds of shops.

Akmerkez in Etiler is an ultra-modern skyscraper where leading Turkish fashion companies and outlets for famous international names can be found. **Forum**, in Bayrampaşa, houses 265 stores, an aquarium and a technology court in a landscape of boulevards, avenues and piazzas. **Galleria**, next to the yacht marina in Ataköy, offers a wide range of well-known clothes stores, including a branch of the French department store, Printemps, and an ice rink (see p222). **Kanyon**, in Levent, boasts 160 stores, a cinema, gourmet restaurants and a fitness centre. The mall is anchored by a Harvey Nichols.

International names alongside Turkish shops in Akmerkez

SEASONAL SALES

Clothes shops are the main places for seasonal sales (indirim), although department stores and a number of speciality shops also have them. They begin in June or July and continue to the end of September. The winter sales start as soon as New Year shopping is over in early January and continue until mid-April. There are no sales in bazaars – every day of the year offers bargains depending on your haggling skills.

Where to Shop in Istanbul

Caviar in the Spice Bazaar

Istanbul is home to a vast range of shops and bazaars. Often shops selling particular items are clustered together, competing for custom. The Grand Bazaar *(see pp98–9)* is a centre for carpets and kilims, gold jewellery and leather jackets, as well as every type of handicraft and souvenir. Nişantaşı and İstiklal Caddesi on the European side, and Bağdat Caddesi

on the Asian side, have a good range of clothes and shoe shops. The best choices for food are the Spice Bazaar *(see p88)* and the Galatasaray Fish Market *(see p215)*.

CARPETS AND KILIMS

One of the best places to buy carpets and kilims in Istanbul is in the Grand Bazaar *(see pp98–9)*, where **Şişko Osman** has a good range of carpets. **Nakkas** offers a range of quality carpets and kilims in a huge variety of sizes, colours and patterns. The **Cavalry Bazaar** *(see p71)* has many kilim shops, and **Hazal Halı**, in Ortaköy, is run by a wonderfully professional lady who knows the history of almost all of the carpets.

FABRICS

As well as rugs, colourful fabrics in traditional designs from all over Turkey and Central Asia are widely sold. **Sivaslı Yazmacısı** sells village textiles, crocheted headscarves and embroidered cloths.

Brightly coloured Central Asian *suzani* wall hangings

Centrally located behind the Blue Mosque, **Khaftan** offers a wide selection of traditional Ottoman textiles. The antiques dealer **Aslı Günşiray** sells both original Ottoman and reproduction embroidered cloths.

JEWELLERY

Istanbul's substantial gold market centres on Kalpakçılar Bası Caddesi in the Grand Bazaar. Here gold jewellery is sold by weight, with a modest sum added for craftsmanship, which is generally of good quality. The daily price of gold is displayed in the shop windows. Other shops in the Grand Bazaar sell silver jewellery, and pieces inlaid with precious stones.

Icons for sale in the Grand Bazaar

Urart stocks collections of unique gold and silver jewellery inspired by the designs of ancient civilizations. **Antikart** specializes in restored antique silver jewellery made by Kurds and nomads in eastern Turkey.

LEATHER

Turkish leatherwear, while not always of the best quality hides, is durable, of good craftsmanship and reasonably priced. The Grand Bazaar is full of shops selling leather goods. **B B Store**, for example, offers a good range of ready-to-wear and made-to-order garments.

Meb Deri sells designer handbags and small leather goods, and **Desa** has classic and fashionable designs.

ANTIQUES AND BOOKS

The best area for antiques is Çukurcuma *(see p107)*, in the backstreets of Beyoğlu. Shops worth a visit are **Aslı Günşiray**, **Antikhane** and **Antikarnas** for their Turkish, Islamic and Western stock. A vast array of Ottoman antique brassware, furniture and pottery, including Turkish coffee cups and vases, are sold in the Grand Bazaar.

The antiquarian bookshops, such as **Librairie de Pera** sell old postcards and prints. One of the very best shops for new books is **Galeri Kayseri**, which sells a wide selection of English-language titles.

HANDICRAFTS AND SOUVENIRS

All types of Turkish arts and crafts can be found in the Grand Bazaar. Ideal gifts and souvenirs include embroidered hats, waistcoats and slippers, mother-of-pearl inlaid jewellery boxes, meerschaum pipes in the shape of heads, prayer beads made from semi-precious stones, alabaster ornaments, blue-eye charms to guard

against the evil eye, nargiles (bubble pipes) and reproductions of icons. At the **Istanbul Crafts Centre** *(see p76)*, watch the traditional art of calligraphy being practised. **Rölyef** in Beyoğlu, the **Book Bazaar** *(see p94)*, **Artrium** and **Sofa** also sell antique and reproduction calligraphy, as well as *ebru* (marbled paintings) and reproductions of Ottoman miniature paintings.

POTTERY, METAL AND GLASSWARE

Hundreds of shops in the Grand Bazaar are stocked with traditional ceramics, including many pieces decorated with exquisite blue-and-white İznik designs *(see p161)*. Other types of pottery come from Kütahya – distinguished by its free style of decoration – and Çanakkale *(see p170)* – which uses more modern designs, often in yellows and greens. To purchase a modern piece of Kütahya ware, visit **Mudo Pera** which stocks a collection by Sıtkı Usta, a master of Kütahya pottery. Most museum shops also have a good range of pottery for sale, including reproduction pieces.

The Grand Bazaar and the Cavalry Bazaar *(see p215)* are centres of the copper and brass trade and offer a huge selection to the browsing visitor. For glassware, **Paşabahçe**, the largest glass manufacturer

in Turkey, creates delicate *çeşmibülbül* vases (decorated with blue and gold stripes) and Beykoz-style ware (with gilded decoration).

FOOD, DRINK, HERBS AND SPICES

The spice bazaar *(see p88)* is the place to buy nuts (especially pistachios) and dried fruits, herbs and spices, jams and the many types of herbal tea produced in Turkey. These include sage

(*adaçayı*), linden (*ıhlamur*) and camomile (*papatya*). However, other foods can be bought here as well, including such luxuries as caviar. Another place with a wide variety of good quality herbs, jams, teas and spices is the Galatasaray Fish Market.

Several shops specialize in particular foods. **Şekerci Hacı Bekir** is renowned for its delectable Turkish delight and baklava. Also popular is **Bebek Badem Ezmesi**, on the Bosphorus, widely acclaimed for its pistachio and almond fondants. Over the course of more than a century in business, **Kurukahveci Mehmet Efendi** *(see p86)* has become the best known producer of Turkish coffee. The quintessential Turkish spirit, raki *(see p197)*, can be bought in any grocery store.

Pickled fruits and vegetables, sold in markets and on street stalls

DIRECTORY

Istanbul's Markets

İznik-style plate, Cavalry Bazaar

Whether you want to lose yourself in the aromas of exotic spices, rummage for old prints and miniatures among secondhand books, hunt for souvenirs or just shop for food, you will find a market or bazaar catering to your tastes somewhere in Istanbul. An obvious first stop is the Grand Bazaar, but several others are well worth visiting for their more specialized produce and their atmospheric settings. Every neighbourhood in Istanbul has its own open-air market on a specific day of the week. At these markets, crowded with budget-conscious housewives, you will find a huge variety of merchandise at the cheapest possible prices.

Spice Bazaar
The Spice Bazaar is an exotic trading house for dried herbs, spices and other foodstuffs (see p88).

Wednesday Street Market
One of Istanbul's colourful neighbourhood markets, the Wednesday market, is next to the Fatih Mosque (see p113) and sells everything from fresh produce and household goods to bulbs and seeds.

THE BAZAAR
QUARTER

GOLDEN HORN

SULTANA

Book Bazaar
Next to the Grand Bazaar, the Book Bazaar (Sahaflar Çarşısı) offers a wealth of printed matter in various languages, from tourist guides to academic tomes and old magazines (see p94).

Grand Bazaar
The largest market in the world, the Grand Bazaar contains about 4,000 shops. In this roofed labyrinth of passages you can find every commodity associated with Turkey, from costly jewellery to basic foodstuffs. It has operated for hundreds of years (see pp98–9).

Şişli Feriköy Organic Market
Istanbul's first organic fruit and vegetables market is open every Saturday in Feriköy.

Ortaköy Flea Market
Every Sunday the main square of Ortaköy is filled with stalls selling souvenirs to suit every budget, from junk to fine jewellery and original Turkish handicrafts (see p122).

EYOĞLU

B O S P H O R U S

Galatasaray Fish Market
The best fish market in Istanbul runs along a historic alleyway. Constantly sprinkled with water to keep them cool, fresh fish from the Sea of Marmara and elsewhere lie waiting to be sold (see p103).

THE ASIAN SIDE

AGLIO
OINT

Kadıköy Street Market
The main market on the Asian side of the city fills the streets around Mahmut Baba Sokağı. Clothes are sold on Tuesdays, and food on Fridays.

Cavalry Bazaar
Converted Ottoman stables are the setting for this bazaar below the Blue Mosque (see pp78–9). Carpets (see pp218–9) are the main items touted, but handicrafts and jewellery are also on sale (see p71).

| 0 metres | 500 |
| 0 yards | 500 |

What to Buy in Istanbul

Turkish slippers

With its endless bazaars, markets, shops and stalls, Istanbul is a souvenir hunter's paradise. If you are seeking a bargain, jewellery and leather can be worth investing in. For something typically Turkish, there is a wide selection of ceramics and copperware based on the designs of traditional Ottoman handicrafts and arts. The city's antique shops *(see p212)* are also worth a visit. Istanbul is possibly most famous for its carpets and kilims *(see pp218–9)*, but check the quality before you buy.

Copperware

Antique copperware can be very expensive. Newer items, however, are also available, at more affordable prices.

Copper goblets

Pipes

Classic nargiles (bubble pipes) are still used by older Turkish men. They make attractive ornaments even if you do not smoke.

Antique copper water ewer

Jewellery

Jewellery includes pendants made from gold, silver, semi-precious stones and other materials. A simple blue glass eye is said to ward off evil.

Blue glass-eye pendants

Ceramics

Ceramics form a major part of Turkey's artistic tradition. The style varies according to the area of origin. Blue and white pottery is in the İznik style (see p161); other areas of production include Kütahya and Çanakkale (see p170).

Colourful Kütahya ware

Green jugs from Çanakkale

Blue and white decorated plate

İznik-style tile

Miniatures

Istanbul has a history of miniature painting, examples of which can be seen in the city's museums, especially Topkapı Palace (see p57). These tiny works of art, often depicting the sultan at court, were once bound in books. Those for sale are copies of originals.

Miniature from the Grand Bazaar

Box inlaid with mother-of-pearl

Box with painted scenes on bone inlay

Handicrafts

Jewellery boxes crafted from wood or bone, alabaster figurines and other hand-made ornaments make unusual souvenirs.

Textiles

Hand-woven cloths, including ikat work (where the cotton is dyed as it is woven), fine embroidery and knits are just some of the range of textiles that can be bought.

Embroidered scarves, known as oyalı

Cotton ikat work

Glassware

This elegant jug is an example of the blue and white striped glassware, çeşmibülbül, made in the Paşabahçe works (see p147).

Çeşmibülbül jug

Local Delicacies

Delicious sweets such as halva, Turkish delight and baklava are very popular. A huge range of fragrant spices, dried fruit and nuts are sold loose by weight in the city's bazaars.

Halva

Nuts in honey

Turkish delight

Mulberries

Sunflower and pumpkin seeds

Chickpeas

Dried red peppers and aubergines

Apricots

Almonds

Pistachio nuts

Turkish Carpets and Kilims

The ancient skill of weaving rugs has been handed down from generation to generation in Turkey. Rugs were originally made for warmth and decoration in the home, as dowry items for brides, or as donations to mosques. There are two main kinds of rug: carpets (*halı*), which are knotted, and kilims, which are flat-woven with vertical (warp) and horizontal (weft) threads. Many foreign rugs are sold in Istanbul but those of Turkish origin come in a particularly wide range of attractive colours. Most of the carpets and kilims offered for sale will be new or almost new; antique rugs are rarer and far more expensive.

A carpet may be machine-made or handmade. Fold the face of the rug back on itself: if you can see the base of the knots and the pile cannot be pulled out, it means that it is handmade.

Carpets are made using three different combinations of material: wool on wool, silk on silk, or wool on cotton.

Weaving a Carpet
Wool for rugs is washed, carded, spun and dyed before it is woven. Weaving is a cottage industry in Turkey; the women weave in winter leaving the summer months for farming duties.

CARPET
This reproduction of a 16th-century Uşak carpet is known as a Bellini double entrance prayer rug.

RUG-MAKING AREAS OF WESTERN TURKEY

The weaving industry in Turkey is concentrated into several areas of production, listed below. Rug designs are traditional to their tribal origins, resulting in a wide range of designs and enabling the skilled buyer to identify the area of origin.

CARPETS
① Hereke
② Çanakkale
③ Ayvacık
④ Bergama
⑤ Yuntdağ
⑥ Balıkesir
⑦ Sındırgı
⑧ Milas
⑨ Antalya
⑩ Isparta

KILIMS
⑪ Denizli
⑫ Uşak

CARPETS AND KILIMS
⑬ Konya

Indigo

Madder

Camomile

Dyes
Before chemical dyes were introduced in 1863, plant extracts were used: madder roots for red; indigo for blue; and camomile and other plants for yellow.

The **"prayer design"** is inspired by a mihrab, the niche in a mosque that indicates the direction of Mecca (see pp38–9).

The tree of life motif at the centre of the kilim is symbolic of immortality.

BUYING A RUG

Before you buy a rug, look at it by itself on the floor, to see that it lies straight – without waves or lumps. Check that the pattern is balanced, the borders are of the same dimensions, and the ends are roughly the same width. The colours should be clear and not bleeding into one another. Bargaining is essential (see p211), as the first price given is likely to be at least 50% higher than the seller really expects.

Buying a good quality old rug at a reasonable price, however, is a job for an expert. The age of a rug is ascertained from its colour, the quality of the weaving and the design. Check the pile to make sure that the surface has not been painted and look for any repairs – they can easily be seen on the back of the rug. Restoration of an old carpet is acceptable but the repair should not be too visible. Make sure the rug has a small lead seal attached to it, to prove its authenticity and that it may be exported, and ask the shop for a receipt.

KILIM

Kilims are usually made using the slit weave technique by which a vertical slit marks a colour change.

The width of a rug is limited by the size of the loom. Most rugs are small because a large loom will not fit into a village house.

Kilim pieces are used to make a variety of smaller craft objects, also for sale in carpet shops.

Burdock motif   **Chest motif**

Motifs

The recurring motifs in rugs – some of them seemingly abstract, others more figurative – often have a surprising origin. For instance, many are derived from marks that nomads and villagers used for branding animals.

Motif from wolf track, crab or scorpion   **Modern motif of a human figure**

ENTERTAINMENT IN ISTANBUL

Istanbul offers a great variety of leisure pursuits, ranging from arts festivals, folk music and belly dancing to sports centres and nightclubs. The main event in the cultural calendar is the series of festivals organized by the Istanbul Foundation for Culture and the Arts *(see pp44–6)*. The festivals take place between March and November, and always draw international performers and large audiences. Throughout the year, traditional Turkish music, opera, ballet, Western classical music and plays are performed at the Atatürk Cultural Centre (AKM,

Belly dancer, Galata Tower

currently closed), the Cemal Reşit Rey Concert Hall (CRR), Haghia Eirene and other venues around the city. Beyoğlu is the main centre for entertainment of all kinds. This area has the highest concentration of cinemas in the city as well as several cultural centres, both Turkish and foreign. In the evening the bars and cafés here play live music. Ortaköy, on the European shore of the Bosphorus, is another popular venue where, on summer nights, dining, music and dancing continue into the small hours of the morning.

Copies of *The Guide*

ENTERTAINMENT GUIDES

Istanbul has a bi-monthly entertainment and listings magazine in English called *The Guide*. This publishes the programmes of the AKM and CRR, and information on other cultural events, as well as bars and nightclubs around the city. *The Guide* is sold at the larger, central newsagents and book shops. The English-language newspaper *Turkish Daily News*, available from news-stands, also has information on entertainment in Istanbul.

Lists of events taking place at individual theatres and cultural centres (including those attached to foreign consulates) can be obtained from tourist information offices *(see p229)*.

The Turkish Airlines in-flight magazine, *Skylife*, has details of major events, and the daily Turkish newspaper *Hürriyet* has listings in Turkish.

BOOKING TICKETS

Tickets for performances at the Atatürk Cultural Centre (currently closed) and Cemal Reşit Rey Concert Hall can be purchased one week in advance from their box offices. Perhaps one of the fastest and most convenient ways to book and pay for tickets to any event is through **Biletix**. **Vakkorama** department store and **Galleria, Akmerkez** and **Capitol** shopping centres sell tickets for large pop and jazz concerts, and also for performances at the Atatürk Cultural Centre and Cemal Reşit Rey Concert Hall.

LATE-NIGHT TRANSPORT

The last late-night buses and dolmuşes leave at mid-night from Taksim, which is close to many entertainment venues. Taxis run throughout the night. During the music festivals in June and July there is a special bus service which runs between show venues and central parts of Istanbul.

FESTIVALS

Five arts festivals, four annual and one biennial, are organized by the Istanbul Foundation for Culture and the Arts. The Film Festival runs from March to April every year, the Theatre Festival is in May and June, the Music and Dance Festival – the original and biggest festival – is in June

and July and the Jazz Festival is in July. The biennial Fine Arts Festival takes place in the autumn. Tickets for all these festivals can be bought over the phone from the **Istanbul Festival Committee**, which also has programme details, and from the venues.

The Yapı Kredi Arts Festival, Akbank Jazz Festival and Efes Pilsen Blues Festival are also in the autumn *(see p46)*.

WESTERN CLASSICAL MUSIC AND DANCE

Every season the Istanbul State Opera and Ballet companies, State Symphony Orchestra and State Theatre perform a wide repertoire of classical and modern works. The companies share the same venue: the 900-seat **Atatürk Cultural Centre** in Taksim, which is currently closed. Early booking is essential for shows here. The **Cemal Reşit Rey Concert Hall** stages concerts of

Classical concert in the church of Haghia Eirene *(see p60)*

Folk dancing at Kervansaray, a long-established venue

Western classical music as well as hosting a wide variety of music and dance groups from all over the world. Concerts, operettas and ballets are also performed at smaller venues throughout the city.

Laser disc screenings of opera, ballet and classical music performances are held most days at 2pm and 6pm at the **Aksanat Cultural Centre**. It also sometimes stages live plays and music recitals.

ROCK MUSIC AND JAZZ

Istanbul has an increasing number of bars and clubs playing good live music. **Hayal Kahvesi** is a bar dedicated to jazz, rock and blues by groups from Turkey and abroad. It also has an outdoor summer branch next to the Bosphorus in Çubuklu. The **Q Jazz Bar**, located in the grounds of the Çırağan Palace Hotel Kempinski (see p190), is an exclusive jazz bar which regularly invites well-known performers. Further up the Bosphorus, in Ortaköy, the **Rock House Café** is an imitation of the famous Hard Rock Café. It has live bands on certain nights of the week.

In the city centre, **Kemancı** features live rock and heavy metal performers. In **Sappho** they play softer, more

Musicians at the Jazz Festival

sophisticated jazz and quality Turkish pop music. Other venues for Turkish pop are **Tribunal** and **Vivaldi**, while at **Beyoğlu Sanat Evi** they play Turkish pop with strong folk music influences.

NIGHTCLUBS

The luxurious, summer-only **Club 29** is probably the most glamorous nightclub in Istanbul. It has a restaurant, swimming pool and torch-lit garden with glorious views of the Bosphorus. Every half-hour a boat ferries guests to and from İstinye on the European side. The bar becomes a disco after midnight. **Reina**, also open in summer only, is the city's biggest nightspot, with a large dancefloor right beside the Bosphorus, as well as several bars and restaurants. **Majesty**, a chic bar and restaurant complex next to the Bosphorus, has a delightful outdoor balcony. Live bands play in the bar and there is dancing to Caribbean music. The restaurant features Turkish music and dance. **Milk** is a popular club open on Thursday, Friday and Saturday nights which plays House, Garage and other electronica.

Avoid the seedier-looking clubs in Beyoğlu, as these have been known to coerce clients into paying extortionate bills.

TRADITIONAL TURKISH MUSIC AND DANCE

Traditional Turkish music is regularly performed at the Cemal Reşit Rey Concert Hall. This includes Ottoman classical music, performed by an ensemble of singers and musicians, mystical Sufi music and folk music from various regions of Turkey. In summer, recitals of Turkish music are occasionally organized in the Basilica Cistern (see p76), which has wonderful acoustics. The Sultanahmet Tourist Office (see p229) has details.

Fasıl is a popular form of traditional music best enjoyed live in *meyhanes* such as **Ece, Istanbulin Dinner Show** and **Asır Rest** (see p201). It is usually performed by gypsies on instruments which include the violin, *kanun* (zither), *tambur* and *ut* (both similar to the lute).

Belly dancing is performed mainly in nightclubs. Though often underrated, the sensuous movements of the female dancers are considered an art. Many clubs and restaurants stage belly dancing together with Turkish folk music and dance. Dinner is often included in the show. One of the best venues is the restaurant in the **Galata Tower** (see p105). Other venues featuring top performers are **Kervansaray, Orient House** and **Manzara**.

A folkloric whirling dervish troupe gives a public performance at the Mevlevi Monastery (see p104) once a month.

The traditional *ut*, a lute-like instrument played in *fasıl* music

CINEMAS

The latest foreign films are on general release in Istanbul at the same time as other European countries. They are screened in their original languages with Turkish subtitles.

The majority of the city's cinemas are on İstiklal Caddesi. Of these, **Alkazar**, **AFM Fitas** and **Atlas** tend to show art-house films. There are also numerous cinemas in Kadıköy, on the Asian side, while all the main shopping centres have multi-screen cinemas.

The first screening of the day is half-price, and many cinemas offer tickets at half-price all day on Wednesdays. Students with a valid card are entitled to a discount for all showings. There is usually an interval.

THEATRE

Plays by Turkish and international playwrights are staged in Istanbul's theatres, but only in Turkish. A popular company is the Istanbul State Theatre, the resident group at the **Atatürk Cultural Centre** (AKM). They will perform at other theatres across the city while AKM undergoes renovations.

HEALTH CLUBS AND SPORTS CENTRES

All the main five-star hotels have good swimming pools and welcome non-residents for a daily fee. Health clubs such as the **Vakkorama Gym**, the **Alkent Hillside Club** and the **Cihangir Sports Center** can also be used by non-members for a daily fee.

At the edge of the Belgrade Forest, the **Kemer Country Riding and Golf Club** has stables and a 9-hole golf course. It also offers riding and golf lessons. For ice-skaters, the rink in the **Galleria** shopping centre (see p211) is open to the public after 7pm. Skates are available for hire.

Yoga and detox centres are cheaper than in the rest of Europe and becoming increasingly popular.

SPECTATOR SPORTS

Football has a very large following in Turkey. The three Istanbul teams, **Beşiktaş**, **Fenerbahçe** and **Galatasaray**, all compete at international level and play in Istanbul most Sundays. Horse racing takes place at **Veli Efendi** race-course between 14 April and 31 October, on Wednesdays and at weekends. The Istanbul **Formula One** racing circuit is on the Asian side of the city, and is where the Turkish Grand Prix is held in August. In summer there are yacht regattas in the Sea of Marmara (see p45). For an unusual spectator sport, head to Edirne at festival time, to see the grease wrestling (see p154).

Galatasaray team logo

BEACHES

The best place to swim, water-ski and windsurf in Istanbul is the Princes' Islands (see p159). Yörükali Plajı, on Büyükada, is a public beach, but it is safe to swim anywhere around the islands.

There are large beaches at Kilyos (see p158) and Gümüş-dere on the Black Sea, about 30 minutes' drive from central Istanbul, and Şile (see p158). The Black Sea can be rough at times, however, with big waves and dangerous undercurrents, so always exercise caution on these beaches. The Marmara Islands (see p169), are also popular for their beaches.

CHILDREN

Little in Istanbul has been designed with children in mind. Nevertheless, there are many things to interest children and increasingly activities and sights that will attract them.

However, children are welcome and will be made a fuss of almost everywhere they go. With a little thought you can find plenty of things for children to do.

The Archaeological Museum (see pp62–5) has a special children's section tracing the history of mankind, with a medieval castle and a Trojan horse to climb on.

The **Turkuazoo Aquarium** at Forum Istanbul shopping centre (see p211) is open daily and boasts an 80 metre (262 ft) underwater tunnel.

There are parks at Yıldız (see pp124–5) and Emirgan (see p141). Another park near Emirgan, the **Park Orman**, is a family complex situated in woods, with picnic areas, a swimming pool and a theatre. **Miniatürk** in Sütlüce, on the edge of the Golden Horn, boasts an extensive model village of miniature replicas of Turkey's cultural land-marks, as well as restaurants, shops and a pool. On the Princes' Islands, where there are no cars, children can cycle safely, or take a tour in a horse-drawn carriage. The **Toy Museum** in Göztepe is the first of its kind in Turkey. In Darıca, 28 miles (45 km) from Istanbul, the **Bosphorus Zoo** has exotic animals in natural habitats.

A theme park near Istanbul

DIRECTORY

BOOKING TICKETS

Akmerkez
Nispetiye Cad, Etiler.
Tel (0212) 282 01 70.

Biletix
Tel (0216) 556 98 00.
www.biletix.com

Capitol
Tophanelioğlu Cad 1,
Altunizade.
Tel (0216) 391 19 20.

Galleria
Sahil Yolu, Ataköy.
Tel (0212) 559 95 60.

Vakkorama
Osmanlı Sok 13,
Taksim. **Map** 7 E4.
Tel (0212) 251 15 71.

ISTANBUL FESTIVAL COMMITTEE

Tel (0216) 454 15 55.
www.istfest.org

WESTERN CLASSICAL MUSIC AND DANCE

Aksanat Cultural Centre
İstiklal Cad 16,
Taksim.
Map 7 D4.
Tel (0212) 252 35 00.

Atatürk Cultural Centre (AKM)
Taksim Meydanı,
Taksim.
Map 7 F3.
Tel (0212) 251 56 00.

Cemal Reşit Rey Concert Hall (CRR)
Darülbedayi Cad,
Harbiye.
Map 7 F1.
Tel (0212) 231 54 97.

ROCK MUSIC AND JAZZ

Beyoğlu Sanat Evi
Abdullah Sok 22/1,
Beyoğlu.
Map 7 E4.
Tel (0212) 252 61 96.

Hayal Kahvesi (Beyoğlu)
Büyükparmakkapı Sok 19,
Beyoğlu. **Map** 7 E4.
Tel (0212) 244 25 58.

Hayal Kahvesi (Çubuklu)
Burunbahçe Mevkii,
Çubuklu. ☐ *May–Oct.*
Tel (0216) 413 68 80.

Kemancı
Sıraselviler Cad 69/1–2,
Taksim. **Map** 7 E4.
☐ *May–Jun.*
Tel (0212) 251 27 23.

Q Jazz Bar
Çırağan Palace Hotel
Kempinski, A Blok,
Beşiktaş. **Map** 9 D3.
Tel (0212) 236 24 89.

Rock House Café
Princess Hotel, Dereboyu
Cad 36–8, Ortaköy.
Map 9 F2.
Tel (0212) 227 60 10.

Sappho
İstiklal Cad, Bekar Sok 14,
Beyoğlu. **Map** 7 E4.
Tel (0212) 245 06 68.

Tribunal
Muammer Karaca Çıkmazı
3, Beyoğlu. **Map** 7 D5.
Tel (0212) 249 71 79.

Vivaldi
Büyükparmakkapı Sok
29/1, Taksim. **Map** 7 E4.
Tel (0212) 293 25 99.

NIGHTCLUBS

Club 29
A. Adnan Saygun Cad,
Ulus Parkı içi, Ulus.
Tel (0212) 358 29 29.
www.club29.com

Majesty
Muallim Naci Cad,
Salhane Sok 10/2,
Ortaköy.
Map 9 F3.
Tel (0212) 236 57 57.

Milk
Akarsu Yokuşu 5,
Galatasaray.
Map 7 E5.
Tel (0212) 292 11 19.

Reina
Muallim Naci Cad 44,
Kuruçeşme. **Map** 9 F2.
Tel (0212) 259 59 19.
www.reina.com.tr

TRADITIONAL TURKISH MUSIC AND DANCE

Ece
Tramvay Cad 104,
Kuruçeşme.
Tel (0212) 265 96 00.

Galata Tower
Galata-Tünel. **Map** 3 D1.
Tel (0212) 293 81 83.

Hasır
Beykoz Korusu, Beykoz.
Tel (0216) 322 29 01.

Istanbulin Dinner Show
Cumhuriyet Cad, Cebel
Topu Sokak 2, Harbiye.
Tel (0212) 291 84 40.
www.istanbulin.org

Kervansaray
Cumhuriyet Cad 30,
Elmadağ. **Map** 7 F2.
Tel (0212) 247 16 30.

Manzara
Conrad Hotel, Yıldız Cad,
Beşiktaş. **Map** 8 C3.
Tel (0212) 227 30 00.

Orient House
Tiyatro Cad 27, next to
President Hotel, Beyazıt.
Map 2 C4 (4 A4). *Tel
(0212) 517 61 63.* www.
orienthouseistanbul.com

CINEMAS

AFM Fitas
İstiklal Cad 24, Beyoğlu.
Map 7 E4.
Tel (0212) 251 20 20.

Alkazar
İstiklal Cad 179, Beyoğlu.
Map 7 E4.
Tel (0212) 293 24 66.

Atlas
İstiklal Cad 209, Beyoğlu.
Map 7 D4.
Tel (0212) 252 85 76.

HEALTH CLUBS AND SPORTS CENTRES

Alkent Hillside Club
Alkent Residential Complex,
Tepecik Yolu, Etiler.
Tel (0212) 257 78 22.

Cihangir Sports Center
Sıraselviler Cad 118,
Mavi Plaza, Cihangir.
Tel (0212) 245 12 55.

Cihangir Yoga
Meclisi Mebusan Yokuşu
51, Cihangir.
Tel (0539) 572 84 37.
www.cihangiryoga.com

Istanbul Sailing Club
Fenerbahçe.
Tel (0212) 336 06 33.

Kemer Country Riding and Golf Club
Göktürk Beldesi,Uzun
Kemer Mevkii, Eyüp.
Tel (0212) 239 79 13.

Vakkorama Gym
Osmanlı Sok 13, Taksim.
Map 7 E4.
Tel (0212) 251 15 71.

SPECTATOR SPORTS

Beşiktaş FC
Spor Cad 92, Beşiktaş.
Map 8 A4.
Tel (0212) 227 87 80.

Fenerbahçe FC
Fenerbahçe Spor Kulübü,
Kızıltoprak, Kadıköy.
Tel (0216) 345 09 40.

Formula One
www.formula1-istanbul.
org

Galatasaray FC
Hasnun Galip Sok 7,
Galatasaray. **Map** 7 E4.
Tel (0212) 251 57 07.

Veli Efendi Hipodromu
Türkiye Jokey Kulübü,
Osmaniye, Bakırköy.
Tel (0212) 543 70 96.

CHILDREN

Bosphorus Zoo
Darica.
Tel (0216) 653 83 15.

Miniatürk
İmrahor Cad, Sütlüce.
Tel (0212) 222 28 83.
www.miniaturk.com.tr

Park Orman
Fatih Çocuk Ormanı,
Maslak Cad, Maslak.
Tel (0212) 223 07 36.

Toy Museum
Dr. Zeki Zeren Sokak 17,
Göztepe.
Tel (0216) 359 45 50.

Turkuazoo Aquarium
Bayrampaşa.
www.turkuazoo.com

SURVIVAL
GUIDE

PRACTICAL INFORMATION

Rapidly expanding Istanbul has the transport, banking and medical facilities of any large modern city. However, in remoter suburbs of the city, and less-visited parts of the Bazaar Quarter, banks and ATM machines may be thin on the ground, so it is worth carrying a day's supply of Turkish lira. It also makes sense to carry the AKBİL travel pass *(see p241)*, a mobile phone and/or phone card.

Büyük Saray Mozaikleri Müzesi

Official sign to a tourist sight

Certain aspects of Turkish culture may seem strange to the foreign visitor, especially if you have never travelled in a Muslim country. It is not considered rude to stare and foreigners are objects of attention in quarters less visited by tourists. *Istanbullus* (Istanbul residents) are subject to the same pressures as any modern urban dweller, but in general are friendly and hospitable, and appreciate any effort to show respect for their traditions.

WHEN TO GO

With its hot, humid summers and cold, wet winters, Istanbul is best visited in May and June or September and October, when the weather is usually warm and sunny enough to enjoy open-air cafés but not too hot to explore on foot. This said, mid-summer temperatures seldom exceed 30°C (86°F) and sightseeing is manageable if you avoid walking around in the midday heat. Bear in mind that you will need to be suitably dressed (shoulders and knees must be covered) when visiting mosques *(see p227)*. The city is at its least busy (and best value) in winter, and the sights are all the better for the lack of crowds. However, fog and rain may be encountered so take a coat and umbrella.

Tourists on the steps of Dolmabahçe Palace on a sunny day

CUSTOMS INFORMATION

Only airports and main road entry points offer a full customs service. At major ports or marinas, customs hours are 8:30am–5:30pm on weekdays. Outside these hours a fee must be paid to consult a customs official. You can buy duty-free items at the airport on entering the country. Visitors over 18 years old can bring in generous amounts of coffee, perfume (5 bottles), spirits (5 litres/180 fl oz) and cigarettes (500). There is no limit on the amount of foreign currency or Turkish lira you can bring in. The maximum when leaving is US$5,000 (or Turkish lira equivalent). In practice, this is rarely enforced.

Turkey is very strict with regard to illegal drugs. Sniffer dogs are used at Atatürk and Sabiha Gökçen airports. You need to have a permit to export antiquities *(see p210)*.

VISAS AND PASSPORTS

Visitors to Turkey should have a full passport with at least six months validity. Overstaying your visa incurs a fine, which escalates rapidly. Citizens of the following countries require visas, paid for in hard currency at the point of entry into Turkey: UK (£10), Canada (US$60), Australia (US$20), USA (US$20) and Ireland (€10). Most tourist visas are issued for three calendar months. Citizens of some countries must apply for a visa before arrival. The process is more complicated

if you arrive by sea. Requirements can and do change, so for up-to-date information contact the Turkish consulate in your country or visit www.mfa.gov.tr.

TOURIST INFORMATION

Tourist information office in Sirkeci

TOURIST INFORMATION

The sign for a tourist information office is a white "i" on a green background in a white box. The offices themselves are named in English and Turkish. They rarely have much printed information to give out but the main office in Sultanahmet Square, in particular, will be able to answer questions on all aspects of your stay in Istanbul. Edirne, Bursa, İznik and Çanakkale have offices near the town centre. Most information offices are open 9am–5pm, Mon–Sat. Some stay open later in summer, while the one in the arrivals terminal of Atatürk airport is open 24 hours daily.

ADMISSION FEES AND OPENING HOURS

Entry fees to Istanbul's major monuments and museums are comparable to elsewhere in Europe, although smaller, less well known establishments are considerably cheaper. In some momuments there is an additional charge for a special section, for example the Harem in Topkapı Palace *(see pp54–9)*.

Most sights are closed one day a week, usually Monday or Tuesday. Exhibits in the most-visited museums are generally labelled in Turkish and English. Museum opening times are usually 8:30 or 9am to 5 or 6pm, with a break for lunch in smaller establishments. Remember that it is best to avoid mosques at prayer times *(see below)*.

Shops open from 8:30 or 9am to 7 or 8pm *(see p210)*. For information on opening times of banks and exchange offices *(döviz) see page 232*.

Public offices are closed on Saturdays and Sundays, and some shops on Sundays, although shopping malls, supermarkets and small grocers' are invariably open seven days a week.

ETIQUETTE

In Istanbul around 10 per cent of women cover their arms, legs and heads in public. Residents of devout areas such as Fatih *(see pp110–13)* may be offended at exposed limbs in the street. In areas like Beyoğlu *(see pp101–7)* most Turkish women dress as they choose and visitors can do the same, except when visiting a mosque *(see below)*.

Although areas like Beyoğlu are lined with bars and restaurants, most Turks drink alcohol in moderation, and overt drunkenness and

Wearing the veil, a matter of personal choice for Turkish women

The venerable Blue Mosque *(see pp78–9)*

rowdiness are frowned upon. Visitors who transgress the law while intoxicated will get little sympathy.

Traditional rules of etiquette and hospitality are still an important aspect of Turkish society. Always show respect for Atatürk *(see p31)*, whose picture you will see often.

Discreet gay and lesbian visitors are unlikely to experience problems and Istanbul has a lively gay scene, though overt displays of affection are best kept to a minimum.

Since 2009 smoking has been prohibited in all enclosed spaces, including government offices, public transport, restaurants, bars and even *nargile* cafés, establishments devoted to smoking the traditional water pipe.

VISITING MOSQUES

Although large mosques are open all day, closing after last prayers in the evening, smaller ones open only for the five daily prayer times *(namaz)*. At these times it may be difficult to gain entrance outside prayer times unless there is a caretaker around to open up for you. Non-Muslims should try not to enter any mosque during prayers.

The times of prayer change throughout the year according to sunrise and sunset. They are displayed on a board either outside or inside the mosque, but are always signalled by the call to prayer

(ezan) from a loudspeaker that is fixed to the minaret of the mosque.

When visiting a mosque women and men should dress appropriately. Most mosques in Istanbul have a prominent notice outside, in English, noting the entry requirements: cover your head (women) and bare shoulders (both sexes); no skirts above the knee or shorts; remove shoes. Some mosques provide shawls to cover head, arms and shoulders. Shoes are usually left on racks in the entryway, but you may prefer to carry them with you as theft is not unknown. Some mosques provide elasticated plastic bags to slip over your shoes instead of removing them. Make as little noise as possible inside and show consideration for anyone who is praying there.

TAXES AND TIPPING

The rate of VAT (KDV in Turkish) varies between 8 and 23 per cent, though the most common rate is 18 per cent. It is included in hotel prices as well as in the purchase price of most goods and services.

A service charge of 10 to 15 per cent is usually charged in upmarket and licensed restaurants and cafés, and it is customary to tip the waiters here a further 5 per cent. Waiters working in more basic establishments will also appreciate a gratuity.

LANGUAGE

As a rule, Turks will make every effort to communicate with foreigners. In areas frequented by tourists it is easy to find English-speakers, but it is worth making an effort to learn a few words and phrases in Turkish. The Phrase Book on pages 279–80 is a useful place to start.

PUBLIC CONVENIENCES

Public toilets are thin on the ground in Istanbul, usually located in prominent underpasses and at transport terminals. Entrances are marked *Bay* for men and *Bayan* for women. The attendant sitting outside, whom you pay on exit (a sign generally shows the charge), may supply toilet paper, but it is a good idea to carry tissues with you. Fortunately, virtually every mosque (of which there are many) has facilities attached for both men and women. Like public toilets, there is usually an attendant and a small fee is charged.

Sign for a public toilet

If you are reluctant to use the squat toilets generally found in public and mosque facilities, you can ask to use the modern flush-style toilets in most restaurants, hotels or cafés. Museums and major sights all have toilets and, outside the city, motorway service areas have excellent, free washroom facilities.

TRAVELLERS WITH SPECIAL NEEDS

Istanbul has few facilities for disabled people and the poor state of the streets can make it difficult to get around. Few mosques allow wheelchairs, and very few museums have disabled access. Toilets with special facilities are also very rare. Conversely, museum staff and the public will go to great lengths to assist with entry to buildings, and there are some low-level public telephones and special access buses (see p239). Trams are accessible to wheelchair

users, although accessing some of the underground stations will be difficult. Other stations have platforms with gentle ramps from street level (see p240).

The **Turkish Tourist Office** in London publishes a guide to facilities for the disabled in Turkey. This contains specific details of hotels as well as general information. The **Turkish Association for the Disabled** (Türkiye Sakatlar Derneği) helps disabled people living in Istanbul, and can arrange bus tours around the city for small groups of disabled tourists.

WOMEN TRAVELLERS

Women travelling in Turkey may receive unwelcome attention from men, but are rarely in danger of physical attack. To avoid harassment, dress respectably and look purposeful when walking around. Avoid being out alone at night. Traditional cafés (see pp208–9) tend to be male preserves, while restaurants often have a section reserved for women and families (see p193). The Beyoğlu area of Istanbul, along with many of the more prosperous suburbs, is a different proposition, and women can and do go out and about without male company, even at night.

Students outside the Moorish-style gateway of Istanbul University

STUDENTS

Apart from a small discount on inter-city trains, an ISIC card is of little use in Turkey. Budget accommodation is easy to find. In July and August you can get a bed in a student dormitory through the Sultanahmet tourist information office. There are also a few youth hostels (see p183), and some cheap hotels and guesthouses in the city centre (see pp184–91).

PHOTOGRAPHY

Museums do not usually charge visitors for using cameras, but there is often a charge for the use of a video camera. Flash is forbidden in most museums, as are tripods. Some mosques do not permit

Groups of friends socializing at a café in Beyoğlu

the use of a flash, but discreet photography is usually allowed. It is polite to ask permission before taking photographs of people.

TIME

Turkey is 3 hours ahead of GMT in summer (March–October) and 2 hours ahead for the rest of the year.

ELECTRICITY

As in Europe, the electric current is 220V AC. Plugs have two round pins and adaptors are readily available in Turkey.

CONVERSION CHART

Imperial to Metric
1 inch = 2.54 centimetres
1 foot = 30 centimetres
1 mile = 1.6 kilometres
1 ounce = 28 grams
1 pound = 454 grams
1 pint = 0.6 litres
1 gallon = 4.6 litres

Metric to Imperial
1 centimetre = 0.4 inches
1 metre = 3 feet, 3 inches
1 kilometre = 0.6 miles
1 gram = 0.04 ounces
1 kilogram = 2.2 pounds
1 litre = 1.8 pints

Colourful display of fruit and vegetables at a market stall

RESPONSIBLE TOURISM

Traditionally, recycling is carried out by members of the Roma community who, pulling hand-carts fitted with giant sacks, scavenge through the large waste-bins left out on the street for collection. Plastics, paper, metal and glass are sold to private operators for recycling. Some Turks help by leaving recyclable materials next to bins rather than putting them in – visitors could do the same.

Environmental awareness in Turkey is improving, with municipality-controlled recycling bins beginning to appear on the streets of Istanbul and other cities. Visitors should make use of these when available.

Electricity is expensive, so many Turks use solar-energy systems for their hot-water needs. If you are serious about energy conservation, check that your proposed accommodation has a system installed. For the same reason low-energy light bulbs have caught on in a big way here.

Street markets are abundant in Istanbul *(see pp214–215)* and buying from them reduces the amount of packaging – try the Wednesday market (Çarşamba Pazarı) in Fatih.

DIRECTORY

CONSULATES

Australia
Asker Ocağı Cad 15, Elmadağ-Taksim. **Map** 7 F3. *Tel (0212) 243 13 33.*

Canada
İstiklâl Cad 189/5, Beyoğlu. **Map** 7 D4. *Tel (0212) 251 98 38.*

New Zealand
İnönü Cad 48/3, Taksim. **Map** 7 F4. *Tel (0212) 244 02 72.*

United Kingdom
Meşrutiyet Cad 34, Tepebaşı. **Map** 7 D4. *Tel (0212) 334 64 00.*

United States
Kaplıcalar Mevkii 2, İstinye. *Tel (0212) 335 90 00.*

TOURIST INFORMATION

Atatürk Airport
International Arrivals Hall. *Tel (0212) 465 31 51.*

Hilton Hotel Arcade
Cumhuriyet Cad, Elmadağ. **Map** 7 F2. *Tel (0212) 233 05 92.*

Karaköy International
Maritime Passenger Terminal (Terminal 2). **Map** 3 E1. *Tel (0212) 249 57 76.*

Sirkeci Station
Sirkeci İstasyon Cad, Sirkeci. **Map** 3 E3 (5 E1). *Tel (0212) 511 58 88.*

Sultanahmet Square
Divanyolu Cad 3, Sultanahmet. **Map** 3 E4 (5 E4). *Tel (0212) 518 18 02.*

RELIGIOUS SERVICES

Anglican Christ Church
Serdar-ı Ekrem Sok 82, Tünel. **Map** 7 D5. *Tel (0212) 251 56 16.*

Greek Orthodox St George's Cathedral
Sadrazam Ali Paşa Cad 35, Fener. *Tel (0212) 525 21 17.*

Jewish Neve Shalom Synagogue
Büyük Hendek Cad 61, Şişhane. **Map** 6 C5. *Tel (0212) 293 75 66.*

Presbyterian All Saints Church
Yusuf Kamil Sok Paşa 10, Moda. **Map** 3 D5 (4 C5). *Tel (0216) 449 39 74.*

Roman Catholic St Anthony of Padua
İstiklâl Cad 325, Galatasaray. **Map** 7 D4. *Tel (0212) 244 09 35.*

TRAVELLERS WITH SPECIAL NEEDS

Turkish Association for the Disabled
Tel (0212) 521 49 12.
www.tsd.org.tr

Turkish Tourist Office
170–73 Piccadilly, London W1V 9DD, UK. *Tel (020) 7839 7778.*

Personal Security and Health

Badge of the Turkish police

Istanbul is safer than many other European cities, and visitors rarely encounter violence. It is, however, a fast-growing city with huge disparities between rich and poor, and burglary, pickpocketing and petty theft are all on the rise. Keep an eye on your valuables in crowded areas and do not wander the streets late at night on your own. The standard of health care in the city is very good, with excellent private hospitals. For minor complaints, pharmacists will be able to provide advice.

POLICE

There are several police forces in Turkey. The Security Police (*Emniyet Polisi*), the city's main force, wear dark-blue uniforms and caps, and pale-blue shirts. The Tourist Police (*Turizm Polisi*) is a branch of the *Emniyet Polisi*. Most officers have some knowledge of one or two European languages. The Tourist Police station in Sultanahmet, opposite the Basilica Cistern (*see p76*), is open 24 hours daily, and has an English–Turkish translator available 8:30am to 5pm Monday to Friday.

The Dolphin Police (*Yunus Polisi*) is a rapid-reaction branch of the *Emniyet Polisi*. Dolphin officers ride motorbikes and wear black biking leathers with a red stripe.

The Traffic Police (*Trafik Polisi*) wear the same blue uniform as the *Emniyet Polisi* but with a white belt, hat and gloves. Officers patrol the streets in black and white cars equipped with loudspeakers.

The navy-blue-uniformed Market Police (*Zabıta*) is a municipal police force, which patrols bazaars and other areas of commerce.

The Military Police (*Askeri İnzibat*) controls Turkey's many conscripts and officers wear an army uniform and white helmet bearing the abbreviation "As İz". The Gendarme (*Jandarma*) polices rural areas.

Dolphin Motorbike Police badge

WHAT TO BE AWARE OF

When looking after your personal safety use common sense as you would in any large city. Be alert for pickpockets, particularly at markets, as well as on public transport and at termini. Keep your cash in a money-belt and other valuables, such as cameras and mobile phones, well out of sight. Carry bags on your front with the strap worn across your shoulder. In the event of any trouble, shout *"imdat"* (help) to alert fellow passengers or officials. If necessary contact the Tourist Police. Women travelling alone or in groups without a male escort may need to take extra care. After dusk, avoid the areas bordering the old city walls as muggings have taken place here. The Tarlabaşı neighbourhood of Beyoğlu is notorious for petty theft, drug-dealing and prostitution, and Taksim Square, especially around the Tarlabaşı Bulvarı exit, can be unsavoury at night. Do not leave valuables in your hotel room (use the hotel safe), and remember that Turkish law requires that you carry ID, preferably your passport (or at least a photocopy of it), at all times. Official tourist guides all carry photo ID around their necks – avoid any who do not. Finally, make sure your taxi driver turns on his meter before setting off.

IN AN EMERGENCY

For emergency telephone numbers see the directory opposite. If your condition is serious or life-threatening you should be treated automatically, but carry your insurance details with you to prove your ability to pay. The state-run **Taksim İlkyardım Hastanesi** (Taksim Emergency Hospital) has a decent reputation. The American and German hospitals listed in the directory have emergency dental practitioners.

LOST AND STOLEN PROPERTY

Turks are generally very honest and will go to great lengths to return lost property. It is worth returning to the last place the item was

Security policeman

Traffic policeman

Dolphin policeman

Fire engine

Turkish Security Police (Emniyet Polisi) car

State ambulance

seen, or going to the Tourist Police. Property left on public transport can be reclaimed from **IETT Buses**. If you have anything stolen, contact the Tourist Police. In order to make an insurance claim, you will need to give (and sign) a statement, preferably at the Tourist Police station in Sultanahmet.

HOSPITALS AND PHARMACIES

The Turkish health system has public and private hospitals. Both are usually well equipped but state-owned hospitals can be overcrowded and bureaucratic. Private establishments tend to be more efficient and more comfortable, have a higher proportion of English-speaking doctors, and some run their own ambulance services.

There are also a number of public clinics (*poliklinik*) all over the city offering treatment for minor ailments, as well as private general

practitioners (*tibbi doktorlar*) offering the same services.

The first port of call with a minor complaint, however, should be a pharmacy (*eczane*). Pharmacists are well-trained, many speak some English and antibiotics can be purchased without a prescription. Outside opening hours, the address of the nearest *nöbetçi eczane* (duty pharmacist) is usually posted in the pharmacy window.

MINOR HAZARDS

Before leaving, make sure that your basic inoculations (diphtheria, polio, typhoid and tetanus) are all up-to-date. Check with your doctor about hepatitis A and hepatitis B vaccinations.

Do not drink tap water (bottled water is readily available everywhere), and exercise care when choosing restaurants and meals. Avoid anything that has been standing around, especially seafood, and only eat salads in more upmarket restaurants.

Some travellers to Turkey experience stomach upsets, often as a result of the amount of oil used in cooking or from drinking tap water. Stick to a bland diet for a few days, eating only bread, yoghurt and rice. Drink lots of fluids and keep alcohol intake to a minimum. Should you suffer from stomach troubles, remedies available from pharmacies include Lomotil, Ge-Oral (oral rehydration salts) and Buscopan. If you are still unwell after 24 hours it is almost certainly some kind of food-poisoning and antibiotics will be required.

Mosquitoes can be a minor irritant, so bring some repellent from your home country or buy a plug-in locally.

Sign for a state hospital in Şişli

Typical sign for a pharmacy in Istanbul

TRAVEL AND HEALTH INSURANCE

The state health system in Turkey has few reciprocal agreements with other countries and private hospital costs are high, so be sure to take out travel and medical insurance before you leave.

Banking and Currency

There is no limit to the amount of currency (foreign or Turkish) you can bring into Turkey. In January 2005, after decades of sky-rocketing inflation, the New Turkish Lira (*Yeni Türk Lirası* or YTL) was introduced, and the many zeros that humbled the old currency were eliminated. Four years later, having successfully combated inflation (which had run at some 10 per cent), the government deleted the *Yeni* (New) and the nation's currency reverted to the Turkish Lira. The lira fared well in the 2009 economic meltdown, holding or increasing in value against most currencies. Visitors will have few problems paying for most things by credit card, using ATMs or making their usual banking transactions.

Cash dispenser with instructions in a range of languages

BANKS AND BUREAUX DE CHANGE

Most private banks, such as Garanti and Yapıkredi, are open 9am–5pm Mon–Fri and some bigger branches also offer limited Saturday opening. State banks, such as Ziraat, close 12:30–1:30pm. Banks can be found in all main areas, on Divanyolu Caddesi in Sultanahmet and on İstiklâl Caddesi in Beyoğlu. The İş Bankası at Atatürk airport is open 24 hours daily. Apart from Turkish banks, there are many foreign banks like Citibank and HSBC, with familiar logos and services.

Most banks have an automated queuing system. Take a numbered ticket from the dispenser (for currency exchange there is usually a button marked *döviz*) and wait for your number to flash up on screen.

Several Turkish banks have outlets at airports, offering a full range of banking services.

With modest inflation, there is no need to worry about exchanging foreign currency at the most beneficial time. Exchange offices (*döviz*) still exist, but not in the numbers they once did. Well-established offices include **Bamka Döviz** in Taksim and **Çetin Döviz** on İstiklâl Caddesi. *Döviz* are open for longer hours than banks, and also on Saturdays, but the exchange rate is often better in banks.

ATMS

ATMs are found outside all banks and near major tourist, business and shopping areas. They accept most debit cards, allowing you to withdraw the equivalent of about £250 daily. There is an English-language option on every machine. You can also use some credit cards such as MasterCard and Visa. It is worth remembering that using a debit or credit card at an ATM involves a fee.

TRAVELLER'S CHEQUES AND CREDIT CARDS

Credit and debit cards, along with ATMs, have made traveller's cheques almost obsolete. Travellers are advised not to bring them into Turkey because they are difficult to cash. If you need to have large sums of money to hand, consider using a money-order (*havale*) service such as Western Union. They have an association with the Turkish Post Office (PTT – *see p235*) and some banks. This is a safe and speedy, although expensive, way to transfer money.

Credit cards, such as VISA and MasterCard, and, to a lesser extent, American Express and Diners Club are

DIRECTORY

BANKS AND BUREAUX DE CHANGE

Bamka Döviz
Cumhuriyet Cad 23, Taksim.
Map 7 E3. **Tel** *(0212) 253 70 00.*

Çetin Döviz
İstiklal Cad 39, Beyoğlu.
Map 7 E4. **Tel** *(0212) 225 64 28.*

Ziraat Bankası
Yeniçeriler Cad 55, Beyazıt
Map 2 C4 (4 B3).
Tel *(0212) 517 06 00.*

CREDIT CARDS

American Express
Tel *(0212) 444 25 25.*

Diners Club, VISA, MasterCard and Eurocard
Tel *(0212) 225 00 80.*

A branch of HSBC in Istanbul

universally accepted in hotels, shops and restaurants. Smaller restaurants and grocery stores, however, may not accept card payment. A number of debit cards issued by international banks, such as HSBC and Citibank, are also accepted, but check before leaving that your card is valid internationally. Ensure you know your PIN number because swipe readers use chip and PIN protocol. It is also a good idea to inform your bank of your travels so that they expect your card to be used in Turkey.

There is no commission on paying with credit cards, though many hotels offer discounts for paying with cash (see p182). If you buy an airline ticket from a travel agent however, they will charge about 3 per cent commission.

CURRENCY

The Turkish currency is known as the Turkish Lira (TL) or, more officially (as your credit card statement will show), TRY. The sub-division of the lira is the kuruş, with 100 kuruş equalling 1 lira. The lowest denomination note is 5 TL, the highest 200 TL. If you are given one of the old YTL notes, which ceased to be legal tender on 1 January 2009, do not be concerned because it can still be exchanged at a state bank. Beware that some Turks, out of habit, still talk in old, hyper-inflated lira terms, asking *bir milyon* (one million) for a glass of tea (1 lira). You are allowed to take up to US$5,000 out of Turkey in cash.

Banknotes

Turkish banknotes come in six denominations: 200 TL, 100 TL, 50 TL, 20 TL, 10 TL and 5 TL, and each denomination has its own distinctive colour. All the notes display the head of Atatürk on the front, with other Turkish notables on the reverse. Those shown here are 50 TL, 20 TL, 10 TL and 5 TL.

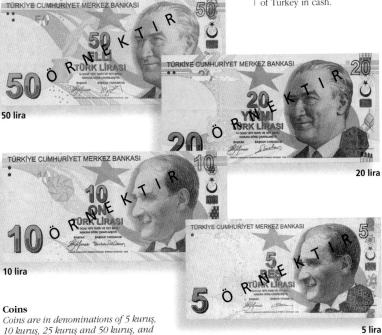

50 lira

20 lira

10 lira

5 lira

Coins

Coins are in denominations of 5 kuruş, 10 kuruş, 25 kuruş and 50 kuruş, and 1 lira (100 kuruş). All coins feature Atatürk on one side.

1 lira **50 kuruş** **25 kuruş** **10 kuruş** **5 kuruş**

Communications and Media

Postal service logo

All major cities in Turkey enjoy easy access to efficient high-speed Internet and broadband connections. Internet cafés abound, though they are now being challenged by an ever-increasing number of places offering wireless connection. The state company, Türk Telekom, has a monopoly on all fixed-line telecommunications.

Post offices are clearly identified by the letters PTT and, although slow, the postal service is fairly reliable. Making phone calls from counter-top metered phones within a PTT building is economical, and many change foreign currency and offer the Western Union service for sending and receiving money.

Dozens of Turkish papers vye for readers' attention, ranging from the pro-Islamic to the staunchly secular, and all persuasions in between. Satellite TV has revolutionized the country's once staid, parochial broadcasting, and many foreign-language channels are widely available.

INTERNATIONAL AND LOCAL TELEPHONE CALLS

Istanbul has two area codes, 0212 (European side) and 0216 (Asian side). When calling a number within the same area, it is not necessary to use the code. When calling the European side from the Asian, you must prefix the number with 0212; use the prefix 0216 when calling the Asian side from the European.

To call another city in Turkey, use the appropriate area code, for example 0224 for Bursa. To make an international call from Turkey, dial 00 followed by the code for the country, eg: Australia: 61; US and Canada: 1; New Zealand: 64; Republic of Ireland: 353 and UK: 44.

MOBILE PHONES

Mobile (cell) phones are essential items in modern Turkey. The market is dominated by three players – **Türkcell**, **Vodafone** and **Avea**. Most visitors with a roaming facility can use their existing mobile phone as they would at home because Turkey uses the standard 900 or 1800 MHz frequencies. Most North American phones are not compatible with the Turkish system and will not work here.

Requiring only a few formalities, visitors have a flexible option of purchasing prepaid SIM cards from local mobile operators. There are numerous outlets around Sirkeci Station in Eminönü. The SIM card can be slipped

into your own phone, but the phone will need to be unlocked first in order for the SIM to work. Calls made using a locally bought SIM are considerably cheaper than using your roaming facility. Be aware that the cards self-cancel after two weeks.

PUBLIC TELEPHONES

Telephone calls in Istanbul can be made from public phone boxes, post offices (PTT) and Türk Telecom (TT) centres using phonecards. The Alokart, with its scratch-off code, allows you to make calls from any landline in Turkey. Chipped Türk Telekom Kontörlü cards are available in units of 50, 100, 200 and 350. Both can be purchased at PTT and TT centres and, for an additional charge, from street sellers and kiosks.

Türk Telekom Kontörlü phonecard

INTERNET ACCESS

Istanbul has plenty of Internet cafés, although they are in short supply in the major tourist hub of Sultanahmet. Two popular, well-established options are **Robin Hood** in Beyoğlu and **Cyber Cafe** in Sultanahmet. Internet cafés charge, very modestly, by the hour, but you can usually negotiate a half-hour rate for minimal usage. The Turkish keyboard can be frustrating to use so ask for help. Look out for the dotless Turkish "ı", for example, which will render web and email addresses invalid if used inadvertently. The "@" sign is usually made by pressing the "alt" and "q" keys at the same time.

Wireless Internet (Wi-Fi) connection is now found in many hotels and guesthouses and, although some luxury hotels charge, it is usually free. Most hotels also have fixed terminals where you can

Public telephone boxes in Istanbul

Woman using free Wi-Fi point

check your mail. Many cafés in the city now offer wireless connection free of charge. VOI (voice-over-Internet) protocol permits you to make phone calls anywhere in the world from a computer providing you have the right software installed and all the necessary adaptors and hardware.

POSTAL SERVICES

Post offices are found throughout Istanbul. There are large branches, with a full range of postal services, in **Sirkeci**, **Taksim**, **Begoğlu** and **Karaköy**. Other locations are marked on the Street Finder (see pp238–48). Opening hours are usually 8:30am–5:30pm Monday to Friday and 8:30am–noon on Saturday. Stamps are only available from post offices.

Letters and postcards can be handed over the counter at post offices or posted in letter boxes, which are yellow and labelled PTT. Common signs indicating which box or slot to put your letter in are: Şehiriçi (local), Yurtiçi (domestic) and Yurtdışı (international).

Use air mail (uçak ile) when posting items abroad as surface post is slow. If you want to send a parcel by surface mail, use registered (kayıtlı) post. The contents of a package must be inspected at the post office, so take tape with you to seal your parcel at the counter. Letters

and postcards to the rest of Europe take around a week, but may take twice as long to reach other continents. A recorded delivery service (called APS) is available from post offices, with delivery in three days within Turkey. Local courier companies such as **Aras** and **Yurtiçi** will deliver letters and parcels in Turkey in a day or so at a comparable price.

Poste restante mail should be addressed with the recipient's name, then: poste restante, Büyük Postane, Büyük Postane Caddesi, Sirkeci, Istanbul, Turkey. A nominal fee is payable on collection of the mail.

NEWSPAPERS AND MAGAZINES

Turkey has two English-language daily papers, the liberal, pro-Islamic Today's Zaman and the nationalist, secular Hürriyet Daily News. Both give round-ups of Turkish and foreign news. Foreign newspapers and magazines can be obtained from newsstands wherever there are substantial numbers of tourists or foreign residents. One of the most convenient outlets is located at the İstiklâl Caddesi exit of the Tünel underground funicular railway (see p241). For current events listings try The Guide (see p220), which also has good features on Istanbul and Turkish culture. It is available from larger newsagents and book shops.

Newspaper stand outside the Topkapı Palace

TELEVISION AND RADIO

Satellite TV has blossomed in Turkey, with dozens of channels vying for viewers. Widely available foreign news channels include BBC World, CNN and Al Jazeera, with English-language entertainment provided by CNBCE, E2, BBC Entertainment and MTV. For foreign sports, look out for Eurosport and Spormax. Most hotels receive global satellite TV but check before booking if you particularly want foreign channels.

The state-owned TRT (Türk Radyo ve Televizyon) has six television channels and three radio stations. TRT2 television and TRT3 radio (FM 88.2) broadcast news bulletins in English, French and German.

GETTING TO ISTANBUL

The easiest way to reach Istanbul is to fly to one of the city's two international airports, Atatürk Airport, on the European side of the city, or Sabiha Gökçen on the Asian side. Turkish Airlines (THY) offers regular, direct flights from more than 100 destinations worldwide. Several major European carriers, such as Lufthansa and KLM, also fly direct to

Emblem of Turkish Airlines

Istanbul. Most carriers fly into Atatürk Airport, but many budget and charter firms use Sabiha Gökçen. Coaches and trains also offer frequent and well-established services between Istanbul and several European capitals. There are no direct ferry sailings from Europe, although cruises of the Aegean and Mediterranean usually include a one-day stopover in Istanbul.

Planes parked at Atatürk Airport

ARRIVING BY AIR

Turkey's main international airline, **Turkish Airlines** (THY), has direct flights to Istanbul from all major cities in Europe and some in Asia. **Lufthansa, KLM** and **British Airways** all have at least one flight daily to Istanbul. A number of budget airlines also serve Istanbul's airports. These include **easyJet**, which connects the UK with Sabiha Gökçen airport, and Turkish carrier **Pegasus**, which flies into both Istanbul airports from the UK and several European cities. German/Turkish carrier **Sunexpress** serves Sabiha Gökçen airport from many northern European countries.

Turkish Airlines flies direct to Istanbul from Chicago and New York, and **Delta Airlines**, among others, also has regular direct flights from New York. **American Airlines, Qatar Airways** and several other international carriers serve the city, but not always directly.

ATATÜRK AIRPORT

Istanbul's **Atatürk Airport** (Atatürk Hava Limanı) lies 25 km (16 miles) west of the city centre in Yeşilköy. Its huge international *(Dış Hatları)* terminal and separate domestic *(İç Hatları)* terminal are internally connected by a series of moving walkways; the journey between them takes about 5 minutes.

The international terminal has all the facilities you would expect, including 24-hour banking, car hire outlets, tourist information and a hotel reservation desk. Allow at least 2 hours to check in for departures from busy Atatürk Airport.

Taxis *(see p238)* wait outside the arrivals hall of the international terminal. The fare to Taksim or Sultanahmet will be about 40 TL.

The airport bus is a cheaper way of getting to the city centre. Buses depart every half-hour between 4am and 1am, take 30–40 minutes and

cost 10 TL. The bus stop, marked "Havaş", is situated outside the main doors of the arrivals hall. Stops include Aksaray, (from where tram/taxis run to Sultanahmet), and it terminates in Taksim Square *(see p107)*.

By far the most economical way to the city centre is by light railway *(hafif metro)* and tramway. Buy two tokens *(jeton)* at the airport terminus of the light railway and take the train to Zeytinburnu. Here use the second token and change to the tramway, which runs into Sultanahmet and across the Golden Horn to Karaköy (for Taksim/Beyoğlu).

SABIHA GÖKÇEN AIRPORT

Many domestic carriers and budget international airlines use **Sabiha Gökçen Airport**. Set in the suburbs of Asian Istanbul, 32 km (20 miles) southeast of the city centre, it has car hire outlets, banks, duty free shops and cafés.

A taxi ride to Taksim takes 1 hour and costs about 95 TL. Havaş buses travel to Taksim half-hourly between 4am and midnight. The 1-hour journey costs 13 TL.

The cheapest option is to take the I.E.T.T. *(see p239)* E3 bus to IV Levent, then the metro to Taksim. Alternatively, take the E10 bus to Kadıköy and the ferry across the Bosphorus to Eminönü (for Sultanahmet). The E3 operates every 15 minutes between 6am and 11:10pm; the E10 runs very frequently between 5am and 3:30am.

The magnificent exterior of Sirkeci Station in Eminönü

ARRIVING BY RAIL

The Orient Express (see p66) no longer runs as far as Istanbul. The best overland route, which takes two days, is from Munich via Vienna, Budapest and Bucharest. Information can be obtained on **The Man in Seat 61** website, but bookings are best done via **European Rail Ltd**.

Istanbul has

Motorway sign showing Turkish and European road numbers

two main-line stations. Trains from Europe arrive at **Sirkeci Station** (see p66), while those from Anatolia and Middle Eastern cities terminate at **Haydarpaşa Station** (see p133), linked by ferry to the European side.

ARRIVING BY COACH

The Turkish coach companies **Ulusoy** and **Varan** operate direct services from several European cities to Istanbul, with tickets available online. Ulusoy coaches depart from Munich and Thessalonica among other European cities, while Varan coaches depart

from Berlin, Prague and Vienna. For services from the UK, contact **Eurolines**.

Coaches arrive at Esenler coach station (otogar), 10 km (6 miles) northwest of Istanbul city centre. Esenler is also the main terminal for domestic connections (see p244). Coach companies usually operate a courtesy minibus to the city centre. If not, take the light railway (hafif metro, see pp240–41) from the otogar to Aksaray, or the I.E.T.T. 91 bus to Eminönü, or 830 bus to Taksim.

ARRIVING BY CAR

Drivers bringing cars into Turkey must show registration documents and a valid driving licence at the port of entry. Your passport will be stamped to show you have brought in a vehicle, and you cannot leave the country without it. You will also be issued a certificate by the Turkish customs authorities and this should be carried at all times, together with your driving licence and passport. You must have a Green Card (available from your insurance company) if arriving from Europe, and appropriate insurance. A fire extinguisher, a first-aid kit and two hazard warning triangles are mandatory. Driving in Istanbul is very taxing and public car parks (otopark or kathotopark) are scarce and often full.

DIRECTORY

ARRIVING BY AIR

American Airlines
Tel (1 800) 433 7300 (US).
www.aa.com

British Airways
Tel (0870) 850 9850 (UK).
www.britishairways.com

Delta Airlines
Tel (0800) 414 767 (UK).
Tel (404) 765 5000 (US).
www.delta.com

easyJet
Tel (0871) 244 2366 (UK).
www.easyjet.com

KLM
Tel (0871) 222 740 (UK).
Tel (1 866) 434 0320 (US).
www.klm.com.tr

Pegasus Airlines
Tel (0845) 0848 980 (UK).
www.flypgs.com

Qatar Airways
www.qatarairways.com

Sunexpress
www.sunexpress.com

Turkish Airlines (THY)
www.turkishairlines.com

AIRPORTS

Atatürk Airport
Tel (0212) 444 08 49.
www.ataturkairport.com

Sabiha Gökçen Airport
Tel (0216) 585 50 00.
www.sgairport.com

ARRIVING BY RAIL

European Rail Ltd
www.raileurope.com

Haydarpaşa Station
Tel (0216) 336 04 75.

The Man in Seat 61
www.seat61.com

Sirkeci Station
Tel (0212) 527 00 50.

ARRIVING BY COACH

Eurolines
Tel (08717) 818181-UK.
www.eurolines.com

Ulusoy
Tel (0212) 444 18 88.
www.ulusoy.com.tr

Varan
Tel (0212) 444 89 99.
www.varan.com.tr

The Bosphorus Bridge, one of two major road bridges

GETTING AROUND ISTANBUL

Street sign at a junction in central Sultanahmet

Central areas are well served by light railway, metro and tram lines. Buses and dolmuşes provide city-wide transport, but roads and vehicles are very crowded at rush-hour times. Ferries and water taxis ply the Bosphorus and, to a lesser extent, the Golden Horn. The massive Marmaray Project, scheduled for completion in 2013, will link the European and Asian sides of the city by an underwater tunnel and create more than 70 km (43 miles) of suburban rail line, with the city centre sections running underground. See the map inside the back cover for more information on Istanbul's ever-expanding public transport network.

Visitors strolling in front of the serene Blue Mosque (see pp78–9)

GREEN TRAVEL

It is possible to walk between many of Istanbul's major sights (see below), and the vast majority of the further-flung points of interest can be easily reached by public transport. Sadly, due to traffic congestion and lack of cycle routes, few people brave the city by bicycle.

Some of the city's buses use natural gas, as do most taxis, and the Metrobuses (see p239) have fuel-efficient, environmentally friendly hybrid engines.

WALKING

The development of semi-pedestrianized zones, such as İstiklâl Caddesi and central Sultanahmet, and walking/jogging routes on the shores of sections of the Sea of Marmara and Bosphorus, has made it possible to walk with ease around some parts of Istanbul. Quieter areas of the city, like Eyüp (see pp120–21)

and parts of Fatih, Fener and Balat (see pp110–13) have relatively little traffic. For specialist tour companies offering walking tours around the city see page 229.

Bear in mind that traffic only stops at pedestrian crossings controlled by lights, and always make use of pedestrian overpasses and underpasses on main roads.

Istanbul, like any city, has parts that should be avoided (see p230). If you are planning to walk in areas off the usual tourist track seek local advice, take extra care and do not walk in unfamiliar streets after dark.

Sign for a pedestrian underpass

TAXIS

Taxis are ubiquitous in Istanbul. Fares are cheap in relation to other major European cities and cabs operate day and night. They can be hailed in the street or found at taxi ranks (see pp246–56). Hotel and restaurant staff can always phone for a taxi.

Cabs are bright yellow, with the word "taksi" on a sign on the roof. They take up to four passengers. The fare is charged according to a meter. If you cross the Bosphorus Bridge the bridge toll will be added to the fare. The driver will not expect a tip unless he has helped you load luggage, but it is usual to round up the fare to the nearest convenient figure.

Most taxi drivers speak little, or no, English. They may not be familiar with routes to lesser-known sights, so carry a map and have the name of your destination written down.

Taxis queueing for customers at a ferry port

A Plan Tours sightseeing bus

DOLMUŞES

Dolmuşes are shared minibuses with fixed routes. The name derives from the Turkish word *dolmuş* ("stuffed" or "full"), and drivers usually wait until every seat is taken before setting off. Dolmuşes run throughout the day until mid-evening, and later on busy routes.

Points of origin and final destinations are displayed in the front windows. Fares generally range between 3 and 6 TL, and you pay by handing your money to the driver or another passenger to pass forward. To stop the vehicle, simply say to the driver "*inecek* (pronounced eenejek) *var*" ("somebody wants to get out").

Dolmuş stops are marked by a blue sign with a black "D" on a white background. From Taksim, destinations include Aksaray, Beşiktaş, Kadıköy and Topkapı, and vehicles depart from the Taksim end of Tarlabaşı Bulvarı, and where İsmet İnönü Caddesi exits Taksim.

GETTING AROUND BY BUS

Inner-city buses are operated by two companies, both under municipal jurisdiction. **I.E.T.T.** (Istanbul Omnibus company) buses are red and the environmentally friendly ones *(yeşil motor)* are green and run on natural gas. Özel Halk (public) buses are mainly light blue and/or green. For a map of useful bus routes see the pull-out map.

I.E.T.T. buses accept only the electronic AKBİL (smart ticket) travel pass *(see p241)*, but drivers might accept cash from tourists. The pass can be purchased from main bus departure centres, newsagents, kiosks and private vendors near bus shelters. Cheaper weekly and 15-day passes are available at major bus depots.

If you cross either of the Bosphorus bridges, expect to pay double fare.

You enter at the front of the bus and exit by the rear doors. Push the button above the door or attached to the railings to alert the driver that you wish to alight at the next stop. A list of stops is displayed on the side of buses or on a video screen. Most buses run from 6am until 10 or 11pm.

The large Metrobuses run on dedicated lanes. The first line completed is of little interest to visitors, but a line planned between Edirnekapı and Vezneciler will link the city walls with the Bazaar Quarter.

USEFUL BUS ROUTES

15 Üsküdar – Beykoz
15/A Beykoz – Anadolu Kavağı
22 Kabataş – İstinye
25/A Levent Metro – Rumeli Kavağı
28 Edirnekapı – Beşiktaş
28/T Topkapı – Beşiktaş
37/E Eminönü – Edirnekapı
40 Taksim – Sariyer
80 Eminönu – Yedikule
81 Eminönu – Yeşilköy
86/V Vezneciler – Edirnekapı

GUIDED TOURS

Several tour operators run special-interest tours of Istanbul, as well as general guided tours of the city and further afield. **Plan Tours** has a variety of tours, including trips to Gallipoli, Troy and Bursa, Jewish heritage tours, and private yacht cruises along the Bosphorus *(see pp144–9)*. Companies running city tours include **Backpackers Travel**, **Fest Travel** and **Turista**. For more companies offering trips outside Istanbul *see page 245*.

If you are approached by people offering their services as tour guides, make sure you see their photo ID, make it clear what you want to see and agree a fee. If you have little time, or do not wish to travel by public transport, it may be worth negotiating a private tour or visit to a sight with a taxi driver. This is best done through your hotel.

DIRECTORY

TAXI COMPLAINTS

Tel (0212) 325 15 15.

GETTING AROUND BY BUS

I.E.T.T. (Istanbul Omnibus Company)
Erkan-ı Harp Sok No. 4, Beyoğlu.
Map 7 D5.
Tel (0800) 211 60 68,
(0800) 211 61 20.
www.iett.gov.tr

GUIDED TOURS

Backpackers Travel
Yeni Akbıyık Cad 22, Sultanahmet.
Map 3 D4 (5 D3).
Tel (0212) 638 63 43.
www.backpackerstravel.net

Fest Travel
Barbaros Bulvarı, 74/20, Beşiktaş.
Map 8 C2. *Tel (0212) 216 10 36.*
www.festtravel.com.tr

Plan Tours
Cumhuriyet Cad 83/1, Elmadağ.
Map 7 F3.
Tel (0212) 234 77 77.
www.plantours.com

Sultanahmet Office (across from Haghia Sophia):
Map 3 E4 (5 E4).
Tel (0212) 458 18 00.

Turista Travel
Divanyolu Cad 16, Sultanahmet.
Map 3 D4 (5 D4).
Tel (0212) 518 65 70.
www.turistatravel.com

Getting Around by Metro, Tram and Train

Metro sign

Rail transport in Istanbul is becoming ever more efficient. The Marmaray Project will revolutionize public transport in the city. Much of the present slow and scruffy suburban rail network is being upgraded and will disappear underground, and the Asian and European sides of the city will be connected by an underwater train, while Beyoğlu will be linked to the old city by Metro, with a tunnel running under the Golden Horn.

To access the tramway purchase a token (*jeton*), which operates the turnstile (these also accept the AKBİL travel pass).

Trams travel on the right-hand side of the street, so be sure to stand on the correct platform. Trams are frequent, running every 5 minutes between 6am and midnight.

LIGHT RAILWAY AND METRO

The light railway (*hafif metro* in Turkish) runs east into the city centre from Atatürk Airport, with a few sections underground. It operates between 6am and 12:30am. The key stops are Zeytinburnu (for connecting to the tramway) and Otogar, for the inter-city bus station. The last stop is Aksaray, which also connects to the tramway but involves a short walk. This can be awkward with luggage because there is a bridge. The Istanbul Metro is a true underground. It runs from Şişhane, at the bottom end of İstiklâl Caddesi, to the suburb

A tram on Istanbul's modern tramway system

TRAMWAY

Istanbul's tramway system is modern and efficient, but it can be very crowded at peak times. The line runs from Zeytinburnu (where it

connects with the *hafif metro* (light railway) coming in from Atatürk Airport) through Aksaray and Sultanahmet. It then crosses the Galata Bridge (*see inside back cover*) and continues to Kabataş.

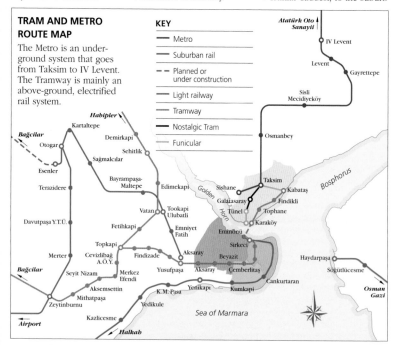

TRAM AND METRO ROUTE MAP

The Metro is an underground system that goes from Taksim to IV Levent. The Tramway is mainly an above-ground, electrified rail system.

KEY

— Metro
— Suburban rail
-- Planned or under construction
— Light railway
— Tramway
— Nostalgic Tram
— Funicular

of IV Levent between 6:15am and 12:30am. The Metro is clean, well run and the cars are air-conditioned. By 2013 it should extend under the Golden Horn and connect to Yenikapı.

Journey tokens, purchased on entry, operate the turn-stiles for both the light railway and the Metro. Alternatively, you can use an AKBİL pass.

CABLE CARS AND FUNICULARS

A cable car connects the shores of the Golden Horn in Eyüp with the Eyüp cemetery and tea gardens, and runs between 8am and 10pm daily. There is also a cable car in Maçka Park, which is open from 8am to 8pm daily.

Inaugurated in 1875, the Tünel is a French-built under-ground railway. It climbs steeply from Karaköy to Tünel Square in Beyoğlu, where it connects with the period tram on İstiklâl Caddesi. The Karaköy station is set back from the main road just off the Galata Bridge *(see p101)*. The Tünel closes at 9pm. A useful modern funicular links Taksim Square with the ferry terminal at Kabataş from 6am to midnight.

THE NOSTALGIC TRAM

The Nostalgic Tram *(Nostaljik Tramvay)* covers a distance of just over 1 km (just under 1 mile) along İstiklâl Caddesi from Tünel to Taksim Square. On the Asian side, the tram runs from Kadıköy along Bahariye Caddesi to Moda. Both run from 7am to 8pm. The trams are the original early-20th-century vehicles, taken out of service in 1966 but revived in 1989. The ticket collectors wear period costume. The AKBİL pass can be used on both lines.

SUBURBAN TRAINS

Suburban trains *(banliyö)* run beside the Sea of Marmara between Sirkeci and Halkalı

(on the European side). The service is slow, the trains are dilapidated and the only useful stops are Yedikule (for Yedikule Museum, *see p115*) and Ataköy (for Galleria mall, *see p211*).

On the Asian side, a line runs from Haydarpaşa to Gebze via Bostancı, one of the ferry piers for the Princes' Islands.

Suburban trains accept only the AKBİL travel pass and tokens. They start daily at 6am and stop at 11:30pm. Both lines will be transformed on completion of the Marmaray Project. For further information on the rail network, see the map inside the back cover.

AKBİL TRAVEL PASS

The AKBİL is a travel pass that can be used on the entire public transport system in Istanbul: light railway, tramway, Metro, suburban trains, city buses, ferries, motor boats and sea buses. Short for *akıllı bilet*, or "intelligent ticket", this token can be bought from main bus stations and other public transport ticket offices.

Turkish Railways sign on the side of a train

DIRECTORY

TRAMWAY

Istanbul Transportation Co.
Tel (0212) 568 99 70.
www.istanbul-ulasim.com.tr

SURBURBAN TRAINS

Haydarpaşa Station
Tel (0216) 336 04 75.

Sirkeci Station
Tel (0212) 527 00 50.

When purchasing an AKBİL, you pay for a number of units in advance and a refundable 6 TL deposit for the token itself. The token can be topped-up at any time. The distinctive orange AKBİL machines are located at the entrances to stations and on buses. To use, place the token in the socket on the front of the machine, near the display panel. The fare will be deducted in units.

AKBİL passes

A new type of refillable travelcard called Beşibiryerde has been introduced in Istanbul, although not all turnstiles are compatible.

Nostalgic Tram travelling along İstiklâl Caddesi in Beyoğlu

Getting Around by Boat

Token (*jeton*)
for İDO ferry

The most pleasant and relaxing means of getting around Istanbul is by the innumerable water-borne craft which ply the Bosphorus between the European and Asian sides. These range from water taxis and small, privately operated ferries to larger ferries and high-speed catamarans. As well as being a relatively fast way to get around, a ride on a boat will also provide some great views of the city.

Passengers disembarking from a ferry

Old ferries at Karaköy

FERRIES

A constant traffic of ferries crosses the Bosphorus and the Golden Horn. Called *vapur*, they are run by the **Istanbul Sea Bus Company (İDO)**. The principal ferry

terminus on the European side is at Eminönü (*see p87*), just east of the Galata Bridge. Destinations served from here, clearly labelled on the relevant boarding halls at each pier, include Haydarpaşa, Kadıköy and Üsküdar on the Asian shore. There is also a pier marked "Boğaz Hattı" for the Bosphorus cruises (*see p243*), and another labelled "Harem" for car ferries to Asian Istanbul. On the west side of the Galata Bridge is the pier for ferries up the Golden Horn (Haliç Hattı).

Another main terminus is Karaköy, opposite Eminönü,

from which ferries run to Haydarpaşa and Kadıköy. The international dock, where cruise liners berth, is also here.

There are ferries from Eminönü to Kadıköy between 7am and 11pm, and from Eminönü to Üsküdar between 6am and 11:30pm, departing every 15 minutes or so. Other services are less frequent. If you want to explore independently using ferries, especially to hop between the villages along the Bosphorus, you will need to arm yourself with a timetable (*see p243*).

FERRY AND SEA BUS ROUTE MAP

There are numerous ferry and sea bus services departing daily from Eminönü and the other ports. In addition, a number of smaller, privately operated motor boats serve the same destinations.

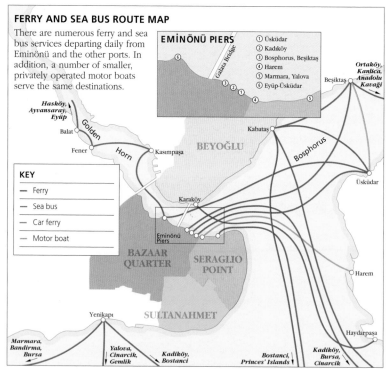

EMİNÖNÜ PIERS
① Üsküdar
② Kadıköy
③ Bosphorus, Beşiktaş
④ Harem
⑤ Marmara, Yalova
⑥ Eyüp-Üsküdar

KEY
— Ferry
— Sea bus
— Car ferry
— Motor boat

SEA BUSES

The modern, Swedish-built catamarans which are known as sea buses *(deniz otobüslü)* are also run by İDO. Their interiors resemble aircraft cabins, with long rows of comfortable, reclining seats, piped music and air-conditioning. Sea buses are considerably faster and more comfortable than ferries, but cost three times as much.

The most useful route is to the Princes' Islands *(see p159)*, with 6–12 departures daily. For destinations outside Istanbul *see pages 244–5.*

MOTOR BOATS

A number of companies, including **Dentur** and **Turyol**, operate motor boats which cross the Bosphorus and Golden Horn at various points, and run up the Bosphorus. These routes are also served by İDO ferries and although cheaper, they are less frequent. Motor boats accept only the electronic AKBİL travel pass or a *jeton* token.

WATER TAXIS

Water taxis are the latest addition to the city's water-borne transport scene. There are 27 designated docks across the city. To book a water taxi either phone or reserve online. They operate a shared rate system for the 10-seater craft, and are very reasonably priced when shared.

Water taxi on the Bosphorous

THE BOSPHORUS TRIP

İDO runs daily ferry excursions up the Bosphorus *(see pp136–49)*. Although prices have increased steeply, they are still reasonable. Light refreshments are served but

One of the many ferries operating on the Bosphorus

no meals. They get crowded in the summer, especially at weekends, so arrive early to book your ticket and to ensure that you get a deck seat with a view. You should retain your ticket during the journey, as you must show it on the return trip. You can disembark at any pier along the way, boarding the next ferry that comes along with the same ticket; but if you make a second stop you will need to buy a new ticket to continue your journey. İDO also offers a trip from Kadıköy in summer at weekends only.

There are several alternatives to the official trip. The small private boats that leave Eminönü just after the İDO ferry sails in the summer months only go halfway up the straits and do not stop on the way. Alternatively you can book a private cruise through a reputable company, such as **Hatsail Tourism**.

TICKETS & TIMETABLES

For ferries and sea buses, buy a flat-fare *jeton* from the booth *(gişe)* at the pier or from one of the unofficial street vendors who sit nearby and sell them at slightly higher prices. Ferry fares cost 1.5 TL, while those for sea buses to the Princes' Islands are 7 TL. You can use *jetons* for all local trips. Better still, use AKBİL, which makes

boarding quicker and offers a discounted fare. Tickets for the Bosphorus trip cost 20 TL and you cannot use AKBİL for it.

To enter the pier, put the *jeton* into the slot beside the turnstile, and then wait in the boarding hall for a boat. A schedule of sailing times is on view at each pier and a copy of the timetable *(tarife)* can usually be bought at the ticket booth.

İDO logo

DIRECTORY

FERRIES AND SEA BUSES

Istanbul Sea Bus Co. (İDO)
Tel (0212) 444 44 36.
www.ido.com.tr

MOTOR BOATS

Dentur
Tel (0212) 227 47 89.
www.denturavrasya.com

Turyol
Tel (0212) 251 44 21.
www.turyol.com

WATER TAXIS

Deniz Taksi
Tel (0212) 444 44 36.
www.deniztaksi.com

PRIVATE CRUISES

Hatsail Tourism
Tel (0212) 241 62 50.
www.hatsail.com

Travelling Beyond Istanbul

TTOK logo

The best way to reach nearby towns and cities from Istanbul is by coach. Further-flung destinations can be reached either by coach or air. A great number of coach companies operate in Turkey, but it is worth paying extra to travel with a reputable company. Many Turkish cities are served by domestic flights from both Atatürk and Sabiha Gökçen airports and fares are competitive. Trains serve fewer destinations and, aside from the fast train between Eskişehir and Ankara, are painfully slow. For destinations across the Sea of Marmara, ferries and sea buses are a relaxing means of transport.

High-speed sea bus on the Bosphorus

INTERCITY COACHES

The main coach station *(Otogar)* for both domestic and international destinations is at Esenler, 14 km (9 miles) northwest of the city centre. There is another at Harem, on the Asian side of the Bosphorus. Both are scruffy and poorly maintained, but all coach companies have city centre branches where you can buy tickets, and they run shuttle services to collection points near the motorway, so you will probably not need to use them.

You must make a booking for all coach journeys. Most companies accept credit cards. Varan and Ulusoy *(see p237)*, the two most reputable bus companies, take bookings and issue tickets from their city centre offices. They operate services between main centres such as Ankara, Antalya and İzmir, as well as to destinations along the Black Sea coast. **Kâmil Koç** has a service to Bursa. The journey goes via Gebze, boarding the ferry to Yalova and takes about 4 hours. **Çanakkale Truva Seyahat** is

the best company to use for getting to Gelibolu (Gallipoli), which takes about 5 hours, or Çanakkale, which takes about 6 hours. **Metro Turizm** is a large and reliable coach company that runs regular schedules to many destinations outside Istanbul. Single pass-engers will usually be seated next to someone of the same sex. Couples can sit together. Refreshments are served free of charge, and there are frequent rest and meal stops. The better companies have some buses with single seats, offer free Wi-Fi and have TVs in the back of the seats. As an example, the fare for the 450-km (280-mile) journey between Istanbul and Antalya is 75 TL with a premium company.

AIR TRAVEL

Flying makes sense in Turkey if you wish to visit distant cities such as Antalya, İzmir, Kayseri (for Cappadocia), Trabzon or Van. Several companies compete on the same routes, so prices are very reasonable (starting from 70 TL) if booked early. **Anadolujet** and **Sunexpress** fly

only from Istanbul's Sabiha Gökçen Airport. **Atlas Jet** and **Onur Air** use Atatürk Airport, while **Pegasus** and **Turkish Airlines** use both. Turkish Airlines have flights to both Bursa and Çanakkale if you are pressed for time.

SEA BUSES AND FERRIES

High-speed ferries *(hızlı feribot)* and sea buses *(deniz otobüsü)* are a convenient means of travelling long distances from a city surrounded by water. Run by **İDO** *(see p242)*, they are good value; cars are also carried on some high-speed ferry routes.

For Bursa, take the twice-daily high-speed ferry from Yenikapı to Güzelyalı (90 minutes), or the sea bus from Kabataş to Güzelyalı (2 hours via Kadıköy), then a bus into Bursa. Alternatively, take the high-speed ferry (seven daily; 1 hour 10 minutes) to Yalova, from where it is 1 hour by bus to Bursa. From Yalova, regular minibuses serve İznik (1 hour). Sea buses also travel to the Marmara Islands from Yenikapı.

TRAINS TO EDİRNE

The daily train to Edirne from Sirkeci Station *(see p66)* takes 6 hours, twice the length of time taken by coach. Advance reservations can be made at the railway stations in either city, or in certain travel agencies displaying the **TCDD** (Turkish State Railways) sign. Bursa, Çanakkale and İznik are not on the rail network.

Café at Istanbul's architecturally interesting Sirkeci Station

CAR HIRE AND ROAD TRAVEL

Turkey's comprehensive intercity coach and air network means that a car is not necessary for travelling to other cities. If you wish to drive, car hire companies including **Avis**, **Budget** and **Sixt** have both airport and city centre offices. You do not need an international driving licence, just your normal one. Turkish roads are hazardous because of fast, reckless driving. Traffic drives on and gives way to the right, even on roundabouts. The Turkish Touring and Automobile Club (Türkiye Turing ve Otomobil Kurumu, or **TTOK**), can give visiting motorists advice on driving in Turkey, as well as offering assistance with breakdowns, accidents and insurance. It has reciprocal agreements with the British AA and RAC.

DAY TRIP TOURS

A number of companies offer day trips from Istanbul to the Princes' Islands, the Dardanelles, Bursa and villages on the Black Sea. These are often good value and offer an efficient and hassle-free method of simplifying your travel arrangements.

Reputable tour operators with English-speaking guides include **Plan Tours**, **Turista** and **Türk Expres**. All offer classical, biblical and heritage tours in Istanbul as well as to regions throughout Turkey.

Some companies offer personalized tours all over Turkey. Plan Tours also operates a double-decker bus tour around Istanbul. **CARED** (Çanakkale Tour Guide Association) can provide tour guides who speak many languages.

Horse-drawn carriage (phaeton) on Büyükada

Car rental company logos

LOCAL TRANSPORT OUTSIDE ISTANBUL

The main means of public transport in both Bursa and Edirne is the dolmuş. These are either minibuses or saloon cars, with the destination displayed on signs on the roof. If you stay in the centre of either city and are moderately fit, you will find that all of the major sights are within easy walking distance.

In Bursa city centre, Heykel, at the eastern end of Atatürk Caddesi, is the main dolmuş terminus. From there you can get dolmuşes to most other parts of the city. There is also an efficient bus service and a metro.

Edirne is much smaller than Bursa, and the public transport system is not as comprehensive. To get from the coach station to the town centre, a distance of 2 km (1 mile), take a Merkez–Garaj minibus dolmuş, or a taxi.

There are no motor vehicles on the Princes' Islands. On Büyükada and Heybeliada phaeton carriages can be hired.

DIRECTORY

INTERCITY COACHES

Çanakkale Truva Seyahat
Tel (0212) 444 00 17.
www.truvaturizm.com

Kâmil Koç
Tel (0212) 444 05 62.
www.kamilkoc.com.tr

Metro Turizm
Tel (0212) 444 34 55.
www.metroturizm.com.tr

AIR TRAVEL

Anadolujet
Tel 444 25 38.
www.anadolujet.com.tr

Atlas Jet
Tel 444 03 87.
www.atlasjet.com

Onur Air
Tel (0212) 633 23 00.
www.onurair.com.tr

Pegasus Airlines
Tel 444 07 37.
www.flypgs.com

Sunexpress
Tel 444 07 97.
www.sunexpress.com

Turkish Airlines (THY)
Tel 444 08 49.
www.turkishhairlines.com

FERRIES

İDO
Tel (0212) 444 44 36.
www.ido.com.tr.

Kabataş Pier
Tel (0212) 249 15 58.

Yenikapı Pier
Tel (0212) 516 12 12.

TRAINS

TCDD
www.tcdd.gov.tr

CAR HIRE AND ROAD TRAVEL

Avis
Tel 444 28 47.
www.avis.com.tr

Budget
Tel (0212) 663 08 58.
www.drivebudget.com

Sixt
Tel (0212) 215 24 19.
www.sixt.com/car-rental/turkey/

TTOK
I. Oto Sanayi Sitesi Yanı,
Seyrantepe Yolu,
IV Levent.
Tel (0212) 282 81 40.
www.turing.org.tr

DAY TRIP TOURS

CARED
Tel (0286) 213 90 40.
www.cared.org.tr

Plan Tours
Cumhuriyet Cad 83/1,
Elmadağ.
Map 7 F3.
Tel (0212) 230 22 72.
www.plantours.com

Turista Travel
Divanyolu Cad 16,
Sultanahmet.
Map 3 D4 (5 D4).
Tel (0212) 518 65 70.
www.turistatravel.com

Türk Expres
Cumhuriyet Cad 47/1,
Taksim.
Map 7 E3.
Tel (0212) 235 95 00.
www.turkexpres.com.tr

STREET FINDER

The map references that are given throughout this guide refer to the maps on the following pages only. Some small streets with references may not be named on the map. References are given for hotels *(see pp180–91)*, restaurants *(see pp192–209)*, shops *(see pp210–19)* and entertainment venues *(see pp220–23)*. The map

Visitor to Istanbul consulting a map

below shows the area covered by the ten maps and the key lists the symbols used. The first figure of the reference tells you which map page to turn to; the letter and number indicate the grid reference. For an overview of Greater Istanbul see pages 108–9. The map on the inside back cover shows public transport routes.

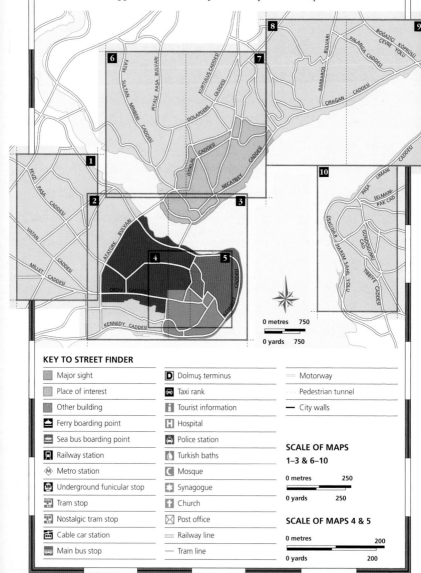

0 metres　750
0 yards　750

KEY TO STREET FINDER

▢	Major sight	**D**	Dolmuş terminus	═══	Motorway
▢	Place of interest	🚖	Taxi rank	⋯⋯	Pedestrian tunnel
▢	Other building	**i**	Tourist information	—	City walls
⛴	Ferry boarding point	**H**	Hospital		
🚢	Sea bus boarding point	▣	Police station		
🚉	Railway station	◖	Turkish baths	**SCALE OF MAPS**
Ⓜ	Metro station	**C**	Mosque	**1–3 & 6–10**
🔲	Underground funicular stop	✡	Synagogue	0 metres　　250
🚊	Tram stop	**i**	Church	0 yards　　250
🚊	Nostalgic tram stop	⊠	Post office	
🚠	Cable car station	═══	Railway line	**SCALE OF MAPS 4 & 5**
🚌	Main bus stop	—	Tram line	0 metres　　　200
				0 yards　　　200

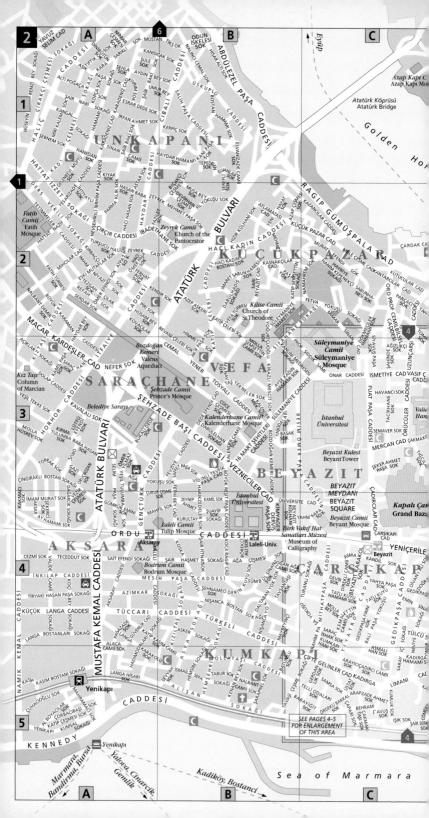

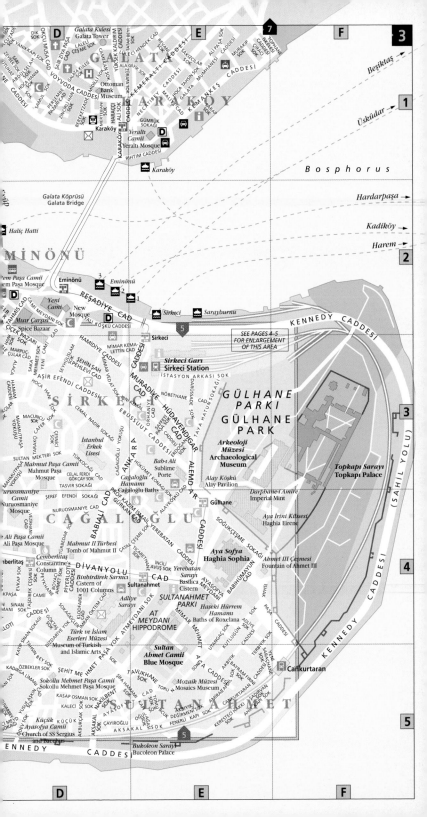

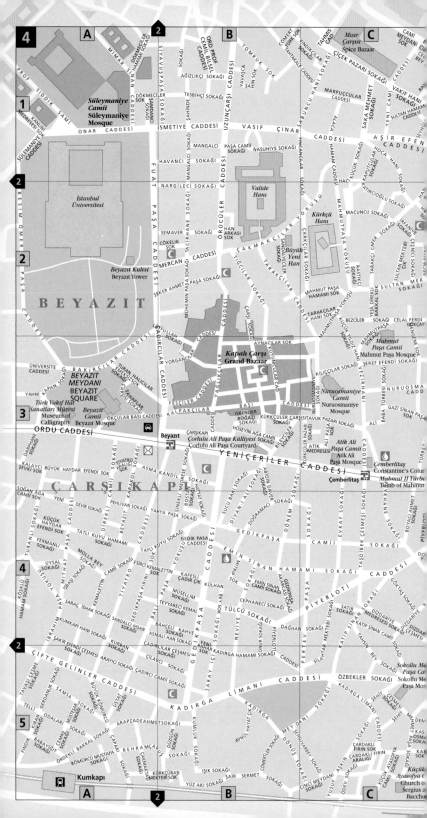

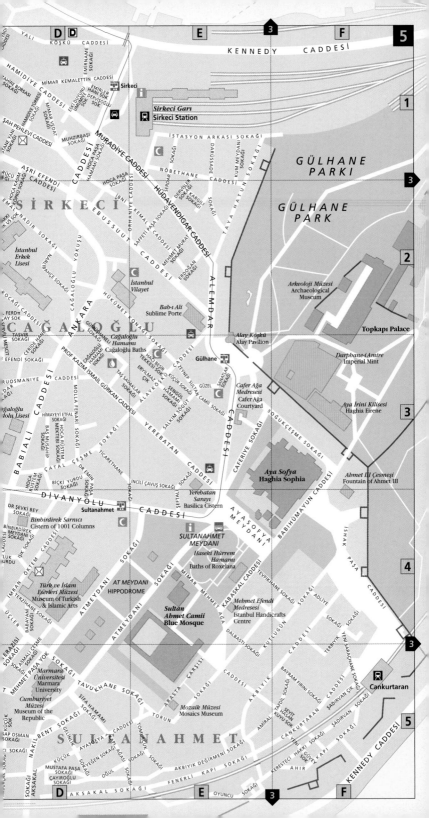

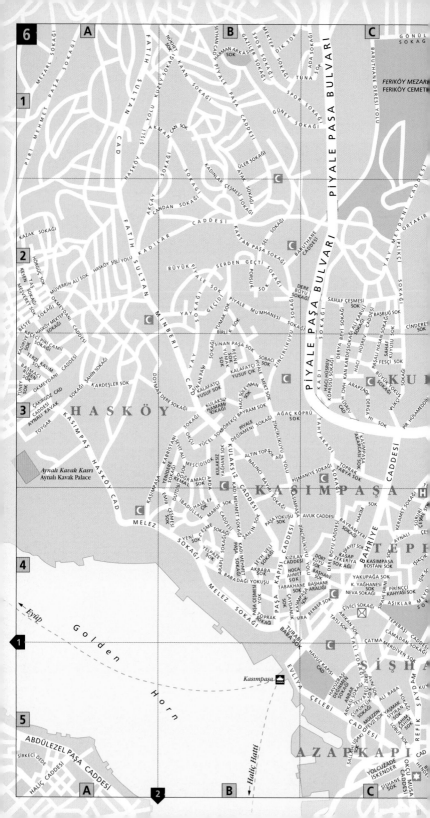

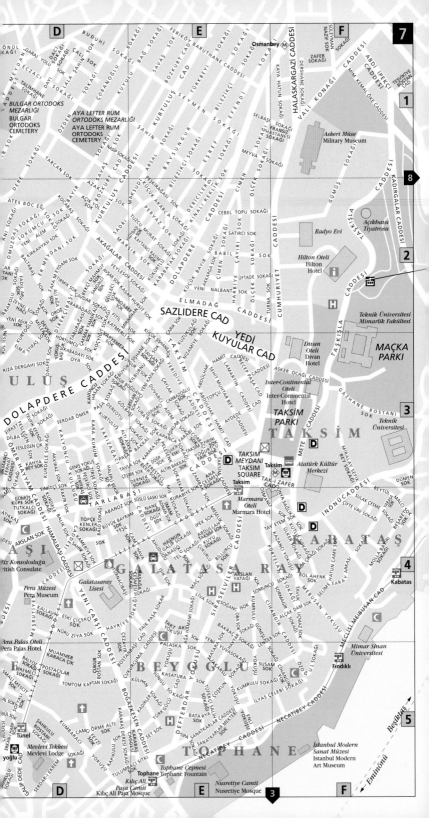

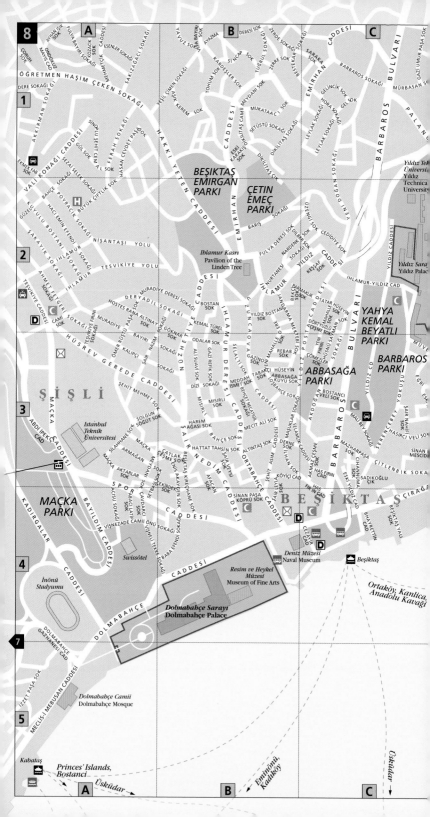

Street Finder Index

In Turkish, Ç, Ğ, İ, Ö, Ş and Ü are listed as separate letters in the alphabet, coming after C, G, I, O, S and U respectively. In this book, however, Ç is treated as C for the purposes of alphabetization and so on with the other letters. Hence Çiçek follows Cibinlik as if both names began with C. Following standard Turkish practice we have abbreviated Sokağı to Sok and Caddesi to Cad. References in brackets refer to the enlarged section of the Street Finder (maps 4 and 5).

A

Abacı Dede Sok	10 C3
Abacı Latif Sok	8 A4
Abanoz Sok	7 D4
Abbasağa Kuyu Sok	8 B3
Abdi İpekçi Cad	7 F1, 8 A3
Abdül Feyyaz Sok	10 C2
Abdülezel Paşa Cad	2 B1, 6 A5
Abdülhak Hamit Cad	7 E3
Abdullah Sok	7 E4
Abdülselah Sok	3 D1
Abidin Daver Sok	4 B3
Açık Türbe Çık	10 B3
Açık Türbe Sok	10 B3
Açık Yol Sok	7 D2
Açıkbaş Sok	1 B2
Açıklar Sok	1 C4, 2 A3
Acısu Sok	8 A4
Ada Sok	6 C1
Adem Baba Sok	1 A3
Adliye Sok	3 E4 (5 F4)
Afacan Sok	8 B3
Ağa Çeşmesi Sok	2 B4
Ağa Çırağı Sok	7 F4
Ağa Hamamı Sok	7 E4
Ağa Yokuşu Sok	2 A3
Ağaç Köprü Sok	6 B3
Ağızlık Sok	1 B1
Ağızlıkçı Sok	2 C3 (B1)
Ahali Sok	10 A3
Ahım Şahım Sok	6 C5
Ahır Kapı Sok	3 E5 (5 F5)
Ahmediye Cad	1 C5
Ahmet Fetgeri Sok	8 A2
Ahmet Hikmet Sok	1 B5
Ahmet Şuayip Sok	2 B4
Ahmet Vefik Paşa Cad	1 A5
Ahrida Synagogue	1 B3
Ahşap Minare Sok	1 B3
Ahududu Sok	7 E4
Aile Sok	1 C4
Ak Koyunlu Sok	1 A5
Akağalar Cad	7 D2
Akarsu Yokuşu	7 E5
Akbaba Sok	6 B4
Akbıyık Cad	3 E5 (5 E5)
Akbıyık Değirmeni Sok	3 E5 (5 E5)
Akburçak Sok	3 D5 (5 D5)
Akçay Sok	6 A2
Akdeniz Cad	1 B4
Akdoğan Sok	8 C3
Akif Paşa Sok	2 B3
Akkarga Sok	7 E2
Akkavak Sok	8 A2
Akkiraz Sok	7 D3
Akkırman Sok	8 A1
Akman Sok	6 B1
Akmaz Çeşme Sok	8 C3
Aksakal Sok	3 D5 (5 D5)
Aksaray Cad	2 A4
Aksaray Hamamı Sok	1 C5, 2 A4
Akseki Cad	1 B3
Akseki Camii Şerif Sok	1 B3
Akşemsettin Cad	1 B3
Aktar Sok	9 E2

Al Boyacılar Sok	2 A5
Ala Geyik Sok	3 D1
Alaca Camii Sok	2 A4
Alaca Hamam Cad	3 D3 (4 C1)
Aladoğan Sok	9 E2
Alay Pavilion	3 E3 (5 E3)
Alayköşkü Cad	3 E4 (5 E3)
Albay Cemil Sakarya Sok	1 B4
Albay Sadi Alantar Sok	8 A1
Alçak Dam Sok	7 F4
Alemdar Cad	3 E3 (5 E2)
Ali Ağa Sok	7 D2
Ali Baba Sok	6 C5
Ali Baba Türbesi Sok	4 C3
Ali Hoca Sok	7 D5
Ali Kabuli Sok	6 C2
Ali Kuşçu Sok	1 A1
Ali Paşa Sok	3 E1 (4 C3)
Ali Suavi Sok	8 B3
Alişah Sok	1 B2
Alişan Sok	2 B5
Altay Cad	1 B3
Altı Asker Sok	7 D3
Altı Poğaça Sok	2 A1
Altın Bakkal Sok	7 E3
Altın Top Sok	6 B3
Altıntaş Sok	8 B3
Ambar Sok	10 B5
Ambarlı Dere Sok	9 E1
Amca Bey Sok	9 F1
Amiral Tafdil Sok	3 E5 (5 E5)
Ana Çeşmesi Sok	7 E3
Anadolu Sok	7 E4
Anbar Arkası Sok	6 C5
Ankara Cad	3 E3 (5 D1)
Arakiyeci Çık	10 C4
Arakiyeci Sok	10 C4
Araplı Sok	6 B4
Arapzade Ahmet Sok	2 C5 (4 A5)
Arapzade Dergahı Sok	6 C3
Arasta Çarşısı	5 E5
Arayıcı Sok	2 C5 (4 A5)
Archaeological Museum	3 E3 (5 F2)
Arda Cad	6 B3
Arı Sok	1 B2
Arif Paşa Sok	4 C3
Arıkan Sok	6 C4
Armağan Sok	8 A3
Armutlu Sok	1 A3
Arpa Emini Köprüsü Sok	1 A3
Arslan Sok	7 D4
Arslan Yatağı Sok	7 E4
Asariye Cad	9 D3
Aşçıbaşı Mektebi Sok	10 C4
Aşık Kerem Sok	8 B1
Aşık Paşa Sok	2 A1
Aşıklar Meydanı Sok	6 C4
Aşıklar Sok	7 E3
Aşir Efendi Cad	3 D3 (4 C1)
Asker Ocağı Cad	7 F3
Asker Sok	2 B4
Asma Kandil Sok	2 C4 (4 A3)
Asmalı Çeşme Sok	5 D5
Asmalı Han Sok	2 C5 (4 B4)
Asmalı Mescit Sok	7 D5
Asmalı Sok	10 A2

Asmalısalkım Sok	9 D3
Astar Sok	2 A1
Asya Sok	2 B4
Atak Sok	6 B2
Atatürk Bridge	2 C1
Atatürk Bulvarı	2 A3
Ateş Böceği Sok	7 D2
Atik Ali Paşa Mosque	3 D4 (4 C3)
Atik Medresesi Sok	4 C3
Atik Valide Mosque	10 C3
Atiye Sok	8 A2
Atlamataşı Cad	2 B2
Atlas Çık	10 B2
Atlas Sok	10 B2
Atmeydanı Sok	3 D4 (4 C4)
Atölyeler Sok	10 C5
Atpazarı Sok	2 A2
Avni Paşa Sok	10 B4
Avni Sok	6 C5
Avşar Sok	7 D2
Avuk Cad	6 C4
Ayan Sok	1 C1
Ayasofya Meydanı	3 E4 (5 E4)
Ayaydın Sok	9 E1
Ayazma Deresi Sok	8 B1
Aybastı Sok	6 C5
Aydede Cad	7 E3
Aydın Bey Sok	2 A1
Aydınlık Sok	9 F2
Ayhan Işık Sok	8 A1
Ayın Sok	10 C3
Aynacılar Sok	4 B3
Aynalı Çeşme Cad	6 C4
Aynalı Kavak Cad	6 A3
Aynalı Kavak Palace	6 A3
Aynülhayat Çık	4 B5
Ayşe Kadın Hamamı Sok	2 B3 (4 A1)
Azak Sok	7 D2
Azap Çeşmesi Sok	2 B2
Azap Kapı Mosque	2 C1
Azat Çık	10 B2
Azat Yokuşu	10 B2
Azep Askeri Sok	2 B2
Azimkar Sok	2 A4
Aziz Efendi Mektebi Sok	10 B3
Aziz Mahmut Efendi Sok	10 B2
Azizlik Sok	10 C2

B

Baba Efendi Sok	8 B4
Baba Hasan Sok	2 A3
Babadağı Sok	7 D2
Babadağı Yokuşu	6 B4
Babayanı Sok	5 D4
Babayiğit Sok	2 C5 (4 A5)
Babıali Cad	3 D4 (5 D3)
Babıhümayun Cad	3 E4 (5 F4)
Babil Sok	7 E2
Babnaibi Sok	1 B3
Bahçeli Kahve Sok	4 B4
Bahriye Cad	6 C4
Baki Bey Sok	1 B5
Baki Dede Sok	1 C1
Bakıcı Sok	10 B2

Bakırcılar Cad	4 A3
Bakkal Bekir Sok	10 B4
Bakraç Sok	7 E4
Balaban Cad	10 B2
Balat Vapur İskelesi Cad	1 C1
Balçık Sok	10 B2
Balcılar Yokuşu	10 C4
Bali Paşa Cad	1 B3
Bali Paşa Yokuşu	2 C4 (4 A4)
Balık Sok	7 D4
Balo Sok	7 E4
Baltabaş Sok	7 D2
Balyoz Sok	7 D5
Bamyacı Sok	9 F5
Bankacılar Sok	4 C1
Barbaros Bulvarı	8 C1
Barbaros Hayrettin Cad	8 C4
Barbaros Sok	8 C1
Barış Sok	8 B2
Baruthane Cad	1 A4, 6 B2
Baruthane Deresi Yolu	6 C1
Baş İmam Sok	1 C3
Baş Müezzin Sok	1 C3
Baş Musahip Sok	5 D3
Başağa Çeşmesi Sok	7 E4
Basak Sok	2 B3
Başbuğ Sok	6 C2
Başhane Aralığı	6 C4
Başhane Sok	6 C4
Başhoca Sok	1 C3
Basilica Cistern	3 E4 (5 E3)
Başkatip Sok	1 B3
Basmacı Ruşen Sok	6 A3
Başvekil Cad	1 A4
Batarya Sok	7 E5
Baths of Roxelana	3 E4 (5 E4)
Battal Gazi Sok	1 B3
Battalin Sok	2 B5
Bayıldım Cad	8 A4
Bayır Sok	7 D1
Bayram Fırını Sok	3 E5 (5 F5)
Bayramyeri Sok	6 C4
Baysungur Sok	7 E1
Bedrettin Sok	6 C5
Behçet Necatigil Sok	8 B3
Behram Çavuş Sok	2 C5 (4 A5)
Bekar Sok	7 E4
Bekçi Mahmut Sok	7 D2
Bekçi Sok	8 B2
Bektaş Sok	10 C3
Bereketli Sok	9 F5
Bereketzade Sok	3 D1
Beşaret Sok	7 F4
Beşiktaş Boğaziçi Köprüsü Bağlantı Yolu	9 D1
Beşiktaş Cad	8 B4
Beşiktaş Kirechane Sok	8 B3
Beşiktaş Yalı Sok	8 C4
Besim Ömer Paşa Cad	2 B3 (4 A2)
Beşirgazi Sok	1 B1
Beste Sok	6 A2
Bestekar Ahmet Çağan Sok	9 E2
Bestekar Rahmi Bey Sok	1 A5
Bestekar Selahattin Pınar Sok	10 A3

General Index

Acknowledgments

Dorling Kindersley would like to thank the following people whose assistance contributed to the preparation of this book:

Main Contributors

Rosie Ayliffe lived in Turkey for three years, during which time she worked as a freelance writer in Istanbul for the English-language weekly *Dateline Turkey* and as a tour guide travelling all over western Turkey. She is one of the authors of the *Rough Guide to Turkey*, and has also contributed to the *Rough Guide to France* and to Time Out's London guides.

Rose Baring is a travel writer who has spent many months exploring Istanbul. She is the co-author of *Essential Istanbul* (AA) and has also contributed to guides to Tunisia, and Moscow and St Petersburg.

Barnaby Rogerson has travelled, written and lectured extensively in the countries of the eastern Mediterranean. He is, with Rose Baring, co-author of *Essential Istanbul* (AA), and has contributed to several other AA and Cadogan guides. He is the author of *A Traveller's History of North Africa*.

Canan Silay worked for many years as the editor-in-chief of the English-language magazine *Istanbul, The Guide*. Previously, she had worked as a journalist with the Turkish daily newspaper *Hürriyet*. She has contributed to several books on Turkey, including Insight guides to Istanbul, Turkey and the Turkish coast.

Managing Editor Georgina Matthews
Managing Art Editor Annette Jacobs
Senior Managing Editor Vivien Crump
Deputy Art Director Gillian Allan

Additional Contributors

Ghillie Başan, Arzu Bolukbasi, Krysia Bereday Burnham, Professor Anthony A M Bryer, Jim Crow, José Luczyc-Wyhowska, Colin Nicholson, Venetia Porter, Dott. A Ricci, Professor J M Rogers, Sargasso Media Ltd, London, Suzanne Swan, Tina Walsh.

Additional Cartography

Robert Funnell, Emily Green, David Pugh, Lee Rowe (ESR Cartography Ltd).

Picture Research

Rachel Barber, Marta Bescos, Rhiannon Furbear, Ellen Root.

Design and Editorial Assistance

Didem Mersin Alıcı, Gillian Andrews, Lydia Baillie, Sonal Bhatt, Tessa Bindloss, Gary Cross, Mehmet Erdemgil, Amy Harrison, Sally Hibbard, Hasan Kelepir, Batur Kiziltug, Maite Lantaron, Jude Ledger, Francesca Machiavelli, Alison McGill, Sam Merrell, Ella Milroy, Mary Ormandy, Catherine Palmi, Marianne Petrou, Mani Ramaswamy, Lee Redmond, Nicola Rodway, Sands Publishing Solutions, Anna Streiffert, Rosalyn Thiro, Dutjapun Williams, Veronica Wood.

Proofreader

Stewart Wild.

Indexer

Hilary Bird.

Additional Photography

DK Studio/Steve Gorton, John Heseltine, Izzet Keriber, Dave King, Ian O'Leary, Fatih Mehmet Akdan, Clive Streeter.

Artwork Reference

Kadir Kir, Remy Sow.

Special Assistance

The Publisher would like to thank staff at museums, mosques, churches, local government departments, shops, hotels, restaurants and other organizations in Istanbul for their invaluable help. Particular thanks are also due to: Feride Alpe; Halil Özek, Archaeological Museum, Istanbul; Hamdi Arabacıoğlu, Association of Mevlevis, Istanbul; Veli Yenisoğancı (Director), Aya Sofya Museum, Istanbul; Nicholas Barnard; Ahmet Kazokoğlu, Bel Bim A.Ş., Istanbul; Poppy Body; Banu Akkaya, British Consulate, Istanbul; Vatan Ercan and Mine Kaner, Bursa Tourist Office; Hanife Yenilmez, Central Bank of the Republic of Turkey, London; Reverend Father Ian Sherwood, Christ Church, Istanbul; Father Lorenzo, Church of SS Peter and Paul, Istanbul; Münevver Ek and Muazzez Pervan, Economic and Social History Foundation of Turkey, Istanbul; Edirne Müze Müdürlüğü; Emin Yıldız, Edirne Tourist Office; Tokay Gözütok, Eminönü Belediyesi, Istanbul; Mohammet Taşbent, Eminönü Zabıta Müdürlüğü, Istanbul; Orhan Gencer, Protocol Department, First Army HQ, Istanbul; Robert Graham; Cengiz Güngör, şevki Sırma and Mustafa Taşkan, Greater Istanbul Municipality; Hikmet Öztürk, İETT Genel Müdürlüğü, Istanbul; Bashir Ibrahim-Khan, Islamic Cultural Centre, London; İsmet Yalçın, İstanbul Balık Müstahsilleri Derneği; Nedim Akıner, İstanbul Koruma Kurulu; Sühela Ertürk Akdoğan and all staff of the Istanbul Tourist Offices; Abdurrahman Gündoğdu and Ömer Yıldız, İstanbul Ulaşım A.Ş.; İznik Tourist Office; Mark Jackson; Sibel Koyluoğlu; Semra Karakaşlı, Milli Saraylar Daire Başkanlığı, Istanbul; Akın Bavur and Recep Öztop, Cultural Department, Ministry of Foreign Affairs, Ankara; staff at the Edirne Müftülüğü and Eyüp Müftülüğü; Mehmet Sağlam and staff at the İstanbul Müftülüğü; Professor Kemal İskender, Museum of Painting and Sculpture, Istanbul; Öcal Özerek, Museum of Turkish and Islamic Arts, Bursa; Dilek Elçin and Dr Celia Kerslake, Oriental Institute, Oxford University; Kadri Özen; Dr İffet Özgönül; Cevdat Bayındır, Public Relations Department, Pera Palas Hotel; Chris Harbard, RSPB; Rosamund Saunders; John Scott; Huseyin Özer, Sofra; Ahmet Mertez and Gülgün Tunç, Topkapı Palace, Istanbul; Doctor Tüncer, Marmara Island; Mr U Kenan İpek (First Secretary), Turkish Culture and Tourism Office in London and Istanbul, Turkish Embassy, London; Orhan Türker (Director of International Relations), Turkish Touring and Automobile Club, Istanbul; Peter Espley (Public Relations Counsellor) and all staff at the Turkish Tourist Office, London; Mustafa Coşkan, Türkiye Sakatlar Derneği, Istanbul; Dr Beyhan Erçağ, Vakıflar Bölge Müdürlüğü; Yalova Tourist Office; Zeynep Demir and Sabahattin Türkoğlu, Yıldız Palace, Istanbul.

Photography Permissions

Dorling Kindersley would like to thank the following for their kind permission to photograph at their establishments: the General Directorate of Monuments and Museums, the Ministry of Culture, the Ministry for Religious Affairs, İstanbul Valiliği İl Kültür Müdürlüğü, İstanbul Valiliği İl Müftülüğü, the Milli Saraylar Daire Başkanlığı and Edirne Valiliği İl Müftülüğü; also the many churches, restaurants, hotels, shops, transport services, and other sights and establishments too numerous to thank individually.

Picture Credits

t = top; tl = top left; tlc = top left centre; tc = top centre; trc = top right centre; tr = top right; cla = centre left above; ca = centre above; cra = centre right above; cl = centre left; c = centre; cr = centre right; clb = centre right below; cb = centre below; crb = centre right below; bl = bottom left; b = bottom; bc = bottom centre; bcl = bottom centre left; br = bottom right; d = detail

The publisher would like to thank the following individuals, companies, and picture libraries for their kind permission to reproduce their photographs:

A Turizm Yayınları: 158b; Archaeological Museum 42b, 62b, 63tr, 64tr, 65t/c; *Aya Sofia from Fossart Album* 74tr; Topkapı

Palace 56b; ABC Basin Ajansi A.Ş.: 44t, 47c/b, 215cr; The Advertising Archives: 102t; Aisa Archivo Icongrafico, S.A., Barcelona: 19, 20c, 24c, 32tr, 33br, 119t, 171t; Louvre Museum 21c; Topkapı Palace 55bl, 57c; AKG, London: 31tl; Erich Lessing 30t, Erich Lessing/Kunsthistoriches Museum, Vienna 32c; Alamy Images: Jon Arnold Images Ltd 79tl; David Crossland 196br, Jeff Greenberg 107br; Ali Kabas 195c; B. O'Kane 228tr; Justin Kase zninez 232bl; Justin Kase zsixz 231cla, 235bc; John Stark 194cl, 195tl; Ancient Art and Architecture Collection Ltd: 20tr, 23tr; Aquila Photographics: Hanneand Jens Eriksen 169b; Archive Photos: 179 inset; Tahsin Aydoğmuş: 4t, 17b, 21b, 22tl, 43b, 71ca, 72t, 75b, 78t, 86tl, 86tr, 119ca, 144b, 170b; Jon Arnold Images: Walter Bibikow 11tr; Avis Budget Group: 245cl, 245clb.

Bel Bim İstanbul Belediyeleri Bilgi İşlem San Ve Tic A.Ş: 241c; Benaki Museum, Athens: 25t; Bridgeman Art Library, London: British Library *A Portrait of Süleyman the Magnificent* (1494–1566), Persian 32br; National Maritime Museum, London *Battle of Lepanto, 7th October, 1571,* Anonymous 27t; Private Collection *Constantine the Great (c.274–337 AD, Roman Emperor 306–337AD), gold aureus* 20tl; Stapleton Collection *Ibrahim from a Series of Portraits of the Emperors of Turkey, 1808,* John Young (1755–1825) 33tl; Victoria and Albert Museum, London *Sultan Mahmud II: Procession,* Anonymous 33tc, 161cbl/cbr; © The Trustees of the British Museum: 161cla; Directorate of Museums, Bursa: 162tl.

Çalıkoğlu Reklam Turizm Ve Ticaret Ltd.: 220b; Jean Loup Charmet: 29t, 33cr; Manuel Çitak: 46b, 103c, 141t, 162b; Bruce Coleman Collection: 141b; Corbis: Lynsey Addario 175br; David Bathgate 238br; Atlantide Phototravel/ Massimo Borchi 227tr; Paul Hardy 172cl; Robert Landau 237bl; Michael Nicholson 10br; Adam Woolfitt 10cla; Alison Wright 177tr.

C.M Dixon Photo Resources: 62tr.

Dreamstime.com: Softdreams 226bl.

ET Archive, London; 18; Bibliotheque de L'Arsenal, Paris 24t; National Gallery 32bl; Mary Evans Picture Library: 142b, 171b, 225 inset; ES Collection/Vatican Library 23tl.

First Army HQ, Istanbul: 133b; Fotolia: Faraways 146tl; Zechal 100.

Getty Images: 9 inset, 30c, 32tl, 49 inset; Photographie Giraudon, Paris: 26c; Bibliotheque Nationale, Paris 33bl; Lauros 29bl; Topkapı Palace 26b, 27c, 28c, 28–9, 32tc; Ara Güler: 23bl, 26tl, 35br, 87b, 128c, 219tr; Mosaics Museum 77c; Topkapı Palace 1, 57t/b, 81t, 95bl, 161bl; şemsi Güner: 43t, 129ca, 140t, 158t.

Sonia Halliday Photographs: 29br, 127b; engraved by Thomas Allom, painted by Laura Lushington 23c, 28br, 59tr; Bibliotheque Nationale, Madrid 21t; drawn by Miss Pardoe, painted by Laura Lushington 104c; Topkapı Palace 33tr, 76b; Robert Harding Picture Library: Robert Francis 35cla; David Holden 150; Michael Jenner 3 inset, 55br; Odyssey, Chicago/Robert Frerck 40br, 168b; JHC Wilson 129cb; Adam Woolfitt 39cl, 91tr, 210b.

İDO-Istanbul Sea Bus Company: 242tr, 243c, 243clb, 243tr, 244cla; Istanbul Foundation for Culture and the Arts: 221b; Istanbul Hilton: 182t; Istanbul History Foundation: 30br; Istanbul Library: 66b, 95tl; Istanbul Metropolitan Municipality: 231tr.

Gürol Kara: 2–3, 98c, 115b, 146ca, 153t, 169t; İzzet Keribar: 5b, 16tr, 47t, 48–9, 50, 52ca, 118tl, 128tr, 134–5, 138b, 139t, 146cb, 172tc, 173br, 173ca, 174tr, 174cl, 174bc, 175tc, 177bc, 214br, 234tl, 240tl.

José Luczyc-Wyhowska: 218tr, 219cl/cr/bl/blc/brc/br.

Magnum Photos Ltd.: Topkapı Palace/Ara Güler 8–9, 28bl, 33cl, 41b, 55t, 56t; Military Museum, Istanbul: 127t.

Nour Foundation, London: The Nassar D. Khalili Collection of Islamic Art Ferman (MSS801) 95tr, Mahmud II (CAL 334) 95cr, Leaf (CAL 165) 95cl; Burnisher (SC1210) 95bra, Knife (SC1297) 95brb.

Dick Osseman: 175clb; Güngör Özsoy: 60t, 70b, 157t/cr, 170c.

Paşabahçe Glassworks: 146t; Pera Museum: 103bc; Photolibrary: Alamer 224-5; Mattes Mattes 34; Pictures Colour Library: 44b, 214tr, 218cl; Plan Tours 239tl; Poseidon: 192bl; Private Collection: 135 inset.

Science Photo Library: CNES, 1993 Distribution SPOT image 12t; Neil Setchfield: 84; Shutterstock: rm 176cla; Sixt AG: 245cla; Antony Souter: 53b; Remy Sow: 180c; Spectrum Colour Library: 153tb; Star Gazete: Murat Duzyol 227br; The Stockmarket: 130t.

Tatilya: 222b; TAV Investment Holding Co.: 236cla; TCDD: - Turkish State Railways: 244br; The Touring and Automobile Club of Turkey: 244tl; Travel Ink: Abbie Enock 35bc; Trip Photographic Library: 154bv; Marc Dubin 45t; Turkish Airlines: 236t; Turkish Information Office: Ozan Sadik 45b. Peter Wilson: 56c, 75t/c, 118c. Erdal Yazici: 44c, 167r, 169c.

Front endpaper: fotolia: Zechel cra.

Jacket
Front Cover: Photolibrary: Jose Fuste Ragat. Back Cover: AWL Images: Michele Falzone clb; Travel Pix Collection cla; Dorling Kindersley: Tony Souter tl; Linda Whitwam bl. Spine: Photolibrary: Jose Fuste Ragat.

All other images © Dorling Kindersley.
For further information see: www.dkimages.com

Phrase Book

Pronunciation

Turkish uses a Roman alphabet. It has 29 letters: 8 vowels and 21 consonants. Letters that differ from the English alphabet are: **c**, pronounced "j" as in "jolly"; **ç**, pronounced "ch" as in "church"; **ğ**, which lengthens the preceding vowel and is not pronounced; **ı**, pronounced "uh"; **ö**, pronounced "ur" (like the sound in "further"); **ş**, pronounced "sh" as in "ship"; **ü**, pronounced "ew" as in "few".

In an Emergency

Help!	**İmdat!**	*eem-dat*
Stop!	**Dur!**	*door*
Call a doctor!	**Bir doktor çağrın!**	*beer dok-tor chah-ruhn*
Call an ambulance!	**Bir ambulans çağrın!**	*beer am-boo-lans chah-ruhn*
Call the police!	**Polis çağrın!**	*po-lees chah-ruhn*
Fire!	**Yangın!**	*yan-guhn*
Where is the nearest telephone?	**En yakın telefon nerede?**	*en ya-kuhn teh-leh-fon neh-reh-deh*
Where is the nearest hospital?	**En yakın hastane nerede?**	*en ya-kuhn has-ta-neh neh-reh-deh*

Communication Essentials

Yes	**Evet**	*eh-vet*
No	**Hayır**	*h-'eye'-uhr*
Thank you	**Teşekkür ederim**	*teh-shek-kewr eh-deh-reem*
Please	**Lütfen**	*lewt-fen*
Excuse me	**Affedersiniz**	*af-feh-der-see-neez*
Hello	**Merhaba**	*mer-ba-ba*
Goodbye	**Hoşça kalın**	*hosh-cha ka-luhn*
Good morning	**Günaydın**	*gewn-'eye'-duhn*
Good evening	**İyi akşamlar**	*ee-yee ak-sham-lar*
Morning	**Sabah**	*sa-bah*
Afternoon	**Öğleden sonra**	*ur-leh-den son-ra*
Evening	**Akşam**	*ak-sham*
Yesterday	**Dün**	*dewn*
Today	**Bugün**	*boo-gewn*
Tomorrow	**Yarın**	*ya-ruhn*
Here	**Burada**	*boo-ra-da*
There	**Şurada**	*shoo-ra-da*
Over there	**Orada**	*o-ra-da*
What?	**Ne?**	*neh*
When?	**Ne zaman?**	*neh za-man*
Why?	**Neden**	*neh-den*
Where?	**Nerede?**	*neh-reh-deh*

Useful Phrases

How are you?	**Nasılsınız?**	*na-suhl-suh-nuhz*
I'm fine	**İyiyim**	*ee-yee-yeem*
Pleased to meet you	**Memnun oldum**	*mem-noon ol-doom*
See you soon	**Görüşmek üzere**	*gur-reush-mek ew-zeh-reh*
That's fine	**Tamam**	*ta-mam*
Where is/are ...?	**... nerede?**	*... neh-reh-deh*
How far is it to ...?	**... ne kadar uzakta?**	*... neh ka-dar oo-zak-ta*
I want to go to ...	**... a/e gitmek istiyorum**	*... a/eh geet-mek ees-tee-yo-room*
Do you speak English?	**İngilizce biliyor musunuz?**	*een-gee-leez-jeh bee-lee-yor moo-soo-nooz?*
I don't understand	**Anlamıyorum**	*an-la-muh-yo-room*
Can you help me?	**Bana yardım edebilir misiniz?**	*ba-na yar-duhm eh-deh-bee-leer mee-see-neez?*

Useful Words

big	**büyük**	*bew-yewk*
small	**küçük**	*kew-chewk*
hot	**sıcak**	*suh-jak*
cold	**soğuk**	*soh-ook*
good/well	**iyi**	*ee-yee*
bad	**kötü**	*kur-tew*
enough	**yeter**	*yeh-ter*
open	**açık**	*a-chuhk*
closed	**kapalı**	*ka-pa-luh*
left	**sol**	*sol*
right	**sağ**	*saa*
straight on	**doğru**	*doh-roo*

near	**yakın**	*ya-kuhn*
far	**uzak**	*oo-zak*
up	**yukarı**	*yoo-ka-ruh*
down	**aşağı**	*a-shah-uh*
early	**erken**	*er-ken*
late	**geç**	*gech*
entrance	**giriş**	*gee-reesh*
exit	**çıkış**	*chuh-kuhsh*
toilets	**tuvaletler**	*too-va-let-ler*
push	**itiniz**	*ee-tee-neez*
pull	**çekiniz**	*cheh-kee-neez*
more	**daha fazla**	*da-ha faz-la*
less	**daha az**	*da-ha az*
very	**çok**	*chok*

Shopping

How much is this?	**Bu kaç lira?**	*boo kach lee-ra*
I would like ...	**... istiyorum**	*... ees-tee-yo-room*
Do you have ...?	**... var mı?**	*... var muh?*
Do you take credit cards?	**Kredi kartı kabul ediyor musunuz?**	*kreh-dee kar-tuh ka-bool eh-dee-yor moo-soo-nooz?*
What time do you open/close?	**Saat kaçta açılıyor/ kapanıyor?**	*Sa-at kach-ta a-chuh-luh-yor/ ka-pa-nuh-yor*
this one	**bunu**	*boo-noo*
that one	**şunu**	*shoo-noo*
expensive	**pahalı**	*pa-ha-luh*
cheap	**ucuz**	*oo-jooz*
size (clothes)	**beden**	*beh-den*
size (shoes)	**numara**	*noo-ma-ra*
white	**beyaz**	*bay-yaz*
black	**siyah**	*see-yah*
red	**kırmızı**	*kuhr-muh-zuh*
yellow	**sarı**	*sa-ruh*
green	**yeşil**	*yeh-sheel*
blue	**mavi**	*ma-vee*
brown	**kahverengi**	*kah-veh-ren-gee*
shop	**dükkan**	*dewk-kan*
till	**kasa**	*ka-sa*
bargaining	**pazarlık**	*pa-zar-luhk*
That's my last offer	**Daha fazla veremem**	*da-ha faz-la veh-reh-mem*

Types of Shop

antiques shop	**antikacı**	*an-tee-ka-juh*
bakery	**fırın**	*fuh-ruhn*
bank	**banka**	*ban-ka*
book shop	**kitapçı**	*kee-tap-chuh*
butcher's	**kasap**	*ka-sap*
cake shop	**pastane**	*pas-ta-neh*
chemist's/ pharmacy	**eczane**	*ej-za-neh*
fishmonger's	**balıkçı**	*ba-luhk-chuh*
greengrocer's	**manav**	*ma-nav*
grocery	**bakkal**	*bak-kal*
hairdresser's (ladies)	**kuaför**	*kwaf-fur*
(mens)	**berber**	*ber-ber*
leather shop	**derici**	*deh-ree-jee*
market/bazaar	**çarşı/pazar**	*char-shuh/pa-zar*
newsstand	**gazeteci**	*ga-zeh-teh-jee*
post office	**postane**	*pos-ta-neh*
shoe shop	**ayakkabıcı**	*'eye'-yak-ka-buh-juh*
stationer's	**kırtasiyeci**	*kuhr-ta-see-yeh-jee*
supermarket	**süpermarket**	*sew-per-mar-ket*
tailor	**terzi**	*ter-zee*
travel agency	**seyahat acentesi**	*say-ya-hat a-jen-teh-see*

Sightseeing

castle	**hisar**	*hee-sar*
church	**kilise**	*kee-lee-seh*
island	**ada**	*a-da*
mosque	**cami**	*ja-mee*
museum	**müze**	*mew-zeh*
palace	**saray**	*sar-'eye'*
park	**park**	*park*
square	**meydan**	*may-dan*
theological college	**medrese**	*med-reh-seh*
tomb	**türbe**	*tewr-beh*
tourist information office	**turizm danışma bürosu**	*too-reezm da-nuhsh-mah bew-ro-soo*
tower	**kule**	*koo-leh*
town hall	**belediye sarayı**	*beh-leh-dee-yeh sar-'eye'-uh*
Turkish bath	**hamam**	*ha-mam*

Transport

airport	havalimanı	*ha-va-lee-ma-nuh*
bus/coach	otobüs	*o-to-bewss*
bus stop	otobüs durağı	*o-to-bewss doo-ra-uh*
coach station	otogar	*o-to-gar*
dolmuş	dolmuş	*dol-moosh*
fare	ücret	*ewj-ret*
ferry	vapur	*va-poor*
sea bus	deniz otobüsü	*deh-neez o-to-bew-sew*
station	istasyon	*ees-tas-yon*
taxi	taksi	*tak-see*
ticket	bilet	*bee-let*
ticket office	bilet gişesi	*bee-let gee-sheh-see*
timetable	tarife	*ta-ree-feh*

Staying in a Hotel

Do you have a vacant room?	Boş odanız var mı?	*bosh o-da-nuhz var muh?*
double room	iki kişilik bir oda	*ee-kee kee-shee-leek beer o-da*
room with a double bed	çift kişilik yataklı bir oda	*cheeft kee-shee-leek ya-tak-luh beer o-da*
twin room	çift yataklı bir oda	*cheeft ya-tak-luh beer o-da*
for one person	tek kişilik	*tek kee-shee-leek*
room with a bath	banyolu bir oda	*ban-yo-loo beer o-da*
shower	duş	*doosh*
porter	komi	*ko-mee*
key	anahtar	*a-nah-tar*
room service	oda servisi	*o-da ser-vee-see*
I have a reservation	Rezervasyonum var	*reh-zer-vas-yo-noom var*
Does the price include breakfast?	Fiyata kahvaltı dahil mi?	*fee-ya-ta kah-val-tuh da-heel mee?*

Eating Out

A table for ... please	... kişilik bir masa lütfen	*... kee-shee-leek beer ma-sa lewt-fen*
I want to reserve a table	Bir masa ayırtmak istiyorum	*beer ma-sa 'eye'-uhrt-mak ees-tee-yo-room*
The bill please	Hesap lütfen	*heh-sap lewt-fen*
I am a vegetarian	Et yemiyorum	*et yeh-mee-yo-room*
restaurant	lokanta	*lo-kan-ta*
waiter	garson	*gar-son*
menu	yemek listesi	*ye-mek lees-teh-see*
fixed-price menu	fiks menü	*feeks meh-new*
wine list	şarap listesi	*sha-rap lees-teh-see*
breakfast	kahvaltı	*kah-val-tuh*
lunch	öğle yemeği	*ur-leh yeh-meh-ee*
dinner	akşam yemeği	*ak-sham yeh-meh-ee*
starter	meze	*meh-zeh*
main course	ana yemek	*a-na yeh-mek*
dish of the day	günün yemeği	*gewn-ewn yeh-meh-ee*
dessert	tatlı	*tat-luh*
rare	az pişmiş	*az peesh-meesh*
well done	iyi pişmiş	*ee-yee peesh-meesh*
glass	bardak	*bar-dak*
bottle	şişe	*shee-sheh*
knife	bıçak	*buh-chak*
fork	çatal	*cha-tal*
spoon	kaşık	*ka-shuhk*

Menu Decoder

badem	*ba-dem*	almond
bal	*bal*	honey
balık	*ba-luhk*	fish
bira	*bee-ra*	beer
bonfile	*bon-fee-leh*	fillet steak
buz	*booz*	ice
çay	*ch-'eye'*	tea
çilek	*chee-lek*	strawberry
çorba	*chor-ba*	soup
dana eti	*da-na eh-tee*	veal
dondurma	*don-door-ma*	ice cream
ekmek	*ek-mek*	bread
elma	*el-ma*	apple
et	*et*	meat
fasulye	*fa-sool-yeh*	beans
fırında	*fuh-ruhn-da*	roast
fıstık	*fuhs-tuhk*	pistachio nuts
gazoz	*ga-zoz*	fizzy drink
hurma	*hoor-ma*	dates
içki	*eech-kee*	alcohol
incir	*een-jeer*	figs
ızgara	*uhz-ga-ra*	charcoal grilled
kahve	*kah-veh*	coffee
kara biber	*ka-ra bee-ber*	black pepper
karışık	*ka-ruh-shuhk*	mixed
karpuz	*kar-pooz*	water melon
kavun	*ka-voon*	melon
kayısı	*k-'eye'-uh-suh*	apricots
kaymak	*k-'eye'-mak*	cream
kıyma	*kuhy-ma*	minced meat
kızartma	*kuh-zart-ma*	fried
köfte	*kurf-teh*	meatballs
kuru	*koo-roo*	dried
kuzu eti	*koo-zoo eh-tee*	lamb
lokum	*lo-koom*	Turkish delight
maden suyu	*ma-den soo-yoo*	mineral water (fizzy)
meyve suyu	*may-veh soo-yoo*	fruit juice
midye	*meed-yeh*	mussels
muz	*mooz*	banana
patlıcan	*pat-luh-jan*	aubergine
peynir	*pay-neer*	cheese
pilav	*pee-lav*	rice
piliç	*pee-leech*	roast chicken
şarap	*sha-rap*	wine
sebze	*seb-zeh*	vegetables
şeftali	*shef-ta-lee*	peach
şeker	*sheh-ker*	sugar
su	*soo*	water
süt	*sewt*	milk
sütlü	*sewt-lew*	with milk
tavuk	*ta-vook*	chicken
tereyağı	*teh-reh-yah-uh*	butter
tuz	*tooz*	salt
üzüm	*ew-zewm*	grapes
vişne	*veesh-neh*	sour cherry
yoğurt	*yoh-urt*	yoghurt
yumurta	*yoo-moor-ta*	egg
zeytin	*zay-teen*	olives
zeytinyağı	*zay-teen-yah-uh*	olive oil

Numbers

0	sıfır	*suh-fuhr*
1	bir	*beer*
2	iki	*ee-kee*
3	üç	*ewch*
4	dört	*durt*
5	beş	*besh*
6	altı	*al-tuh*
7	yedi	*yeh-dee*
8	sekiz	*seh-keez*
9	dokuz	*doh-kooz*
10	on	*on*
11	on bir	*on beer*
12	on iki	*on ee-kee*
13	on üç	*on ewch*
14	on dört	*on durt*
15	on beş	*on besh*
16	on altı	*on al-tuh*
17	on yedi	*on yeh-dee*
18	on sekiz	*on seh-keez*
19	on dokuz	*on doh-kooz*
20	yirmi	*yeer-mee*
21	yirmi bir	*yeer-mee beer*
30	otuz	*o-tooz*
40	kırk	*kuhrk*
50	elli	*eh-lee*
60	altmış	*alt-muhsh*
70	yetmiş	*yet-meesh*
80	seksen	*sek-sen*
90	doksan	*dok-san*
100	yüz	*yewz*
110	yüz on	*yewz on*
200	iki yüz	*ee-kee yewz*
1,000	bin	*been*
100,000	yüz bin	*yewz been*
1,000,000	bir milyon	*beer meel-yon*

Time

one minute	bir dakika	*beer da-kee-ka*
one hour	bir saat	*beer sa-at*
half an hour	yarım saat	*ya-ruhm sa-at*
day	gün	*gewn*
week	hafta	*haf-ta*
month	ay	*'eye'*
year	yıl	*yuhl*
Sunday	pazar	*pa-zar*
Monday	pazartesi	*pa-zar-teh-see*
Tuesday	salı	*sa-luh*
Wednesday	çarşamba	*char-sham-ba*
Thursday	perşembe	*per-shem-beh*
Friday	cuma	*joo-ma*
Saturday	cumartesi	*joo-mar-teh-see*

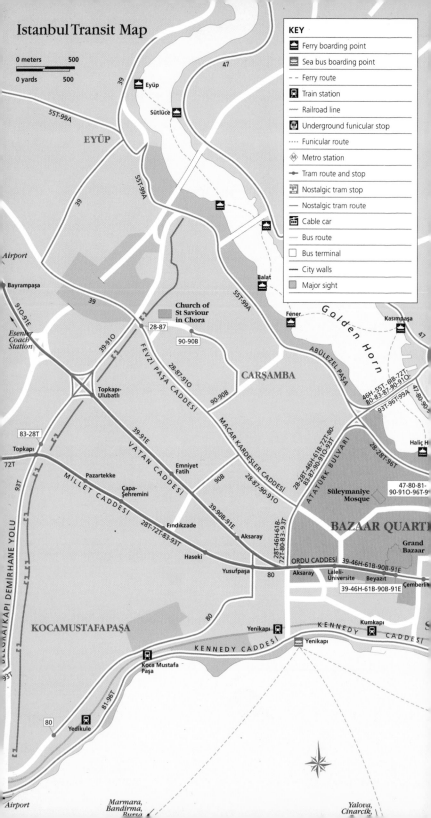